Human Rights and US Foreign Policy

This book analyzes the role of human rights in the foreign policy of the George W. Bush Administrations.

References to human rights, freedom and democracy became prominent explanations for post-9/11 foreign policy, yet human rights have been neither impartially nor universally integrated into decision making. Jan Hancock addresses this apparent paradox by considering three distinct explanations. The first position holds that human rights form a constitutive foreign policy goal, the second that evident double standards refute the first perspective. This book then seeks to progress beyond this familiar discussion by employing a Foucaultian method of discourse analysis to suggest a third explanation. Through this analysis, the author examines how a discourse of human rights has been produced and implemented in the presentation of US foreign policy. This illuminating study builds on a wealth of primary source evidence from human rights organizations to document the contradictions between the claims and practice of human rights made by the Bush Administrations, as well as the political significance of denying this disjuncture.

Presenting three detailed investigations on the role of the human rights discourse in the wars waged against terror, Afghanistan and Iraq that have dominated the foreign policy initiatives undertaken by the George W. Bush presidency, this book will be of interest to advanced students and researchers of US foreign policy, human rights, international relations and security studies.

Jan Hancock is the Hallsworth Research Fellow at the Centre for International Politics, University of Manchester, UK.

Routledge research in human rights

1 **Human Rights and US Foreign Policy**
Jan Hancock

Human Rights and US Foreign Policy

Jan Hancock

Routledge
Taylor & Francis Group

LONDON AND NEW YORK

First published 2007
by Routledge
2 Park Square, Milton Park, Abingdon, Oxon OX14 4RN

Simultaneously published in the USA and Canada
by Routledge
270 Madison Ave, New York, NY 10016

Routledge is an imprint of the Taylor & Francis Group, an informa business

Transferred to Digital Printing 2009

© 2007 Jan Hancock

Typeset in Times by Wearset Ltd, Boldon, Tyne and Wear

British Library Cataloguing in Publication Data
A catalogue record for this book is available from the British Library

Library of Congress Cataloging in Publication Data
A catalog record for this book has been requested

ISBN10: 0-415-36577-5 (hbk)
ISBN10: 0-415-54342-8 (pbk)
ISBN10: 0-203-96319-9 (ebk)

ISBN13: 978-0-415-36577-2 (hbk)
ISBN13: 978-0-415-54342-2 (pbk)
ISBN13: 978-0-203-96319-7 (ebk)

For Rhiannon with love, peace and hope

Contents

Acknowledgments viii
List of abbreviations ix

Introduction 1

PART I
Human rights discourse in foreign policy theory and practice 11

1 The hegemonic discourse 13

2 The hegemonic discourse of Wilson and Carter 32

3 Inconsistent application of human rights 53

4 Consistent application of human rights 68

PART II
Case studies 85

5 War on Terror 87

6 War on Afghanistan 109

7 War on Iraq 123

Conclusion 148

Notes 156
Bibliography 202
Index 224

Acknowledgments

Many thanks are extended to the Hallsworth Committee at Manchester University for providing the funding and professional support that made the production of this monograph possible. Many thanks are extended to the colleagues who have contributed to the formulation of ideas that find expression in the following pages, especially to Tony Evans and Neil Stammers. The vitally important work on human rights done by *Human Rights Watch*, *Amnesty International*, the *American Civil Liberties Union* and *Human Rights First* is also acknowledged. Many thanks to Erika Hancock and Sheila Travis for aiding the preparation of the text and to John Baker for providing much needed IT support. Special thanks to Morwenna for everything.

Abbreviations

ABC	American Broadcasting Corporation
ACLU	American Civil Liberties Union
AEI	American Enterprise Institute
AHRC	Afghanistan Human Rights Commission
AIDS	Acquired Immune Deficiency Syndrome
AU	African Union
AUC	United Self-Defense Forces of Colombia
AWAC	Airborne Warning and Control
BP	Beyond Petroleum
CBS	Columbia Broadcasting System
CEO	Chief Executive Officer
CIA	Central Intelligence Agency
CPA	Coalition Provisional Authority
CPI	Committee on Public Information
CSP	Center for Security Policy
CSRT	Combatant Status Review Tribunal
DEP	Department of Environmental Protection
DIA	Defense Intelligence Agency
DoD	Department of Defense
DRC	Democratic Republic of Congo
ELN	National Liberation Army
EPA	Environmental Protection Agency
EU	European Union
FARC	Revolutionary Armed Forces of Colombia
FBI	Federal Bureau of Investigation
GDP	Gross Domestic Product
HIV	Human Immuno-deficiency Virus
IAEA	International Atomic Energy Agency
ICC	International Criminal Court
ICRC	International Committee of the Red Cross
IDF	Israeli Defense Force
IPCC	Intergovernmental Panel on Climate Change
JINSA	Jewish Institute for National Security Affairs

KBR	Kellogg Brown and Root
MCA	Millennium Challenge Account
MNC	Multi National Corporation
MP	Military Police
MSF	Médecins Sans Frontières
NATO	North Atlantic Treaty Organization
NBC	National Broadcasting Company
NED	National Endowment for Democracy
NEPDG	National Energy Policy Development Group
NGO	Non Governmental Organization
NSC	National Security Council
OECD	Organization of Economic Cooperation and Development
OSCE	Organization for Security and Cooperation in Europe
OSHA	National Institute of Occupational Safety and Health
OSP	Office of Special Plans
PAC	Political Action Committee
PDPA	People's Democratic Party of Afghanistan
PIPA	Program on International Policy Attitudes
PNAC	Project for the New American Century
PoW	Prisoner of War
PUC	Person Under Control
UDHR	Universal Declaration of Human Rights
UK	United Kingdom
UN	United Nations
US	United States
USAID	United States Agency for International Development
USA PATRIOT	Uniting and Strengthening America by Providing Appropriate Tools Required to Intercept and Obstruct Terrorism
WMD	Weapons of Mass Destruction

Introduction

Aims and focus

The aim of this book is to provide a systematic analysis of the human rights discourse expressed by the George W. Bush Administrations. There exists a twofold rationale for this investigation. First, officials in the George W. Bush Administrations (hereafter referred to simply as the Bush Administrations) ascribed a prominent position to 'human rights' alongside 'freedom', 'democracy' and 'liberty' when explaining US foreign policy. Such prominence commends the systematic analysis of these normative explanations as an issue of significant scholarly and public interest. The second rationale resides in the tendency of the foreign policy and international relations sub-disciplines to neglect the normative explanations provided by administration officials as a focus for examination in favor of interest based or quantifiable analysis.

The argument presented in the following pages holds that the human rights discourse expressed by the Bush Administrations should be taken seriously but not literally. The book details how the concept of human rights has been co-opted as an instrument of foreign policy. This study will consequently be of most use to (i) those with an interest in the role of human rights in the foreign policy of the Bush Administrations, (ii) those with an interest in the role of human rights in contemporary world politics and (iii) those with an interest in the application of social power in world politics. As its normative basis, the book takes seriously the advancement of human rights as an important goal, a position it shares with numerous statements from Bush Administration officials.

The following text does not seek to provide an historical narrative of the internal struggles and disagreements between Bush Administration officials.[1] Instead, the study analyzes the commonalities in the human rights discourse expressed by administration officials. The book focuses on the period between September 2001 to the completion of the text in August 2006 and, following the continuities evident in the human rights discourse, does not distinguish between the first and second administration except where this is required to aid the analysis. The study focuses on the post-September 11, 2001, hereafter referred to as 9/11, era, since it is from this point that appeals to concepts of freedom, democracy and human rights became more prominent and consistent in official explanations of foreign policy.

The focus of this study is placed on the US executive rather than the legislature or judiciary for three reasons. First, this focus helps guard against unsustainable generalizations. Second, it is the narrative expressed by administration officials and most especially the president himself that receives the most prominent coverage in the popular media and therefore presents itself as most pressing for political analysis and explanation. Third, the Bush Administrations have continued the trend of asserting broad executive powers to pursue foreign policy.[2] Interventions by the legislature and the judiciary in the policymaking process will, however, be noted when relevant to the analysis.

The remainder of this introductory chapter will fulfill three functions. It will (i) provide definitions, (ii) briefly explain the method of analysis adopted in the study and will (iii) outline the structure of the following chapters. Attention turns first to defining the key terms used in the subsequent analysis.

Ethics

The word 'ethics' is derived from the Greek word 'ethos', which refers to an accepted custom or common practice. 'Ethical' can subsequently be defined as an appeal to a normative principle of right conduct.[3] Understood as a claim for 'the right thing to do', ethical reasoning is clearly implicated throughout all aspects of politics including foreign policy. For example, maintaining a position that the right foreign policy is that which best advances a perceived national interest is not a rejection of ethical reasoning. Instead, the position advances an ethical claim since it asserts that foreign policy ought to reflect the stated interests of a specific population. In contrast to defining 'right' in terms of state interests, the concept of human rights holds instead that right can be derived from a focus on the dignity of all humans irrespective of their nationality or status.

Values

Defined as a general rule of conduct, the term 'value' will be used in this study to refer to identifiable political principles and ethical positions.[4]

Human rights

Human rights are an example of that which Gallie termed an 'essentially contested concept'.[5] According to this classification, a number of competing definitions for human rights are evident, while no universally accepted criterion exists through which to validate the competing rights claims. The natural rights tradition has, for example, defended individual rights to life and liberty on the basis of such rights being given by God to humanity.[6] While natural rights claims remain unproblematic for individuals who have internalized a specific religious doctrine, they are more problematic from other perspectives. Marx for example denied not only the existence of God but also the very premise that human nature can be identified and abstracted into a universal or essential form. Instead, Marx perceived nature as a structural function of historical process and social conditioning.[7] In contrast to Marx, proponents of negative human rights argue, characteristically on the basis of liberal political theory, that human rights can be defined in terms of protecting the autonomy of individuals from the undue interference of society. Ingram, for example, claims that 'the best scheme of rights is one that protects the autonomy interests of citizens'.[8]

Advocates of positive rights focus on the rights of the impoverished to access such goods as food, shelter, education and health care on the basis that these goods are more urgently required than defending the autonomy rights of individuals.[9] Basic rights theorists such as Shue, Vincent and Galtung deny an ethically significant dichotomy between negative and positive human rights and instead adopt a framework derived from biological needs to validate specific human rights claims.[10] Utilitarian and consequentialist theorists question the ontological primacy of a focus on human rights and instead suggest aggregate good as a more fundamental criterion of justice.[11] Other theorists assert a mutual compatibility between utilitarianism and human rights by claiming that overall social happiness is best achieved through the recognition of individual rights.[12]

Bauer argued that to validate rights it is 'not necessary to agree on the foundation of human rights so long as we can agree on the norms'.[13] Through a consequentialist focus, Kuhonta claimed that human rights are justified not because of their intrinsic self evidence, but because they promote positive values such as public spiritedness.[14] For Bauer and Kuhonta, the absence of any consensual philosophical basis for universal human rights therefore posed no real problems for recognizing such rights, since these can be validated by criterion independent of their intrinsic self-evidence. There is no shortage of suggestions by theorists as to what this criterion could consist of. Gewirth, for example, advanced human rights in terms of prerequisites necessary to act as a moral agent.[15] Donnelly has suggested rights in terms of guarantees required to protect humans from threats to their dignity posed by the state and market.[16]

As briefly summarized above, a plethora of competing bases for human rights can be seen to exist, each of which advances a different ethical criterion or account of human dignity through which to prioritize one particular definition of rights over competing claims. One possible solution to this problem of defining human rights is by recourse to those rights stipulated in international human rights legislation. The political and selective manner in which such laws have been formulated and enforced reveal that legal human rights are, however, as much a result of political bargaining and compromise as they are mechanisms to protect the oppressed and vulnerable.[17] Consequently, international human rights legislation will certainly be referred to by this study, but it will not be adopted as the analytical basis from which to conduct the subsequent investigation.

Instead, human rights will be defined in this book in terms of *necessary* rather than *sufficient* conditions. Whereas sufficient conditions would define a substantive list of human rights, such definitions are vulnerable to the charge of reflecting the contingent political predilections of the observer masquerading under a cloak of universal interest. In contrast, all coherent claims to promote human rights, irrespective of which specific rights are subsequently advocated, are necessarily compelled to respect two basic principles. These principles hold that (i) all people possess human rights solely by virtue of their shared humanity (universal application) and that (ii) human rights abuses are seen as equally significant irrespective of where they occur (impartial application). A claim to advance human rights on a selective or politicized basis that does not meet the requirements of these two conditions is internally contradictory. Asserting, for example, that only some humans possess human rights, that some people possess more human rights than others, that different people possess different human rights or that the human rights of some people are more urgent than the same rights of other people, demonstrates that a criterion other than simple membership of the human race is being used to advance rights claims. Consequently, such a claim would be inconsistent with the necessary conditions of human rights as described above. By defining human rights in terms of these two necessary conditions, human rights will be used in this study as an analytic instrument through which to examine the specific claims made by policy makers.

Discourse

This book adopts David Howarth's definition of discourse as 'systems of meaning which form the identities of subjects and objects'.[18] Under this definition, discourse does not simply refer to the use of language to describe a corresponding reality. Instead, discourse refers to an internally consistent set of mythological and ideational assumptions that impart meaning to events from a particular perspective.[19] Thus defined, discourses can produce meanings through a narrative that relates events to contingent, or mythological, points of reference.[20] It is through presenting mythological simplifications as accepted factual truths that discourse is itself involved in the process of producing understanding.

A number of distinct and competing discourses can subsequently be identified to explain the role of human rights in US foreign policy. One maintains that human rights concerns constitute an important, if not always overriding goal in policy making. In contrast, a second holds that decisions made by successive administrations have themselves been responsible for serial violations of human rights.[21] The very different claims made by each of these discourses reflect the divergent assumptions of the observers on the possible and legitimate role of human rights in foreign policy.

Hegemonic discourse

The terms hegemonic discourse and hegemonic mythology will be used interchangeably in the following text to refer to the messages or rules that constitute the internally consistent account of human rights in post-9/11 foreign policy decisions as repeatedly asserted by Bush Administration officials. Internal consistencies refer to the implicit or explicitly stated account of human rights that are repeated within the administration's foreign policy narrative. External consistencies refer in contrast to the adequacy of the hegemonic discourse as an accurate account of reality. This study identifies three internally consistent rules as constituting the hegemonic discourse, (i) that human rights are advanced as independent foreign policy goals; (ii) that human rights promotion realizes a pre-existing US identity and (iii) human rights advocacy complements foreign policy goals of freedom, justice and democracy promotion. These three messages are consistent within (i) the body of official statements, speeches and declarations expressed by the president and administration officials and (ii) the public reports, briefing papers and official websites authored by the executive branch.

Myths

Myths are referred to here not as factual inaccuracies but rather as repeated simplifications that present a contingent understanding of reality as a singular and unproblematic truth. Myths are therefore discourses since they advance specific interpretations that impart meaning and purpose to events. Myths can be mobilized to serve an overtly political function as, for example, in the claim that the deployment of military power is a force for good when used by the US, but is proof of evil intent when utilized by enemies of the US. It is in this sense of insisting upon a politicized interpretation of reality over other possible interpretations that myths act as a mechanism of governance to discipline the process of belief formation in the minds of the audience.

Social power

This book adopts a Foucaultian definition of social power as 'a mode of action on the actions of others ... to structure the possible actions of others'.[22] Various techniques of power can structure the possible actions of others. For example, threatening physical coercion or offering incentives can encourage desired behavior. Coercion is, however, a generally inefficient form of power since it does little to produce voluntary compliance and tends instead to produce resistance from those over whom it is exercised.[23] At the very least, coercive power eradicates any enthusiasm and support among those over whom it is exercised.

The inducement of conformity through structured incentives relies, in contrast, on the notion that individuals are rational actors constantly making instrumental calculations as to the costs versus the benefits of compliance relative to non-compliance. Power can be exercised through appeals to self-interest by ensuring that incentives, punishments and sanctions lead subjects to perform such actions as desired by those exercising the power.[24] In contrast to these two manifestations of social power, the Foucaultian definition focuses attention on how power operates by disciplining subjects to internalize dominant modes of understanding the world.[25] According to Foucault, subjects understand the world on the basis of the social values and norms characteristic of the communities within which they have been immersed, since people tend to assume that these contingent norms are in fact universal truths.[26]

Under this Foucaultian interpretation, the most effective expression of social power is that which is least visible since the subjects will be unaware of the processes through which they are being influenced. The most powerful influences over the thoughts and actions of individuals can subsequently be identified as those ethical beliefs that have attained an unquestioned status as truth and removed from any further critical scrutiny.[27] Competing interpretations of reality will be instinctively dismissed when these contradict fundamental beliefs that are erroneously viewed by the subjects as truths. Nowhere in this account of power must people necessarily internalize social norms. Indeed, Foucault noted that individuals can react to dominant social codes of conduct through resistance. Indeed, it is precisely in resistance that normalizing practices become visible and denaturalized.[28] Nonetheless, the undoubted strength of the Foucaultian definition of power is that it allows us to understand how social power operates through authorizing discursive frames of reference to present myths as accepted truths.[29]

This somewhat abstract discussion of power is central to understanding US foreign policy since the definition of power provided allows us to comprehend the hegemonic discourse in terms of producing understanding in the minds of the audience. In particular the hegemonic discourse can insist on one contingent interpretation of events and political identities in terms of a singular unproblematic truth. The Foucaultian account of power therefore provides a radical way of understanding discourse in terms of producing reality, rather than limiting the function of language to describing a corresponding reality.

Legitimacy

Legitimacy can be defined as, 'the tendency of individuals or groups to accept and follow the rules of a political order'.[30] Legitimacy is a significant aspect of politics to the extent that it causes individuals or groups to internalize as normative beliefs the principle that an authority, imperative or institution is right and ought to be obeyed. According to the categorization of social power provided above, legitimacy exists not as a function of coercive capability or by appeals to self-interest but rather to the degree to which an authority or action is perceived by the audience as right and proper.[31]

Although from the perspective of political analysis it may be methodologically cleaner to quantify power in terms of military and economic statistics, it may be simultaneously less significant than focusing on primary questions of legitimacy perceptions. Finnemore, for example, demonstrated how the effectiveness of force is not an inherent, objectively-dictated given but instead depended on the subjective and normative perceptions of others.[32] In the absence of force being seen as legitimate it is unlikely to achieve its goals since the deployment of naked force devoid of perceived legitimacy has rarely fared well over the long term as a means of social control.[33] One technique by which administration officials can be subsequently hypothesized to generate legitimacy for policies is to present them in terms that are perceived by the audience as conferring legitimacy, such as through the language of democracy, freedom and human rights, for example.

Method

Constructing an appropriate methodology to investigate the purpose and meaning of human rights in US foreign policy is itself a politicized matter and rests on a number of prior assumptions made by the observer.[34] Such assumptions include the extent to which the promotion of human rights is seen as an appropriate or even possible function of foreign policy, how human rights can be defined and how abuses occurring in different states can be ascertained and measured. As Farer reminds us, the many contested definitions of human rights, combined with the imagery and intangibility of the concept means that as a symbol 'they remain available for appropriation by advocates of almost any position'.[35] Compounding such problems of heuristics are further issues of how best to understand the discourse expressed by policy makers.

The method subsequently adopted in this book is to analyze over 220 primary sources for internally consistent and repeated features of references made by administration officials to human rights. These internal consistencies will then be juxtaposed with (i) the necessary conditions of human rights as detailed above and (ii) the human rights consequences of actual foreign policies as ascertained by a variety of sources independent of the administration. The results can then be examined to establish either the consistent application of human rights in foreign policy or else significant patterns evident in the inconsistent application of human rights. Analyzing the patterns in how human rights have been applied internally consistently in the official narrative but externally selectively in actual foreign policy practice can then explain how the concept has been politically co-opted.

The objection that no state can be expected to promote human rights on the basis of impartial and universal application is in no way denied here. To the extent that this is the case, this should be properly acknowledged as an inherent contradiction between (i) human rights as a rules-based system characterized by the universal application of a specific set of standards for all people and (ii) the states system as an interest-based system characterized by the geographical accumulation of wealth and power. The alternative option of redefining human rights so as to facilitate their selective integration into foreign policy would render the concept internally incoherent.

Discourse analysis methodology has been criticized by a number of political scientists and it is appropriate to address these objections at the outset. Keohane and Mearsheimer have argued that discourse analysis is bad science since it lacks testable theories and is short on empirical analysis.[36] Walt adds that the method is dangerously self-indulgent.[37] Discourse analysis has moreover been questioned as cynical, 'Un-American' or even as entertaining conspiracy theory.[38] Such criticisms are unhelpful for three reasons.

First, such criticisms unduly dismiss the political significance of the evident disjuncture between (i) the ethical, even idealistic narrative through which policy makers present foreign policy decisions and (ii) the tendency of international relations and foreign policy analysis to sideline value-based investigations in favor of a focus on power politics, interests or more quantifiable data analysis. Discourse analysis offers a method through which to systematically investigate the internal workings and political significance of the normative discourse expressed by administration officials.

Second, discourse analysis is validated by Howarth's observation that words can change their meaning over time. The English word 'cattle' for example originated in reference to all forms of property and then changed its meaning to refer only to four legged animals owned by people, before changing again and denoting only domesticated bovines.[39] It can subsequently be established that as, 'a system of signs expressing ideas', the meaning of a word cannot be described as fixed to a corresponding object existing independently in the real world.[40] Meaning instead occurs within language itself by virtue of the differences and relations between distinct words as expressions of ideas. That is to say, meaning is contingent upon the context and ideational assumptions held by the speaker and listener.[41] Since the meaning of a relatively unproblematic idea such as 'cattle' can vary widely between time and place, understanding the meaning of references by administration officials to more complex notions of human rights becomes a pressing priority. This is especially the case since the language of human rights is highly loaded with emotive and powerful connotations.

Third, and following from point two, appeals made by politicians to values can themselves determine how the audience understands and responds to policy decisions.[42] Scholastic enquiries that are restricted to the study of that which can be falsified can overlook more complex social processes through which people understand certain interpretations as established truths, rather than as contestable or contingent claims. Rather than seeing truth as a social reality existing external to discourse, Foucault defined truth as an, 'ensemble of rules according to which the true and the false are separated and specific effects of power attached to the true'.[43] This position effectively re-conceptualizes cause and effect in the politics of power and ethics. Rather than focusing on traditional subjects of how political philosophy can limit the rights of the powerful, the question was inverted by Foucault to examine how ethical norms, including those of human rights, are themselves devised and implemented as mechanisms of social power. That is to say, dominant ways in which reality is discussed and presented in society can be itself an expression of power since this provides the frames of references through which the audience processes information.[44] Discourse analysis therefore provides a useful method to explain how social power operates not just as coercion or inducements but also by validating or rejecting interpretations of truth and legitimacy.

Structure

This book is structured into two parts. Chapters 1 to 4 detail the internal consistencies and evident patterns in the application of a human rights discourse in the foreign policy of the Bush Administrations. Chapter 1 examines the three internally consistent rules that together constitute the hegemonic discourse. The chapter proceeds to evaluate three competing explanations of these rules, (i) that they describe a corresponding reality; (ii) that the expressed rules depart from describing a corresponding reality and can on these grounds be dismissed as insignificant; and (iii) that the rules are significant not for their capacity to describe reality, but instead to produce an understanding of that reality. Chapter 2 revisits the foreign policy discourses of Presidents Woodrow Wilson and Jimmy Carter to illustrate previous examples of the productive capacity of a human rights foreign policy discourse. The chapter considers how these examples can inform our understanding of the significance of human rights to the foreign policy of George W. Bush.

Chapter 3 uses a country specific focus to detail how the Bush Administrations applied human rights selectively in the policies adopted toward different states, thereby contradicting the necessary conditions for human rights defined in terms of universal and impartial application. The chapter goes on to argue that the human rights discourse expressed by administration officials has not been random in the sense of without political pattern. In particular, the chapter finds that a human rights discourse has been consistently applied to validate predetermined identities and to coalesce support and legitimacy around foreign policies. Chapter 4 investigates connections between the Bush Administrations and dominant elements of domestic civil society. The chapter then examines how a focus on these elements can help us to understand the role played by human rights in foreign policy. As a part of this analysis, the chapter details how the Bush Administrations expressed human rights in terms of US exceptionalism and as a distinctly American concept.

Part I of the book thereby details the consistencies, evident patterns and inconsistencies in the roles assigned to human rights by the Bush Administrations. The analysis does not deny a political significance to human rights in foreign policy. Instead, the hegemonic discourse is found to operate as an important technique of governance in the sense of producing an understanding of foreign policy reality in terms of freedom, human rights and democracy promotion. Part II of the book applies this analysis to three case studies that have come to define the foreign policy of the Bush Administrations. These studies consider how the official narrative has politicized the concept of human rights in the conduct of the wars fought against terror (Chapter 5), Afghanistan (Chapter 6) and Iraq (Chapter 7). The final chapter concludes by summarizing the research in terms of six findings.

Part I

Human rights discourse in foreign policy theory and practice

1   The hegemonic discourse

Introduction

The aim of this chapter is twofold. It seeks first to identify the consistencies in which the language of human rights has featured in the official foreign policy narrative expressed by the Bush Administrations and second to consider the relative merits of three differing interpretations of the resultant hegemonic discourse. The chapter is split into two sections. The first defines the hegemonic discourse in terms of three internally consistent messages or rules, (i) that human rights are impartially promoted as independent foreign policy goals; (ii) that rule one is derived from a pre-existing US identity; and (iii) that championing human rights complements distinct foreign policy goals of freedom, justice and democracy promotion.

All but the most dogmatic observers agree that policy makers have not applied human rights concerns on the basis of impartiality and universality identified in the introduction as the necessary conditions for human rights. Three possible accounts of the hegemonic discourse then become apparent and each will be examined in the second part of this chapter. The first of these, termed the reflective explanation, holds that human rights need not be impartially or universally applied in foreign policy decisions for these to nonetheless constitute independent policy goals existing alongside other competing goals. The contradictions between the reflective position and the necessary conditions of human rights lead the second approach, termed the rejectionist explanation, to reject the hegemonic discourse as simply rhetoric. The third explanation, termed the productive explanation, accepts that the hegemonic discourse does not impartially describe a corresponding reality but asserts that it is politically significant for producing an understanding of the real world. For the productive account, the political significance of the hegemonic discourse resides not in its literal meaning but instead in how its internal consistencies work as a technique of governance by disciplining the minds of those who internalize its logic as unproblematic truth.

Rule one: human rights are promoted as independent foreign policy goals

The first internally consistent feature of the hegemonic discourse asserts that the Bush Administrations promote human rights as independent policy goals. This rule has been asserted in a succession of public statements from administration officials, some of which pre-date 9/11. The head of the US delegation to the 57th Session of the UN Commission on Human Rights, for example, affirmed in March 2001 that 'the Administration of George W. Bush is fully committed to the cause of human rights'.[1] The secretary of state likewise announced that 'America's emphasis on human rights in the world will not wane during this administration. President Bush will always be mindful of the sanctity of the individual as opposed to the state and the precious rights that keep that sanctity intact'.[2] Repeating this message, the undersecretary of state for global affairs asserted that

> [w]e shall continue to be the world's leading advocate for democracy and human rights. We shall continue to meet foreign government officials, and insist that our views on human rights be known. We shall speak up for the dissidents, the victims of persecution, the tortured and the dispossessed.[3]

The message underlying these comments is one of support for human rights as an independent foreign policy goal.

After 9/11, the discursive endorsement of human rights became more prominent and was adopted by administration officials who had previously been seen as human rights skeptics. Included in this group was the president himself, who announced on one occasion that '[w]e believe in ... the duty of nations to respect the dignity and the rights of all'.[4] Colin Powell affirmed that 'on every continent we make important immediate and long-term investments in democracy and human rights'.[5] On another occasion the secretary of state announced 'we commit ourselves to democracy, development, global public health and human rights'.[6] The director of the office for the promotion of human rights and democracy closed his April 2004 statement before the Congressional Human Rights Caucus 'by stressing that the promotion of democracy and the protection of fundamental human rights is a central, defining element of our foreign policy'.[7] The assistant secretary for democracy, human rights and labor declared that 'I can wholeheartedly attest to the fact that in the Bush Administration human rights and democracy work is alive and well' and that 'human rights is and will remain a pillar of American foreign policy'.[8] The 2002 *National Security Strategy* asserted a forthright defense of values when it declared that states lose rights to non-intervention if they 'brutalize their own people' or 'reject basic human values'.[9] In correspondence with the author, Minister Counselor for Public Affairs at the US embassy in London, Daniel Sreebny, reported that '[t]he promotion of universal human rights is an integral and important part of contemporary U.S. foreign policy'.[10] The underlying message in these statements locates the promotion of human rights as a constitutive foreign policy goal of the Bush Administrations.

Administration officials have, moreover, affirmed that human rights are promoted in foreign policy on a universal rather than selective basis. When submitting a resolution on human rights violations in China to the UN Commission on Human Rights in 2001, the head of the US delegation for example urged 'other Commission members to join us in upholding the principle of universality of human rights'.[11] The assistant secretary for democracy, human rights and labor asserted the commitment of the administration to the universality of human rights by identifying 'our work promoting the universal observance of human rights',[12] and by stating that '[w]e employ a wide range of strategies to promote human rights and democracy',[13] and by affirming that the administration is 'maintaining the focus on human rights and democracy worldwide'.[14]

The Bureau of Democracy, Human Rights and Labor repeated the message that universal human rights are promoted as independent foreign policy goals by announcing that 'we share the common goal of promoting respect for human rights' and highlighted 'those set forth in the Universal Declaration of Human Rights, and international humanitarian law' as receiving particular attention.[15] This same message has been expressed in various human rights reports produced by the State Department. Since 1975, Congress has required the State Department to produce an annual *Country Reports on Human Rights Practices* to document human rights violations occurring around the world. In 2004, the State Department published an additional report, *Supporting Human Rights and Democracy*.[16] This document described how the US was responding to those issues raised in the *Country Reports* and 'highlights US efforts to promote human rights and democracy in the 101 countries and entities with the worst human rights record'.[17] The document concluded that these efforts demonstrated 'the United States is pursuing a broad strategy of promoting respect for human rights that is both appropriate in itself and beneficial for US security'.[18]

In a *Foreign Affairs* article, Paula Dobriansky labeled as 'incorrect' the criticism that the Bush Administration cooperated with authoritarian regimes and turned a blind eye to the anti-democratic practices carried out by US allies.[19] The undersecretary of state for global affairs clarified that 'this administration, whenever it encounters evidence of serious human rights violations or anti-democratic practices in specific countries, has raised a voice of opposition to such violations and sought to address these problems'.[20] Moreover, this principled position was maintained 'irrespective of the identity of the offender'.[21] The internally consistent message in this discourse affirmed the promotion of universal human rights as an independent policy goal of the Bush Administrations.

Rule two: rule one is derived from a pre-existing US identity

The second internally consistent rule in the hegemonic discourse holds that human rights are constitutive foreign policy goals (rule one) not out of choice alone but instead to realize a pre-existing US identity. This rule rests on two pillars. First, the rule requires that identities can be established as matters of fact, rather than of interpretation. The second pillar requires that US identity can be defined in terms of the good, while those of its enemies can be defined in terms of evil. In one notable expression of this rule asserted during his 2002 State of the Union address, the president juxtaposed the US against 'evil doers', 'terrorists' and 'rogue states' that together constituted an 'axis of evil'.[22] This discourse differentiates the world into binary opposites with the US defending human rights as a component of its struggle against evil. As Craner explained

> [t]he United States stands up for democracy and human rights around the world, and we maintain a fundamental belief that freedom is better than oppression, that liberty is better than tyranny, that rule of law works better than power and that respect for human rights is better than arbitrary abuse of individuals.[23]

Having established specific identities, the second hegemonic rule holds that the US must promote human rights as an aspect of its identity both as a state and as a people. The president has advanced this rule through stating that '[t]his nation is freedom's home and defender',[24] and that 'our nation is committed to an historic, long-term goal – we seek the end of tyranny in our world'.[25] Here, the president is contextualizing foreign policy not in terms of choices made by the administration but rather by recourse to beliefs and values that are attached to the nation.

On other occasions the president has articulated US identity in terms of human rights by declaring that 'advocating human rights around the world allows all Americans to celebrate the universal principles of liberty and justice that define our dreams and shape our hopes as we face the challenges of a new era'.[26] In his 2005 inaugural speech President Bush similarly announced that '[a]ll who live in tyranny and hopelessness can know: the United States will not ignore your oppression, or excuse your oppressors. When you stand for liberty, we will stand with you'.[27] This repeated the identity of the US described by the president in his 2002 State of the Union address when he proclaimed that 'America will always stand firm for the non-negotiable demands of human dignity: the rule of law; limits on the power of the state; respect for women; private property; free speech; equal justice and religious tolerance'.[28] The message shared by these assertions held that a pre-existent US identity validated and justified the support for human rights evident in the foreign policy of his administrations.

Repeating this link between national identity and human rights, the head of the US delegation stated in remarks to the UN Commission on Human Rights that 'ours is a country with global interests and a deep and abiding concern for the promotion of universal human rights in every country of the world'.[29] The assistant secretary for democracy, human rights and labor likewise linked human rights to US identity by asserting that 'human rights have the deep and strong backing of both parties, all branches of government, and, most importantly, the American people'.[30] According to this message, the promotion of human rights is hard wired into the nature of the US state and civil society. It is in this context that Colin Powell asserted that '[t]he United States values the sanctity of the individual and is committed to preventing human rights abuses'.[31] The secretary of state likewise derived support for human rights from US identity when he commemorated 2004 human rights week by reaffirming 'our commitment to the principles which have come to characterize our nation'.[32] Reifying hegemonic rule two, Powell included human rights in these principles since '[o]ur fight for human rights will continue so long as tyrannical regimes infringe upon the freedom of citizens'.[33]

Indeed, the US has been defined in the hegemonic discourse not as a territorial state geographically located to the south of Canada and to the north of Mexico but instead in terms of ideals of human rights and freedom. National Security Advisor, Condoleezza Rice, for example, announced following 9/11 that, 'we are not going to stop talking about the things that matter to us – human rights and freedom and so forth. We're going to press those issues. We would not be America if we did not'.[34] There is simply no alternative, Rice explained on another occasion, 'America's power and purpose must be used to defend freedom'.[35] Consistent with defining US identity partly in terms of human rights, the president rejected allegations that US intelligence officers tortured foreign prisoners on the grounds that 'the values of this country are such that torture is not a part of our soul and our being'.[36]

Hegemonic rule two equates US identity with the promotion of human rights through employing simplified renditions of the origins of the state. Articulating this myth, Dobriansky proclaimed that 'US commitment to human rights dates from the Declaration of Independence and our nation's founding. This reflects our nation's values'.[37] Repeating this message that US commitment to human rights derives from the origins of the state, the president asserted that, 'from the day of our Founding, we have proclaimed that every man and woman on this earth has rights, and dignity, and matchless value'.[38] On another occasion President Bush stated that '[d]uring Human Rights Day, Bill of Rights Day and Human Rights Week, we celebrate the founding ideals of our Nation and emphasize the importance of protecting human liberty throughout the world'.[39] Again conflating human rights with the founding of the US, the president used the occasion of his 2003 State of the Union address to announce that, '[o]ur founders dedicated this country to the cause of human dignity, the rights of every person and the possibilities of every life'.[40] On a further occasion the president repeated the underlying message by calling upon 'the people of the United States to honor the legacy of human rights passed down to us from previous generations'.[41]

The version of history that asserts US identity in terms of freedom and human rights has been subsequently appealed to when explaining foreign policy decisions. For example, in a news conference after the 2003 invasion of Iraq, President Bush announced that for nearly a century, the United States and Great Britain have been allies in the defense of liberty. We've opposed all the great threats to peace and security in the world. . . . In every challenge, we've applied the combined power of our nations to the cause of justice, and we're doing the same today.[42]

The internally consistent message established the US as the vanguard of human rights. Craner can, therefore, state that

the United States has been the unquestioned leader of the movement to expand human rights since the Second World War. We pushed it in the UN Charter, the Universal Declaration of Human Rights and into the conventions and treaty bodies that have ensued.[43]

Dobriansky likewise asserted the underlying message that '[s]ince the end of the Second World War, the United States has been without equal in articulating a vision of international human rights and having the grit to carry it out'.[44]

Rule three: US championing human rights complements distinct foreign policy goals of freedom, justice and democracy promotion

After the Cold War, the Bureau of Human Rights and Humanitarian Affairs changed its name to the Bureau of Democracy, Human Rights and Labor. This conflation of human rights with democracy constitutes the third, internally consistent, rule in the hegemonic discourse, often combined with additional commitments to justice, human dignity, freedom and liberty promotion as constitutive foreign policy goals. The third internally consistent hegemonic rule asserts not only that these ethical principles are mutually compatible but moreover that the promotion of these principles, rather than self-interest or power concerns, explains the basis of US foreign policy. Vice President Cheney for example announced that a power-based frame of analysis was an inappropriate paradigm through which to understand foreign policy when he announced in 2004 that 'our choice is not between a uni-polar world and a multi-polar world. Our choice is for a just, free and democratic world'.[45]

Expressing this message that ethical values rather than power considerations best explain foreign policy, President Bush announced that 'our commitment for freedom is complete' and 'Americans stand united with those who love democracy, justice and individual liberty. We are committed to upholding these principles'.[46] On other occasions the president has announced that, '[w]e're pursuing a strategy of freedom around the world' and that 'liberty is the right and hope of all humanity'.[47] When addressing the UN, President Bush listed as 'callings' for the US, the 'defeat of terror', the protection of 'human rights', 'the spread of prosperity' and 'the advance of democracy'.[48] Similarly, the 2002 *National Security Strategy* expressed support for an array of liberal values when it declared US commitment to 'the common rights and needs of men and women' and to the 'non-negotiable demands of dignity, the rule of law, limits on the power of the state, respect for women and private property and free speech and equal justice and religious tolerance'.[49] The secretary of state likewise announced in a *Foreign Affairs* article that '[w]e want to promote human dignity and democracy in the world',[50] and that '[w]e commit ourselves to democracy, development, global public health and human rights, as well as to the prerequisite of a solid structure for global peace'.[51]

The internally consistent message in this discourse holds that the asserted ethical principles constitute an independent concern in foreign policymaking. That is to say, the promotion of democracy, liberty, justice and freedom by the US complements the promotion of human rights asserted in hegemonic rules one and two. Rather than addressing the complexities and contradictions inherent to political choices, the third rule of the hegemonic discourse thereby insists on a black and white explanation of foreign policy decisions that expunges any such contradictions of political significance.

The reflective explanation

The question then presents itself as to the meaning and political significance of the three hegemonic rules described above and the chapter turns in its second part to consider three distinct explanations. The first explanation, hereafter referred to as the reflective explanation, readily concedes that lack of resources or competing security concerns may preclude the promotion of human rights in certain cases, but maintains that the three rules describe a corresponding reality nonetheless. Burke-White interprets the hegemonic discourse as reflecting a genuine commitment to ideals by pointing to the prominence assigned to values in the 2002 *National Security Strategy*.[52] Freedman likewise asserts that the value-based language of policymakers should be considered on its own grounds and cannot be dismissed as 'simply surface froth, designed to beguile and bemuse public and wider international opinion'.[53] Foot argues that the Bush Administration is compelled to consider human rights concerns because of the political, bureaucratic and legislative commitments that it operates under.[54] Since human rights are interpreted as constitutive foreign policy goals, it follows that hegemonic rule one can be understood literally in the sense of articulating the value basis of policy decisions.

A number of observers have likewise taken the second hegemonic rule to reflect the corresponding reality that the US promotes human rights by virtue of its pre-existent identity. Wolfson, for example, defines US traditions in terms of 'reverence for individual rights' and consequently sees the state as 'a force for good' across the world.[55] Condron relies on this same interpretation to conclude that '[t]his explains why human rights have become such an issue in foreign policy – they lie at the basis of the American nation and are a logical goal for our moral feelings'.[56] Schweller likewise interprets rule two as describing reality by contending 'if forced to choose between peace, on the one hand, and justice and liberty, on the other, Americans will choose the latter as they have consistently done in the past'.[57] By virtue of the nature and identity of US society, the promotion of human rights can, under this account, be seen as a constitutive element of foreign policy. Rosenblatt goes so far as to extend the applicability of rule two to the foreign policies of all US administrations by claiming that political leaders must represent the liberal values held by the citizenry. Rosenblatt moreover contends that US politics has disloyalty to leaders 'built into its system' and that consequently 'whenever we find leaders straying from principles, we are encouraged, indeed obliged, to smack them down'.[58] Under this explanation, a vigilant and empowered population ensures that political leaders adhere to the liberal principles that define US national identity.

The reflective explanation likewise interprets hegemonic rule three as representing a corresponding social reality. Warner contends that '[i]deas like the rule of law, human rights, economic liberty and democracy are what free societies export to the rest of the world'.[59] Mazarr suggests that President Bush believes in a directional history where good will succeed in its battle over evil.[60] According to Mazarr, 'this is utopian, transformative language, derived from a perspective that sees history as a contest of ideas and minds more than of battalions and budgets'.[61] Thus, the hegemonic discourse is interpreted literally to signify a commitment to ethical principles.

Under the reflective interpretation, principles are hypothesized to provide a basis for foreign policy decision making independent of power concerns. In the words of Deputy Secretary of Defense Paul Wolfowitz, 'in international relations, as in other human activities, principles count'.[62] Goldstein and Keohane conclude that in terms of the design of policies 'ideas serve the purpose of guiding behavior under conditions of uncertainty by stipulating causal patterns or by providing compelling ethical or moral motivations for action'.[63] Colin Dueck identifies the 'independent influence of ideas' as 'the crucial, missing element' in understanding the post-September 2001 foreign policy decisions made by the Bush Administration.[64]

Those theorists accepting the contention that the hegemonic discourse reflects a corresponding reality include many who oppose such a direction for foreign policy. In cases of previous administrations, Morgenthau famously argued that a commitment to human rights was a form of sentimentality that cost the US resources and lives and on those grounds threatened the national interest. Morgenthau interpreted such sentimentality as both a destructive and influential force in foreign policymaking.[65] Morgenthau consequently urged the US government to respond to the interests of its people rather than pursue what he perceived to be an illusionary universal moral code.[66]

According to the reflective explanation, the hegemonic discourse can be interpreted literally since policymakers are motivated in part by principles, including those of human rights. Debate then ensues as to the wisdom of this course of action, typically on the basis of the definition of the national interest advanced. One group contends that national interests are best served through the promotion of human rights while another group takes the opposing position. The meaning of the hegemonic discourse provided by policymakers is, however, taken as a given by both groups and removed from further scrutiny.

Before being seduced by the seemingly axiomatic interpretation of the hegemonic discourse as describing a corresponding reality, we would be wise to remind ourselves of how Antonio Gramsci demonstrated the capacity for ideology to substitute partial aspects of reality for the comprehensive true account. In particular, Gramsci highlighted the political significance of constructing mythological discourses around superficial ideas and presenting the resultant simplified interpretation of reality as the full story.[67] How the three hegemonic rules described above constitute such mythological simplifications can be highlighted through detailing sources of evidence that contradict the myths advanced. Such evidence analyzed in subsequent chapters of this book include the use of cluster bombs, the decision not to compile authoritative statistics on the number of civilian deaths caused in the wake of wars fought in Afghanistan and Iraq and the authorization of military orders providing for non-US nationals suspected of involvement in international terrorism to be held indefinitely without trial.

The proposition that the Bush Administrations have worked to promote human rights, but have at times been thwarted in this ambition by circumstances beyond their control, suffers from three notable inadequacies. First, the explanation fails to account for the hostility of the administrations to international legal mechanisms that have sought to define and advance universal enforcement of stipulated human rights.[68] Second, the account erroneously asserts that at certain times human rights concerns can enter the policymaking process but at other times must be sidelined due to competing national interest concerns. Attempts at explaining the selective integration of human rights into foreign policy are erroneous since they contradict the necessary conditions for human rights.[69] Third, the reflective explanation overlooks, and thereby depoliticizes, the patterns evident in the inconsistent application of human rights under the Bush Administrations.[70]

The politically significant simplifications evident in the hegemonic discourse can be identified in the internal construction of each individual hegemonic rule. As the introduction explained, human rights can mean very different things to different people, with internal fault lines running between social and economic rights on the one hand and civil and political rights on the other. Taxes to provide resources for social education and health rights subsequently conflict with the private property rights claims of individuals. Rather than defining how conflicts between competing categories of rights are to be reconciled or detailing how universal human rights are to be enforced in practice, hegemonic rule one discards nuances and instead simply repeats its defining message that human rights are promoted as independent foreign policy goals.

That the reflective explanation offers an inadequate interpretation of hegemonic rule one can be demonstrated through examining how the president's assessment on the role of human rights in foreign policy has changed over time. In the 2000 presidential debates against Al Gore, George W. Bush repeatedly criticized his opponent for focusing too much on nation building adventures overseas.[71] In one debate Bush stated, for example, 'I don't think we can be all things to all people in the world. I think we've got to be very careful when we commit our troops'.[72] In another debate Bush voiced his opposition to the interventions in Somalia and Haiti by claiming that 'I don't think nation-building missions are worthwhile' and that 'I don't think our troops ought to be used for what's called nation-building. I think our troops ought to be used to fight and win war'.[73] These statements evaluate questions of war and peace not by a criterion of human rights but instead by perceptions of the national interest.

Likewise prior to 9/11, Condoleezza Rice opposed deploying coercive US power in instances where the only potential gain would be the protection of human rights.[74] Writing in *Foreign Affairs*, Rice explained that foreign policy under a Republican Administration 'will proceed from the firm ground of the national interest, not from the interests of an illusionary international community'.[75] These statements are not consistent with the reflective explanation of a foreign policy based around promoting respect for human rights as an independent goal since the perceived interests of US citizens are privileged over the needs of non-US citizens. The reflective explanation of the hegemonic discourse cannot explain why the linguistic change from ambiguous skepticism pre-9/11 to principled human rights promotion post-9/11 occurred at precisely that time when the administration resolved to deploy US military force.

The inadequacy of the reflective explanation of the second hegemonic rule relates to the assertion that the US has a singular identity, rather than a rich plurality of competing and indeed contradictory identities. Attempts to attach one particular identity to a state are problematic since they overlook how both identity and history are themselves inherently contestable rather than fixed variables. Contentions that the US is founded on ideals of democracy, human rights and freedom are as vacuous as claims that locate the origins of that state in values of capitalism, slavery and genocide since each interpretation falsely presents a simplified mythology as an exclusive truth. The word 'democracy' was for example mentioned neither in the Declaration of Independence nor was it mentioned in the 1787 Constitution. It is at best unlikely that the framers of the Constitution intended for indigenous peoples, slaves, women or blacks to be included as full citizens or to play a meaningful role in political affairs. Indeed, slavery was an integral economic institution until the passing of the thirteenth amendment in 1865, exemplified by the quantifying of slaves as three-fifths of a person for the purpose of calculating the representation and taxation of each state in the Union. Whereas the reflective explanation of rule two necessarily holds that US identity is a pre-existent fact that can be described through language, identity is more accurately understood as a socially constructed variable that is only given meaning by an internally coherent discourse.

The reflective explanation is likewise open to charges of immunizing from critical scrutiny the political mythology contained in hegemonic rule three. Conflating commitments to distinct ethical concepts of human rights, freedom, justice and democracy and thereafter asserting that these values underpin foreign policy does little to define what is actually understood by these contested concepts. Neither does the conflation explain how conflicts between these concepts are to be resolved. Indeed, acknowledging that a choice exists between promoting either democracy or human rights would contradict hegemonic rule three that rejects such nuances by instead maintaining that foreign policy promotes both. In contrast to this expression of mythology, conflating distinct ethical terms is problematic for the impartial and universal realization of human rights since it moves attention away from a deontological focus on rights in favor of vague commitments to 'freedom', 'democracy promotion' or 'dignity' that can be applied on an ad hoc basis to defend virtually any policy. Illustrating the extent to which linguistic appeals to freedom can invert reality, the words 'arbeit macht frei' or 'freedom through work' greeted victims entering concentration camps built by the National Socialist government of Germany to implement the final solution to the Jewish question. References to 'human dignity' can be similarly problematic for the realization of human rights since dignity, unlike rights, need be neither egalitarian nor universal in nature.[76] Moreover, 'dignity' lacks any recognized enforcement mechanism, which further facilitates its linguistic manipulation to promote virtually any policy.[77] Therefore, the discursive insistence in hegemonic rule three that universal ethical values act as the foundation for foreign policies coexists with a reluctance to systematically define these concepts in practice.

The rejectionist explanation

Given the shortcomings of the reflective explanation to account for the three hegemonic rules, a second explanation, hereafter termed the rejectionist explanation, dismisses the hegemonic discourse as a distraction. According to the rejectionist explanation, concerns of self-interest and limited resources prevent policymakers from integrating human rights into foreign policy decisions.

First and foremost for theorists following in the footsteps of Kenneth Waltz, the actions of states are constrained by the anarchical nature of the international system. This system leaves individual states with little choice but to compete with other states for the coercive power capabilities that are thought to ensure their own security.[78] Accordingly, states simply do not have the option of promoting respect for human rights since international politics, unlike domestic politics, is restricted to ensuring conditions for survival. Rather than being of independent concern, oppressive conditions in foreign states only become politically significant to the extent that they affect conditions of international order that can impinge on the security of states. Claims by politicians to promote respect for human rights as an actual foreign policy goal, independent of power concerns, can be subsequently dismissed as either a convenient cover for less philanthropic goals, or else, as idealistic aspirations that cannot be realized in practice because of the nature of the international system.

John Pilger and William Blum reach this same conclusion of rejecting the political significance of the hegemonic discourse, albeit on very different grounds from Waltz. These notable critics of US foreign policy see human rights violations occurring around the world as a direct consequence not of the constraints of the international system but rather of the choices made by successive administrations.[79] According to both Pilger and Blum, the US is itself identified as a serial violator of human rights in its quest for economic and political gain. From this perspective, the difference between the words and actions of officials leads inexorably to the rejection of the hegemonic discourse as rhetoric.

Despite the chasm between their normative foundations, Waltz, Blum and Pilger share the same analytical explanation for the role of the hegemonic discourse, notably that it tells us little about foreign policy. In support of this explanation it is known that George W. Bush grew up with oil and little league baseball in the West Texas town of Midland and vehemently opposed liberal, 'intellectual snobbery'.[80] It can subsequently be hypothesized that political consistency may not be particularly high on the list of priorities for a president who cares more about pragmatism and workable compromises.

It could also be argued that the significance of the hegemonic rules identified above can be rejected on grounds that they do little to allow for nuances within the administrations. It could be argued further that if the reflective explanation is inadequate, then the rejectionist account must, by default, be valid, or that some messy combination of the two explains the hegemonic discourse. It is the contention here that rejecting the political significance of the hegemonic discourse on any of these grounds is inadequate for three reasons.

First, the rejectionist explanation cannot adequately account for the centrality ascribed by President Bush to how and why post-9/11 foreign policy was presented as a generational battle between good and evil. Second, the rejectionist account does not explain why, if human rights are simply a political irrelevance, a minimum level of treatment for military prisoners is even considered, or why the US military does not deploy the full extent of its vast military arsenal against designated enemies. Third, the rejectionist account overlooks the significance of the internal consistencies of the hegemonic discourse identified above in terms of the three hegemonic rules. Although it is unquestionably the case that individual administration officials have their own personal ideas about the meaning and role of human rights in foreign policy, there is little contradiction of the mythology underlying the hegemonic discourse from any administration officials. There is, for example, very little evidence of administration officials making post-9/11 public statements that the human rights of non-nationals are simply an irrelevance to US foreign policy.

The productive explanation

The reflective and rejectionist explanations of the hegemonic discourse begin with the assumption that ideas can only exist in the real world external to the discourses constructed by actors. That is to say that both explanations perceive references to human rights made by administration officials in terms of explaining a corresponding reality. The rejectionist explanation adds that, because of the evident contradictions between the human rights rhetoric and practices of the administration, the political significance of the hegemonic discourse can be dismissed.

In contrast to these interpretations, Michel Foucault stressed the constitutive role of discourse in producing, rather than reflecting, the meanings of ideas and understandings of reality.[81] The third interpretation advances this productive explanation of the hegemonic discourse to explain (i) the prominence ascribed to the ethical basis of foreign policy by administration officials, (ii) the internal consistencies within the hegemonic discourse as expressed through the three rules detailed above and (iii) the externally inconsistent application of human rights in actual foreign policy practice. On these three grounds, the productive explanation is argued here to provide a more comprehensive account for understanding the hegemonic discourse than either the reflective or rejectionist perspectives.

The productive explanation interprets the hegemonic discourse not as describing a corresponding reality but instead as a technique of governance that produces an interpretation of events and identities. The remainder of the chapter explains this claim by detailing how mythologies can become confused with factual truths in the minds of the audience. It does this in four stages, the first of which explains how accepted truths can be a function of deeply held beliefs rather than a reflection of a corresponding reality. The second stage details how the process of belief formation is in part a function of governance. The third proceeds to review evidence that officials connected to the Bush Administrations have recognized that power operates through influencing popular beliefs. The fourth stage illustrates how accepted truths have been produced by political discourse.

Questioning cause and effect in truth and beliefs

Daalder and Lindsay noted in a rightly celebrated work on George W. Bush that the fixation during the 2000 election campaign was on how informed the then governor of Texas was of foreign policy, on the assumption that beliefs must be built on a foundation of facts. Daalder and Lindsay observed that 'this assumption is usually wrong' and that 'people generally come to their beliefs about how the world works long before they encounter facts'.[82] In particular, Daalder and Lindsay observe the tendency for personal beliefs to construct the truth rather than vice versa. Highlighting the relative importance of instinct over systematic analysis, George W. Bush reported in conversation to Bob Woodward that he was a 'gut player' rather than an intellectual.[83]

Beliefs are commonly formed not from an objective inspection of all available evidence but rather through the lens of conceptual frameworks that are dominant in society.[84] Exemplifying this point, Campbell demonstrates how the desire to find a westward route to Asia from Europe led Christopher Columbus to retain the conviction that, despite all evidence to the contrary, he had landed in India rather than America, and hence the application of the name 'Indians' to the indigenous population.[85] Columbus, Campbell explains, 'knows in advance what he will find; the concrete experience is there to illustrate a truth already possessed, not to be interrogated according to pre-established rules in order to seek the truth'.[86]

Political culture theorists have suggested that this propensity to interpret real world evidence to support pre-existent beliefs applies to US society in general. Gabriel Almond for example insisted that the American populace tends to react to foreign policy in a manner based upon instinct and emotion rather than reflection. The emotion may be that of resignation, anger or of indifference but, Almond concluded, it was invariably a 'superficial and fluctuating response'.[87] Factual evidence relating to the real world that does not conform to deeply held beliefs can subsequently be silenced without the need for any formal censorship, since such evidence will be instinctively distrusted. Congressman Otis Pike revealed, for example, that when he chaired a 1975 committee that uncovered a litany of US covert actions, few members of Congress had shown an interest in reading the subsequent report. Pike explained that 'they are asked to believe that their country has been evil. And nobody wants to believe that'.[88] To the extent that scholars neglect the productive function of the hegemonic discourse expressed by policymakers, they simultaneously overlook the political significance of the creation and validation of social beliefs.[89]

Governing through the production of social beliefs

Under the Foucaultian account, power is most effectively employed when it remains hidden by virtue of being perceived as normal to those over whom it is exercised.[90] Since beliefs contextualize how the world is understood by an audience, it follows that power can be exercised through attempting to influence those beliefs. The godfather of public relations, Edward Bernays, for example, hypothesized that understanding how the group mind operates can allow the political elite 'to control and regiment the masses according to our will without their knowing about it'.[91] In particular Bernays identified as a consistent rule in mass psychology that the voice of the people 'is composed of inherited prejudices and symbols and clichés and verbal formulas supplied to them by the leaders'.[92]

Graham Wallas likewise maintained nearly a century ago that the citizenry tended to formulate their understanding of the world from an emotional rather than a reasoned basis and contended that emotional associations could be artificially made in the minds of the audience.[93] Wallas explained that such associations could be made by politicians referring repeatedly to emotional points of reference after which it would be difficult for the minds of an audience 'not to confuse acquired emotional association with the full process of logical inference'.[94] Rather than public opinion being a reflective check on the power of government, according to Bernays and Wallas such opinion can be itself a product of the imagery, symbols, clichés, verbal formulas and emotional associations provided by political authorities. Wallas consequently noted that, 'advertisement and party politics are becoming more and more closely assimilated in method'.[95] Gabriel Almond concurred, advising political leaders not to provide overly detailed information about foreign affairs to the public since all that was required were 'cues for mood responses'.[96]

The significance of this discussion to the productive explanation of the hegemonic discourse resides in how Bernays, Wallas and Almond theorize discourse as a means to produce a desired interpretation of reality in the minds of the audience.[97] In particular, the hegemonic discourse can be seen as a technique of governance in the sense of producing the beliefs and interpretations held by an audience. Convincing people to think in a certain manner is the function of discipline. As Allen explains, the point of discipline is not to force people to do what you want them to do or to control their behavior by appeals to their self-interest. Instead discipline operates by making people think in a desired manner.[98] The productive interpretation does not deny that the hegemonic discourse can be selectively applied as a cover for the promotion of other foreign policy goals,[99] but it adds that the discourse performs a more basic function in terms of disciplining an audience by producing identities and meaning.

Political recognition that power operates by influencing belief

Identifying a productive function of discourse in theory is, of course, insufficient to demonstrate the applicability of that theory in practice. Evidence indicates however that the architects of the hegemonic discourse in the Bush Administrations have recognized the productive function of political discourse. Chief speechwriter for George W. Bush, Michael Gerson, thought that in order for the US to become involved in the world, the US public 'had to be convinced that both its security interests and its ideals were in jeopardy'.[100] Exemplifying the productive function of discourse, the purpose of speech identified by Gerson is therefore to persuade rather than to describe.

Similarly acknowledging the productive function of discourse, the Defense Department issued a directive early in the first Bush Administration for the military to establish an Office of Strategic Influence. Hiebert reports the specific remit of this office was to influence public opinion around the world.[101] In a further example acknowledging the productive function of discourse, a 2004 report written by the Defense Science Board sought to address reasons for 'America's negative image in world opinion and diminished ability to persuade' following the 2003 invasion of Iraq.[102] The report identified 'global public opinion', 'the role of culture, values and religion in shaping human behavior', 'media trends and influences on audiences' as constituting 'issues vital to national security'.[103] The report goes on to recommend 'a sophisticated method that maps perceptions and influences networks' so that the US could win what was termed a 'global struggle about ideas'.[104] This 'struggle' was to be built upon 'in-depth knowledge of other cultures and factors that motivate human behavior' and was to be implemented by adapting, 'techniques of skilful political campaigning'.[105] The creation of perceptions and public opinion was therefore

identified in the report not only as an entirely possible function of political discourse but moreover as an issue vital to national security.

In light of this evidence, it is consistent to interpret the hegemonic discourse
in terms of a governance mechanism that operates by disciplining how an audience interprets the world around it. Indeed, the Department of Defense operates
a National Defense University at Fort McNair, Washington, where it employs
professors of psychological operations specifically to research and teach techniques of mind control and persuasion.[106] Hiebert reminds us that government
propaganda techniques are especially effective in the US, since most citizens
think such techniques are only practiced by other states.[107]

Examples of power operating by influencing belief

This final section reviews specific cases that exemplify the productive function
of discourse employed by the Bush Administrations. In one notable case, Lang
demonstrates how Bush Administration officials branded Iran as a terrorist state
in the axis of evil, not because of a sole focus on terrorist activities, but rather
because the US has traditionally not seen the Palestinian or Shi'ite Lebanese
rights, advanced by Iran, as a legitimate area of political concern.[108] In particular
Lang details how the discourse provided by the administration differentiated the
legitimate from the illegitimate to create the necessary context in which the contention that Iran is a terrorist state could be understood in the minds of the
audience.[109]

In another instance, Campbell uses the example of neighboring Iraq to
demonstrate how identity can be discursively produced. In the case of its 1990
invasion of Kuwait, Iraq was presented by the George H.W. Bush Administration as an aggressive violator of international laws and a threat to the peace and
security of the Middle East, a classification that led to the 1991 Gulf War. A
decade earlier when Iraq invaded revolutionary Iran, Campbell notes there was
'no call to action, let alone a military response from the United States'.[110]
Indeed, the US sent military aid to Iraq to fund its war against Iran. Campbell
uses this juxtaposition to illustrate how identity is produced through discursive
political interpretation rather than simply reflecting a pre-existing reality. This
same conclusion can be validated through examining the identity of Iraq as an
ally of al Qaeda, as repeatedly suggested by the Bush Administration in the run
up to the 2003 Iraq War.

Despite extensive searches by the US intelligence community and two commissions investigating Iraq and the 9/11 attacks, credible evidence linking
Hussein to the events of that day remained elusive.[111] Indeed, there was more
evidence linking Florida to 9/11 than there was Iraq, given that a number of the
hijackers had trained at flying schools based in that state. In contrast, the discourse of the Bush Administrations repeatedly conflated the wars on terror and
Iraq. A section of a January 2004 speech by the president detailing progress in
the war on terror was, for example, entitled 'Making Real Progress in Iraq – the
Front Lines of the War on Terror'.[112] On other occasions the president described

the Iraq War as 'the central front in the war on terror',[113] claimed that '[t]he liberation of Iraq removed ... an ally of al Qaeda',[114] and that 'there's no question that Saddam Hussein had al Qaeda ties'.[115] Donald Rumsfeld alluded to a similar association, claiming in September 2002 that the CIA had 'bullet-proof' evidence of a connection between al Qaeda and Saddam Hussein.[116] The secretary of defense subsequently warned that '[w]ithin a week, or a month, Saddam could give his WMD to al Qaeda'.[117] Rice implied the same link between Hussein and al Qaeda by asserting that 'Saddam was a danger in the region where the 9/11 threat emerged'.[118] Vice President Cheney likewise contended that '[t]here's overwhelming evidence ... of a connection between al Qaeda and Iraq',[119] that the Iraqi leader had 'an established relationship with al Qaeda',[120] and that Hussein had 'long-established ties with al Qaeda'.[121] Speaking in June 2003, General Wesley Clark summarized the underlying political message from the administration as 'a concerted effort' to 'pin' the 9/11 attacks on Saddam Hussein.[122] Clark claimed that, as early as September 11, 2001, he received calls from the White House requesting that '[y]ou got to say this is connected. ... This has to be connected to Saddam Hussein'.[123]

Without administration officials making direct public allegations that Hussein was responsible for the 9/11 attacks but in the context of the constant conflation of Saddam Hussein and 9/11 as outlined above, polls indicate that an initially skeptical American public came increasingly to accept the links alluded to in the discourse as established fact. Whereas in the week of the 9/11 attacks only 3 percent of American citizens surveyed, named Saddam Hussein as the most likely perpetrator, an August 2002 poll found that the number of respondents believing Hussein to be personally involved in the 9/11 attacks had risen to 53 percent.[124] By March 2003 60 percent of American citizens surveyed thought of Hussein as an immediate threat to the US and almost half thought that the 9/11 hijackers included Iraqis.[125] By September 2003 a *Washington Post* poll found that 69 percent of Americans believed that Saddam was involved in the 9/11 attacks.[126]

As Pillar points out, public understanding of US foreign policy relies not upon forensic examination of all available evidence but instead upon vague associations, the blurring of important distinctions and by suggestive references made by trusted figures.[127] Further, detailing this productive function of discourse, cognitive scientists have demonstrated that the neural circuitry, the synapses, of the human brain works by processing frames rather than isolated facts. Hiebert explains, 'we don't think about facts; the mind switches to the way those facts are framed'.[128] That is to say, the human brain thinks through looking at context and linkages rather than at facts in isolation. It is in this sense of framing understanding that repeatedly suggesting linkages between al Qaeda and Hussein can be understood as an effective technique of governance.

That the hegemonic discourse is itself constitutive of the production of reality can be exemplified in the interpretation provided by the Bush Administration to the loss of the US seat on the UN Commission on Human Rights in May 2001. The Chinese delegation explained the reason for this in terms that the Bush

Administration was 'politicizing' human rights, having 'undermined the atmosphere for dialogue'.[129] The episode was, in contrast, presented by the administration as resulting from its unwavering principled support for human rights. In particular, President Bush explained the loss of the seat in terms of hegemonic rule one as 'the price paid' for US support of a previous resolution condemning human rights abuses in Cuba.[130] Expressing hegemonic rule two, the president asserted the identity of the US as promoting human rights by stating that 'repressed people around the world must know this about the United States: We might not sit on some commission, but we will always be the world's leader in support of human rights'.[131] This identity was sustained by administration officials portraying other members of the UN as the parties responsible for the politicization of human rights and for punishing the administration for taking a principled stance. Thus, the undersecretary of state for global affairs asserted in Congressional testimony, 'we did pay a price for taking forthright, principled positions at the Commission this year'.[132]

Conclusion

This chapter began by identifying three internally consistent features or rules in the account of human rights in foreign policy provided by Bush Administration officials. Together, these three rules constitute that which has been referred to as the hegemonic discourse. Three different explanations of the political significance of the hegemonic discourse were then discussed in the second part of the chapter. The reflective explanation readily acknowledged the hegemonic discourse as a summarized account of reality but denied that the simplifications made in the discourse were imbued with political significance. Instead, the hegemonic discourse was seen as describing the constitutive and independent, if at times aspirational, role that human rights perform in foreign policy. The rejectionist interpretation in contrast saw the notable disjuncture between the claims made in the hegemonic discourse and the reality of foreign policy as evidence to dismiss the discourse as devoid of explanatory value.

Both the reflective and rejectionist explanations were found to suffer notable inadequacies. The productive account suggested that the hegemonic discourse could be taken seriously, unlike its interpretation under the rejectionist explanation but not literally, unlike its interpretation under the reflective explanation. Under the productive explanation, the evident chasm between rhetoric and real world evidence does not lead inexorably to the conclusion that the hegemonic discourse can be ignored as a focus for scholarly enquiry. In particular it was argued that rejecting the significance of the hegemonic discourse either overlooks or unduly denies the capacity of language to produce, rather than describe, the socially accepted nature of the real world.

The reflective and rejectionist explanations of the hegemonic discourse were subsequently found to overlook not only that the productive function of discourse is openly acknowledged within policymaking circles but indeed that its political importance is highlighted. One report written by the Defense Science

Board, for example, affirms that '[n]othing shapes US policies and global perceptions of US foreign and national security objectives more powerfully than the President's statements and actions, and those of senior officials'.[133] As Bernays summarized some years ago, it is now less important for successful politicians to know how to please the public as it is for them to know how to sway the public.[134]

A value-based language of human rights, justice and freedom can be applied to contextualize foreign policies that could, in the absence of such a context, be interpreted as examples of aggression, brutality, domination, inequality and exploitation.[135] The political significance of such evident contradictions as fighting wars in the name of peace, killing in the name of human rights, supporting the human rights of some while denying those same rights to others, and supporting certain categories of human rights while denying the validity of other categories can be obfuscated through insistence upon the rules of the hegemonic discourse.

Rather than power and ethics being located on opposing ends of the political spectrum, the productive explanation identifies that the disciplinary function of power operates in part through the capacity to define the good from the evil, the threats from the normal, the friends from the enemies, the terrorists from the freedom fighters, the legitimate from the illegitimate, the dangerous from the safe and the oppressors from the oppressed.[136] Administration officials enjoy a privileged capacity to exercise this disciplinary power to the extent that they can set the political agenda, define identities, contextualize issues and enjoy instant access to the popular media to get their message across to the audience. Administration officials subsequently enjoy considerable discretion to deploy the hegemonic rules as an instrument of governance. National Security Advisor, Condoleezza Rice is thus able to state that 'there is an old argument between the so-called "realistic" school of foreign affairs and the "idealistic school". . . . As a policymaker, I can tell you that these categories obscure reality. In real life, power and values are married completely'.[137] The remaining chapters of this book detail how the hegemonic discourse has co-opted human rights in the service of power.

2 The hegemonic discourse of Wilson and Carter

Introduction

Discourses of natural rights, the rights of man and, more recently, human rights have been cited by successive administrations to explain the basis, intents and motivation underlying foreign policy decisions. Analysis of the rights-based discourses expressed by all previous US administrations is neither possible within the confines of one chapter nor is it the purpose here. Instead, this chapter has two more specific aims. First, it will explain how the hegemonic discourse expressed by George W. Bush was heralded in the foreign policy discourses of Presidents Woodrow Wilson and Jimmy Carter. Second, the chapter aims to analyze the rights-based discourses of the Wilson and Carter Presidencies utilizing the reflective, rejectionist and productive theoretical explanations described in Chapter 1. In the cases of both Presidents Wilson and Carter the chapter defends a productive explanation and proposes that the reflective account evidences both external inconsistencies and internal contradictions.

To avoid selecting historical examples on the basis of fitting a predetermined conclusion, this chapter provides evidence in support of all the explanations before testing the consistency of each in the light of the necessary conditions of human rights.[1] The chapter will address its stated aims by analyzing (i) the internal consistencies of the hegemonic discourses articulated by Presidents Wilson and Carter and (ii) how these internal consistencies produced a politicized understanding of reality.

The focus on the Democrat Administrations of Woodrow Wilson and Jimmy Carter has been chosen for two reasons. First, the internal consistencies of the rights based discourses articulated by Presidents Wilson and Carter share notable characteristics with the hegemonic discourse of George W. Bush. Second, Woodrow Wilson and Jimmy Carter provide the strongest examples of twentieth century presidents who have stated an independent influence of rights in the policymaking process, as evidenced in the enduring caricatures of these presidents as liberal idealists.

The chapter is structured into three sections. The first section details how the reflective explanation resonates in prominent interpretations of the role of human rights in modern US foreign policy history. This section goes on to analyze how the reflective explanation attempts to reconcile its stated account with the selective integration of human rights in actual policy practices and explores the limitations to such attempts. The second and third sections examine the human rights discourses expressed by the Wilson and Carter Administrations. The chapter concludes that the radical challenge posed by the project of universal human rights has been eviscerated and that the concept has instead been co-opted by these administrations as an instrument of governance. The chapter thereby details notable commonalities in the hegemonic discourse expressed by the Wilson, Carter and George W. Bush Administrations.

Reflective techniques

The reflective explanation interprets the human rights claims made by successive administrations in terms of describing the independent integration of rights concerns into the policymaking process, albeit with the concession that these commitments may at times be overridden by competing concerns of US national security.[2] Indeed, this literal interpretation of the hegemonic discourse is taken as a given by the reflective account, and attention turns to investigate how human rights norms emerge, are sustained and become integrated into the policy process.[3]

Ideas and ethics are therefore seen to play a role in the policymaking process independent of power concerns. Policymakers are, for example, hypothesized to operate in a world constrained by ethical norms, if not necessarily by the multilateral regimes that institutionalize and codify those norms in the form of laws.[4] Robert McElroy, for example, locates 'the roots' of US foreign policy in 'support for freedom, human rights and anti-colonialism'.[5] Stephen Ambrose and Douglas Brinkley likewise contend that, 'the concept that every human being has certain unalienable rights is essentially Jeffersonian and American'.[6] Philip Bobbitt presents the US as a unique power that stands for human rights within a broader constitutional theory which rates democracy and human rights above state sovereignty.[7] Mary Kaldor similarly asserts that, 'America is the Crusader State – a state based on an idea rather than a national identity: and that idea is democracy'.[8] These theorists recognize norms of freedom, human rights and democracy as exercising independent roles in the design of US foreign policy.[9] The selective integration of human rights into the actual practice of US foreign policy has been accommodated by the reflective account in terms of four techniques, (i) the separation of ethics from power, (ii) competing goals, (iii) isolated exceptions and (iv) through asserting a default position.

Separation of ethics from power

The first technique employed to explain how human rights can be selectively integrated into foreign policy is to separate ethics and power in the policymaking process. McElroy, for example, suggests that ethical norms rather than power concerns can enter the political process on grounds that (i) domestic public opinion reflects human rights norms; (ii) policymakers care about their reputations and do not wish to be considered as immoral in 'the courtroom of world opinion'; (iii) national leaders have consciences; (iv) leaders wish to be associated with human rights norms and (v) 'norm entrepreneurs' have a capacity to highlight specific issues, and to thereby bring US foreign policy into compliance with international human rights norms.[10]

Since power and ethics can be separated, the influence of ethics can be identified in foreign policy decisions where no geopolitical or economic interests are apparent. McElroy highlights the 1975 decision by President Ford to order the Joint Chiefs of Staff to accept his decision to return the sovereignty and control of the Panama Canal to Panama. At the time, those urging a focus on US power concerns urged Ford not to relinquish control yet, finding the contradiction between continued US control of the canal increasingly difficult to reconcile with the right to self-determination, the president chose policy on grounds of the latter.[11]

McElroy likewise contends that a norm to help starving people compelled decision makers to act during the 1921–23 Harding Administration.[12] In 1921 the US spent 1 percent of its federal budget on food and medical supplies to mitigate famine in Russia. McElroy points out that, at the time, there was widespread economic hardship in the US, the Bolsheviks were undertaking a campaign to undermine capitalist governments in Central Europe and had confiscated US assets. McElroy observes that this aid was not motivated by a self interested desire to subsidize the domestic grain industry since much of the grain was bought from Canada.[13] Since, in these two instances, policy decisions were made that contradicted the evident self-interest of the US, McElroy interpreted human rights as exercising an independent function in the policymaking process. Thus, a clear distinction between power and human rights is made. Thereafter the independent pursuit of human rights is identified to explain policy decisions that work to the detriment of power concerns.

Competing goals

Sikkink accounts for the inconsistent integration of human rights in US foreign policy in terms of competing foreign policy goals.[14] This argument holds that whereas human rights do not determine all of foreign policy, neither do power concerns. This second technique therefore builds upon the distinction made between power and ethics to assert that the hegemonic discourse describes the ideals underlying the policymaking process. It adds that, due to competing power concerns, these ethical commitments cannot be consistently or impartially applied in practice.[15] The criticism that human rights have been applied inconsistently by successive US administrations is therefore accepted, but the position asserts that human rights concerns can enter the policymaking process nonetheless, albeit on a selective basis.

Exceptions

The third technique categorizes as exceptions any examples that demonstrate the subjugation of human rights concerns in foreign policy decisions. Callahan, for example, points out that where the US has not been as forthright in its defense of human rights as it could otherwise have been, these constitute 'exceptions to a firm human rights policy', caused by 'short-sighted temptations'.[16] This technique asserts that the hegemonic discourse generally describes a corresponding reality. Evidence to the contrary can be accommodated as exceptional.

Default

The fourth technique applied to accommodate the selective application of human rights in policy decisions is to assert a default position. Since stated intents can be neither proved nor disproved, this technique effectively provides policy-makers with the benefit of the doubt. According to this position, human rights concerns enter the policymaking process whenever and however policymakers say they do. In a variation of this technique, Kathryn Sikkink counters the criticism that the US government has failed to promote human rights impartially on the grounds that officials could be pursing 'quiet diplomacy' behind the scenes.[17] This technique can be mobilized even in circumstances where little evidence exists to support such an interpretation, since it requires none for its validation.

It is suggested here that the four techniques described above offer inadequate explanations for the selective integration of human rights in foreign policy. In particular, the underlying reasoning demonstrates three shortcomings, (i) it depoliticizes the disparity between language and practice, (ii) the separation of ethics from power is artificial and (iii) internal contradictions.

Depoliticizing the disparity between language and practice

The reflective explanation can acknowledge that the hegemonic mythology provides a simplified version of reality. The explanation cannot, however, acknowledge a political significance to this disparity since to do so would be to depart from the interpretation of the language of policymakers as reflecting a corresponding reality. Through depoliticizing the disparity between the claims and practice of human rights in foreign policy, the reflective explanation provides a sanitized history that internalizes, rather than independently critiques, the hegemonic mythology.

The separation of ethics from power is artificial

Separating power and ethics may provide for much interesting debate over foreign policy causality, but it is an ultimately artificial activity that explains more about the ideological predilections of the observers than it does about the basis of the policymaking process. Social power, as defined in the introduction to this book, is itself involved in both the validation and implementation of ethical frameworks, including those of human rights. Since the substantive meaning of human rights is inherently contestable, validations of the concept are products of social and political struggle rather than of objective reflection. Social power is, for example, exercised in authorizing notions of when a human rights problem exists in the first instance. That is to say, discourse *produces* coherent notions of human rights violations as distinct from acts of, for example, political necessity, counter terrorism, criminality, political upheavals or risk.[18] It is in this sense of governing interpretation that ethical discourse is itself an instrument of power.

Power is exercised not only in the formulation but also in the practical implementation of a human rights discourse as can be illustrated in the decision by the Harding Administration to provide humanitarian aid during the 1921 Russian famine mentioned by McElroy above. As detailed below in the context of the Wilson Administrations, a key priority in Europe was to ensure the continued viability of Russia as a bulwark against Germany, which was perceived as the main threat to US interests in the aftermath of World War I. Political dislocation caused by mass starvation would pose a serious threat to this role ascribed to Russia.

Indeed, ethical concerns cannot be integrated or implemented into the policy-making process independent of power concerns if the word 'independent' is to hold meaningful currency. Illustrating the symbiotic relationship between ethical discourse and power, Chandler cogently explains how militaristic states have deployed means of violence across the world in the name of advancing human rights. Chandler demonstrates how appeals to human rights have been co-opted to justify the selective erosion of the norm of state sovereignty.[19] The selective advocacy of human rights provides policymakers with the discretionary power to decide when to act on grounds of human rights with little accountability for the making of such decisions. In this sense of legitimizing violence, ethical discourse is again implicated in the power politics of foreign policy.

Internal contradictions

Whereas the above two criticisms of the four reflective techniques problematize the account provided from an external perspective, the third is based upon an internal contradiction. The introduction to this book argued that, for human rights to be advanced as a coherent concept, they must be recognized for all people in all circumstances. Human rights that are advanced in certain circumstances, but not in others, are not being asserted as political trumps and are therefore not being recognized as human rights at all. That is to say, a selective integration of human rights into foreign policy fails to comply with the necessary conditions of impartiality and universality and on these grounds cannot be coherently understood as support for human rights at all. Indeed, the only rights conferred are to US policymakers who can select when to intervene, when to remain on the sidelines or indeed when to oppose an intervention on grounds of human rights that require no consistency in application. The chapter turns in its second and third sections to expand on this point by illustrating how the Wilson and Carter Administrations politicized human rights.

Woodrow Wilson 1913–1920

Perhaps more than any other president, Woodrow Wilson has been characteristically identified as promoting the rights of man in foreign policy decisions. President Wilson systematically integrated a language of freedom, the rights of man and democracy promotion (hegemonic rule three) into explanations of his administrations foreign policy (hegemonic rule one) and of US identity (hegemonic rule two). Substitute 'the rights of man' for 'human rights' and this foreign policy discourse preludes the hegemonic discourse expressed by the George W. Bush Administrations described in Chapter 1.

Articulating the first of these rules, President Wilson advanced the rights of man as independent foreign policy goals when accounting for his decision to commit the US to World War I. In this instance President Wilson announced that, '[w]e are fighting for what we believe and wish to be the rights of mankind'.[20] Prior to US entry into the war, President Wilson had spoken of the 'inhumanity' of submarine warfare utilized by the German fleet to sink neutral merchant and passenger ships, including the steamers Sussex and Lusitania, in the seas around Britain.[21] Responding to this use of submarine warfare and to defend 'a just conception of the rights of mankind', President Wilson urged Congress in 1916 to authorize his administration to sever diplomatic ties with Germany.[22]

The second hegemonic rule holds that human rights are promoted in foreign policy not out of choice alone but rather to realize a pre-existent US identity. In accordance with this rule, Woodrow Wilson designated the US as, 'the responsible spokesman of the rights of humanity',[23] asserted that the US was built on 'elevated ideals' and was dedicated to 'righteousness'.[24] This message asserting a national identity in terms of the rights of man was repeated in an address to Congress in 1916. In this address the president stated

> [i]t was as if in the Providence of God a continent had been kept unused and waiting for a peaceful people who loved liberty and the rights of men more than they loved anything else, to come and set up an unselfish commonwealth.[25]

As in the manifestation of this rule under the Bush Administrations, this mythology was asserted by making invisible the history and existence of First Nation Americans as well as the violence inflicted upon their peoples in the name of civilization by the European settlers.

Also, as in the case of the Bush Administrations, President Wilson defined the identity of the US not in terms of geographical location, but rather by recourse to ideals of liberty and freedom. In the Tampico affair, for example, a number of US citizens were arrested, although later released with an apology, after landing at Tampico, Mexico in 1914. Woodrow Wilson responded to the incident by requiring the Mexican authorities to salute the US flag. Making the link between US identity and liberty explicit, the president explained the rather unusual demand that the authorities of a foreign state salute the US flag on the grounds that

> we seek to maintain the dignity and authority of the United States only because we wish always to keep our great influence unimpaired for the uses of liberty, both in the United States and wherever else it may be employed for the benefit of mankind.[26]

Consistent with the identity of the US asserted in the second hegemonic rule, the only possible function of US power is therefore to promote liberty for the benefit of mankind. This production of reality renders unclear whether the stars and stripes is a representation of a geographical state or of the concept of freedom since there exists little substantive difference between the two in the asserted discourse.

The third hegemonic rule states that the goal of advancing human rights complements distinct foreign policy goals of democracy promotion and extending freedom abroad. In a speech to a joint session of Congress, President Wilson stated, in line with this rule, that the object of US entry into World War I was 'to vindicate the principles' of peace, justice, the rights of mankind and to make the world safe for democracy.[27] Woodrow Wilson subsequently declared that the US had entered the war 'for democracy and human rights'.[28] President Wilson used his second inaugural address to state that 'we shall be the more American if we but remain true to the principles in which we have been bred' which he went on to define in terms of peace, equality and democracy.[29] As described above, all three hegemonic rules can, therefore, be located in the foreign policy narrative expressed by Woodrow Wilson.

The reflective explanation

As detailed in the first section of this chapter, the reflective explanation interprets the meaning and significance of the three hegemonic rules in terms of describing a corresponding social reality. Such accounts characteristically refer to the 14 Point Plan presented by President Wilson at the Paris Peace Conference following the conclusion of hostilities during World War I. This plan promoted a liberal agenda for ending secret diplomacy, required international agreements to be open to public scrutiny, stipulated freedom for navigation on the sees, required barriers to free trade to be removed, stated that armaments should be reduced to the lowest point consistent with domestic safety and required for colonial and territorial claims to be settled with due regard to the principle of self-determination of peoples.[30]

The 14 Point Plan led Kenneth Thompson to conclude that '[w]ith Wilson, idealism and sometimes moralism replaced political realism as the cornerstone of a new world order'.[31] Freedman similarly endorsed the reflective explanation, concluding that Woodrow Wilson 'believed that American power could be used to promote justice and democracy abroad'.[32] McElroy claimed that for President Wilson 'the motivating power of conscience will provide a very strong incentive for action in favor of an international moral norm'.[33] Kissinger appealed to 'Wilsonian idealism' as an unproblematic point of reference for understanding foreign policy decisions based upon ethical values rather than power concerns.[34] According to Kissinger, Wilson's 'crusading ideology' held that 'America's special mission transcends day-to-day diplomacy and obliges it to serve as a beacon of liberty for the rest of mankind'.[35] Mead concurred by identifying as a basis of foreign policy 'Wilsonian support for humanitarian interventions'.[36] Wolfson contends that Wilson promoted values 'for the sake of democracy and human rights in and of themselves'.[37] Cole agreed on grounds that '[t]o Wilson, foreign policy was not just pursuing American national interests but the interests of humanity at large'.[38] Warner likewise referred to 'Wilsonian aspirations for democracy and human rights' as independent foreign policy goals.[39]

References to 'Wilsonian values' as independent commitments to liberal principles have existed ever since his presidency when members of domestic civil society spoke of 'Wilson's principles of national and international righteousness'.[40] It is in this sense that the caricature identity of Wilson as an idealistic advocate of liberal principles is immediately recognizable. Indeed, this interpretation is taken as a given by Warner and Wolfson who subsequently contend that President Wilson's foreign policy can offer insights into that of George W. Bush since both are interpreted as driven more by values of freedom, democracy and human rights than by power interests.[41]

The rejectionist explanation

A literal interpretation of the hegemonic discourse provides for a selective account of the historical evidence as can be exemplified through examining President Wilson's advocacy of self-determination in the 14 Point Plan. Whereas, it is indeed the case that point five advanced the principle of self-determination, the applicability of this principle is ambiguous and restricted to specific 'colonial claims' rather than advanced as a universal human right.[42] The interpretation that Woodrow Wilson promoted self-determination as an independent policy goal faces considerable difficulties in explaining why the president stated in his private correspondence that

> since trade ignores national boundaries, and the manufacturer insists on having the world as a market, the flag of his nation must follow him, and the doors of the nations which are closed against him must be battered down.... Concessions obtained by financiers must be safeguarded by ministers of state, even if the sovereignty of unwilling nations be outraged in the process.[43]

The interpretation also faces difficulties in explaining why, if President Wilson held a deep conviction for the principle of self-determination, the US bought the Virgin Islands from Denmark in 1916 for $25 million. The interpretation faces still more difficulties explaining why, when Secretary of State Robert Lansing explained that the basis of the Monroe doctrine derived from US self-interest, Woodrow Wilson found the account to be 'unanswerable', or why the president insisted that this should never be mentioned to the US public.[44] Further problems are encountered in explaining why an idealistic advocate of liberal values would only oppose the use of force between the major powers rather than against smaller states. For example, President Wilson proved so eager to operationalize an assertive version of the Monroe doctrine that he deployed the US marines to prevent a liberal political revolution in Nicaragua in 1912 and left them there in support of US business interests for the rest of his first administration and for the full duration of his second.[45] Between 1914–18 the president also sent the marines into the Dominican Republic, Haiti and twice into Mexico.[46]

The reflective interpretation of the hegemonic discourse faces similar problems in explaining why Woodrow Wilson opposed Japanese efforts to have a clause on racial equality inserted into the Covenant of the League of Nations.[47] The interpretation faces further problems explaining why the president objected to black suffrage on the grounds that the mind of blacks was, 'dark, ignorant, uneducated and incompetent to form enlightened opinion' or accounting for why President Wilson spoke approvingly of 'white civilization and its dominion over the world'.[48] Further problems are encountered when trying to explain why Woodrow Wilson had argued that efforts aimed at racial equality in domestic society were misguided and that most African Americans should remain as an obedient and subservient labor force.[49] More problems are encountered in explaining why the president accepted segregation in government departments during his tenure in office and did little to stop a wave of anti-black violence that swept across the US.

Unless history is rewritten to overlook these contradictions or to make them invisible by virtue of constituting simple exceptions, the reflective explanation must be viewed as offering, at best, an unreliable and incomplete explanation of the hegemonic discourse. However, the rejectionist explanation offers a similarly inadequate account for the manifestation of the hegemonic discourse under President Wilson for two reasons. First, dismissing the hegemonic discourse fails to explain why, in the light of a mass of evidence to the contrary, the reflective explanation can be asserted in renditions of history as unproblematic truth. Second, the rejectionist explanation overlooks politically significant patterns in the application of the hegemonic discourse.

Chapter 1 suggested that discourse does more than describe motives and events. In particular, discourse can be used to produce a mythological understanding of reality. Moreover, this mythology can be revealed through analysis of the internal consistencies to the discourse. The chapter therefore now turns its attention to analyze patterns in the application of the hegemonic discourse under the Wilson Administrations.

The productive function of mythology

We know that the Wilson Administrations possessed a keen awareness of the capacity to produce reality through discourse. This can be demonstrated through the public relations operations established by President Wilson during World War I. Especially notable was the creation in 1917 of the Committee on Public Information (CPI) under the chairmanship of George Creel, a former journalist turned campaign strategist. The posters created by the CPI sanitized the war effort by rarely mentioning violence and war. The posters instead focused on resource conservation, army recruitment and the sale of war bonds, which had been renamed liberty bonds.

The archival record similarly demonstrates President Wilson's awareness of the capacity to produce reality through discourse. In particular, one strategy document prepared for Woodrow Wilson by S.E. Mezes, D.H. Miller and Walter Lippmann[50] revealed awareness of how ethical principles could be used not to describe a corresponding reality but instead to produce meaning. The Mezes document advocated the use by President Wilson of what it refers to as 'liberal utterances', to 'stimulate American pride and interest' with US involvement in World War I. 'Such a liberal offensive' the document reasons 'will do more than any other thing to create in this country the sort of public opinion that this President needs in order to carry through the program he has outlined'.[51] The purpose of linguistic appeals to liberal ideals advanced in the document was, therefore, neither to describe corresponding real world events nor the political priorities of the administration. The express purpose was instead to create perceptions and public opinion.

Furthermore, five factors present the Mezes document as a credible source for informing the strategy behind the 14 Point Plan. First, we know that the document was delivered to the president four days before he made his 14 points speech and that Woodrow Wilson had the document before him when he wrote the speech.[52] Second, the document was personally delivered to President Wilson by his trusted and influential advisor, E. House. Third, the original document kept in the Library of Congress has Woodrow Wilson's amendments and shorthand on it, demonstrating that the president paid it close attention. Fourth, there exist notable similarities between the Mezes document and the contents of the 14 Point Plan.[53] Finally, as a private document written for the president by close political allies, rather than for public consumption, the document represents an open statement of strategic thinking devoid of much of the spin that distorts public speeches.

By drawing from the Mezes document, the following section analyzes the internal consistencies to the application of the hegemonic discourse by President Wilson. In particular, the hegemonic mythology was applied consistent with three political imperatives, (i) producing US identity, (ii) producing support for President Wilson's political leadership and (iii) producing geopolitical change. By explaining Woodrow Wilson's hegemonic discourse in terms of these three imperatives, the productive explanation can offer a more internally comprehensive and externally consistent account than that proposed by either the reflective or the rejectionist explanations.

Producing identity

The hegemonic discourse expressed by Woodrow Wilson is only inconsistent when understood as a literal description of a corresponding reality. It is, in contrast, consistent when understood in terms of producing a benevolent understanding of US identity and by extension, of the deployment of US power. That the benevolent messages contained in the hegemonic discourse infiltrates everyday situations is reflected through identifiable patterns. During Woodrow Wilson's second administration, German measles for example became 'liberty measles' and sauerkraut 'liberty cabbage'. With a change of administration, target and vegetable, 'French fries' became 'freedom fries' following the refusal of the French government to support the March 2003 invasion of Iraq. In both of these cases, the name of everyday foodstuffs had been altered to assert the internal rules of the hegemonic discourse.

Linguistic expressions are politically significant to the extent that they frame identity in the minds of the audience. In particular, to the extent that the audience internalized the identity of the US projected in the hegemonic mythology, a political program that failed to respect the necessary requirements for human rights could be understood precisely in terms of defending those rights. After joining World War I, for example, the Wilson Administration sponsored the Espionage and Sedition Acts that prohibited interference with the draft mechanism and curtailed criticism of the government, its armed forces and of US participation in a war that was, as we have seen, explicitly fought on the basis of promoting the rights of mankind and democracy. Under the Espionage and Sedition Acts, numerous publications were banned and one and a half thousand US citizens were imprisoned. In a similar inversion of comprehension, the Uniting and Strengthening America by Providing Appropriate Tools Required to Intercept and Obstruct Terrorism Act sponsored by the Bush Administration curtailed civil liberties and extended the surveillance capacity of governmental agencies in part by recourse to the identity of the US as the champion of liberty and rights.[54]

Producing support for Wilson's political leadership

The Mezes document discussed matters of nationalism, imperialism and democracy in a section entitled 'a program for a diplomatic offensive'.[55] This section recommended the use of 'liberal utterances from the United States' for three productive rather than reflective reasons. The first of these was to 'show the way to the Liberals in Great Britain and in France and therefore restore their national unity of purpose'.[56] The second reason constituted a means to cement foreign support for US political leadership. In particular the Mezes document cogently suggested that President Wilson's natural allies, the British and French liberals 'will readily accept the leadership of the President if he undertakes a liberal diplomatic offensive because they will find in that offensive an invaluable support for their internal domestic troubles'.[57]

Third, 'liberal utterances' are recommended in the Mezes document in order for Woodrow Wilson's political program to be made more acceptable to the domestic American audience. The section on a diplomatic offensive, for example, finished by suggesting that

> a powerful liberal offensive on the part of the United States will immensely stimulate American pride and interest in the war and will assure the administration the support of that great mass of the American people who desire an idealistic solution.[58]

These are then three ways in which liberal discourse is explicitly recognized in terms of a diplomatic offensive to produce desired perceptions and understandings of reality among identified audiences. Speech acts are being advocated not according to the criterion of describing foreign policy goals, but instead on grounds of their productive function to coalesce domestic and international support around the administration.

Producing geopolitical changes

The Mezes document provided a compelling explanation for the selective integration of the right to self-determination in the 14 Point Plan. First and foremost, self-determination was presented in the document as a useful instrument through which to advance perceived US interests by manipulating the nationalist sentiments that were rife throughout Europe. Nowhere is this more apparent than in the case of Germany's close military ally, Austria–Hungary, which was facing increasingly organized secessionist movements among its constitutive nationalities. The Mezes document recommended that US policy should aim at threatening the Austro-Hungarian government with the prospect of nationalist uprisings within its borders through plentiful references to self-determination while simultaneously 'refusing to accept the extreme logic of this discontent, which would be the dismemberment of Austria–Hungary'.[59] This agenda, the document reasons, would 'reduce to a minimum' the resistance of Austro-Hungary to US war demands since the US would be perceived as offering the best guarantee for maintaining the status quo desired by Austro-Hungary in terms of keeping its territory intact while simultaneously 'enormously accelerating' the motive for independence from Berlin in foreign affairs, a key US goal in isolating Germany militarily.[60] Consistent with this line of reasoning, number 10 of the 14 points explicitly provided the Austro-Hungarian people with 'the freest opportunity of autonomous development'.[61]

Addressing the prewar alliance system, point one of the 14 Point Plan stipulated that there should be 'no private international understandings of any kind'.[62] The Mezes document labeled as an 'intangible asset' the 'almost universal feeling' that 'old diplomacy is bankrupt' since 'this is a sentiment fundamentally anti-Prussian in its nature and should be capitalized for our side'.[63] The specific geopolitical aim promoted by the advocacy of open diplomacy in the Mezes document was to prevent Berlin from being able to reform alliances to 'establish a power in central Europe which will be the master of the continent'.[64] Points 6–13 of President Wilson's proposed plan did not stipulate rights possessed by all human beings by virtue of their common humanity or define conditions for democracy and freedom. Instead, these eight points used specific appeals to self-determination and national independence to specify conditions for Russia, Belgium, France, Italy, Austria–Hungary, Romania, Serbia, Montenegro, Turkey and Poland that would preclude precisely the military dominance of central Europe by Germany that was identified as a threat in the Mezes document.

The specific application of the principle of self-determination to those European states neighboring Germany in the 14 Point Plan is both consistent with the use of self-determination as a mechanism to promote perceived US geopolitical aims and inconsistent with its advocacy as a universal principle. For the principle of self-determination to be advanced as a universally applicable right, it would logically be stated as such in the 14 Point Plan rather than explicitly being applied to certain states, namely those surrounding Germany. To consequently interpret President Wilson's integration of self-determination in the 14 Point Plan as an idealistic advocacy of human rights neglects the weight of evidence to the contrary that, instead, suggests its instrumental use as a means to isolate Germany militarily. Indeed, if President Wilson was an advocate of self-determination as a general principle, it is unclear why a political representative, later to become known as Ho Chi Minh, was unceremoniously ejected from the Paris Peace Conference when he called for international support for a Vietnam free from French colonial rule.[65]

Likewise, the democratization of Germany was specifically advocated in the Mezes document not out of naïve commitment to democracy but instead as a means of dealing with the threat posed by a militaristic Germany to US geopolitical interests, and in particular as a means of minimizing the possibilities for a future military alliance between Austria–Hungary and Germany.[66] Indeed, the Mezes document highlighted the military isolation of Germany as the predominant US interest in Europe following World War I to the extent that revolutionary Russia was perceived not as a threat but instead as a potential ally in containing any possible future German expansionism. It is in this sense of containing a militaristic Germany that the Mezes document referred to the 'military impotence' of Russia as a liability to the United States.[67] Consistent with the identification of Germany rather than Russia as the principal European threat, Woodrow Wilson's point six called for the German evacuation from all of the territories it had seized from Russia. The Mezes document provides some insight into the apparent paradox of US support for the revolutionary Bolshevik state. In particular, the second Russian revolution was seen in the Mezes document as 'inherently difficult for the Germans to manage and master' since (i) this was perceived as inherently antagonistic to German capitalism, (ii) the nationalistic love of Russia was 'spiritually antagonistic' to Protestant Germany and (iii) the nationalist sentiments could be molded by the Russian moderates 'who will either return to power or at least exercise a strong influence in Russia'.[68]

The Mezes document also revealed knowledge of how the offer of free trade stipulated in point three of the 14 Point Plan could be used as a political instrument through which to extract political concessions from a defeated Germany. The carrot of economic access to overseas markets on the one hand combined with the stick of economic exclusion on the other were presented in the Mezes document as 'our strongest weapon' against the Germans: 'held over them, it can win priceless concessions'.[69] In particular the Pacific, Central and South American economies were referred to as 'our assets outside of Europe', access to whose markets were valuable bargaining chips through which to compel Germany to accept US war demands.[70]

Contradicting the reflective explanation of Woodrow Wilson's professed commitment to free trade, the so called 'Wilson corollary' to the Monroe doctrine dictated that 'only American oil interests receive concessions' within the US sphere of influence in Latin America.[71] When President Wilson operationalized this corollary by driving British influence out of oil rich Venezuela, he supported the corrupt and repressive dictator Juan Gomez, who reciprocated by extending a warm welcome to US petrochemical corporations.[72] Again, the productive rather than reflective explanation stands out as providing the more externally consistent account of the hegemonic discourse.

From the neo-Gramscian theoretical perspective, Gill, Rosenberg and Evans have all coherently demonstrated how a succession of US administrations have professed rights to self-determination and free trade as a means through which to dismantle the colonial empires that had hitherto benefited European markets. In particular, dismantling colonial empires would provide US corporations with new foreign markets to help solve domestic crises of overproduction and allow US capital access to new sources of raw materials, sub soil resources and cheap labor.[73] The language of rights and self-determination was consistently advanced in the 14 Point Plan not in terms of describing the naïve idealism underlying foreign policy but instead as a technique of governance, the constitutive methods of which have been detailed above.

James Earl Carter 1977–1980

This final section details how the independent pursuit of universal human rights has been commonly identified as a defining characteristic of the 1977–80 Carter Administration and questions the accuracy of this conclusion. Sikkink states that under President Carter, human rights became 'an integral and legitimate part of foreign policy'.[74] McElroy states that Jimmy Carter came to power 'deeply committed to formulating a more forthrightly moral foreign policy for the United States'.[75] Warner concurs, observing that 'Jimmy Carter shifted the ballast of our policies back to the Wilsonian emphasis on human rights'.[76] Diamond speaks of 'Jimmy Carter's human rights efforts' to 'save many victims of indiscriminate repression and reinforce pressures for democratic change,' particularly in Latin American states.[77] Indeed, one observer raised some disquiet over the 'threat' posed to foreign policy by the 'over-involvement' of Jimmy Carter 'with his pursuit of human rights'.[78] This caricature of President Carter as an idealistic advocate of human rights interprets the numerous presidential statements made in support of human rights as literal descriptions of the basis of policymaking. The following examples illustrate how the statements made by Jimmy Carter in support of human rights conform to the three hegemonic rules common to the discourse expressed by Woodrow Wilson and George W. Bush.

President Carter used his inaugural address to assert the first hegemonic rule that his administration would promote universal human rights as an independent goal by declaring that '[o]ur commitment to human rights must be absolute'.[79] Reinforcing this message, President Carter announced in a March 1977 address to the UN that '[n]o member of the United Nations can claim that mistreatment of its citizens is solely its own business'.[80]

President Carter advanced the second hegemonic rule that the promotion of human rights by his administration realized a pre-existent US identity by declaring that 'America did not invent human rights.... Human rights invented America'.[81] The origins and essence of the US can therefore be defined in terms of the concept of human rights. On another occasion Jimmy Carter conflated human rights and US nationhood by stating that '[h]uman rights is the soul of our foreign policy because human rights is the very soul of our sense of nationhood'.[82]

The discursive promotion of human rights by President Carter complemented the distinct foreign policy goals of promoting freedom and peace across the world as asserted in hegemonic rule three. President Carter declared on one occasion that '[w]e ought to be a beacon for nations who search for peace and who search for freedom, who search for individual liberty, who search for basic human rights'.[83] The president subsequently called for the US to 'set a standard within the community of nations of courage, compassion, integrity and dedication to basic human rights and freedoms'.[84] In his farewell address the president identified '[t]he love of liberty' as the 'common blood' that flows through American veins.[85]

The reflective explanation of Jimmy Carter's hegemonic mythology finds support not only in these words but also in identifiable foreign policy actions, including the signing, by the president, of the two most significant international human rights covenants.[86] Other actions included changes in US relations with Central and Latin American military dictatorships. President Carter for example distanced his administration from Nixon's open support of the Pinochet regime in Chile. A degree of US pressure was placed on the leaders of military regimes in Latin America to improve their observance of human rights. Heads of military regimes were, for example, not invited to Washington. When diplomatic efforts failed to halt human rights abuses in Latin America, multilateral loans were suspended and military aid was cut to offending states such as Uruguay and Argentina.[87]

Military credits to Guatemala were banned when the military regime brutalizing the country refused to accept human rights conditions attached to the continuation of US aid in 1978. For the following two years the Carter Administration refused to authorize multilateral loans to Guatemala on the explicit basis of the systematic human rights abuses perpetrated by the military junta. In 1977 President Carter announced that aid to the Somoza dictatorship in Nicaragua would be made contingent upon human rights improvements, leading to the cutting off of US military and economic aid to that state in February 1978.[88] The president placed considerable political capital in securing the passage of the Panama Canal Treaty that returned full sovereignty over the Canal back to Panama in line with the principle of self-determination.[89]

The reflective explanation of Jimmy Carter's human rights discourse can also highlight changes made to the foreign policy bureaucracy during his time in office. The coordinator for human rights and humanitarian affairs was, for example, upgraded to the position of assistant secretary. Prior to President Carter's entry to the White House the State Department had one officer to take responsibility for human rights issues. By 1977, the assistant secretary of state for human rights and humanitarian affairs presided over a new State Department bureau with a staff of over thirty and the responsibility of preparing an annual human rights report for every state receiving US assistance. Kathryn Sikkink summarizes the reflective explanation of the hegemonic discourse under President Carter by stating that 'in the seven years from 1973 to 1980, the US fundamentally altered its external policy by explicitly incorporating human rights criteria into the foreign policy calculus'.[90]

The rejectionist explanation

Interpreting President Carter's human rights discourse as describing a corresponding basis of policymaking has been questioned by the rejectionist explanation. In particular, the notable disjuncture between rhetoric and reality is highlighted to illustrate the selective manner in which human rights were integrated into actual policy decisions. In support of its position, the rejectionist explanation can point to President Carter's declaration, in his inaugural address, of his ultimate aim to eliminate nuclear weapons from the Earth and to restrict US arms sales abroad. In reality, the US nuclear arsenal during the Carter Administration grew at roughly the same rate as under Nixon and Ford while arms sales increased.[91] With respect to the steps taken against Latin American dictators noted above, many of the loans from international development banks, that the US initially voted against, were eventually approved. This applied to 23 loans to Argentina, 11 to Paraguay and five to Chile.[92]

Much of the original impetus for halting military aid to repressive Latin American regimes was moreover due to elements in Congress rather than a commitment by the executive branch.[93] Carleton and Stohl concluded, in their study of whether US military aid was dependent upon the human rights situation in recipient states, that President Carter was 'long on rhetoric and short on action'.[94] These two researchers found that the most important determinant in how much military aid was given by the US to a recipient state was how much aid had been provided to that state in the previous year. Carleton and Stohl found little difference between the Carter and 1981–84 Reagan Administration in the targeting of US military aid on human rights grounds.[95] Other notable studies that have found a link between US aid and degrees of repression in recipient Latin American states have found this linkage to be in fact positive. In other words, aid from the US was disproportionately distributed to states with poor human rights records during the tenure of the Carter Administration. Lars Schoultz concluded that

> US aid was clearly distributed disproportionately to countries with repressive governments, that this distribution represented a pattern and not merely one or a few isolated cases, and that human need was not responsible for the positive correlations between aid and human rights violations.[96]

Moreover, the study by Schoultz was restricted into violations of 'anti-torture rights' in recipient states rather than social and economic categories of human rights.

National Security Advisor Zbigniew Brzezinski became increasingly skeptical of integrating human rights into foreign policy when the geopolitical and economic trade-offs became apparent.[97] Writing some 20 years after leaving office, Brzezinski described the 'three great imperatives' of geopolitics as being, 'to prevent collusion and maintain security dependence among the vassals, to keep tributaries pliant and to keep the barbarians from coming together'.[98] The rejection of human rights concerns in favor of this foreign policy focus on geopolitics was exemplified in opposition to the January 1979 invasion of Cambodia by Vietnam, which finally brought Pol Pot's atrocities to an end.[99] The people of Indo China once again suffered the consequences when Washington policymakers chose to support the ousted Khmer Rouge against the Vietnamese in this manifestation of war by proxy against the Soviet Union. During their rule in Cambodia the Khmer Rouge had killed between one and two million out of a total population of only seven million people.[100]

The voting record of US delegates to the UN during the Carter Administration also contradicts the rhetorical advocacy of human rights. The US was the sole dissenting state on a 1979 General Assembly resolution calling for alternative approaches within the UN system for improving the enjoyment of human rights and fundamental freedoms.[101] The US and Israel were the only two states dissenting from a December 1979 General Assembly resolution demanding that Israel desist from human rights violations.[102] That same month the US joined the UK and France in voting against a General Assembly resolution that strengthened the arms embargo against South Africa and the US stood as the sole state voting against safeguarding the rights of developing states in multinational trade negotiations.[103]

The same sidelining of human rights was evident in the August 1980 response to a hurricane in the West Indies. In this instance emergency US aid was made conditional on the understanding that Grenada under the socialist government of Maurice Bishop would be excluded. When the recipient countries opted for solidarity over self-interest and refused to exempt Grenada from receiving aid, President Carter sent none.[104]

The rejectionist explanation can highlight these numerous contradictions in the application of human rights by President Carter to reason that the hegemonic discourse does not describe a corresponding reality. Consequently, the hegemonic discourse is seen by this explanation as either rhetoric or else wishful delusions and in either case offers few insights into policymaking.

The productive function of mythology

As the reflective account points out, the saliency ascribed by the president to the promotion of human rights, as well as specific foreign policy initiatives undertaken in their name, means that human rights cannot be simply dismissed when understanding the foreign policy of the Carter Administration. However, as the rejectionist explanation observes, the reflective account confuses symbolic and partial efforts taken at the margins of policymaking with the actual integration of human rights into foreign policy. Attempting to resolve this apparent paradox by claiming that human rights concerns have been asserted wherever possible but that this intent is thwarted by competing security concerns is both unsatisfactory and contradicts the impartial and universal prerequisites for human rights recognition.

The productive explanation analyzes how President Carter's human rights discourse has been applied consistently in terms of constructing one interpretation of events and in that sense producing reality in the minds of the audience. In particular, the internal rules of the hegemonic mythology are consistently applied as an explanation of foreign policy irrespective of the extent to which these reflect or depart from describing a corresponding reality. In this respect, the insistence by President Carter on the hegemonic discourse shares similar patterns with the application of the 'rights of man' discourse by Woodrow Wilson. In terms of coalescing domestic support for example, Thompson demonstrated how Jimmy Carter promoted human rights as an electioneering tactic during his second presidential debate with Ford in 1976.[105] In this instance, Jimmy Carter appealed to human rights to counteract Ford's criticisms that he was soft on Communism. In particular, Carter used appeals to human rights to attack Ford and Kissinger for not sufficiently protesting Soviet violations of basket three of the Helsinki agreements which dealt with freedoms of travel, marriage and the reunification of families.[106]

The insistence by Jimmy Carter on the applicability of the hegemonic mythology came in the continuing wake of Nixon, Vietnam and Watergate when the claimed benevolence of both US identity and foreign policy was under unprecedented public skepticism. The productive explanation of Jimmy Carter's human rights discourse as a technique through which to reassert the doctrines of the hegemonic discourse is more able than either the reflective or the rejectionist explanations to explain the patterns evident in the selective integration of human rights into the practice of foreign policy. Nowhere is this better exemplified than in the application of foreign policy in the Middle East.

In line with previous administrations, President Carter subordinated a focus on endemic violations of human rights in Middle Eastern states to the objective of ensuring the steady flow of oil to world markets. Under what became known as the Carter doctrine, the possible use of any means necessary, including force, was asserted to ensure US access to Gulf oil supplies. The Carter doctrine held that any Russian incursion into the Middle Eastern region would be repelled since the area was, as the president went on to clarify, within the zone of vital US interests and contained 'our oil'.[107] In practice the Carter doctrine entailed a permanent US military presence in the Middle East region, the commitment to keeping the Strait of Hormuz open for oil transportation and the creation of a Rapid Deployment Force to deal with any emergencies.[108] Implementing the doctrine also involved sending AWAC communication planes and F-15 fighter jets to protect the undemocratic Saudi Arabian monarchy that feared for its hold on power following the success of the 1979 Islamic revolution in Iran.[109]

President Carter's public concern for the human rights of Iranians only emerged after the 1979 revolution. This event ushered in an Islamic regime that was considerably less inclined to follow orders from Washington than was the unelected regime of the shah that it replaced. Prior to the revolution, the shah had enjoyed the full support of the Carter Administration.[110] President Carter had, for example, spoken of the love of the Iranian people for the shah and, on a 1977 New Year's Eve trip to Iran, the president announced that 'because of the great leadership of the shah, [Iran] is an island of stability in one of the more troubled areas of the world'.[111]

Under the literal account of the hegemonic discourse, selective amnesia of human rights violations can only be categorized as an exception. In contrast to depoliticizing the significance in the disparity between the hegemonic discourse and a corresponding reality, the productive account can highlight the consistencies internal to the discourse. In particular, President Carter consistently applied human rights in terms of producing a benevolent understanding of US foreign policy in line with the hegemonic mythology. The identities of states as repressive or benign were produced in the discourse not according to the independent application of a set of human rights criteria but instead in the context of broader political and economic concerns.

Conclusion

This chapter has sought to explain how the internal rules that constitute the hegemonic discourse provided by the George W. Bush Administrations appeared in the foreign policy discourses provided by Presidents Woodrow Wilson and Jimmy Carter. It has been argued that a human rights discourse was formulated and implemented under the Wilson and Carter Administrations in a manner that failed to comply with the necessary prerequisites of human rights. A literal interpretation of the human rights discourse provided by the Wilson and Carter Administrations must subsequently be seen as internally contradictory. Unless it can be demonstrated that the necessary conditions of human rights defined in terms of impartiality and universality can be refuted, the claims made under the hegemonic discourse asserted by both presidents cannot be accurately understood in terms of describing a corresponding reality. The extent to which the productive rather than rejectionist explanation can account for the role of a human rights discourse in these administrations is subsequently directly proportional to the extent to which the audience understood the hegemonic discourse as corresponding with an unproblematic truth. The productive explanation alone, can account for how the hegemonic discourse insisted on a mythological account of reality that disciplined the minds of the audience.

This chapter has presented and discussed evidence that policymakers or close advisers in the Wilson and Carter Administrations have (i) demonstrated an awareness of the productive rather than simply descriptive function of discourse, (ii) consistently appealed to the hegemonic discourse as an explanation of events and thereby (iii) applied the hegemonic discourse consistently as a mechanism of governance. The key mechanism of power at work here, is not reducible to the rhetorical rendition of human rights as a cover for less philanthropic foreign policies. Instead, the hegemonic discourse operated on a more fundamental level by infiltrating the very processes by which an audience understood political events and identities.

The productive account of the hegemonic discourse provided by both Presidents Wilson and Carter is, however, not itself unproblematic. By its very nature of focusing on the production of values, language and meaning, the productive explanation instinctively rejects a singular and unproblematic account of the truth in favor of acknowledging the merits of differing interpretations. Moreover, in subjecting the discourse of policymakers to critical analysis, the productive explanation runs foul of a positivist methodology that rejects the significance of such enquiry as cynical, UnAmerican or even conspiracy theory. At best, examining the internal structures of discourse can be seen as a poisoned chalice by a methodological orthodoxy that instead values falsifiable claims and statistical analysis.

Two points can be made in defense of those who choose to drink from this chalice nonetheless. First, it can be noted that the default positions to either, accept the hegemonic discourse as reflecting a corresponding reality, or else to neglect this discourse entirely as an appropriate subject for scholarly analysis are neither politically nor ideologically neutral. Instead, a perspective that internalizes rather than subjects the hegemonic mythology to independent scrutiny becomes itself a component part of normalizing that mythology as truth.

Second, the productive function of discourse, so fundamental to political understanding, remains largely invisible to a methodological approach that denies the merits of discourse analysis. There are of course limits to the capacity of an administration to designate and create identities and thereby assign meaning to political events, not least the difficulties in reconciling the projected image with contradictory real world evidence. Indeed, in these limits lies the basis for political resistance. The remaining capacity of an administration to produce meaning through the hegemonic mythology is, however, exemplified nowhere better than through the enduring caricatures of Presidents Wilson and Carter as idealistic practitioners of universal human rights.

3   Inconsistent application of human rights

Introduction

This chapter aims to explain how the George W. Bush Administrations have applied human rights selectively in foreign policy, thereby contradicting the necessary conditions for human rights defined in terms of universal and impartial application. The criterion adopted by the administrations to interpret human rights abuses has not been an independent assessment of violations but instead the broader political context in which they have occurred and in particular, the predetermined identities of the actors involved in the abuse. This approach is hostile to the notion that all people have fundamental inalienable rights since it subordinates human rights to political contingencies.

The chapter demonstrates the selective application of human rights through the use of country specific examples differentiated into three groups. The first group contains states of peripheral concern to Washington policymakers, where even severe violations of human rights are not deemed to constitute an imperative to intervene. The second group comprises states where administration officials have selectively highlighted human rights violations as proof of evil and repressive regimes. The third group consists of designated friendly states in which the Bush Administrations have discursively authorized acts of human rights violations as serious as those witnessed in the second group. This authorization derives from the reclassification of human rights violations as counter terrorism, cultural diversity, necessary acts of self-defense, unproved allegations, tragic mistakes or as regrettable exceptions to an otherwise improving trend. Reclassifying human rights violations along these lines has allowed the Bush Administrations not only to maintain close relations with this third grouping of states but moreover to account for these cordial relations in terms of the hegemonic mythology.

The chapter makes two findings. The first demonstrates that the Bush Administrations have not applied human rights consistently as independent foreign policy goals. The second holds that discursive appeals to the concept of human rights by administration officials have not been random in the sense of without political pattern or significance. This pattern is made evident through analyzing the politicization of human rights as a mechanism of governance. Previous chapters have explained this mechanism in terms of producing legitimacy for foreign policy actions in the minds of the audience who internalize its mythology as truth. This chapter details the practical application of this mechanism in the foreign policies adopted toward a range of states and thereby addresses the aim of the chapter stated above.

Human rights tragedies

Tackling endemic violations of basic human rights would first require addressing the multidimensional problems facing Africa. High levels of poverty, HIV/AIDS infection and a lack of adequate preventative health care facilities combine with military conflicts to cause avoidable deaths on a massive scale on the continent. Yet policymakers have been keen to avoid US military commitments in the Democratic Republic of Congo (DRC) where an estimated two million people have died from violence, war-related hunger or disease between 2001 and 2005.[1] In those cases where officials have focused on human rights abuses in Africa,[2] the rhetoric has often followed rather than led public opinion and has lacked decisive action. It is perhaps the Darfur region of western Sudan that offers the most lucid example of where the hegemonic discourse contrasts most sharply with the absence of purposive action to end human rights atrocities.

Between January 2000 and July 2006 an estimated 300,000 civilians have been killed in Sudan during a civil war involving numerous separate factions. During this conflict the Janjaweed, a group of Arab militia armed in part by the Sudanese government, destroyed villages and perpetrated the mass rape and killing of refugees in internal displacement camps. By 2001 the situation had become so serious that relief organizations became unable to provide aid to all those suffering in the conflict zone. Secretary of State Colin Powell acknowledged the gravity of the worsening humanitarian crisis when he referred to the conflict in Darfur as 'perhaps the greatest tragedy on the face of the Earth'.[3] With respect to humanitarian intervention however, the US joined other Western governments in avoiding any obligations.

During 2003 the killings in Darfur reached such proportions that calls from human rights organizations for foreign governments to recognize these as constituting genocide became unanswerable. It was, however, only in the summer of 2004 that Colin Powell finally acceded to such requests and simultaneously accepted the obligations conferred under international humanitarian law to intervene to prevent further genocide. The secretary of state concluded that with respect to US military commitments 'no new action is dictated' by the determination that the killings in Darfur amounted to genocide.[4] Instead, according to an agreement signed in the summer of 2004 under the auspices of the international community, Sudanese government troops complemented by 7000 troops sent by neighboring African Union (AU) states were identified as the appropriate bodies to monitor a cease-fire of hostilities.

President Bush welcomed the 2004 cease-fire and called on the government of Sudan to enforce the agreement and 'stop the killing in Darfur'.[5] Reasoning that 'while we in the international community must intensify our efforts to help,' Secretary Powell likewise concluded that 'the government of Sudan bears the greatest responsibility – to face up to this catastrophe and save the lives of its own citizens'.[6] Given the evident ties between the Sudanese government and the Janjaweed militia, this placing of onus provided, all too predictably, the ideal conditions for the continuation of what had already been acknowledged to constitute genocide.[7] The AU mission in Sudan mandated to protect the cease-fire was wholly inadequate to cover the conflict zone, lacking in both resources and experience. The head of the AU contingent, Baba Gana Kingibe, made repeated unsuccessful requests for the Sudanese government to disarm the Janjaweed militia who, in 2006, had broadened their range of targets to include AU troops and humanitarian workers.[8] Indeed, while Western government officials were busy washing their hands, Janjaweed violations of the cease-fire had extended to attacks against villages in neighboring Chad.

In the cases of both the DRC and Darfur, rhetorical recantations of the hegemonic discourse by administration officials contrasted with the lack of purposive actions to solve the multidimensional problems facing the areas. In direct contrast, the human rights failings of a second group of states have not only been highlighted by the White House, but have been emphasized by administration officials in accounting for US involvement in the internal politics of these states.

Demonizing enemies

Administration officials have consistently highlighted the human rights failings of left wing regimes in Latin America. The US permanent representative to the UN offices in Geneva accordingly explained that, in the western hemisphere, Cuba 'remains and stands out as the one country that not only continues to systematically violate the fundamental human rights of its people, but moreover continues systematically to reject any outside scrutiny'.[9] This assessment was not based upon state provision of health care to Cuban citizens, since this is exemplary. Neither was the assessment based upon the operations of death squads, extra judicial killings or massacres by paramilitary groups since, unlike the modern histories of many neighboring states, these have not been features of revolutionary Cuban society. Instead 'harsh government restrictions on freedom of speech, press, assembly and association' were identified as conferring the status of systematic human rights violator on Cuba.[10] The Bush Administrations further tightened US sanctions against the island in line with this assessment.

Outspoken critic of neo-liberal economics, Hugo Chávez, was elected president of Venezuela in July 2000 after an election process that was recognized as free and fair by international monitors. Venezuela is the third largest supplier of oil to the US and the newly elected president fully understood the political significance of the state owned oil company.[11] On April 11, 2002 anti-government protests across Venezuela caused 18 deaths and precipitated a coup against Chávez. Before the president was able to regain control on April 13, the pro-business opposition leader Pedro Carmona had set up an unconstitutional government with the aid of the military.[12] During his two days in office Carmona had already found the time to announce the privatization of the Venezuelan oil industry. The Bush Administration immediately recognized the authority of the unconstitutional Carmona regime.[13]

Prior to the coup, a stream of Venezuelan opposition leaders, many with the support of the National Endowment for Democracy (NED), had met with a range of US officials in Washington, DC.[14] The State Department publicly denied any prior knowledge of the coup, announcing that it was an internal matter.[15] Yet documents released in 2005 revealed that the Central Intelligence Agency (CIA) had indeed known in advance that dissident military officers had planned the coup, leading Chávez to openly accuse the US of planning to overthrow him.[16] Washington stepped up its support for anti-Chávez elements of Venezuelan civil society following the failed coup. NED and USAID contributed $12 million to subcontracted civil society groups pressing for a 2004 referendum to remove Chávez from office, a referendum that Chávez subsequently won with a convincing majority. Chávez has since accused the US of fomenting a series of strikes across Venezuela.[17]

The Bush Administration and its allies in civil society presented this intervention in the internal political economy of Venezuela in terms of the hegemonic discourse. The director of the office for the promotion of human rights and democracy stated before the Congressional Human Rights Caucus that, with respect to Venezuela, 'the United States will continue to use all available bilateral and multilateral tools at our disposal to strengthen democracy and to institutionalize democratic reform'.[18] Chávez was allocated the identity of a tyrant. After Chávez made overtures to Castro, one think tank spoke of 'a rabidly anti-US, pro-axis of evil regime under Hugo Chávez'.[19] During a National Press Club appearance, Secretary of Defense Donald Rumsfeld described Chávez as, 'a person who was elected legally – just as Adolf Hitler was elected legally'.[20] Free and fair elections therefore have limited relevance as signifiers of democracy. US administration officials can instead differentiate true democracy from a situation where a populist tyrant has cynically manipulated democratic politics by engendering a cult following. Thus, predetermined identities are produced in terms of the hegemonic discourse.

The linguistic use of democracy and human rights as a technique to legitimize foreign relations can be demonstrated through a juxtaposition of Venezuela with Bolivia under President Gonzalo Sanchez. The Sanchez Administration protected freedoms of the press and private property rights while eroding the economic rights of Bolivian citizens to health, education, housing and food. A swath of privatizations had sold off state owned rail, mining, oil, electricity, telecommunication, airline and water services to mostly foreign investors.[21] In 2002, 60 percent of Bolivians subsequently lived below the poverty line and over half of the population had no domestic access to electricity. It is in this context of adherence to neo-liberal economic policies that when the Bolivian army killed 78 anti-poverty protestors on October 11–12, 2003, Condoleezza Rice warned demonstrators against any attempt to use force to remove a 'democratically elected government'.[22]

Whereas the Bush Administration conferred legitimacy on the Sanchez Government by virtue of its classification as 'democratically elected', the Chávez Government was demonized as tyrannical and its rise to office equated with that of Adolf Hitler. To the extent that administration officials are able to produce reality in the minds of the audience, US foreign policy toward both Bolivia and Venezuela can be understood in terms of rule three of the hegemonic discourse as the US promotion of democracy alongside human rights in its enduring struggle against tyranny.

As with the 2000 Venezuelan election, the Bush Administration disregarded the democratic relevance of the 17 million Iranian voters who delivered a landslide election victory to Mahmoud Ahmadinejad on June 25, 2005.[23] Also, as in the case of Venezuela, this disenfranchisement was conducted in the name of expanding democracy and the will of the people consistent with the third hegemonic rule.[24] For example, in his 2006 *State of the Union Address*, President Bush referred to Iran as 'a nation now held hostage by a small clerical elite that is isolating and repressing its people'.[25] When 'democracy', 'freedom' and 'the people' are understood as techniques to produce legitimacy for foreign policy rather than in their literal sense, it becomes clear why George W. Bush was able to declare to the people of Iran that '[w]e respect your right to choose your own future and win your own freedom'.[26]

Consistent with the use of human rights as a legitimizing technique, Secretary Rice requested $75 million in funds from Congress in February 2006. These funds were to be used for radio and satellite television broadcasting into Iran and 'to develop a network for political dissidents and human rights activists'.[27] Rice explained to the Senate Foreign Relations Committee that '[t]he United States wishes to reach out to the Iranian people and support their desire to realize their own freedom and to secure their democratic and human rights'.[28] Thus, intervention in internal Iranian politics was legitimized in terms of the hegemonic mythology.

Categorizing away human rights violations

The human rights record of Iran under Mahmoud Ahmadinejad is indeed a matter of concern from any political perspective seeking to promote the impartial and universal implementation of human rights, as indeed are those of Venezuela and Cuba. But highlighting the human rights failings of designated enemy states does nothing to explain why these states have been identified for urgent concern in the first instance. This is especially the case since the abuses conducted in these states pale when juxtaposed to the genocidal practices witnessed in the DRC or Darfur. Furthermore, a literal interpretation of the hegemonic discourse cannot explain why an *elected* leader in Iran or Venezuela is less democratic than an *unelected* regime elsewhere in the world. Consider, for example, the case of Saudi Arabia.

Violations of human rights to speech, assembly and association are noticeably absent as a cause for urgent concern to the Bush Administrations when they

occur in Saudi Arabia. The feudal monarchical government in this Middle
Eastern state tolerates no elections or dissent. Severe restrictions are placed on
the rights, movement and employment of women. Subversion, rebellion and
heresy are all capital offences. The Saudi security forces practice public behead-
ings, torture prisoners, hold prisoners of conscience, 'disappear' people, execute
opposition dissidents and detain people without charge or trial.[29] Under a literal
understanding of the hegemonic discourse, such an egregious and longstanding
violator of human rights would be expected to be subject to serious sanctions
from the Bush Administrations. In fact the US has major military garrisons in
Saudi Arabia alongside the other feudal monarchical Gulf states of Kuwait,
Bahrain, Qatar, the United Arab Emirates and Oman with whom the Bush
Administrations maintain similar cordial relations.[30]

The subordination of human rights concerns in foreign policy toward Saudi
Arabia stands both in logical contradiction to a literal interpretation of the hegemonic discourse and consistent to ensuring continued US access to Saudi oil. In
2002, Saudi Arabia supplied 1.2 million barrels per day to the US, one-sixth of
total US oil imports.[31] The *Report of the National Energy Policy Development
Group* described the Persian Gulf as 'vital to US interests' and highlighted Saudi
Arabia as a 'linchpin of supply reliability to world oil markets'.[32] In this context
the US stations two kinds of troops in Saudi Arabia, the first of which consists of
regular Air Force units to protect the kingdom from external threats. The second
set of US troops are military advisers and military contract personnel who work
with the Saudi Arabian National Guard to provide security directly to the Saudi
royal family.[33]

The Saudi regime has enjoyed a clear exemption from anything more than
symbolic criticism on human rights grounds from US administrations ever since
World War II, when Franklin D. Roosevelt met with Abdul-Aziz ibn Saud and
agreed to protect the royal family in return for privileged US access to Saudi
oil.[34] Roth points out that when it comes to Saudi Arabia, under the Bush
Administrations, 'even rhetorical US support for human rights has been sparing
– often nothing more than the State Department's once-a-year pronouncements
in its global human rights report'.[35] The State Department has neglected to
explain why the human rights of Saudi dissidents are seen as less pressing than
those in Iran with one document blandly stating that 'US officials routinely highlight the need to improve human rights conditions' in Saudi Arabia.[36] Whereas
Bush Administration officials have highlighted state repression in Iran as proof
of an inherently evil regime, equally draconian measures in Saudi Arabia have
been exempted from criticism by virtue of being reclassified as expressions of
cultural heritage and legitimate diversity.[37] Indeed, the 2006 *National Security
Strategy* goes so far as to praise Saudi Arabia for having 'taken some preliminary steps to give its citizens more of a voice in their government'.[38] Again, we
see that rather than being applied on an independent basis, human rights criteria
are used to justify the predetermined identity of the state in question.

Since administration officials enjoy broad discretion in interpreting events,
those human rights abuses carried out by friendly states or states with a per-

ceived significance to US geopolitics can be downplayed or otherwise excused. Carothers consequently observed that in practice, 'the Bush Administration has sought closer ties and enhanced security cooperation with a host of authoritarian or semi-authoritarian regimes'.[39] The Mubarak regime in Egypt practices systematic torture.[40] The Bush Administration elected to adopt a policy of 'quiet diplomacy' with the regime, given the significance of Egypt to regional politics and to efforts to resolve the Israeli–Arab conflict on terms favorable to Israel. Administration officials made, for example, no public announcement when the Mubarak regime renewed emergency decrees that facilitated continued authoritarian rule.[41] Forsythe consequently summarized US democracy promotion as 'non-existent' in Egypt.[42]

Systematic human rights abuses and the canceling of parliamentary elections in Algeria in 1992 led to the implementation of a ban on US aid to that state. In the ensuing ten years an estimated 120,000 people lost their lives in political violence. During this time the Algerian security forces have been implicated in the systematic use of torture, disappearances and arbitrary killings against the Islamic opposition in the name of counter terrorism.[43] In December 2002 Assistant Secretary of State William Burns responded to this campaign of extra judicial violence not with sanctions or even public criticism but instead by announcing that the US would resume weapon sales and security assistance to Algeria and by explaining that 'Washington has much to learn from Algeria on ways to fight terrorism'.[44] Systematic human rights violations in Algeria have therefore been reclassified and authorized as progressive counter terrorist measures. Again, the consistency lies not in the impartial promotion of human rights but instead in the application of discourse to reaffirm the predetermined identity of a regime. Nowhere is this consistency more evident than in the case of foreign policy toward Israel.

George W. Bush used a 2000 presidential debate to announce that, 'I'm going to stand by Israel' and informed his subsequent administration that '[w]e're going to correct the imbalance of the previous administration on the Mideast conflict. We're going to tilt back toward Israel'.[45] In line with these statements, the White House did little to rebuke the policies of assassinations and collective punishments against Palestinians that had become 'standard operating procedure' under the Israeli government of Ariel Sharon.[46] Thomas Neumann, executive director of the Jewish Institute for National Security Affairs (JINSA) concluded that the first George W. Bush Administration was the 'best administration for Israel since Harry Truman'.[47] Indeed, in May 2004, the disregard for even the pretence of impartiality in the Middle East policy of the Bush Administration led 53 former US diplomats to publicly accuse the administration of sacrificing US credibility in the Arab world.[48]

The Israeli Defense Force (IDF) responded to the July 2006 kidnapping of two Israeli soldiers by members of the Lebanese based Hezbollah armed organization with an extensive bombing campaign. Lebanese targets in this campaign included roads, ports, bridges, a water plant and a power generating plant. Widespread destruction of the civilian infrastructure prevented the distribution of humanitarian aid and made refugees out of one third of the Lebanese population. Civilian housing and a UN observation station were destroyed in the bombing, causing loss of life to civilians and UN observers. Hezbollah responded to the bombing campaign by firing hundreds of Katyusha rockets at Northern Israeli towns causing further civilian deaths. This use of Katyusha rockets against civilian areas was in direct contravention of the requirements of international humanitarian law to discriminate between civilians and combatants in choosing targets.

The Bush Administration appealed to the plight of Israeli civilians to condemn Hezbollah's firing of rockets into Northern Israel as acts of terrorism. However, the acts of violence conducted by the IDF were not likewise condemned by the administration as acts of international terrorism. Neither was the IDF campaign condemned as aggression, a crime against humanity, a war crime nor as a human rights atrocity. Instead, the actions of the IDF were interpreted as proportionate acts of self-defense and throughout July 2006 the Bush Administration refused calls to use the diplomatic weight of the US to force an immediate cease-fire.[49] That the position adopted by the Bush Administration insisted on a politicized interpretation, that eschewed the impartial application of human rights, can be demonstrated through detailing three features of how the official narrative produced identities, (i) defining Hezbollah as terrorists, (ii) defining the initial kidnapping of two soldiers as a threat to the future security of Israel and (iii) defining the intent of Israelis in terms of self defense.

First, in contrast to its classification by the White House, Hezbollah described itself not as a terrorist group but rather as a resistance organization engaged in, what it perceived to be, a legitimate struggle against Israeli occupation. To define a terrorist organization from a resistance movement is itself a fundamentally contested matter of interpretation, with far-reaching consequences for how the audience understands political events.

Second, to interpret the Hezbollah kidnapping of two IDF soldiers as an urgent threat to the security of Israel is not itself unproblematic. It is unclear why the kidnapping of two soldiers must necessarily be interpreted as a terrorist threat to the future security of Israel, requiring massive military retaliation not negotiation. It is similarly unclear how the destruction of Lebanese infrastructure carried out in the IDF bombing campaign advanced either the defense of Israel or the security of Israeli citizens. This is especially the case since the Hezbollah firing of Katyusha rockets into northern Israeli towns followed, rather than predated, the launch of the July 2006 IDF bombing campaign.

Third, establishing intent is itself a politically contested activity that frames how the audience subsequently understands events. In reducing the intent of the IDF to a necessary and proportionate response of self-defense, the narrative from the Bush Administration presented those Lebanese civilian deaths resulting from the IDF bombing campaign as unavoidable, if tragic, mistakes rather than as a consequence of political choices. In particular, the account of intent advanced by the administration failed to address why the principle of non-combatant immunity was neglected in the conduct of the IDF campaign. This neglect was expressed linguistically by the promise of Israel's chief of staff to 'turn back the clock in Lebanon by 20 years' and, in practice, through the IDF air strike on the village of Qana in which 60 civilians, including 34 children, were killed.[50] Indeed, civilian areas in Lebanon were bombed to such an extent that the IDF had killed 20 times as many civilians in Lebanon in July 2006 as had Hezbollah rockets in Israel.[51] A classification of the civilian deaths caused in the IDF bombing campaign as tragic mistakes overlooks how the principle of civilian immunity was consciously subordinated to military contingencies as evidenced in the widespread use of cluster munitions by the IDF. A cluster bomb consists of a canister that opens to release hundreds of individual bomblets that explode molten metal and fragments over a wide area. Bomblets that fail to explode in the air or upon contact with the ground remain until they are disturbed. Unexploded bomblets pose a particular danger to children whose vital organs are closer to the ground and are protected by less body tissue than those of an adult. The UN estimates that the IDF dropped two million bomblets on Lebanon, of which up to a million have yet to explode. Following the cease-fire, these unexploded munitions injured or killed an estimated two or three Lebanese civilians per day.[52]

Human rights abuses and undemocratic reforms in Pakistan were overlooked by a Bush Administration keen not to offend an ally in the war on terror. General Pervez Musharraf had overthrown an elected government in Pakistan in 1999. Three years later Musharraf pushed through constitutional amendments that (i) extended his presidential term by five years, (ii) gave him the power to dissolve the elected Parliament and (iii) created a National Security Council to oversee the civilian government.[53] In November 2002 an Anti-Terrorism Act was introduced allowing the police to arrest and detain terrorist suspects for one year without charge.[54] This concentration of political power in Pakistan was accompanied by the strengthening of US ties.[55] In return for support from Musharraf following 9/11, Washington wrote off $1 billion of bilateral debt and the Bush Administration promised to ask Congress to allocate a further $3 billion in aid.[56] President Bush clarified his priorities during a press conference in August 2002 when, in response to a direct question about the constitutional changes enacted under Musharraf, he replied '[m]y reaction about President Musharraf, he's still tight with us on the war against terror, and that's what I appreciate'.[57]

In contrast to the focus by the Bush Administrations on Cuba and Venezuela as sources of human rights violations in Latin America, Colombia has been highlighted for particular concern by independent human rights NGOs. Colombian citizens suffer under an ongoing civil war between the military, the Revolutionary Armed Forces of Colombia (FARC), the National Liberation Army (ELN) and the United Self-Defense Forces of Colombia (AUC). Citizens involved in community activities have been seen as suspected sympathizers of leftist guerrillas and many have been executed by the paramilitary AUC forces.[58] Corruption is rife among officials and honest police, judges and lawyers have been targeted for assassination.[59] Amnesty International estimates that in 2003, 3000 civilians were killed, 175,000 displaced and 600 civilians 'disappeared'.[60]

Since 2001, Colombia has consistently had the highest death rate for trade unionists, journalists and mayors in Latin America. The state also has the highest homicide rate in the Americas and the highest kidnapping rate in the world. Politically related deaths rose from eight per day in 1996 to 18 in 2001.[61] The Bush Administrations responded to this record of violence not by encouraging conflict resolution, mediation or human rights strategies but instead by increasing funding and support for the Colombian military. In 2003, US financial aid to Colombia reached $583 million, 75 percent of which was directed at the nation's military and police forces.[62] In the same year the US military provided training to 13,000 Colombian troops, 4000 more than that provided for Iraq and 8000 more than for Afghanistan.[63]

The State Department has accommodated US support for the Colombian state within the hegemonic discourse by downplaying the role of the Colombian authorities in human rights abuses and by instead focusing on positive human rights developments. On August 11, 2002, Colombian President Alvero Uribe declared a state of internal disturbance and granted the executive branch special powers. Using these powers, the President issued decree 2002 that restricted freedoms of movement and expression while eliminating a number of due process safeguards.[64] The State Department gave a positive spin to this development by noting in its *2002 Country Reports on Human Rights Practices* that the Colombia Constitutional Court struck down elements of decree 2002 as unconstitutional.[65] The *Country Reports* however remained silent on the numerous attempts by the Uribe Administration to (i) reject the Constitutional Court's rulings, (ii) reinstate those powers deemed unconstitutional through presenting bills to Congress, (iii) criticize the Constitutional Court for its ruling, (iv) slash funding for the Constitutional Court following its ruling and (v) offer support to attempts at extending police powers declared unconstitutional by the Constitutional Court.[66]

The Lawyers Committee for Human Rights observe that the Colombian chapter of the State Department's *Country Reports* similarly underreported the serious human rights abuses committed by the Colombian military.[67] In particular, the State Department played down the ties between Colombian paramilitary and military units by only referring to such ties in the context of individual members of the security forces.[68] Another document produced by the State Department distances Colombian paramilitaries from military units by instead conflating paramilitary and leftist guerrillas as 'terrorists' against whom the Colombian Office of the Prosecutor General is conducting 'major operations'.[69] In contrast to this supposed separation of military and paramilitary units, the UN Commission for Human Rights identified 'coordination' between the two forces.[70] Similarly, Human Rights Watch reported that paramilitary forces 'operate with the tolerance and often support of units within Colombia's military' and cite 'joint military-paramilitary operations'.[71] Amnesty International likewise referred to 'army-backed paramilitaries' as responsible for human rights abuses.[72] There are also reported efforts to regularize the paramilitary system within the formal Colombian military structure through enlisting 15,000 peasants to fight in their home areas with regular troops.[73]

There are therefore evident disparities between the assessment made by the State Department and independent human rights organizations with respect to (i) the extent of efforts by the Uribe Administration to restrict the legal rights of Colombian citizens and (ii) the extent of the collaboration between the Colombian military and paramilitary units. The consistency in this disparity lies in the State Department denying or downplaying involvement by the Colombian government in human rights abuses relative to those reports produced by independent human rights sources. This consistency is in line with producing a benign understanding of US support for the Uribe Administration. Producing such a benign understanding is politically significant given that Colombia is the seventh largest oil supplier to the US and given that its military is charged with protecting oil pipelines from guerrilla attacks. Moreover, in 2002, $98 million of US aid was authorized by Congress for 60–100 US Special Forces troops to train the 300-strong Critical Infrastructure Brigade in Colombia. This brigade was to act specifically as a rapid deployment force to protect the 500-mile-long Cano Limon–Covenas oil pipeline linking the interior oilfields to the refineries on the Caribbean coast operated by Occidental Petroleum.[74]

Foreign policy practices have therefore politicized human rights as detailed in the cases reviewed above. Human rights cannot, however, be rejected as politically insignificant since this overlooks the evident consistency within the politicization of the narrative provided. Namely, the human rights narrative, expressed by the Bush Administrations, has consistently produced ethical identities and explanations for policy decisions as required by the hegemonic mythology. The production of reality can therefore be seen as a function of the hegemonic discourse since it is this predetermined discourse that defines the intentions, objectives and identities of friendly and enemy states alike. The chapter finishes by illustrating this politicized function of human rights with respect to the central Asian state of Uzbekistan under the regime of Islam Karimov. The case of Uzbekistan is instructive since in this instance the Bush Administration publicly voiced human rights criticisms against a state that was highly significant for strategic reasons including (i) the development of oil infrastructure from the Caspian Sea Basin, (ii) its location for US military bases and (iii) sharing a border with Afghanistan.

A massacre of anti-government protestors in Andizhan, Uzbekistan, on May 12–13, 2005 by the security forces resulted in 500 deaths and focused worldwide media attention on the systematic human rights abuses carried out by the Karimov regime.[75] Three days after the massacre, State Department spokesman Richard Boucher condemned the incident by announcing, '[w]e certainly condemn the indiscriminate use of force against unarmed civilians and deeply regret any loss of life'.[76] In the weeks following the massacre, thousands fled to neighboring Kyrgyzstan in fear of further repression. Relieving the possibility of a humanitarian catastrophe, the US organized for the refugees to be airlifted to Romania. The Karimov regime responded to this unwanted interference by ordering the US military to leave its Karshi-Khanabad air base in Uzbekistan and by snubbing diplomatic relations with the US.

Diplomat Nicholas Burns defended the decision to support the refugees irrespective of these repercussions by stating that, as a matter of principle, 'we are not willing to overlook these very important human rights concerns'.[77] Rejecting human rights as meaningless rhetoric is inconsistent with both the words and actions of policymakers in this instance. Indeed, human rights constituted the explicit reason for a policy shift toward a strategically significant state with which the Bush Administration had previously enjoyed amicable relations. Yet, as will now be detailed, the reflective account of this manifestation of the hegemonic discourse is also deficient. In particular the reflective account fails to explain (i) close US–Uzbek relations prior to the Andizhan massacre, (ii) that moves to integrate human rights into US policy toward Uzbekistan originated in Congress rather than the executive and (iii) the politicization of the human rights discourse expressed by the Bush Administrations.

First, systematic repression in Uzbekistan was occurring long before Bush Administration officials expressed public condemnation. Between 2001 and 2004 there were an estimated 600 political arrests in the state per year.[78] Religious activity in Uzbekistan was only allowed in government-approved mosques and at least 7000 Muslims had been incarcerated for failing to abide by state designated religious regulations.[79] In 2002, a UN special rapporteur described the torture of political prisoners in Uzbekistan as 'widespread and systematic', with favored techniques including boiling until dead.[80] Prisoners were tortured to extract recantations of faith, to provide information, to incriminate accomplices and to swear loyalty to the president.[81]

This record of human rights violations did little to obstruct close relations between the Bush Administrations and the Karimov regime. Indeed, former UK ambassador to Uzbekistan, Craig Murray, described Karimov as 'very much George Bush's man in central Asia'.[82] In exchange for the tripling of US aid to a total of $160 million per annum, Karimov allowed the US to use military bases in Uzbekistan as a launch pad for operations into Afghanistan.[83] A spokesperson for the Human Rights Society of Uzbekistan summarized two years before the Andizhan massacre that 'the attitude of the whole US administration shows that they have traded human rights in Uzbekistan for airfields'.[84] Indeed, one possible function of the torture practiced in Uzbekistan was to provide information to the US and UK intelligence services. Murray was relieved of his post after revealing that on at least three occasions prisoners had been transferred by the US from Afghanistan to Uzbekistan where '[t]hey almost certainly would have been tortured'.[85] When he raised these concerns with the CIA, Murray reports that '[t]here was no reason to think they were perturbed'.[86]

Second, the reflective account of the hegemonic discourse fails to explain why those limited efforts that had been made to integrate human rights into foreign policy toward Uzbekistan prior to the Andizhan massacre had originated from outside the Bush Administrations. Funds for human rights training in Uzbekistan were only provided under pressure from Congress. Indeed, the human rights abuses occurring in Uzbekistan were only acknowledged by administration officials when members of Congress pressed them on why the administration was 'dancing with dictators' in maintaining close relations with the Karimov regime.[87]

Third, the reflective explanation fails to explain politicized efforts to create the impression rather than the actuality of an improving human rights situation in Uzbekistan prior to the Andizhan massacre. After legislation in 2002 made US assistance to the Karimov regime conditional upon human rights improvements in Uzbekistan, efforts were placed on creating the impression of such developments. While attending the opening of a human rights center in the Ferghana valley of Uzbekistan in 2003, for example, US ambassador Jon Purnell reportedly interrupted a local speaker who was critical of governmental repression. Eviscerating the concept of human rights of all coherence and purpose, the ambassador explained that political points were not allowed at the function.[88]

In another example of creating the impression of an improving human rights situation in Uzbekistan, the *2002 Country Reports on Human Rights Practices* simply reclassified repressive practices away. Members of the Muslim group Hizb ut-Tahrir seeking to establish a Muslim state through non-violent means, had long been targeted for repression by the Karimov regime.[89] Until 2002, Hizb ut-Tahrir had been classified as a 'pious Muslim' or 'independent Muslim' organization in the *Country Reports*. This changed in 2002 when the group was reclassified by the State Department as 'a banned extremist Islamic political party'.[90] Thereafter, state repression of group members could be categorized as counter terrorism rather than as oppression. This categorization produced the appearance of an improving human rights situation in Uzbekistan, which could in turn be taken as retrospective evidence to justify the conciliatory approach to Karimov adopted by the Bush Administrations prior to the Andizhan massacre.

The Bush Administration shifted its position from ambivalence to a forthright principled focus on Uzbek human rights at precisely that time when front-page headlines were highlighting the above three contradictions between the hegemonic mythology and reality for public attention. The hegemonic discourse only functions as an instrument of governance to the extent that it is normalized as truth and not systematically investigated or demonstrated to provide a politicized rather than objective description of reality.

Explaining the shift in policy toward Uzbekistan in terms of reasserting the credibility of the hegemonic mythology accounts for the above three failings of the reflective explanation since the apparent rather than actual promotion of human rights is all important. The productive explanation is furthermore consistent with administration delays in condemning or indeed offering so much as a mild rebuke immediately following the Andizhan massacre, when the position was to still maintain cozy relations with Karimov. When pressed on the issue immediately following the massacre, the White House for example declined to comment, with press secretary Scott McClellan simply urging both sides to exercise restraint.[91] When McClellan first provided commentary after the massacre, it was to explain that those shot dead in Andizhan included 'Islamic terrorists' and that protestors should seek democracy 'through peaceful means', despite the fact that opposition had not been allowed to take part in the elections of December

26, 2004.[92] The change to vocal and principled advocacy of human rights occurred only after it became politically untenable to attempt to reconcile the contradictions between actual policy and the hegemonic mythology. By accounting for the hegemonic discourse as a technique of governance, the productive explanation alone can account for (i) the three contradictions to the reflective explanation of human rights policy towards Uzbekistan identified above, (ii) why the principled response from the Bush Administration to the Andizhan massacre came belatedly and (iii) why, when the policy shift eventually came, the principled focus on human rights was asserted so vociferously.

Conclusion

The politicization of human rights as a technique of governance is evident in the production of the annual *Country Reports on Human Rights Practices* by the State Department. During the Cold War, the politicization of human rights in the reports became so overt that the Lawyers Committee for Human Rights issued annual critiques detailing how human rights abuses were selectively highlighted or downplayed in the documents. Responding to such criticisms, the State Department issued guidelines in 1993 requiring authors to cover standardized human rights criteria relating to, for example, discrimination, labor rights and problems of impunity for past human rights violations. In turn, the Lawyers Committee for Human Rights stopped producing its annual critiques in 1995 on the grounds that the *Country Reports* had become more thorough and impartial. The contents of the *Country Reports* produced during the tenure of the first George W. Bush Administration led the Lawyers Committee to announce that it needed 'to reconsider this judgment'.[93] In particular, coverage of some states in the *2002 Country Reports* were found to be marred by a 'misrepresentation of the facts or political spin' and distortion caused by omissions.[94] In particular the group identified a 'serious misrepresentation of the human rights situation' in those states where US military and security personnel were present, following on from the introduction by the State Department of new guidelines that censored mention of the human rights consequences of counter-terrorism measures.[95] These new guidelines required that 'actions by governments taken at the request of the United States or with the expressed support of the United States should not be included in this report'.[96] The *Country Reports* thereby censored mention or comment on the role played by the US and the war on terror in those human rights violations noted in its pages.[97] Thus the *Country Reports* produced a predetermined reality, rather than reflected a corresponding reality.

This chapter has employed a country specific focus to detail precisely how the Bush Administrations have used human rights to produce a politicized interpretation of reality. Severe violations of human rights in areas of peripheral concern have been interpreted by the administrations as tragic humanitarian events but this designation has been insufficient to warrant urgent action. Human rights violations in designated enemy states have, in contrast, been highlighted as proof of evil and despotic regimes, identities that have subsequently been utilized by officials explaining US support for opposition movements in such states. Similar or worse violations of human rights in designated friendly states have been re-categorized as counter terrorism, necessary self-defense or as isolated exceptions to an otherwise improving trend. The criterion consistently adopted to classify human rights violations has not been an independent assessment of the actual acts themselves but instead the predetermined identity of the state responsible for that abuse. Amnesty International, for example, identified Chechnya, Colombia and Nepal as the breeding grounds for the worst human rights atrocities in the world. The NGO explains that the Bush Administrations have said little on Nepal, have done even less, and have actively supported repression in Chechnya and Colombia as a part of the 'war on terror'.[98]

The evident disparities between the human rights rhetoric and practice of the Bush Administrations may appear to validate the rejectionist account of human rights discourse as a meaningless focus for understanding foreign policy. This chapter has argued against drawing such a conclusion since this overlooks the fundamental political function of human rights discourse in producing an understanding of policy decisions in the minds of the audience. Deputy Secretary of Defense Paul Wolfowitz identified this importance of human rights when, writing in the *National Interest*, he identified 'human rights as an important *tool* of American foreign policy'.[99] The assistant secretary for democracy, human rights and labor similarly highlighted the instrumental significance of human rights when, in a speech to the Heritage Foundation, he announced that 'our focus on national interests will come by concentrating on advancing human rights and democracy in countries important to the United States'.[100] Human rights are thereby co-opted as an instrument through which to advance the politics of power. Attention turns in Chapter 4 to analyze the specific interests and values that have been articulated under a language of universal human rights.

4 Consistent application of human rights

Introduction

Chapter 3 detailed how the George W. Bush Administrations applied human rights inconsistently in foreign policy. The chapter hypothesized that the hegemonic discourse was, however, consistently applied in the sense of a mechanism of governance that allocates identities to political actors and thereby produces an internally coherent reality of foreign policy in the minds of the audience. This analysis may appear abstract and unhelpful to those readers more interested in the underlying interests and values advanced by the Bush Administrations. To be of help to such readers, Chapter 4 aims to detail the connections between the Bush Administrations and particular elements of domestic civil society focusing upon evangelical religious groups, think tanks and corporate interests. This chapter analyzes how a focus on these elements of domestic civil society can reveal patterns in how human rights have been applied in the foreign policy of the Bush Administrations. This chapter is structured into two sections. The first section looks at how specific values advanced by favored groups have found representation in policies sponsored by the White House and resonate in the human rights discourse expressed by the Bush Administrations. The Millennium Challenge Account (MCA) will be incorporated as a particular study to illustrate how favored elements of domestic civil society have influenced the application of human rights in a specific foreign policy initiative.

Whereas describing associations between organizations and administration officials may prove useful in explaining the general political outlook and priorities of the administrations, it is insufficient to demonstrate that a language of human rights has been co-opted in the furtherance of elements of domestic civil society. The second section of the chapter therefore examines how the hegemonic discourse has articulated human rights in terms of US exceptionalism as a distinctly American concept. This second section briefly details the hostility from the Bush Administrations to international human rights legislation and to the International Criminal Court (ICC). The chapter thereby demonstrates how the Bush Administrations have sidelined legal mechanisms in favor of asserting human rights on a more selective and discretionary basis. Henry Kissinger once remarked, 'What is presented by foreign critics as America's quest for domination is very frequently a response to domestic pressure groups.'[1] This chapter argues that the two interpretations of US foreign policy considered by Kissinger are far from mutually exclusive. This chapter finds instead that the hegemonic discourse allows policymakers a wide remit to advance favored elements of domestic civil society under a language of human rights, democracy promotion and freedom.

Favored elements of domestic civil society

US civil society covers a rich plurality of groups promoting an array of distinct agendas. Despite their relative lack of influence over policy formulation, environmental activists, human rights NGOs and west coast punk rock bands are as much features of domestic civil society as are fundamentalist Christian groups and corporate organizations pursuing the accumulation of capital. From the myriad and contradictory elements of domestic civil society, three specific institutions can be identified for their significant connections with Bush Administration officials. These institutions relate not to human rights advocacy NGOs but instead to (i) evangelical religious groups, (ii) ideologically sympathetic think tanks and (iii) corporate America.

Religion

One third of the US electorate is now thought to hold to fundamentalist Christian beliefs including the denial of evolution in favor of some variant of creationism or intelligent design.[2] President Bush enjoyed strong electoral support among evangelical voters, especially from among those belonging to the subcategory of white evangelical Protestants. According to exit polls, 68 percent of this subcategory voted for him in the 2000 election, a figure that rose to 78 percent in 2004.[3] In exit polls conducted for both the 2000 and 2004 elections, 23 percent of the electorate described themselves as white evangelical Protestants.[4] However, the Pew Research Center notes that the growing significance of evangelical Christians lies not in their rising numbers but rather in their increasing political cohesiveness as a group in the Republican Party.[5]

Links between the Bush Administrations and the evangelical Christian movement are exemplified in the prominent support provided by Billy Graham and Christian Coalition founder Pat Robertson for George W. Bush in his 2000 election campaign.[6] The Christian Coalition was founded in 1989 for the purpose of giving 'Christians a voice in government' and claims two million members across the US.[7] There is ample evidence suggesting that the evangelical Christian movement is pushing its agenda at an open door in the Bush White House. The president has consistently used the terminology, imagery and symbolism immediately familiar to evangelical Christians in expressing a foreign policy discourse, for example, in likening Osama bin Laden to Satan as 'the evil one'.[8]

The importance of religion to the political outlook of the president himself was exemplified in his declaration during the 2000 election campaign that his favorite philosopher thinker was Jesus Christ on the stated grounds that 'he changed my heart'.[9] The significance of religious belief was exemplified on another occasion when the president was questioned on whether he had asked for his father's advice before launching the Iraq War. The president reportedly replied that his earthly father was 'the wrong father to appeal to for advice ... there is a higher father that I appeal to'.[10] In a similar account of divine intervention, former Palestinian Foreign Minister Nabil Shaath, reported that President Bush announced to Palestinian Prime Minister Mahmoud Abbas in June 2003, 'God would tell me, "George, go and end the tyranny in Iraq" and I did.'[11] President Bush is reported to have added, 'Now again I feel God's words coming to me: "Go get the Palestinians their state and get the Israelis their security and get peace in the Middle East." '[12] When the president ordered the US military invasion of Iraq on March 19, 2003 he prayed 'for the strength to do the Lord's will' and to be 'as good a messenger of His will as possible'.[13] In addition to being asserted in the context of authorizing acts of organized political violence, the religious beliefs of the president have also featured as a rationale for the recognition of human rights. In his 2005 inauguration speech the president, for example, affirmed a belief in the 'rights, and dignity, and matchless value' of 'every man and woman on this earth' on the stated grounds that 'they bear the image of the maker of heaven and earth'.[14] On another occasion the president opposed human cloning on the grounds that '[h]uman life is a gift from our Creator'.[15]

Neo-conservative think tanks

In domestic civil society, neo-conservatism can be defined in terms of the promotion of Judeo-Christian culture in contradistinction to secular humanism and ethical relativism.[16] In terms of foreign policy, neo-conservatism is characterized by the advocacy of US power and influence around the world in the stated furtherance of freedom. Neo-conservatism can be differentiated from liberalism through its instinctive skepticism of international law and multilateral institutions, and its sanction of unilateral US militarism as an acceptable means to affect desired changes across the world.[17] Washington-based think tanks promoting a neo-conservative agenda include the Center for Security Policy (CSP), the American Enterprise Institute (AEI) and the Project for the New American Century (PNAC). The AEI declares its aims as 'preserving and strengthening the foundations of a free society-limited government, competitive private enterprise, vital cultural and political institutions and vigilant defense'.[18] The foreign policy aims of the AEI were candidly presented in a July 2003 forum entitled '[t]he US is and should be an Empire'.[19] Promoting the forum, the AEI declared that '[t]o protect the global trade routes of democratic capitalism and its own security interests, the US can intervene anytime, anyplace'.[20]

There exists a revolving door for officials in the Bush Administrations and for personnel in these think tanks. Donald Rumsfeld, for example, affirmed to the CSP that '[i]f there was any doubt about the power of your ideas, one has

only to look at the number of Center associates who now people this administration – and particularly the Department of Defense – to dispel them'.[21] The close
ties between the AEI and the Bush Administration were likewise acknowledged
when, in 2003, the president announced that '[a]t the American Enterprise Institute, some of the finest minds in our nation are at work on some of the greatest
challenges to our nation. You do such good work that my administration has
borrowed twenty such minds'.[22] Such minds included Leon Kass who chaired
the Council on Bioethics, Defense Policy Board member Richard Perle and Vice
Chairman of the US–China Security Commission, Michael Ledeen. AEI Public
Affairs Director, Veronique Rodman, was a member of the Broadcasting Board
of Governors. Former AEI trustee John Snow was appointed secretary of the
treasury in 2003. Former Chairman of the Council of Economic Advisers, R.
Glenn Hubbard, returned to the AEI in 2003 to research tax policy and health
care. Former member of the Council of Economic Advisers, Randall Kroszner,
joined the AEI in 2003 as a visiting scholar to research international trade, regu-
lation and corporate governance.[23] Economic adviser to President Bush,
Lawrence Lindsey, formerly held the Arthur F. Burns chair at the AEI.[24] Staff
Chief to the Council of Economic Advisors, Diana Furchgott-Roth, was for-
merly a resident fellow at the AEI.[25] Before joining the Bush Administration,
John Bolton was vice president of the AEI.[26] Administration support for Bolton
was exemplified through his controversial recess appointment to the position of
US ambassador to the UN in August 2005 following weeks of deadlock in the
Senate over his proposed appointment.

The PNAC was created in 1997 upon calls for a return to 'Reaganite policies
of military strength and moral clarity' in furtherance of shaping 'a new century
favorable to American principles and interests'.[27] The PNAC obtained both its
name and inspiration from Henry Luce Booth. Writing in 1942 against the isola-
tionism that he considered to be characteristic of the Franklin Roosevelt Presidency, Luce Booth advocated that the US should 'exert upon the world the full
impact of our influence, for such purposes as we see fit and by such means as we
see fit'.[28] Promoting this agenda, one PNAC document stated that, 'if an American peace is to be maintained, and expanded, it must have a secure foundation
on unquestioned US military pre-eminence'.[29] Numerous signatories to statements of principles and letters authored by PNAC have subsequently served as
officials in the Bush Administrations.[30] Signatories to a 1998 PNAC letter urging
an attack on Iraq who subsequently served in the first George W. Bush Administration, for example, included Elliott Abrams,[31] Richard Armitage,[32] John
Bolton,[33] Paula Dobriansky,[34] Donald Rumsfeld,[35] Paul Wolfowitz,[36] Richard
Perle,[37] William Bennett[38] and Zalmay Khalilzad.[39]

Corporate America

Smith points out that in US politics the conflation of democracy, human rights
and capitalism is commonly accepted as unproblematic.[40] Illustrating the validity
of this claim, the 2006 *National Security Strategy* identified the protection of

'private property, independent business and a market economy' as constitutive signifiers of 'effective democracy'.[41] Thus defined, democracy refers to particular modes of economic organization rather than to a general will of a people. As capably demonstrated by Donnelly, this confusion between very separate categories has allowed successive US administrations to support a plethora of repressive military dictatorships and civilian oligarchies conducive to US economic interests in the name of democracy and human rights.[42]

Social and economic human rights that prioritize the provision of basic goods and services to the needy over the private property rights of individuals have consequently been categorized as undemocratic, Un-American or communist by an enduring current in American politics. This trend can be traced back to at least the 1950s when Senator Bricker led a campaign to amend the constitution. Senator Bricker was especially concerned that social and economic human rights could be incorporated into federal legislation through the back door route of international treaties. The Bricker constitutional amendment consequently proposed that a treaty should become effective in the US only through legislation that would be valid in the absence of that treaty.[43] Senator Bricker explained that 'my purpose in offering this resolution is to bury the so-called covenant on human rights so deep that no one holding high office will ever dare to attempt its resurrection'.[44] President Eisenhower only defeated the proposed amendment with the pledge that the US would not accede to human rights conventions. Henkin has duly noted that through the packages of reservations, understandings and declarations attached to those few human rights treaties that have been subsequently ratified by the US, Senator Bricker has been remarkably successful in achieving the stated purpose of his proposed amendment.[45]

The hostility of the Bush Administrations toward social and economic human rights can subsequently be seen in terms of this enduring trend in American politics. Such hostility from Bush Administration officials can be identified in the adoption of three discursive strategies toward social and economic rights, (i) co-option, (ii) subjugation and (iii) critical exclusion. First, social and economic rights have been made incoherent by virtue of being co-opted by Bush Administration officials into, instead, promoting corporate interests and the market mechanism. When questioned at a press briefing on the administration's record on economic rights, the assistant secretary of state for democracy, human rights and labor asserted that 'we're also trying to help on that end of things' citing support for 'free trade agreements' in defense of the claim.[46] Thus conceptualized, the social provision of resources to the marginalized and vulnerable as a fundamental right is inverted into, instead, promoting an agenda for expanding the neo-liberal market. In a similar act of co-option, President Bush has conflated human rights with economic freedom. Explaining foreign policy in the Middle East, the president stated on one occasion that '[w]e applaud those in the region striving to advance human rights and economic freedom, fight corruption, and advance equal justice under law'.[47] This mirrors a pledge in the 2002 *National Security Strategy* that the United States will 'actively work to bring the hope of democracy, development, free markets and free trade to every corner of the world'.[48] This conflation of very different imperatives discursively denies even the possibility that a free people may choose not to endorse 'free trade' or 'free markets' and similarly denies that the market can itself act as a causal factor in human rights violations.[49]

Weeks before a September 2005 international summit designed to advance the implementation of millennium development goals, US officials proposed no fewer than 750 changes and objections to the main document to be discussed at the forum. The director of the Earth Institute at Columbia University commented that he considered the intent of the administration was 'to try to gut this document … to try to eliminate the momentum behind the millennium development goals and to wriggle free of the commitments they have made'.[50] The Bush Administration deemed that a section on poverty alleviation contained in the document was 'too long'.[51] The administration consequently set about lobbying for the removal of the goal for developed states to donate 0.7 percent of their GNP in aid to the developing world. The administration maintained that the development agenda should instead be placed upon implementing the Monterrey Consensus in reference to the 2002 summit held in Mexico that stressed the role of neo-liberal economic reforms in alleviating poverty.[52] Thus, the focus of the millennium development goals was co-opted from addressing the immediate needs of the worlds poorest toward promoting a corporate driven agenda of market expansion.

The second discursive strategy adopted by administration officials to subjugate social and economic rights was by defying logic and categorizing these human rights in terms of their civil and political counterparts. Thus, the US permanent representative to the UN offices in Geneva explained in 2001 that 'the protection of basic civil and political rights is indispensable to sustainable growth. This all-important link between human rights and economic development is sometimes missing from the discussions'.[53] This followed, the ambassador reasoned, since the protection of private property and the freedom to contract would give individuals the confidence to invent, innovate and invest.[54] Thus the market mechanism is presented in terms of a solution to poverty and the role of the market in denying essential resources to the impoverished is discursively excluded. The US delegation to the 59th session of the UN Commission on Human Rights were still less reserved in articulating open hostility to the economic right to development. The delegation asserted that, 'in our estimation the right to development is not a "fundamental", "basic" or "essential" human right'.[55] The delegation went on to explain that economic, social and cultural rights were 'progressive and aspirational' and not, in their view, 'entitlements that require correlated legal duties and obligations'.[56]

The third discursive strategy adopted to undermine social and economic rights was to insist that these are counterproductive in providing for basic human needs. According to one official, 'we know that government-controlled economies never seem to work over the long term. There is no substitute for free markets, transparent financial institutions and respect for the rule of law'.[57] This strategy attacks rights-based policies guaranteeing essential provisions for all human beings. In particular, such economic rights are conceptualized to neglect the fight against poverty. Through this inversion of comprehension, a language of human rights, development and freedom can be mobilized to promote policies that compound the desperate position of those suffering most under the viscidities of the global economy. Implementing this inverted logic of helping the vulnerable, US delegates stood almost alone in 2001 in opposing a UN resolution to lower the costs of accessing anti-viral AIDS drugs and opposing a resolution endorsing the human right to food.[58]

While social and economic rights designed to benefit the economically vulnerable have been co-opted, subjugated and criticized by administration officials, private property rights have been defended. The 2002 *National Security Strategy* spoke of 'free trade' as 'a moral principle'.[59] President Bush defended this principle when calling upon the Cuban government to respect private property rights.[60] The apparent contradiction of asserting one type of economic human right (that of individuals to private property) while simultaneously denying the validity of economic rights as a legitimate category of human rights is consistent with the mobilization of a rights-based discourse to promote the market mechanism and corporate interests. In particular, the legitimate role of the state is thereby limited to protecting market outcomes and any state intervention to provide economic justice for the impoverished is delegitimized. The internal consistency of the discourse outlined above lies in the co-option of human rights to promote favored characteristics of domestic civil society. Nowhere is this more evident than through one specific project cited by the State Department as evidence of US commitment to human rights;[61] the MCA.

On January 23, 2004, President Bush signed legislation creating the Millennium Challenge Corporation to administer the allocation of development aid under a new initiative, the MCA. To be eligible for aid under the MCA, recipient states must demonstrate a strong commitment in three categories, (i) good governance defined as 'rooting out corruption, upholding human rights and adherence to the rule of law'; (ii) health and education and (iii) to 'economic policies that foster enterprise and entrepreneurship', with this third category defined as 'more open markets, sustainable budget policies and strong support for individual entrepreneurship'.[62] The MCA does not advance development or poverty alleviation as an enforceable human right Under the program, aid is instead distributed on a discretionary basis independent of immediate human need.

The funds allocated to the MCA for the financial years 2003–06 totaled $5.2 billion, a figure that compares to a 2006 Department of Defense budget of $441.5 billion. Overall US aid under the Bush Administrations remains at the bottom of the league of developed states overseas aid as a proportion of national income. In 2001 US aid totaled 0.11 percent of Gross Domestic Product (GDP), approximately half of the 0.2 percent averaged throughout the 1980s, one third the average of Organization of Economic Cooperation and Development (OECD) states and compares to a UN recommended target of 0.7 percent.[63] For these reasons, the MCA is unlikely to prevent the continued systematic violation of basic economic rights such as the right to be free from hunger.

The MCA is, however, a highly effective mechanism to provide incentives for states to abide by market principles, thereby realizing the objective articulated by George W. Bush in a 2000 presidential debate that '[f]oreign aid needs to be used to encourage markets and reform'.[64] In order to offer such encouragement, the MCA has been formulated in line with recommendations from the Heritage Foundation. Indeed, the foundation claimed without hyperbole that the MCA program was 'lifted straight from the Heritage playbook'.[65] The Heritage Foundation was hostile to what it termed 'merit-based aid' that allocated foreign aid on the basis of urgent human needs. The organization instead suggested targeting resources at 'the best run and most promising of the world's poorest countries',[66] and those 'pursuing economic reform',[67] concerns that are embedded in the MCA criteria for allocating aid as detailed above. Aid, thereby, becomes a rather indiscrete incentive to encourage developing states to abide by favored neo-liberal economic principles. As the Heritage Foundation puts it, 'less developed countries willing to open their economies would be rewarded with financial aid ... countries that back-pedal on reform, however, would see their aid cut'.[68] Ideological governance is being transmitted through the MCA since states that adopt redistributive policies and prioritize provisions for basic human needs over market reforms are at a clear disadvantage to qualify for aid under the criteria advanced.

Furthermore, potential recipient states will be evaluated against the stipulated criteria by institutions, whose ethos reflects the favored values of economic neo-liberalism. The World Bank Institute and Freedom House are the sole reference sources used under the MCA for establishing the extent of 'good governance' in recipient states. The sources used to establish 'economic freedoms' are the Institutional Investor, the International Monetary Fund, the World Bank Institute, the World Bank and the Heritage Institute. The common neo-liberal economic sympathies of these organizations led one member of the Foreign Relations Committee to point out that these sources would necessarily impart 'immediate political considerations' to the implementation of the MCA.[69] The MCA initiative is, therefore, as effective a mechanism to advance economic neo-liberalism as it is an ineffective tool to advance economic human rights.

The manipulation of political discourse was illustrated in the appointment of Charlotte Beers, an advertising expert with little prior diplomatic experience, to a prominent position in the State Department. Colin Powell explained the reasoning for this appointment in terms of the State Department 'selling a product. That product we are selling is democracy. It's the free enterprise system, the American value system'.[70] Thus conceptualized, the value system of domestic civil society is commodified as a product and thereafter equated with democracy and the free enterprise system to be sold and exported by the State Department. As detailed above, the discourse of human rights constructed by the administration is one technique through which the free enterprise system has been advertised and sold abroad. If the values of corporate America are articulated by the Bush Administrations then so too are the underlying interests, as will be detailed in the following section by reviewing (i) associations between Administration officials and corporate entities, (ii) funding associations with corporate bodies and (iii) a pattern of decision making favoring corporate interests.

Illustrating ties between corporate America and the Bush Administrations, Secretary of Defense, Donald Rumsfeld, had previously acted for eight years as chief executive officer (CEO) of GD Searle, a pharmaceutical corporation, now a subsidiary of Pharmacia.[71] Between 1990 and 1993 Rumsfeld acted as CEO of the telecommunications parts supplier General Instrument Corporation.[72] Attorney General, John Ashcroft, reportedly received campaign contributions from Enterprise Rent-A-Car and Monsanto.[73] Chief of Staff, Andrew Card, was chief lobbyist for General Motors and CEO of the American Automobile Manufacturers Association before serving in the first George W. Bush Administration.[74] Stephen Hadley, national security advisor in the second administration, had previously been a partner in the lobbyist firm Shea and Garner whose corporate client list included Lockheed Martin.[75]

Prior to her appointment as agriculture secretary, Ann Veneman served on the International Policy Council on Agriculture, Food and Trade. This Council is funded by, among others, Cargill, Nestle and Kraft. Veneman had previously served as a board member of the agribusiness corporation Calgene, now a subsidiary of Monsanto.[76] Environmental Protection Agency Administrator, Christine Whitman, was governor of New Jersey 1993–2001. During her tenure as governor Whitman saw fit to abolish the state environmental prosecutor's office and replaced the state public advocate with a business ombudsman.[77] The Center for Responsive Politics reports that, as former Wisconsin governor, Health and Human Services Secretary Tommy Thompson accepted over $72,000 in campaign donations from Philip Morris.[78] Elaine Chao acted as president and CEO of United Way prior to her appointment as secretary of labor.[79] Director of the Office of Management and Budget, Mitch Daniels, was formerly senior vice president for the pharmaceutical MNC Eli Lilly.[80] The appointment of Interior Secretary Gale Norton followed her position as national chairwoman on the Coalition of Republican Environmental Advocates. This lobbying group is funded by, among others, BP, Amoco and Ford.[81] Prior to his appointment as commerce secretary, Don Evans had previously spent 25 years at the Denver based petrochemical corporation Tom Brown Inc., where he was CEO and chairman.[82] Paul O'Neill was a chair of Alcoa prior to his arrival in the Treasury Department.[83]

Hartung and Ciarrocca report that eight officials had direct or indirect ties to Lockheed Martin before joining the Bush Administration. Former Chief Operating Officer of Lockheed Martin, Peter Teets, was appointed undersecretary of the air force and director of the national reconnaissance office in the first administration.[84] Arms manufacturer Northrop had seven former officials, consultants or shareholders in the first Bush Administration.[85] Secretary of the Air Force, James Roche, was a former vice president of Northrop.[86] Assistant Secretary of the Air Force for Installations, Environment and Logistics, Nelson Gibbs, had previously served as corporate comptroller at Northrop.[87] Deputy Secretary of Defense Paul Wolfowitz, Pentagon Comptroller Dov Zakheim and Undersecretary of Defense, Douglas Feith, held consultancy contracts or served on paid advisory boards for Northrop before joining the administration.[88]

The George W. Bush electoral machine received considerable financing from corporate America. During the 2000 electoral cycle, the Bush campaign team out raised Al Gore among all business sectors of the US economy.[89] The disparity was especially notable in the energy sector in which industry sources donated $13 to Bush for every $1 donated to Gore.[90] PAC and individual contributions from the oil and gas sector to the Bush campaign in the 1999–2000 electoral cycle amounted to $1,929,451. This compares with similar contributions during the same electoral cycle to Gore of $138,514.[91] During the 1999–2000 electoral cycle, Bush received more in contributions from the oil and gas sector than any other federal candidate had received over the entire decade 1990–2000.[92] During the 2002 electoral cycle the coal industry reportedly contributed $3,740,084 to the election campaigns of federal candidates or political parties. While $427,607 (11 percent) of these donations went to the Democrats, $3,311,477 (89 percent) went to Republicans.[93] The 2003 lobbying expenditure of Lockheed Martin stood at $3.3 million and its 2003 campaign contributions amounted to $420,000, 58 percent of which went to the Republican Party or Republican candidates.[94] The 2003 lobbying expenditure of Boeing stood at $4 million and its 2003 campaign contributions were $114,000, 65 percent of which went to either the Republican party or Republican candidates.[95] Northrop was the second largest US defense contractor with sales of $17 billion in 2002. The 2003 lobbying expenditure of the corporation was $6.5 million and its campaign contributions that same year totaled $343,000.[96]

Corporate America received significant support from the Bush Administrations. The steel lobby succeeded in persuading President Bush to impose 30 percent tariffs on imported steel.[97] Revenue from sales of military equipment resulting from the 2003 Iraq War offset the loss that Boeing made in commercial plane sales.[98] Northrop similarly turned a $59 million loss in the third quarter of 2002 into a $184 profit in 2003 on the back of Iraq related military contracts.[99]

The mutual ties between corporate America and the Bush Administrations were revealed on December 7, 2002 when General Amin of the Iraqi Armed Forces handed over a document to the UN compound in Baghdad. This document detailed Iraqi weapons programs as required under UN Security Council resolution 1441. President Bush and Secretary of State Powell ordered US Ambassador to the UN, John Negroponte, to take charge of these papers. Despite the explicit requirement under resolution 1441 for the document to be passed to the Security Council,[100] and a protest by Secretary General Kofi Annan, the document was duly passed to US representatives. The US only copied the full document to representatives of Russia, China, the UK and France. The ten non-permanent members of the Security Council only saw censored highlights of the document.[101]

The explanation provided by US officials for why one state, rather than the Security Council, should receive the document was based on the rationale that, if distributed in its entirety, the document could be used by states to construct

WMD.[102] This explanation is, however, inconsistent with a prior agreement made in the Security Council, that weapons inspectors would remove sensitive technical data that could be used by non-nuclear weapon powers.[103] The explanation is furthermore inconsistent with the actual censorship conducted by the US authorities that left significant technical data on WMD production in the document. Indeed, one official at the International Atomic Energy Agency criticized the distributed version of the document as 'a very dumb idea' on grounds that the Americans 'forgot they also had obligations on non-proliferation'.[104] The censored version of the distributed document had, however, systematically expunged information relating to how MNCs had armed Saddam Hussein in the 1980s, consistent with the attempt to protect the reputations of corporate allies.[105]

The Bush Administration similarly advanced the interests of military industrial corporations in its November 2001 decision to withdraw the US from negotiations on a verification protocol designed to enforce the 1995 Biological Weapons Convention. Citing commercial confidentiality, US biological laboratories had long opposed opening their premises to international inspections as required under protocol proposals.[106] Furthermore, the Bush Administration saw fit to withdraw from a plethora of arms control treaties. In December 2001 the administration gave Russia six months notice that it was abrogating the 1972 Anti-Ballistic Missile Treaty. The administration similarly announced its opposition to the Comprehensive Test Ban Treaty on the stated grounds this would limit US nuclear research options.[107] The administration also announced that it would invest in the Star Wars system of national missile defense. The Bush Administration rejected a 1997 landmine treaty that calls for the destruction of all anti-personnel landmines. The administration agreed in principle to a UN 2001 agreement to halt the illegal flow of small arms but, under pressure from the National Rifle Association, blocked two key provisions seeking to regulate the trade in weapons.[108] This systematic withdrawal from multilateral arms control treaties, combined with a steep increase in military spending, led to an income bonanza for corporations operating in the military industrial sector.

The Bush Administrations prioritized corporate interests over environmental protection by calling repeatedly for oil drilling in the Arctic National Wildlife Refuge. The administrations have been sympathetic to the corporate position on climate change by withdrawing the US from the Kyoto protocol and acting to preclude the Inter Governmental Panel on Climate Change (IPCC) from adopting a more critical position on carbon reductions. In light of concerted efforts by the IPCC under the 1996–2002 chairmanship of Robert Watson to tackle global carbon dioxide emissions, Exxon Mobil sent a memo to the White House requesting that candidates deemed more acceptable replace those on the IPCC with 'aggressive agendas'.[109] After the Bush Administration received the Exxon Mobil memo, the State Department announced it was supporting the appointment of Rajendra Pachauri, rather than Robert Watson, for the post of chairman of the IPCC, when the office came up for re-election in 2002.[110] Pachauri was duly elected.

When President Bush arrived in office at a time of periodic electricity blackouts in California, he announced that solving the energy crisis was his top priority.[111] The president established the National Energy Policy Development Group (NEPDG) headed by Dick Cheney to develop a long-term energy plan for the US. Task Force meetings were held in secret in early 2001 and the White House refused to release a list of participating groups or representatives. However, leaked documents suggest that whereas environmental groups were excluded from Task Force meetings, corporate representatives received a warm reception.[112] One White House document obtained by the *Washington Post* in November 2005 revealed that executives from petrochemical multinationals including Exxon Mobil, Conoco (before its merger with Phillips), Shell Oil and BP America 'met in the White House complex with the Cheney aides'.[113] This document contradicted previous public denials made by petrochemical managers of their involvement with the Task Force, a revelation that led Senator Frank Lautenberg to observe that 'the White House went to great lengths to keep these meetings secret and now oil executives may be lying to Congress about their role in the Cheney Task Force'.[114]

The Bush Administrations found a balance between workers safety and cutting corporate costs by tipping the scales toward the latter. The administration, for example, saw fit in 2002 to break with 32 years of precedent and disregard management–union balance on the workplace safety advisory committee of the National Institute of Occupational Safety and Health (OSHA) by placing seven management representatives and only two union representatives on the panel.[115] Even after shifting the balance of the OSHA against the protection of workers, the administration did not see fit to follow OSHA recommendations to toughen laws relating to worker exposure to silica dust.[116] The administration similarly disregarded recommendations by the OSHA to strengthen the protection of workers handling metal working fluids that contain potentially toxic materials.[117]

In another instance, the executive defended corporate interests when responding to a case brought by Burmese citizens against the California based Unocal Corporation. The plaintiffs alleged in the Ninth Circuit Court of Appeals that during the building of a $1.2 billion petrochemical pipeline in Burma, Unocal and the Burmese military regime committed serious human rights abuses, including the use of forced labor.[118] The Department of Justice responded to the allegations by filing a brief calling for the Court to limit the ability of foreign citizens to access the US judiciary on the stated grounds that such lawsuits harm US foreign policy and undermine the war on terror.[119]

Although demonstrating an evident pattern, none of the connections highlighted above prove a causal link between the favored interests and values of domestic civil society on the one hand and the human rights discourse produced by the Bush Administrations on the other. To conclude that civil society connections are irrelevant to understanding the genealogy of the hegemonic discourse is, however, to unduly neglect the complexity of how background cultural assumptions, ideologically sympathetic think tanks, financial connections, religious beliefs and economic values have all played a constitutive role in developing the political agenda advanced by the Bush Administrations. Unduly discounting the influence of favored elements of domestic civil society in the construction of the hegemonic discourse furthermore hides how the myth of US exceptionalism has been embedded in the human rights discourse articulated by the Bush Administrations.

US exceptionalism

According to the myth of exceptionalism, the US was created and developed in a manner different to other states. In particular, the myth presents the US as a shining beacon on the hill: a polity offering the rest of the world an example of a different kind of state based upon worthy ideals and values.[120] The mythology of US exceptionalism attaches an exceptional moral character to domestic American civil society and allows human rights to be understood as the specific inheritance of US citizens. Wolfson, for example, states that 'Americans rise to the defense of the universal rights of man because they are their own particular inheritance'.[121] In her former capacity as Deputy Assistant Secretary of Human Rights and Humanitarian Affairs in the Reagan Administration, Paula Dobriansky likewise stated that, in the field of human rights, the US has 'something unique to offer the world'.[122] President Bush forthrightly articulated the myth of exceptionalism when, in a West Point speech, he announced that the US was 'the single surviving model of human progress'.[123] To the extent that this myth of US exceptionalism is understood as established truth, human rights can be neither validated according to international legislation, nor through inclusive debate between distinct cultures. Instead, human rights can be understood in terms of those cherished interests and values of domestic civil society. Making this point explicit in a speech presented to a select Heritage Foundation audience, the assistant secretary for the bureau of democracy, human rights and labor maintained that the focus for human rights in the Bush Administration would be to 'protect the values that underpin civil society at home'.[124]

Since the internal consistencies of the hegemonic discourse hold that (i) moral absolutes exist as matters of fact and (ii) the favored elements of domestic civil society as interpreted by the administration define the 'good', the president can assert that '[a]nybody who tries to affect the lives of our good citizens is evil'.[125] The president repeated these messages when announcing in May 2003 that 'American values and American interests lead in the same direction: We stand for human liberty'.[126] With respect to human rights, President Bush has asserted the myth of US exceptionalism by equating human rights with those civil rights stipulated in American law, pronouncing on one occasion that '[w]e value our own civil rights, so we stand for the human rights of others'.[127] The president thereby discursively equated US civil rights and universal human rights, repeating the message that he had previously announced to the UN General Assembly in September 2001. On that occasion, President Bush identified the American Declaration of Independence and the Universal Declaration of Human Rights (UDHR) as both proclaiming the dignity of human life which he went on to define in terms of 'the rule of law, limits on the power of the state, respect for women, protection of private property, free speech, equal justice and religious tolerance'.[128] Following on from the internal logic of US exceptionalism, there exists no contradiction between promoting the favored elements of US civil society in foreign policy and promoting universal human rights, since the latter can be composed in terms of the former. The concept of exceptionalism therefore confers a unique capacity to US policymakers to authorize the human rights agenda in terms of favored elements of domestic civil society as detailed above.

Opposition to international human rights law

When presented with evidence demonstrating the selective and politicized integration of human rights concerns into policy decisions, theorists advancing the reflective explanation reply that the administration is damned either way. In those circumstances where it intervenes to support human rights, the administration is condemned for politicizing human rights and when it does not intervene it is condemned for lack of action while a humanitarian disaster unfolds.[129] This explanation cannot, however, accommodate the ambivalence demonstrated by the Bush Administrations toward signing key international human rights legislation nor can it explain why so much effort has been allocated into undermining the efficacy of the International Criminal Court (ICC).

Serious problems of definition, co-option and enforcement notwithstanding, one potential mechanism through which the universal and impartial implementation of human rights standards could be advanced is through international human rights law.[130] If human rights values had an independent status as a foreign policy goal, it could be expected that enforceable multilateral rules-based mechanisms would be supported by the administration to promote adherence to those human rights norms. In contrast and as Forsythe notes, the administration has defended international human rights law via 'affectionate generalities' while simultaneously acting to block moves toward the more effective and impartial implementation of legislation.[131]

The Bush Administrations have not seen fit to press for the US to ratify the International Covenant on Economic, Social and Cultural Rights or the Convention on the Elimination of All Forms of Discrimination Against Women. While the State Department lists the promotion of children's rights as a central policy goal, the US is one of only two states not to have signed the UN Convention on the Rights of the Child.[132] The Bush Administrations have also declined to sign protocol one to the Geneva Convention.[133] Lobe reports that no fewer than two dozen key policymakers in the Bush Administrations have been affiliated to the Federalist Society for Law and Public Policy. A recurrent theme within this legal association is opposition to international human rights legislation.[134]

The Bush Administrations have actively opposed the Rome Statute that established the remit for the International Criminal Court. The explicit purpose of the ICC is to prosecute individuals accused of war crimes, crimes against humanity and crimes of genocide in cases where the domestic state is unwilling or unable to prosecute.[135] The 2001–04 Bush Administration reversed the policy of the Clinton Administrations by 'unsigning' the US from the ICC on grounds that a signature could circumscribe the freedom of the US to act in world affairs.[136] Undersecretary of State for Arms Control and International Security, John Bolton, was permitted by Colin Powell to sign the letter formally announcing Washington's withdrawal from the ICC, an act Bolton went on to recall as 'the happiest moment of my government service'.[137]

The Bush Administrations have since led a campaign to weaken the remit of the ICC. For example, the administration lobbied unsuccessfully to extract a specific exemption for US nationals from article 12 of the Rome Statue. Article 12 places citizens of non-state parties within the jurisdiction of the ICC if the acts under investigation were committed in the territory of a state party to the treaty.[138] In the final phase of the Rome negotiations, the US secretary of defense indicated that the US could withdraw its troops from Germany if the German government continued to press for a broader base of jurisdiction for the ICC than the consent of the national state of the accused.[139] The administrations have extracted special bilateral agreements from over a dozen states signatory to the Rome Statute granting US nationals immunity from possible extradition to the ICC.[140] By June 2003 US military assistance had been withdrawn from 35 states party to the Rome Statute who had refused to sign such bilateral agreements.[141] The Bush Administrations also threatened to end UN peacekeeping operations unless US soldiers were exempted from ICC jurisdiction and even sponsored domestic legislation authorizing the use of military force to free any US suspects should they be held by the ICC at some future date.[142]

Opposition from the administrations to international war crimes courts that are independent of the political control of the US extends beyond the ICC. One observer notes that in response to Belgian laws granting Belgian courts jurisdiction to try foreign nationals accused of war crimes, Rumsfeld threatened that he might move the NATO headquarters from Brussels unless the laws were changed. Faced with this extraordinary threat, the Belgian government acted swiftly to implement the requested changes.[143]

Conclusion

Chapters 3 and 4 have detailed how human rights have not been incorporated into the foreign policy of the Bush Administrations in a manner consistent with the necessary conditions of impartial and universal application. The chapters have argued that this disparity need not lead to the rejection of the hegemonic discourse as a political irrelevance. In particular, the chapters have detailed how the political function of the hegemonic discourse lies not in its capacity to describe a corresponding reality but rather in its capacity to write the desired reality as a technique of governance.

According to the productive interpretation of the hegemonic discourse, the reflective explanation suffers from a restrictive, indeed simplistic, view of the function and capacity of language. The notable failing of the reflective account derives from its overlooking or otherwise denying how language produces an interpretation of events rather than impartially describing those events. The productive account, in contrast, employs a method of discourse analysis to examine how a discourse of human rights has been politicized. Three notable consistencies have subsequently been identified in the human rights discourse expressed by the Bush Administrations, (i) that US policymakers are empowered to decide when and how to promote human rights, (ii) US policymakers have the discretion to articulate favored elements of domestic civil society through the language of human rights and (iii) that the vulnerable and marginalized around the world are disempowered from any capacity to claim enforceable human rights in practice.

US officials are empowered with the discretion to decide when and how to enforce human rights since the myth of exceptionalism grants them, rather than any international body or universal rules-based mechanism, the authorization to define the human rights agenda. The subsequent importance of human rights as an instrument to account for the deployment of the US military was demonstrated during September 2005 negotiations on UN reorganization. On this occasion, US Ambassador to the UN, John Bolton, sent no fewer than six letters to UN delegates proposing amendments to the negotiated draft on changes to the permissibility of humanitarian intervention. In these letters Bolton assured the delegates that the US 'stands ready to intervene in *select* cases where governments fail to halt mass killings on their soil'.[144] Bolton did however go to some lengths to clarify that US force would not be deployed on any impartial or universal basis to prevent human rights atrocities, highlighting that the UN Charter 'has never been interpreted as creating a legal obligation for Security Council members to support enforcement action' in all cases.[145] In facilitating the entirely discretionary deployment of US force overseas on humanitarian grounds, Bolton added that world leaders should not foreclose the use of military force by the US even when this is 'absent authorization by the Security Council'.[146] Under the logic advanced by Bolton, the US is empowered to deploy military force on a discretionary basis with little accountability to any multilateral body or rules based mechanism, provided that the stated grounds for the action are humanitarian, as evaluated by the US government.

Advancing a similar logic, the 2006 *National Security Strategy* announced the commitment of the US to 'promote freedom, democracy, and human rights in *specific* countries and regions'.[147] The internal consistency of this discourse lies not in promoting the universal or impartial conditions for human rights but rather in legitimizing US interventions in sovereign states through a selective and discretionary appeal to human rights. As Chandler points out, it remains the intervening power that chooses where and when to intervene, defines the victims and prescribes the rights and ethical principles that it chooses to uphold.[148] This co-option of human rights remains hidden to the extent that the hegemonic mythology is confused with an unproblematic description of a corresponding reality. The political stakes in this endeavor to write reality could not be higher. Success in producing reality in terms of the hegemonic discourse determines whether the US military is welcomed as liberator or attacked as occupier, whether US capital is welcomed as a source of prosperity or expropriated as imperialist exploitation, and whether foreign policy will enjoy popular support from around the world or whether domestic protests and foreign resistance will instead make policy goals unattainable.[149]

The second notable consistency in the human rights discourse expressed by the Bush Administrations articulates favored elements of domestic civil society. This feature of the discourse was examined in two sections of this chapter. The first section detailed notable associations between elements of domestic civil society and the Bush Administrations. Whereas describing such associations may help to reveal the interests and values embedded in the administrations, it is insufficient to demonstrate that a human rights discourse acts as a surrogate for the promotion of these elements. The second section of the chapter therefore looked at how human rights had been presented by the Bush Administration in terms of US exceptionalism rather than, for example, in terms of international legislation or forging a global consensus between distinct cultures. That is to say, the chapter detailed how the internal structuring of the human rights discourse advanced by administration officials allowed the concept to be understood as distinctly 'American'. The promotion of human rights could thereafter assert favored domestic civil society interests and values since the discourse has been structured so as to compose the former in terms of the latter.

The third notable consistency in the human rights discourse expressed by the Bush Administrations lies in disenfranchising the vulnerable from any capacity to enforce universal human rights through recourse to any political or juridical institutions. Human rights have been eviscerated of their requirements for impartial and universal implementation and have thereby been made incoherent as an independent political concept. US authorities are instead empowered to promote and enforce human rights on a discretionary basis as a technique of governance as explained above. The second part of this book turns to detail the application of this technique in case studies of the three wars that have dominated the foreign policy agenda of the Bush Administrations, the wars on terror, Afghanistan and Iraq.

Part II

Case studies

5　War on Terror

Introduction

This chapter analyzes how human rights have featured in the foreign policy response of the Bush Administrations to the atrocities of 9/11. The specific aims of this chapter are twofold. The first is to examine how the hegemonic discourse has been asserted in the official narrative of the war on terror. The second is to detail how the hegemonic discourse produced a politically contingent understanding of the war on terror. This chapter therefore focuses not solely upon how policies implemented by the Bush Administrations in the conduct of the war have impacted upon human rights, but also the analysis seeks to contribute to the existing literature on the subject by focusing on the political function of the discourse through which these policies have been explained to the public.

In order to address these stated aims, the chapter is structured into two sections. The first examines how the hegemonic discourse has featured in the official narrative of the war on terror and considers the capacity of the reflective explanation to account for this discourse as a literal description of a corresponding reality. Focusing on the treatment of detainees held in Guantanamo Bay and the program of rendition, this first section highlights evidence of policies that appear to contradict a universal and impartial commitment to human rights. The second section identifies why the hegemonic discourse should not be dismissed as inconsistent rhetoric. This section details how the hegemonic discourse has produced caricature identities of the protagonists in the war on terror. These identities articulate the hegemonic mythology as factual truths in the minds of the audience. In so doing the hegemonic discourse precludes nuanced understandings of the causes of 9/11 while silencing criticisms of the foreign policies subsequently enacted in its name.

Accounting for the war on terror in terms of advancing human rights

Human rights have featured as a component part of the official narrative provided by the Bush Administrations in the war on terror, also referred to as the long war. In particular the official narrative holds that (i) the US military

upholds the highest standards and has not been authorized to torture enemy suspects and that (ii) the war on terror is itself based upon the principled defense of
human rights and freedom. Asserting that the US military does not engage in
acts of torture, the president for example affirmed during a 2005 visit to Panama
that, 'any activity we conduct is within the law. We do not torture'.[1] On another
occasion the president voiced his opposition to torture by calling upon 'all
nations to speak out against torture in all its forms and to make ending torture an
essential part of their diplomacy'.[2] Colin Powell likewise rejected the use of
torture by US forces on the grounds that '[t]he struggle for freedom requires
scrupulous adherence to human rights'.[3]

Human rights perform, however, a more fundamental role in the official
narrative of the war on terror than simply codifying boundaries for the US military in the conduct of that campaign. US war aims have themselves been presented in terms of advancing values of civilization, freedom, democracy, human
dignity and human rights. Indeed, the war on terror has been presented not pri-
marily as a war between two opposing armed groups but instead as a more fundamental conflict between values. In this conflict, values of freedom, human
rights and democracy, identified with the US, contrast to the evil and hatred of
terrorists. Asserting the war on terror as a battle between clearly distinguishable
values, the assistant secretary of state explained that US commitment to 'the
cause of human dignity on every continent' required in practice that the US will
'prevail in the war against terrorism'.[4]

The official narrative of the war on terror articulates the rules that Chapter 1
identified as constituting the hegemonic discourse. The assistant secretary for
democracy, human rights and labor asserted human rights as a basis for the war
by stating that, '[m]aintaining the focus on human rights and democracy worldwide is an integral part of our response to the attack and is even more essential
today than before September 11th'.[5] Likewise, President Bush focused on
human rights as a rationale for the war by explaining that his administration was
involved in creating a coalition that is 'waging war on terrorism and defending
international human rights'.[6] In December 2001 the president accounted for the
9/11 attacks on the basis that, 'enemies of freedom do not respect or value individual human rights. Their brutal attacks were an attack on these very rights.
When our essential rights are attacked, they must and will be defended'.[7] Thus
conceptualized, 9/11 was an attack not principally against a state but instead
against the values of human rights that are synonymous with the US in the hegemonic mythology. The president has accordingly explained the military response
to 9/11 not just in terms of defending the US but also of defending 'essential
rights'.[8]

The reflective explanation of the hegemonic discourse holds that its three
component rules describe a corresponding reality. Promoting this view among
the scholarly community, the Institute for American Values interprets 9/11 as an
attack upon US values rather than simply upon its foreign policies.[9] This group
greeted the declaration of the war on terror with the message that '[w]e fight to
defend ourselves, but we also believe that we fight to defend those universal

principles of human rights and human dignity that are the best hope for humankind'.[10] The group accounted for the inconsistent application of these principles in the realities of US foreign policy in terms of 'the all too frequent gaps between our ideals and our conduct'.[11]

Individuals in the foreign policy establishment have similarly accepted the internal rules of the hegemonic discourse as a literal explanation for the war on terror. Henry Kissinger urged policymakers to eradicate terrorism for the sake of, not only, security but also for the promotion of freedom, since, 'for the entire post-war period the security of free peoples anywhere has depended upon America's willingness to defend them'.[12] The assistant secretary of state for human rights and humanitarian affairs in the Clinton Administration similarly accepted the hegemonic discourse as a literal description of purpose in the prosecution of the war on terror. John Shattuck subsequently concluded that the Bush Administration was engaged in fighting 'human rights wars'.[13]

In direct contrast to the reflective explanation, the *2003 Human Rights Watch Annual Report* charged that 'Washington has waged war on terrorism as if human rights were not a constraint'.[14] The report concluded that for Washington, 'human rights are dispensable in the name of fighting terrorism'.[15] Far from constituting an underlying rationale for the war on terror, according to this leading NGO, human rights have been a notable casualty of the war. The following examples of (i) the restrictions placed upon civil rights, (ii) the treatment of prisoners in Guantanamo Bay and (iii) the rendition program, all demonstrate inconsistencies in the reflective explanation of the hegemonic discourse.

Civil rights

Presidential orders and legislation sponsored by the Bush Administrations in the aftermath of 9/11 have curtailed the civil rights and freedoms enjoyed by US citizens. In December 2005 a political scandal broke over a presidential order authorizing the National Security Agency to eavesdrop, without court approval, on e-mails and telephone calls to overseas destinations made by US citizens. This presidential order, issued at the end of 2001, was in contravention of statute.[16] President Bush and Attorney General Alberto Gonzales argued that the program included proper checks and balances, since select Congressional leaders had been briefed on its details. Several of those members of Congress receiving the briefs disputed that this constituted Congressional oversight on grounds that they had been sworn to secrecy over all aspects of the briefs and consequently had little effective capacity to block the program.[17]

The Uniting and Strengthening America by Providing Appropriate Tools Required to Intercept and Obstruct Terrorism Act (USA PATRIOT Act) is perhaps the most well known piece of domestic legislation passed in the aftermath of 9/11 to extend government powers over US citizens. The USA PATRIOT Act took rights away from US citizens and empowered the government in a broad range of areas including (i) authorizing FBI agents to obtain business and educational records of individuals without first needing to certify that suspects are considered to be foreign agents or terrorists, (ii) authorizing roving wiretaps to conduct surveillance on individuals anywhere in the US, (iii) lifting restrictions preventing intelligence and criminal justice officials from sharing information on investigations and (iv) stipulating that the designation of a 'terrorist' is the preserve of the secretary of state and is not open to review or challenge from others.[18] Subsequent to becoming statute, this legislation has been applied in a plethora of circumstances that have little to do with organized political violence. In May 2003, the Department of Justice, for example, acknowledged to Congress that the provisions of the USA PATRIOT Act had been utilized 'in a variety of criminal cases' including computer hacking, fraud, identity theft and failure to appear at court.[19] The act was even invoked in attempts to force homeless people out of train stations in New Jersey.[20]

Guantanamo Bay detention facility

On November 13, 2001, President Bush issued a military order calling for non-US nationals suspected of involvement in international terrorism to be held indefinitely without trial. Camps Delta, Echo and X-Ray were subsequently constructed at Guantanamo Bay Naval Base, Cuba, for the purpose of detaining and interrogating terrorist suspects. Some 680 men and children taken mostly from Afghanistan have since been imprisoned and interviewed at the base. Although official secrecy and highly restricted external monitoring of Guantanamo detainees prevents full knowledge of the actual conditions and practices faced by inmates, corroborating sources point to the systematic abuse of detainees, with this amounting in some cases to torture.

Authorized practices

Army Field Manual 34–52 prohibits US military personnel from conducting 'physical torture' which is defined to include 'forcing an individual to stand, sit or kneel in abnormal positions for prolonged periods of time', 'food deprivation' and 'any kind of beating'.[21] In October 2002 the authorities at Guantanamo Bay requested approval of strengthened interrogation techniques that went beyond these stipulated limits. Secretary of Defense, Donald Rumsfeld, responded in December 2002 by authorizing enhanced interrogation techniques which included (i) keeping detainees in stress positions, (ii) hooding detainees, (ii) 20-hour-long interrogation sessions, (iii) the removal of detainee clothing, (iv) prolonged isolation of detainees, (v) sensory deprivation and (vi) inducing stress through exploiting phobias, such as a fear of dogs.[22]

The *2002 Country Report* authored by the State Department identified and criticized, as forms of 'torture and abuse', the same practices occurring in other states that were authorized for use in Guantanamo Bay, under the enhanced interrogation techniques. For example, the Palestinian Authority was criticized for hooding prisoners, tying inmates in painful positions and forcing prisoners to stand for long periods of time.[23] China was criticized for subjecting prisoners to practices of 'torture and other cruel, inhuman or degrading treatment' including 'prolonged periods of solitary confinement', 'shackles' and 'incommunicado detention'.[24] The same document criticized Egypt for stripping and blindfolding prisoners and criticized Jordan for its 'methods of torture' that were found to include, 'sleep deprivation, extended solitary confinement, and physical suspension'.[25] Sleep deprivation and 'suspension for long periods in contorted positions' had also been identified by the State Department as common methods of torture used against detainees by state authorities in Iran.[26] Thus, acts of prisoner abuse that were condemned when practiced by other states had become authorized operating procedure in Guantanamo Bay.

Subsequent allegations of the abuse of detainees made by Federal Bureau of Investigation (FBI) agents to the Department of Defense in December 2002 did little to improve conditions for those held at Guantanamo Bay. Likewise, objections to the authorized techniques made by Judge Advocates were reportedly 'ignored' by Pentagon officials.[27] Internal working group reports and challenges from military lawyers did, however, result in some modifications being made by Rumsfeld to the techniques authorized for use in Guantanamo Bay. In January 2003, the secretary of defense rescinded his blanket approval of enhanced interrogation techniques and instead required his approval for the application of those techniques in individual cases.

Protocol was once again changed in April 2003 with the approval of 24 techniques to be used against all detainees held in Guantanamo. Included among these techniques were 'dietary and environmental manipulation', 'sleep adjustment', 'isolation' and 'false flag'.[28] Under the policy of false flag, inmates were led to believe they would be delivered to the authorities of a third state where they would be tortured. In an open letter to President Bush, Amnesty International mentioned the false flag case of Guantanamo inmate Mohammed al-Kahtani, allegedly the 'twentieth hijacker' on 9/11, who was placed upon a plane and made to believe he was being sent to be tortured in Egypt. In this case, the plane was reported to have landed not in Egypt but to have returned to Guantanamo Bay, whereupon people who al-Kahtani was encouraged to believe were Egyptian security personnel subjected the detainee to interrogation.[29]

Alleged practices

In addition to those practices officially authorized for use in Guantanamo Bay, corroborating eyewitness accounts, provided by guards, leaked reports, FBI agents and released inmates, paint a picture of institutionalized mistreatment. According to two former guards, detainees held in the facility were tied with 'ankle shackles and handcuffs with an additional chain connecting all restraints to the D ring in the floor'.[30] In a leaked 2005 report, the International Committee of the Red Cross (ICRC) informed the US government that prisoners in Guantanamo Bay had been subjected to levels of psychological and physical coercion 'tantamount to torture'.[31] In June 2005, an 84-page document outlining interrogation practices used against al-Khatani was leaked to the public. The document described the detainee being strip-searched, deprived of sleep and having bags of fluid intravenously pumped into his body to force him to urinate while clothed.[32] Rather than being treated as a human being, al-Khatani was made to bark during interrogation sessions to identify alleged terrorists from photos.[33]

According to an FBI e-mail dated December 2003 and obtained under the Freedom of Information Act, interrogators from the Defense Department used 'torture techniques' to extract information from one inmate at Guantanamo.[34] This e-mail revealed that Defense Department personnel had impersonated FBI agents during the interrogation session so that if anything became public, 'DoD interrogators will not be held accountable' and 'the FBI will [sic] left holding the bag before the public'.[35] The American Civil Liberties Union noted that, in the light of other documentation similarly obtained under the Freedom of Information Act, a total of 26 FBI agents had witnessed Guantanamo inmates being mistreated. Forms of reported abuse included grabbing of genitals, bending back of fingers and the placing of duck tape over the mouths of individuals who recited the Koran.[36] In late 2002, one FBI agent reported that a detainee was kept in isolation for three months in a cell that was flooded with light 24 hours a day, leading the prisoner to crouch in a corner and talk to imaginary people.[37]

Private interviews with Guantanamo inmates are strictly controlled and no such access is provided to the public media or human rights groups other than the ICRC. Subsequent to their release, freed inmates have, however, provided mutually corroborating accounts of abuse. One reported technique of abuse is water boarding. Under this practice, detainees are held under water and made to believe they will drown.[38] Other reported techniques include: being left naked; having hair shaved; being subjected to cavity searches and other forms of degrading treatment; being kept on a restricted diet; being kept in rat, snake and scorpion infested cages; being subjected to loud music and being deprived of sleep through being moved every two hours.[39] One former inmate, Rhuhel Ahmed, has alleged that a gun was held to his head while an interrogator pressed him to admit to having gone to Afghanistan to fight a holy war.[40] Moazzam Begg, a former inmate of Camp Echo, alleged that he was forcibly stripped before being paraded in front of cameras.[41]

Based on interview evidence obtained from released detainees, a 2006 report from the UN Commission on Human Rights cited a litany of abuses carried out at Guantanamo Bay including 'the use of dogs, exposure to extreme temperatures, sleep deprivation for several consecutive days and prolonged isolation'.[42] Other forms of abuse, highlighted in the report, included sensory deprivation and the denial of access to independent tribunals, practices that were perceived as causing severe suffering among detainees, leading to 'serious mental health problems'.[43] Corroborating evidence for this conclusion came after the publication of the report when three detainees hanged themselves from the steel-mesh of their cells.

The UN report observed that detainees engaged in hunger strikes in protest of their treatment were force-fed using abusive methods that 'amount to torture'.[44]

The report concluded that the 'excessive violence used in many cases during transportation, in operations by the Initial Reaction Forces and force-feeding of detainees on hunger strike must be assessed as amounting to torture as defined in article 1 of the Convention against Torture'.[45] According to the report, the absence of any impartial investigations into allegations of torture at Guantanamo Bay amounted to impunity for alleged perpetrators of abuse and consequently constituted a violation of articles 12 and 13 of the Convention against Torture.[46]

The response of the Bush Administration to this report was one of dismissal rather than of welcoming recommendations of how to improve human rights standards. State Department spokesman, Sean McCormack, saw fit to discredit the report by arguing that it erroneously presented allegations from released prisoners as facts.[47] White House spokesman, Scott McClellan, similarly attempted to undermine the evidence used in the report as little more than the unproven allegations of terrorist propagandists by stating '[w]e know that al Qaeda terrorists are trained in trying to disseminate false allegations'.[48] A spokesperson for the Department of Defense attempted a different technique for undermining the report by declaring that it had no merit since its authors had not visited Guantanamo Bay.[49] Co-author of the report, UN special investigator Manfred Nowak, replied that the invitation to visit Guantanamo Bay specifically excluded private interviews with detainees. Nowak added 'what's the sense of going to a detention facility and doing fact-finding when you can't speak to the detainees? It's just nonsense'.[50] Another Pentagon spokesperson simply dealt with the UN report by reciting the hegemonic mythology as established fact, stating that 'all detainees are treated humanely'.[51] The authorities have only permitted the ICRC to conduct private visits to prisoners and Congress has deemed this access to constitute sufficient oversight despite the fact that the ICRC does not make its reports publicly available.[52] This leaves a black hole in the public knowledge of the exact treatment facing detainees in Guantanamo Bay. Whereas administration officials have publicly maintained that inmates are treated humanely, this conclusion is questioned by the leaked reports and mutually corroborating evidence reviewed above.

Legal void

Official assertions of human rights as a basis of the war on terror are inconsistent with the legal void evident in the process of dealing with Guantanamo detainees. The 2006 UN report on Guantanamo Bay concluded that the facility should be closed since the legal regime 'seriously undermines the rule of law and a number of fundamental universally recognized human rights' including rights to challenge the legality of detention and to a fair trial.[53]

Detainees occupy a legal void between Cuban and US law and between criminal and military law. Cuban laws that require prisoners to be either charged with an offence or released do not cover Guantanamo Bay. Bush Administration officials have argued that detainees should not benefit from legal rights, such as the presumption of innocence and the right to trial by jury, accorded by US law to criminal suspects.[54] Alberto Gonzales justified this designation in a speech to the American Bar Association by pointing out that critics of the Guantanamo process failed to understand that detentions should not be viewed in civilian terms. Rather, the White House counsel explained, the rules of war apply where people can be detained indefinitely 'and they need not be guilty of anything'.[55]

Yet the administration has simultaneously announced that the war on terror is a new sort of war in the sense that those detained in Guantanamo Bay are not entitled to Prisoner of War (PoW) status. On February 7, 2002 President Bush announced that neither the Geneva Conventions nor PoW status applied to al Qaeda suspects.[56] PoW status requires prisoners to provide only name, rank, serial number and date of birth and could thus preclude further interrogation by US personnel. Gonzales has stated that the need to obtain information in the fight against terrorism renders 'obsolete' and 'quaint' the limitation in the Geneva Convention on the interrogation of prisoners.[57] Moreover, the administration refused to accept the authority of a tribunal that could determine the legal status of detainees.[58] This position is in contravention of the third Geneva Convention that requires all captured combatants to be treated as PoWs until a 'competent tribunal' determines otherwise.[59]

Instead of being treated as criminal suspects or as PoWs, categories of 'detained personnel,' 'enemy combatant' and 'unlawful combatant' that have no standing in international law have been applied to Guantanamo detainees. The president has stated that detainees would be treated 'in a manner consistent with the principles of Geneva to the extent appropriate and consistent with the principles of military necessity'.[60] Given that (i) the concept of military necessity is itself open to a broad range of interpretation and (ii) there is little by way of external public monitoring of the treatment of detainees, the authorities in Guantanamo Bay face little effective accountability in their treatment of detainees to anyone outside the US government.[61]

Since detainees have been deprived of both PoW and criminal status, they cannot be tried in the US court martial system nor in federal courts. Under the Guantanamo process the accused are, instead, to be tried under a system of military commissions. In March 2002 the Defense Department issued an order outlining a set of procedures under which these military commissions would operate.[62] Under the rules, a military panel will judge the guilt of the accused. The rules of the military commissions do not allow for suspects to appeal to a civilian court but, instead, only to another military panel who must answer in turn to the US executive.[63] Thereby, as Roth points out, '[t]hrough his surrogates, the president becomes prosecutor, trial judge and appellate judge' in the military commission process.[64] This neglect of due process is an expression of arbitrary power and violates a protocol addition to the Geneva Convention that entitles the accused to 'an impartial and regularly constituted court respecting the generally recognized principles of regular judicial procedure'.[65] The National Association of Criminal Defense Lawyers consequently described the military commission process as unethical.[66]

Under the stated rules for military commissions, defense attorneys are hampered in their capacity to mount a robust defense since they (i) are subject to the

Department of Defense monitoring their communications with clients, (ii) are required to reveal to the Department of Defense any information that may result in 'significant impairment of national security', (iii) may be excluded from parts of the military commission proceedings and (iv) may be denied access to any 'protected information' deemed by the Department of Defense as 'necessary to protect the interests of the United States'.[67] Such 'protected information' is defined broadly to include, for instance, any information concerning 'national security sources'.[68] Furthermore, according to a March 2002 Department of Defense order, 'national security' can dictate that an entire trial be conducted in secret, without the presence of either the accused or civilian counsel.[69] As well as violating the US Constitution's sixth amendment right to be confronted with the witness, this stipulation contravenes the rights of the accused under the Geneva Convention to 'defense by counsel of his own choice'.[70]

The possibility for detainees to have fair hearings is further compromised by multiple high profile assertions that those held in Guantanamo Bay are terrorists prior to such allegations being tested in a properly convened court. Guards at Guantanamo Bay have reportedly been told by Military Police (MP) commanders that prisoners were 'the very men responsible for 9/11'.[71] The president has defended the trial process at Guantanamo on the grounds that '[j]ustice is being done. These are illegal combatants'.[72] Vice President Dick Cheney similarly stated in June 2005 that 'if you were to release those 520 that are currently held at Guantanamo that have been deemed to be enemy combatants, we're putting a lot of bad guys back on the street to do exactly what they started to do in the first place'.[73] White House spokesman, Scott McClellan, has referred to Guantanamo inmates as 'dangerous terrorists'.[74] Senior Pentagon spokesman, Bryan Whitman, likewise defended the treatment of inmates on the grounds that '[t]hese are dangerous people'.[75] When declaring in May 2006 that he would like to close the detention facilities at Guantanamo Bay, President Bush reported that the inmates 'will get their day in court. One can't say that of the people that they killed'.[76] The presumption underlying all these statements demonstrates hostility to the procedural right to a fair trial, since it assumes the guilt rather than innocence of the accused. The assumed guilt of Guantanamo detainees is furthermore problematic in light of the release without charge of a number of inmates. Indeed, as of June 2006, only ten of those held in Guantanamo have been formally charged before a military commission.

It is precisely the purpose of trials to assess the alleged guilt of the accused. The cases of British citizens Shafiq Rasul, Ruhal Ahmed and Asif Iqbal illustrate how the presumption of guilt can be erroneous. These three were arrested in Afghanistan and held in Guantanamo Bay for 26 months after being falsely identified by US authorities as appearing in a video-taped meeting between bin Laden and the 9/11 hijacker Mohamed Atta. The three initially protested their innocence before providing false confessions under interrogation. The US authorities only acknowledged that the three were not terrorists after proof was supplied that the accused had been in the UK at the time that the bin Laden video was taken.[77]

Rather than being combatants, Rasul, Ahmed and Iqbal had decided to travel across the border to provide humanitarian assistance to Afghans while on a holiday visiting friends and family in Pakistan in October 2001. After the outbreak of the 2001 war in Afghanistan, the three were found by Northern Alliance forces in a Taliban stronghold area and assumed to be foreign al Qaeda fighters whereupon they were handed over to the US military. This error was only made apparent because the accused came from Britain where a high degree of public surveillance enabled the UK government to provide camera footage of one of the suspects working at a Curry's store in Tipton at the time that he was alleged to have been featured in the video with bin Laden. Detainees domiciled in states lacking such an extensive surveillance network or government resources have no similar chance of disproving unfounded allegations without recourse to a free and fair trial. By virtue of being open to convict the innocent, the system of military commissions established for Guantanamo inmates should also be criticized for simultaneously providing the guilty with the ideal compliant through which to attack their convictions.

A number of US District and Supreme Court rulings have highlighted how the military commission process contravenes the rights of the accused. In November 2004, District Court Judge James Robertson ruled that detainees should have been presumed as PoWs unless a competent tribunal had determined otherwise.[78] The Bush Administration responded not by implementing the judgment but by lodging an immediate appeal against the verdict. Outgoing Attorney General John Ashcroft criticized the ruling as 'intrusive judicial oversight and second-guessing of presidential determinations'.[79]

On June 28, 2004 the Supreme Court ruled that prisoners suspected of terrorism could be held initially without charge or trial, but not indefinitely, as was the case in Guantanamo. The Supreme Court added that prisoners had rights to challenge their treatment through US civilian courts and had rights of access to attorneys during their detentions.[80] This ruling was followed by the case of Yasser Hamdi, in which the Supreme Court ruled that the accused must be given the opportunity to contest the basis of his detention in a neutral forum.[81] The administration responded to these court rulings by establishing Combatant Status Review Tribunals (CSRT). The CSRTs consisted of three non-commissioned officers who would examine the legality of ongoing detentions at Guantanamo Bay. Out of 317 cases heard in the six months following June 2004, only one CSRT found against continued detention.[82] A US District Court subsequently ruled that the CSRT proceedings failed to comply with the Supreme Court ruling on the grounds that they denied the accused fair opportunities to challenge their continued incarceration.[83]

A June 2006 decision by the Supreme Court ruled that military commissions were unauthorized by federal statute and violated international laws.[84] This ruling highlighted flaws in the military commissions system including (i) failure to guarantee defendants the right to attend their trials and (ii) acceptance of hearsay evidence, unsworn testimony and evidence obtained through coercion.[85] The Supreme Court ruled that, contrary to the claims made by the Bush Administrations, Article 3 of the Geneva Conventions prohibiting trials except by proper court applied to detainees as a matter of law.[86] As detailed in the above section, there are evident contradictions between official explanations of the role of human rights in the prosecution of the war on terror and the treatment of those detained in the conduct of that war.

Rendition

The application of the hegemonic discourse by administration officials in the conduct of the war on terror also stands in notable contradiction to the outsourcing of torture exemplified through the program of rendition. As one former intelligence official explained, following 9/11 the CIA had limited detention facilities for suspects, leading to a debate 'about how to make people disappear'.[87] A presidential finding of September 15, 2001 and military order number one issued by President Bush in November 2001 responded to this debate by providing the CIA with the authority to detain, on an indefinite basis, any non-US citizen anywhere in the world.[88]

It is contrary to US statue to hold people in isolation or to torture prisoners in secret prisons in the US. Legal memorandums, prepared for the administration, advised that US officials would not, however, be responsible for violating US statutes 'if it can be argued that the detainees are formally in the custody of another country'.[89] Individuals held under the program of rendition have subsequently been delivered to the intelligence services of foreign states including, it is thought, Uzbekistan, Jordan, Syria, Morocco and Egypt where torture is routine.[90] The Lawyers Committee for Human Rights reported that some suspects were even transferred to states with lists of specific questions that the US authorities wanted answering.[91] One diplomat explained '[a]fter September 11, these movements have been occurring all the time. It allows us to get information from terrorists in a way we can't do on US soil'.[92]

The CIA acknowledges that it conducts rendition, but provides few details and adds that the intention is never for captives to be tortured. The agency has further explained that guarantees have been obtained from states collaborating in the rendition program certifying that suspects will not be tortured.[93] No explanations have been forthcoming as to why states with a demonstrated record of torture have been identified as suitable destinations for prisoners or why state authorities that routinely engage in torture are considered to find the provision of false guarantees to be in any way problematic.

Under the policy of extraordinary rendition, prisoners termed 'ghost detainees' simply disappear, hidden in some cases even from the ICRC.[94] 'Disappearing' people evades even the most rudimentary legal processes of accountability and oversight. As a former UN special rapporteur on torture stated, 'the more hidden detention practices are, the more likely that all legal and moral constraints on official behavior will be removed'.[95] Former CIA lawyer, John Radsan, confirmed this assessment when he summarized that 'there are hardly any rules for illegal enemy combatants. It's the law of the jungle. And right now we happen to be the strongest animal'.[96] At least 11 individuals are thought to have been 'disappeared' under the program of extraordinary rendition although official secrecy ensures that the full number is not publicly known and may be considerably higher.[97]

After leading an investigation into extraordinary rendition on behalf of the Council of Europe, Swiss Senator Dick Marty concluded that 'individuals have been abducted, deprived of their liberty and all rights and transported to different destinations in Europe, to be handed over to countries in which they have suffered degrading treatment and torture'.[98] A fleet of Gulfstream V turbo jets, thought to be operated by the CIA, transports prisoners to secret detention facilities around the world.[99] One such jet is listed as owned by Premier Executive Transport Services, a brass plaque company based in Delaware with nonexistent directors.[100] Another jet is registered to a series of dummy US corporations and has clearance to land at US military bases.[101] As a component part of the rendition program, the CIA is also thought to operate secret detention facilities, termed 'black sites', in Eastern European states.[102] One former victim of the rendition program, German national Khalid Masri, spent five months in an Afghan jail after being seized by the CIA in Macedonia.[103] In another case, a former inmate of Guantanamo Bay reports receiving a knockout injection at the facility in April 2004. The detainee awoke in Sana'a, Yemen, where he alleges he was beaten and deprived of food by the authorities.[104]

Maher Arar, a Canadian engineer born in Syria, was arrested on September 26, 2002 at John F. Kennedy airport while returning to Canada from a family holiday. Since his name appeared on a watch list of terrorist suspects he was detained and questioned for 13 days before being placed in handcuffs and leg irons and transported on a Gulfstream V jet to Amman, Jordan. Arar reports that he heard the pilots refer to their jet during the flight as the 'special removal unit'.[105] Ten hours after landing in Jordan, Arar was driven to Syria where Arar alleges that he was threatened, then beaten and whipped repeatedly with two-inch thick electric cables. During his incarceration Arar confessed to anything his torturers asked him. Arar was eventually released in October 2003 after the Canadian government took up his case. Imad Moustapha, Syrian Ambassador in Washington, simply commented that Arar had been sent to Syria under 'a secretive program called extraordinary rendition'.[106] Upon his eventual release Arar was 40 pounds lighter than before his arrest, had a pronounced limp and suffered chronic nightmares.[107]

Australian citizen Mamdouh Habib was detained in Pakistan on October 5, 2001 as a suspected al Qaeda trainer and rendered to Egypt. In Egypt, Habib alleges he was hung by his arms from hooks, repeatedly rammed with an electric cattle prod, doused with cold water whenever he fell asleep, was nearly drowned and was repeatedly beaten. After six months of such treatment Habib signed a confession. Incredibly, the US authorities took this confession not as proof that people will sign anything to stop further torture, but instead as evidence of guilt. Habib was subsequently transferred to Guantanamo Bay in May 2002.[108] According to a Guantanamo detainee who has since been released, Habib was subjected to a regime of sleep deprivation at the base, that left him with 'blood coming from both his nose and ears'.[109]

The program of rendition has been defended by President Bush by recourse to the familiar terrain of the hegemonic discourse in terms that '[w]e operate within the law and we send people to countries where they say they're not going to torture the people'.[110] The authority under which renditions may be legally performed is detailed in a memo that the administrations have refused to make public despite Congressional request.[111] It is not known whether the White House ever approved a specific list of interrogation methods to be employed by collaborating states and officials have repeatedly refused to comment on the question.[112]

Article 3 of the UN Convention against Torture prohibits signatory states from sending anyone to another state in cases where there exist, 'substantial grounds for believing that he would be in danger of being subjected to torture'.[113] This article is therefore being contravened to the extent that the US authorities have 'substantial grounds' for knowing that victims of the rendition program will be tortured. Martin Lederman, employed at the Justice Department's Office of Legal Counsel until 2002, revealed that 'there are ways to get around' this provision, for example 'what if you kind of know' rather than definitively know that a suspect will be tortured?[114] Such quests for legal loopholes are inconsistent with a commitment to the absolute prohibition on torture.

The rendition program has demonstrated similar disregard for the domestic laws of foreign states prohibiting the rendition of citizens. In June 2003, five suspects were taken from Malawi in direct contravention of a Malawi court order refusing their removal. This incident followed the January 2002 removal of six Algerians from Bosnia who, under diplomatic pressure, were handed over to US authorities by the Bosnian government in violation of an order from the Bosnian Supreme Court requiring the release of the men for lack of evidence.[115]

In light of the cases reviewed above, the rejectionist explanation interprets human rights as an irrelevance rather than as a foundation for the conduct of the Bush Administration in the war on terror. Supporting evidence for this interpretation is not hard to find. US representatives opposed a resolution introduced by Mexico at the Easter 2002 session of the UN Commission on Human Rights. The proposed resolution highlighted the importance of fighting terrorism in a manner consistent with human rights. Concerted opposition from the US joined by Algeria, India, Pakistan and Saudi Arabia led Mexico to withdraw the proposed resolution.[116] At the Quito conference of American defense ministers held in November 2004, the US delegation rejected a proposal made by their Canadian counterparts to balance anti-terror agreements with explicit support for international human rights laws. One observer at the conference, Argentine lawyer Gaston Chillier, concluded that the underlying message from the US delegation was that 'international human rights law is not a requirement in combating terrorism'.[117]

This chapter has thus far reviewed evidence testifying to the notable contradictions in attempting to explain the hegemonic discourse as a literal description of foreign policy in the conduct of the war on terror. As we have seen, the universal and impartial requirements of human rights have been readily subjugated in the conduct of that war. The focus of attention turns in the second section of the chapter to detail why the hegemonic discourse should not be subsequently rejected as a political irrelevance for understanding the war.

The discursive production of identity

The principal battleground in the politics of the war on terror is not military or economic strength, but rather the capacity to produce how events and identities are understood, since it is this ideological understanding that determines levels of popular support for different political groupings. After 9/11, UK Prime Minister Tony Blair sent a five-page memo to President Bush outlining his ideas about how a campaign against terrorism should be organized. In this memo, Blair stressed how it is 'critical to shape world opinion'.[118] The 2002 *National Security Strategy* picks up the theme of shaping opinion when it stated that 'we will also wage a war of ideas to win the battle against international terrorism'.[119] The second section of this chapter details how the hegemonic discourse has been applied to produce an understanding of the war on terror in the minds of the audience. The section does this by examining how the narrative provided by administration officials has produced the identities of the protagonists in the war on terror. The analysis begins by examining the production of US identity before attention turns to that of the terrorist enemy.

US identity

The official narrative of the war on terror provided by Bush Administration officials reifies US identity by virtue of differentiating a benevolent 'us' from an evil 'them'. The war on terror has been presented as a principally moral battle in line with the message from the president that 'we fight against evil'.[120] The ethical identity of the US in this battle has been asserted in terms that 'Americans always do what is right'.[121] The US is consequently affirmed as 'a nation which is willing to sacrifice not only for its own security, but for the freedom of others'.[122] In his 2006 *State of the Union* address, the president contextualized the war on terror in terms of realizing the pre-existing US identity asserted in the hegemonic mythology. In this instance President Bush characterized the US as

> the nation that saved liberty in Europe, and liberated death camps, and helped raise up democracies, and faced down an evil empire. Once again, we accept the call of history to deliver the oppressed and move this world toward peace.[123]

US identity is thereby produced in terms of freedom, democracy, human rights and peace. The case of the prohibition of torture illustrates how reality has been selectively produced to conform to this predetermined identity.

Officially reiterating adherence to the prohibition of torture while
putting in place policies that effectively weaken the prohibition

The Convention against Torture stipulates an absolute ban on torture, which it defines as

> any act by which severe pain or suffering, whether physical or mental, is intentionally inflicted on a person for such purposes as obtaining from him or a third party information or a confession, punishing him for an act he or a third person has committed or is suspected of having committed, or intimidating or coercing him or a third person ... when such pain or suffering is inflicted by or at the instigation of or with the consent or acquiescence of a public official or other person acting in an official capacity.[124]

Under the stipulations of the ICCPR, the right not to be tortured cannot be overridden under any circumstances.[125] As detailed in the first section of this chapter, the Bush Administrations have implemented policies that appear incompatible with the absolute prohibition of torture asserted in these legal texts. The approach of the Bush Administration to the prohibition on torture has been subsequently summarized by a UN report as 'officially reiterating its adherence to the absolute prohibition of torture' while simultaneously 'put[ting] in place a number of policies that effectively weaken the prohibition'.[126]

One internal document circulated within the Bush Administration and later leaked to the public provides an explanation for the apparently paradoxical behavior identified by the UN report. This internal document, authored by Department of Justice Lawyers, found that neither the Torture Convention, nor domestic criminal statues, nor Congress could disallow the president from legally authorizing service personnel to inflict even severe pain on unlawful combatants.[127] The document noted that the US conditioned its ratification of the Convention against Torture on the understanding that 'in order to constitute torture, an act must be specifically intended to inflict severe physical or mental pain or suffering'.[128] An act inflicting severe pain that was principally intended to extract information was argued in the document to demonstrate only general rather than specific intent. That is to say, the pain inflicted was simply a by-product of the specific intent of the interrogator, which was to elicit information from the detainee. Thus, such an act was argued not to contravene the agreements entered into by the US under its ratification of the Torture Convention.[129]

The same document reasoned that domestic criminal statute could not preclude the president from legally authorizing harmful interrogation acts against unlawful combatants. Based upon the constitutional designation of military management powers to the president, the document asserted that '18U.S.C §2340A [prohibition of torture] must be construed as inapplicable to interrogations undertaken pursuant to his Commander-in-Chief authority'.[130] Thus, the document reasoned, should the president order an act that contravened domestic statute prohibiting torture, that act would be nonetheless legal by virtue of the allocation of military powers under the US Constitution.

If neither international nor domestic laws could prevent the executive from legally ordering acts that involved inflicting pain on unlawful combatants, the same document reasoned that neither could the legislature. The document contended that, '[a]ny effort by Congress to regulate the interrogation of unlawful combatants would violate the Constitution's sole vesting of the Commander-in-Chief authority in the president'.[131] Moreover, the document continued that it might be 'necessary' to torture or kill detainees in order to prevent future terrorist attacks, given that the use of force could be used to prevent harm to others.[132] This document, declared secret by Donald Rumsfeld, was subsequently leaked to the *Wall Street Journal*. In light of its evident contradictions with the hegemonic discourse, the Bush Administration was forced to provide a revised version of the legality of interrogation practices subsequent to the public leaking of the document.[133]

In another instance, White House Counsel Alberto Gonzales exploited a loophole to the Convention against Torture when he observed that the US defined the 'cruel, inhuman or degrading treatment' prohibited under the convention in terms of treatments that would violate the fifth, eighth or fourteenth amendments to the US Constitution.[134] In responses to Senate enquiries, Gonzales maintained that since the US Constitution does not apply to non-US citizens, neither could the Convention against Torture's prohibition on ill treatment. According to the interpretation provided by Gonzales, US officials interrogating non-US citizens abroad could subsequently engage in cruel and inhuman treatment short of torture without violating pledges made by the US in its ratification of the convention.[135]

In response to the legal rulings noted in the first part of this chapter, the formal rules on the permissible treatment of detainees have been constantly changed, amended, added and redrafted, thus confusing serving personnel and further eroding the absolute prohibition on torture. As Senator McCain put the matter, '[w]e have so many differing legal standards and loopholes that our lawyers and generals are confused. Just imagine our troops serving in prison in the field'.[136] Further attempts by the Bush Administrations to weaken the absolute ban on torture can be exemplified in the reaction to the campaign run by Senator John McCain in Autumn 2005, for an amendment to the Department of Defense Appropriations Bill. The proposed amendment would end all ambiguities by prohibiting any US government employee from using torture and inhumane treatment against prisoners. According to defense, state, intelligence and Congressional officials, Vice President Cheney responded to the proposed amendment by leading a counter campaign.[137] In November 2005 Cheney reportedly lobbied at a senatorial luncheon for an exemption to the proposed ban on torture in CIA operated black sites.[138] The administration went so far as to threaten a presidential veto of the McCain proposals.[139] The White House changed its position only after both Houses of Congress defied the threatened veto and passed the McCain measure with overwhelming majorities.[140]

Announcing its newfound support for this 'important legislation' on December 15, 2005 the administration took the opportunity to reassert the hegemonic mythology by stating that the legislation 'make[s] it clear to the world that this government does not torture'.[141]

Similar presidential pronouncements that 'we don't do torture',[142] that '[t]he United States is committed to the worldwide elimination of torture and we are leading this fight by example',[143] and that 'our values as a Nation, values that we share with many other nations in the world, call for us to treat detainees humanely',[144] can be subsequently seen to perform two political functions. First, such pronouncements produce in the minds of the audience the benevolent identity of the US articulated in the hegemonic discourse. Second, these pronouncements rule out very little, with respect to actual policy practices, since, as we have seen through the various legal loopholes and definitions detailed above, the potential for serious or even fatal acts of prisoner abuse to be categorized as illegal acts of torture has been virtually eliminated as a possibility. The Bush Administrations have therefore combined public assurances that the US does not torture with behind the scenes efforts to redefine the meaning of torture unduly narrowly. Thus, legal loopholes are exploited to allow abusive interrogation techniques that would be prohibited under the internationally accepted definition of torture. This strategy is consistent with facilitating the abusive treatment of detainees held in US custody on the one hand while simultaneously producing a public understanding of US identity in terms of the hegemonic mythology on the other.

Lack of accountability

The production of reality in line with the hegemonic discourse is facilitated by the lack in public knowledge of, or accountability for, the treatment of those detained in the prosecution of the war on terror. For example, the CIA has not had to answer any questions in open testimony about the conditions in which ghost detainees are held. CIA and White House officials have consistently objected to such questions when raised by Congress on grounds of 'national security concerns'.[145] When questioned on the matter during a December 2005 trip to Europe, Secretary of State Condoleezza Rice defended the use of rendition but refused to provide any details, even on the question of whether or not the CIA runs secret interrogation facilities.[146]

Based on reports from intelligence officials and diplomats, the covert prison system operated by the CIA was predicated upon 'keeping even basic information about the system secret from the public, foreign officials and nearly all members of Congress charged with overseeing the CIA's covert operations'.[147] According to one report, the president himself informed the CIA that he did not want to know where the black sites operated by the agency were located.[148] Dick Cheney reportedly urged Senator John Rockefeller to drop the matter after the Senator requested that the full Senate Select Committee on Intelligence be briefed on the specific interrogation techniques practiced by the CIA on detainees.[149] Giving testimony to a September 2003 hearing of the House and Senate Intelligence Committees, the head of the CIA counter terrorist center reported that the treatment of detainees was a 'highly classified area' adding simply 'all you need to know is there was a before 9/11 and there was an after 9/11. After 9/11 the gloves came off'.[150]

The Bush Administrations have acted to preclude international inspection of US detention facilities. An Optional Protocol to the Convention against Torture aiming to establish mechanisms for inspecting suspected places of torture was opposed by the administration when it was debated in the UN General Assembly. The protocol was entirely optional, and the administration could have simply declined to add US signature to the text. However, the policy adopted by the administration was instead an attempt to deprive all states of a mechanism that might be used to criticize its own conduct in detention facilities.[151]

The secrecy and public unaccountability of the treatment of detainees extends beyond the US government and to its allies overseas. In presenting the Council of Europe investigation on the issue of extraordinary rendition, Dick Marty noted that he had 'very limited logistical support' or help from European governments in the conduct of his inquiries.[152] One leaked briefing paper from December 2005 revealed that contrary to unambiguous public denials made previously on the matter by British ministers, the Blair government had in fact been aware of US rendition to secret interrogation centers.[153] The high degree of secrecy surrounding the holding of detainees precludes public knowledge of the precise treatment of prisoners. This lack of meaningful public accountability allows for evidence of malpractice to be dismissed as isolated exceptions, hearsay, unproven allegations, terrorist propaganda or conspiracy theory. Thus a sanitized US identity is again produced in line with the defining messages of the hegemonic discourse.

Terrorist identity

The identity of the enemy in the war on terror has been discursively produced by the Bush Administrations in binary opposition to the moral rectitude that is said to define the identity of the US. That is to say, the enemy in the war on terror is motivated by a hatred of freedom, democracy and human rights. Since the hegemonic discourse asserts values of freedom and human rights as synonymous with the US, hatred of these values explains both why terrorists attacked the US on 9/11 and why any other interpretation of the intent of terrorists can be rejected. The president, for example, stated that 'America was targeted for attack because we're the brightest beacon for freedom and opportunity in the world'.[154] In another instance the president described the intent of the terrorist enemy in terms that '[t]his new enemy seeks to destroy our freedom and impose its views. We value life; the terrorists ruthlessly destroy it.'[155] According to this narrative, the enemy that the US faces holds to an ideology that 'hates freedom, rejects tolerance and despises all dissent'.[156] Rice explained the underlying message by stating that 'ruthless enemies seek to destroy not only our nation and not only to destroy all free nations but to destroy freedom as a way of life'.[157] Thus the intent of the terrorist enemy has been asserted in binary opposition to the values that define the identity of the US in the hegemonic discourse.

The reader may enquire why this designation of identity is in any sense problematic. After all, 9/11 was a human rights atrocity in the sense of a wanton massacre of civilians. Proponents of the reflective explanation have subsequently charged that critics fail to understand how the Bush Administrations have engaged in the fight against terrorism as a genuine political battle.[158] Countering this claim, two factors can be highlighted that reveal identity as a politicized function of discourse rather than as an unproblematic assertion. First, that al Qaeda demonstrates no regard for human rights can certainly be accepted as unproblematic, but this does nothing by itself to demonstrate that the Bush Administrations necessarily respect human rights. Indeed, organized political violence has been historically characterized by violations of human rights among all warring factions. As this chapter has already documented the policies of the Bush Administrations, adopted in the conduct of the war on terror, offers no compelling exception to this trend.

Second, the intents and motivations ascribed by the Bush Administrations to the enemy in the war on terror are as inconsistent with the symbols, logic and rationale asserted by Osama bin Laden himself, as they are consistent with the requirements of producing an understanding of foreign policy in line with the hegemonic discourse. The 9/11 attacks targeted not the Statue of Liberty as could be expected from a symbolic attack on freedom, but rather the military and economic centers of US power. The aim of his campaign of violence and killings, as expressed by bin Laden himself, is not the eradication of freedom but instead the overthrow of corrupt feudal monarchies in the Middle East that are considered to be puppets of the US.[159] The issues highlighted by bin Laden in his numerous tirades relate not to a hatred of human rights but instead to US foreign policy in the Middle East. Such policies include the support demonstrated for Egypt and Israel and to the presence of non-Muslim US troops in Saudi Arabia and other parts of what is considered to be the Holy Land. In an interview broadcast in 1998, bin Laden stated that his aim was 'that our land be liberated from enemies'.[160] US foreign policy in the Middle East is therefore opposed by bin Laden not because it is perceived to promote freedom but because it does not.

On Sunday, October 7, 2001, President Bush gave a televised address announcing the military response to the 9/11 attacks. This was immediately answered with a pre-recorded message from bin Laden that responded

> A million innocent children are dying at this time as we speak, killed in Iraq without any guilt. We hear no denunciation, we hear no edict from the hereditary rulers. In these days, Israeli tanks rampage across Palestine, in Ramallah, Rafah and Beit Jala and many more other parts of the land of Islam and we do not hear anyone raising his voice or reacting.[161]

After this response was broadcast in the US, the Bush Administration requested news networks not to broadcast any further tapes from bin Laden without appropriate commentary.[162] Such management techniques led to the US public becoming immediately familiar with the caricature image of a mad mullah, an anti-christ figure whose insane hatred of freedom and readiness to die for some incomprehensible cause meant that neither he nor his evil followers could be reasoned with.[163] Since, according to the official narrative, terrorists are fighting a 'war against humanity',[164] and terrorists 'are offended by our existence as free nations',[165] it logically follows that '[n]o concession will appease their hatred. No accommodation will satisfy their endless demands'.[166] The identities of the terrorist enemy have, therefore, been discursively produced by virtue of their intents being rewritten away from their stated motives and to conform instead to the requirements of the hegemonic mythology. Since motives can be neither proved nor disproved, this selective rewriting of intent can be identified as a constitutive technique of producing identity.

Conclusion

Depending upon the political perspective of the observer, state infringement on internationally recognized human rights may or may not be deemed an appropriate response to the threat and use of violence by non-state organizations. This chapter has not sought to contribute to this discussion. The chapter has instead aimed to demonstrate how the Bush Administrations have politicized the language of human rights in the conduct of the war on terror. This chapter has subsequently detailed how the hegemonic mythology has formed an integral part of the official narrative of the war on terror as expressed by Bush Administration officials.

The first section of the chapter examined how the implementation of the war contradicted a literal interpretation of the hegemonic discourse. The treatment of prisoners in Guantanamo Bay, the tightening of restrictions on civil rights within the US and the program of rendition all illustrated how human rights were seen as contingent rather than absolute attributes. Illustrating the subjugation of human rights to military concerns, the administration floated a proposal in 2001 to suspend, for up to five years, legislation restricting the provision of US military aid to a state with a poor human rights record when that state was deemed to be an important partner in the war on terror.[167]

The second section of this chapter cautioned against using the evidence provided in the first to dismiss the political significance of the hegemonic discourse. The hegemonic discourse was instead found to perform a political function in terms of producing the identities of the protagonists in the war on terror. The chapter reviewed how the identity of the US was selectively produced in line with human rights and freedom and how the identity of the enemy was defined in terms of a hatred of that freedom. The hegemonic discourse subsequently acts as a technique of governance to the extent that the audience internalizes its politicized interpretation of the war on terror as unproblematic fact.

International efforts of addressing the problem of political violence in terms that the administration does not directly control, have met, at best, a muted reception in the White House. In February 2002, the Non-Aligned Movement, for example, proposed a major international conference to combat terrorism. This initiative proposed to examine how to distinguish a terrorist from a freedom fighter, and terrorism from political resistance, counter terrorism or state terrorism. The aim of the conference was to establish ground rules to define the phenomena of terrorism as a prerequisite to the design of policies to bring about its eradication. The US government rejected the planned conference out of hand, stating that it could not provide 'practical benefits'.[168] Washington policymakers thereby retained the capacity to define and apply the agenda of the war on terror on an entirely discretionary basis.

Other regimes have taken and accentuated the example set by the Bush Administrations in justifying repressive practices through appeals to the terrorist enemy. Liberian President Charles Taylor, cracked down on press and political dissent by applying terms of 'terrorist' and 'illegal combatants' to political opponents and placing such designated individuals beyond the reach of courts.[169] In Zimbabwe, aides of President Robert Mugabe have labeled members of lawful opposition parties as 'terrorists'. Mugabe also justified the November 2001 arrest of six critical journalists by accusing them of being terrorists.[170] Prior to his death, former Yugoslav President Slobodan Milosevic defended himself against war crimes charges on grounds that he had been merely combating terrorism.[171] In Russia, the administration of Vladimir Putin used the language and logic of the war on terror to insulate itself from international criticism of the brutal tactics adopted against rebel forces in Chechnya.[172] Such tactics included forced disappearances, extra judicial killings and acts of torture.[173]

States have employed not only the language of the war on terror to justify internal repression but have also mirrored the tactics used by the Bush Administrations. Through issuing military order 1500 on April 5, 2002, Israel, for example, authorized the holding of persons for up to 18 days with no access to attorneys or courts. This order allowed for an IDF officer to authorize the incommunicado holding of a prisoner from the West Bank, if 'from the circumstances of his arrest arose a suspicion that he endangers or could potentially endanger the security of the region, of IDF forces or of the public'.[174] Imitating the system of military commissions used at Guantanamo Bay, Tunisia instituted trials for civilians on terrorism charges in military courts that fail to conform to requirements of due process.[175] On June 24, 2002 Liberian security agents detained Hassan Bility, editor of the Monrovian newspaper *Analyst*, in incommunicado detention.[176] Bility was held at an undisclosed location, refused access to a lawyer and tortured under interrogation.[177] In light of these and other actions, UN General Secretary Kofi Annan, highlighted the concern that governments across the world were dealing with political opposition through recourse to the war on terror.[178]

This case study has detailed how discourse is itself a politicized instrument of foreign policy. Discourse operates as an instrument of governance in the sense of framing the context within which the audience understands policies. According to the internal structure of the hegemonic discourse, the single biggest danger to human rights in the world lies in preventing the US military from being able to assert its defense of freedom against the forces of hatred and evil.[179] In the words of Attorney General John Ashcroft, any criticism of US foreign policies, however well intentioned, 'only aids terrorists'.[180] Any meaningful debate on US foreign policy is, thereby, shut down. Dissent or criticism of foreign policies implemented in the name of the war on terror can instead be dismissed as unpatriotic, cynical, anti-American, denying the political significance of 9/11, irresponsibly neglecting the future security of the American people or as terrorist propaganda.

6 War on Afghanistan

Introduction

The final two case studies analyze the strategic and politicized integration of the hegemonic discourse in the official narratives provided by the Bush Administrations for the wars fought against Afghanistan (this chapter) and Iraq (Chapter 7). The aims of this chapter are twofold. The first aim is to identify the application of the hegemonic discourse in the 2001 Afghanistan War and its immediate aftermath. The second is to analyze how the official discourse asserted by the Bush Administrations produced a contingent understanding of reality. The chapter addresses the aims from the relative perspectives of the reflective, rejectionist and productive explanations described in the first part of this book.

The chapter details notable inconsistencies with interpreting the hegemonic discourse in terms of describing a corresponding reality. However, the chapter also urges against drawing the conclusion that the hegemonic discourse can be subsequently rejected as rhetoric devoid of pattern or political significance. Instead the productive explanation of the hegemonic discourse details how its internal consistencies operate as a technique of governance in the sense of producing a benevolent interpretation of US power. The chapter begins with a brief introduction to the modern history of Afghanistan and an outline of the application by the Bush Administration of the hegemonic discourse in the official narrative of the 2001 war.

Human rights discourse in the 2001 Afghanistan War

The April 1978 revolution in Afghanistan installed the Moscow backed People's Democratic Party of Afghanistan (PDPA) that ruled the country by decree. The PDPA was perceived as hostile to Islam and was soon confronted by guerrilla mujahedin groups supplied in part by the US and trained in camps located in Pakistan. This growing instability on its southern flank led to a full scale Soviet invasion of Afghanistan in December 1979.

US policymakers responded to the Soviet invasion by increasing support for the Islamic mujahedin groups. During the 1980s, the mujahedin received total funding of $2.8 billion in cash and weapons from the CIA to fight the Soviet

military with much of this aid funneled through the Pakistani intelligence services.[1] US agencies also coordinated the Pakistani, Saudi Arabian and Egyptian
financing and transporting of fundamentalist groups to fight the anti-Soviet
jihad.[2] The flood of arms into Afghanistan by both superpowers throughout the
1980s reduced the historical influence of tribal Afghan leaders relative to the
power of emerging regional warlords and their military commanders.

Violence and endemic human rights violations at the hands of warlords out-
lasted the presence of Soviet troops in Afghanistan.[3] Promising to end the lawlessness and killings, elements of the mujahedin reformed into a distinct
religious and political organization known as the Taliban and seized control of
Afghanistan in September 1996. The Taliban regime systematically violated
human rights norms by imposing an uncompromising interpretation of Sharia
law that included public floggings, executions, punitive amputations, arbitrary
detentions and mass displacements. In 1999 the Security Council further compounded the human suffering of Afghans by imposing sanctions against the state
in response to the refusal of the Taliban to hand over Osama bin Laden who was
the main suspect for August 1998 attacks against US embassies in Kenya and
Tanzania.[4]

Two days after 9/11, Colin Powell announced bin Laden as the chief suspect
of the atrocity and required the Taliban to deliver bin Laden and other suspected
leaders of al Qaeda to the US. Taliban leaders requested evidence of bin Laden's
guilt from the US government and offered to hold a trial in Afghanistan, a proposal that was subsequently rejected by the Bush Administration. Mediators
from Pakistan were unable to convince the Taliban to hand over bin Laden. On
October 7, President Bush announced the start of the 2001 war between Coalition Forces and Afghanistan. Three US cruisers, a destroyer and the British sub-
marines Triumph and Trafalgar launched a salvo of missiles against the state
from the Arabian Sea. A wave of land based bombers swept across Afghanistan.
US ground forces attacked later in October and their newfound local allies, the
Northern Alliance, seized the capital, Kabul, from the Taliban on November 15,
2001.[5] The legality of the invasion was predicated upon the individual and
collective right to self-defense.[6] UN Security Council Resolution 1378 condemned the Taliban for 'allowing Afghanistan to be used as a base for the export
of terrorism' and stated a 'deep concern' for 'the grave humanitarian situation
and the continuing serious violations by the Taliban of human rights and international humanitarian law'.[7]

The Bush Administration explained the war in terms of the hegemonic
mythology. The stated intent was to extend freedom and human rights to
Afghans as well as to ensure US security, exemplified in the names 'Infinite
Justice' and 'Enduring Freedom' assigned to the military operation. In his
October 7 address to the nation, President Bush stated that 'we defend not only
our precious freedoms but also the freedom of people everywhere to live and
raise their children free from fear'.[8] Four days later, Bush described war aims in
terms that 'we went into Afghanistan to free people, because we believe in
freedom. We believe every life counts, everybody has worth, everybody matters,

whether they live in America or in Afghanistan'.[9] Consistent with this message that the war was being fought on grounds of liberation, Department of Defense officials were keen to stress that civilian casualties were being avoided in the US bombing campaign. The secretary of defense stated that 'no nation in human history has done more' to avoid civilian deaths.[10] One general asserted that, 'the last thing we want are any civilian casualties. So we plan every military target with great care'.[11]

Formal developments in the institutions of democracy and human rights also featured in postwar Afghanistan. In May 2003 Afghanistan acceded to the ICC. The Afghan authorities ratified the UN Women's Convention in the following March.[12] In June 2002 an independent Afghanistan Human Rights Commission (AHRC) was established to protect the human rights of Afghan citizens and investigate alleged violations. The AHRC received US Congressional funding in 2003. Hamid Karzai won presidential elections held in October 2004. An elected Afghan parliament was inaugurated in December 2005.

The Bush Administration also diverted resources into providing humanitarian assistance for Afghans.[13] The US spent $246 million on such assistance during the months of October and November 2001.[14] In the year following the war, the US Agency for International Development (USAID) sent emergency food assistance worth $138 million to Afghanistan. During the same period the Department of Defense delivered 2.4 million food rations to Afghans at a cost of $10 million. The State Department provided $124.5 million to the UN and international NGOs for the repatriation of refugees displaced by the war and spent $7 million clearing land mines.[15] In the 14 months following the war, the US government had spent a total of $848 million on humanitarian relief, rehabilitation and reconstruction in Afghanistan. This included 6100 water projects, the construction of four mountain passes, 142 schools, 72 health clinics and 4000 km of road. These actions have all been presented as evidence of the US commitment to humanitarian efforts in line with the messages comprising the hegemonic discourse outlined above.[16]

Reflective explanation

There is plentiful evidence to confirm the systematic human rights abuses conducted under the Taliban.[17] This abuse has been taken by some observers as reason enough to validate the Afghanistan War as necessary to free an oppressed population.[18] In a letter to President Bush on behalf of the United States Conference of Catholic Bishops, Bishop Joseph Fiorenza stated that the use of force against Afghanistan was 'regrettable but necessary'.[19] Cardinal Francis George of Chicago concurred that 'this is a just war'.[20] Elshtain agreed, arguing that any civilian deaths incurred during the war were unintended.[21] Elshtain added that ongoing assessments made by the US military as well as international observers acted to minimize civilian casualties.[22] Under this explanation, the discourse of policymakers reflects the aim of the war to liberate an oppressed people.

Rejectionist explanation

According to the rejectionist explanation, the reflective interpretation provides an unduly sympathetic account of the hegemonic discourse that overlooks notable contradictions. In particular, the following three features of the war and its aftermath refute the messages contained in the hegemonic discourse, (i) the continued brutalization of postwar Afghanistan, (ii) that some of the most egregious violators of human rights during the 1990s were adopted by Coalition Forces as key allies in Afghanistan and (iii) the abuse of prisoners held in US custody.

Continued brutalization of Afghan society

Non-military attempts to end the endemic violence besetting Afghanistan have been under resourced and pushed to the margins of policy by Coalition Forces. In the absence of tackling the social causes of violence, the establishment of the formal institutions of democracy and human rights noted above has had little impact on alleviating the suffering of the Afghan population living outside of Kabul. The situation for women remains little changed from the Taliban days. Misogynistic marriage and divorce laws remain in place. Where legislation designed to protect women has been forthcoming, these are flouted with impunity.[23] Two years after the war, Amnesty International described rape and sexual violence directed against women as 'common', noted that women and girls were traded to resolve family disputes and reported that women faced widespread discrimination in the justice system.[24]

The resources allocated to the AHRC were wholly inadequate for its assigned remit of protecting the human rights of Afghans. Despite the best efforts of the AHRC, it has been largely ineffectual in improving the human rights situation in Afghanistan. Niland cogently describes the establishment of the AHRC as an institutional sleight of hand. Through establishing the AHRC, Niland argued that Coalition Forces, the UN and the Afghan government could all distance themselves from the responsibility of improving the human rights situation in Afghanistan which was perceived as a poisoned chalice from which none of these organizations wished to drink.[25]

Instead of establishing and prioritizing resources for human rights and conflict resolution mechanisms, official policy focused instead around militarizing security and further fueling endemic cycles of violence. In the five years following the war, reports of killings, explosions, shootings and attacks on Coalition Forces, Afghan officials and foreign aid workers continued on an almost daily basis. Attacks by resurgent Taliban forces increased significantly in the south of the country in 2006. In 2003 Amnesty International described the security situation faced by Afghan civilians as 'deteriorating', and explained that '[s]erious human rights abuses and armed conflict continued in many areas. The criminal justice system remained ineffective and was a source of violations rather than a mechanism for providing justice'.[26] People disappeared frequently and anyone investigating disappearances risked their lives. Bombing raids by Coalition Forces continued to cause civilian deaths.[27]

In the five years following the war there was little improvement in the economy or infrastructure of Afghanistan outside Kabul. Child labor continued to be unchecked and endemic. The only sector of the economy that was performing well was the illegal opium trade, which compounded the civilian suffering caused by organized crime.[28] Police failed to protect human rights and were at times complicit in committing violations themselves by using torture and arbitrary detention to extract confessions and money.[29] In the three years following the war, there remained little international security presence outside of Kabul, allowing control of rural areas to fall into the hands of warlords and their local commanders whose combined militias were estimated at 200,000 strong in May 2003.[30] The lack of funds available to the central Afghan government prevented President Karzai from addressing the dire security situation or indeed from paying civil servants, further compounding problems of corruption. Rather than directly fund the Karzai government, Western officials elected to instead recycle to foreign agencies some $5 billion of funds pledged at a 2002 donors conference for the rebuilding of Afghanistan.[31]

Choice of allies

The rejectionist explanation can also highlight the difficulties in reconciling a genuine commitment by the Bush Administration to liberate Afghans with its choice of allies. The Coalition Forces allied with the militias of the Northern Alliance which were constituted, in no small part, by the warlords and military commanders responsible for the violence and human rights abuses endemic in Afghanistan in the early 1990s.[32] With the removal of the Taliban, the Northern Alliance forces carried on where they had left off. On November 13, 2001 the ditches of Kabul were filled by the bodies of Taliban fighters, many of who had been lynched before being shot.[33] That same month 400 captured Taliban fighters were killed in a secure fort after they turned on their captors. Journalists reported that some 50 of the dead were found with their hands bound behind their backs.[34] There were further reports that up to 3000 Taliban prisoners held in metal transport containers died when these were sprayed with gunfire from Northern Alliance fighters. Eyewitnesses have alleged that US military personnel were present at the time that these war crimes occurred.[35] Mass graves containing the remains of captured Taliban prisoners were discovered in the Dasht-I Leili district of northern Afghanistan.[36] The various militia elements allied to the warlords have been identified by human rights organizations as responsible for arbitrary detentions, confiscation of property, rape, abduction of girls and women and forced conscription.[37]

It is difficult to reconcile support for these warlords with the stated intent to liberate the Afghan people. Yet the Bush Administration responded to a direct request from President Karzai to confront the most abusive warlords not by offering support but instead by providing the warlords with money and arms.[38]

Roth points out that one warlord, Ismail Khan, based in Heart, west Afghanistan, used death threats, detention and torture to stamp out dissent and forced women to wear burqas. In a visit to the region in April 2002, Donald Rumsfeld described Khan as an 'appealing person'.[39] Gunmen belonging to another local warlord were employed to protect US bases located outside Kandahar.[40]

In part because of US financial and military support for the warlords, the Karzai government has been unable to tackle endemic attacks on civilians. One report into human rights abuses produced by Minister Noorzai in March 2002 was, for example, shelved since the central government lacked the resources required to disband the militia elements identified in the report as responsible for serious violations.[41] Thus the rejectionist explanation points to the apparent hypocrisy in the use by the Bush Administrations of the language of liberation to explain policies that funded the same militias that were responsible for widespread human rights violations. As Niland summarizes, the stated commitment to human rights in Afghanistan 'was paralleled by military, financial and political support for lawless factions that have again killed and raped women and girls with impunity in Afghanistan'.[42]

Prisoner abuse

As in the treatment of prisoners subjected to rendition discussed in Chapter 5, there exists a public lack of knowledge and accountability of the treatment of prisoners held by US military forces in Afghanistan.[43] Human Rights Watch reports that the US operates its detention facilities in Afghanistan, 'in a climate of almost total impunity'.[44] A body of evidence suggests that an environment where prisoner abuses could take place was subsequently allowed to flourish. This evidence is derived from corroborating reports provided by (i) released prisoners, (ii) leaked medical reports, (iii) human rights organizations, (iv) Afghan authorities and (v) ex-administration officials. Prisoner abuse has been further facilitated by the ambiguous legal status accorded to Afghan prisoners.

Released prisoners

Bagram airbase, located an hours drive from Kabul on a plain beneath the Panjshir mountains, was originally built as a base for invading Soviet forces. Following the 2001 war, US forces converted the base into a makeshift prison. Prisoners have described the cells in the Bagram detention hanger as being five by ten meters in length, each housing ten to 15 prisoners, with a bucket in a corner for a toilet and only separated from other cells with wire fencing.[45] Prisoners held at both Guantanamo Bay and Bagram airbase have reported that their treatment at Bagram was significantly worse.[46] One uncooperative detainee held at Bagram was reportedly stripped naked by guards under the orders of a CIA case officer, chained to a concrete floor and left overnight without blankets where he subsequently froze to death.[47] When relatives came to collect his body, they were given $100 for a taxi ride and no explanation for the death.[48] There have been reports that other prisoners have simply disappeared from the base without trace.[49] UK citizen Moazzam Begg stated that he was forced to sign documents under duress and that during interviews he was 'subjected to pernicious threats of torture, actual vindictive torture and death threats'.[50] Prisoners kept in Bagram have reported being deprived of sleep; being kept in stress positions through the use of shackles; being hooded; being exposed to severe beatings and kickings, such as the peroneal strike to the leg; being exposed to cold and water; being forced to sign false confessions; being stripped naked and photographed and being threatened with barking dogs.[51] Detainees held in US run detention centers at Kandahar military base and in the cities of Jalalabad and Asasdabad have reported similar patterns of abuse on a lesser scale.[52]

Leaked reports

Announcing that two prisoners died in Bagram airbase in December 2002, the military authorities claimed that the deaths were the result of natural causes. On February 7, 2003, the US commander in Afghanistan, Lt Gen. Daniel McNeill stated that there was 'no indication' that either prisoner had been injured in custody.[53] The *New York Times* subsequently obtained army pathologist reports that categorized the deaths as cases of homicide.[54] In particular, the peroneal strike was identified by the pathologists as having caused severe damage to the legs of both victims. One death was of an individual known as Dilawar who was detained in Bagram after being suspected of launching rockets at an American base. For much of the four days previous to his death, the detainee was chained by his wrists to the top of his cell and his legs were repeatedly beaten. During his final interrogation, the guards attempted to force the detainee to the ground, but his legs were so damaged from the beatings that they would no longer bend. After interrogation he was taken back to his cell where he was chained once again to the ceiling. Several hours later he was pronounced dead. His autopsy found that his heart had failed due to 'blunt force injuries to the lower extremities'.[55] One of the coroners reported that his legs had 'been pulpified' adding that, 'I've seen similar injuries in an individual run over by a bus'.[56] A subsequent report into the incident found that 'harsh treatment by some interrogators was routine and that guards could strike shackled detainees with virtual impunity'.[57] Most alarming was a statement made by Lt Gen. McNeill that the treatment of Dilawar had been 'in accordance with what is generally accepted as interrogation techniques'.[58]

The public controversy resulting from the leaked pathologist documents led to an investigation by the Criminal Investigative Command into the two detainee deaths. The resulting report was ruled classified but a copy was again leaked to the *Washington Post* and to the *New York Times*. Abuses revealed in the report included 'slamming prisoners into walls, twisting handcuffs to cause pain, kneeing prisoners, forcing a detainee to maintain painful contorted positions, shackling the detainees arms to the ceiling and forcing water into the mouth of the detainee until he could not breathe'.[59]

Human rights organizations

A 2004 report from Human Rights Watch began with the words that the system of arrests and detention operated by the US military in Afghanistan 'violates international human rights law and international humanitarian law'.[60] The report goes on to describe numerous allegations of abuse committed by Coalition Forces including the use of excessive force during arrests as well as arbitrary and indefinite detention.[61] The report cites repeated examples of the use by Coalition Forces of lethal force from helicopter gunships when apprehending people in uncontested residential areas. Afghan soldiers deployed alongside US troops were found to have used excessive force during arrest operations and to have looted the homes of those detained.[62]

Afghan authorities

Rafiullah Bidar, the director of the AHRC for the Gardez region of Afghanistan, reported that '[a]ll I do nowadays is chart complaints against the US military' stating that '[m]any thousands of people have been rounded up and detained by them'.[63] Bidar continued, '[p]eople who have been arrested say they've been brutalized – the tactics used are beyond belief'.[64]

Ex-administration officials

According to Colin Powell's chief of staff, Colonel Lawrence Wilkerson, prisoner abuse arose as the result of an 'alternative decision-making process' led by Dick Cheney and Donald Rumsfeld.[65] Wilkerson went on to estimate between 70 and 90 prisoners from the wars on terror, Afghanistan and Iraq, held in US custody had died under 'questionable circumstances'.[66]

Legal ambiguities

A string of policies and leadership failings created the environment for the abuse of prisoners.[67] US soldiers lacked both clear guidance and effective oversight in their treatment of detainees. When the war started, the Bush Administration rescinded the standards of prisoner treatment, stipulated in the *US Army Field Manual on Intelligence Interrogation*, that military personnel had been previously trained to adhere to. Instead, the administration declared that prisoners were to be treated humanely but declined to provide clarification of what humane treatment included or excluded. The requirement for prisoners to be treated humanely was further compromised by a February 2002 presidential memo, which made humane treatment conditional upon 'military necessity'.[68] Exemplifying the resultant widespread confusion and ambiguities surrounding the proper treatment of prisoners, the army judge overseeing one pre-trial inquiry into prisoner abuse at Bagram recommended that criminal abuse charges against a former MP commander be dropped. The judge explained it would be difficult to prosecute soldiers for breaking rules at Bagram since those rules were not at all clear.[69]

Despite official recognition by the Bush Administration that the Geneva Conventions applied in the Afghanistan War, Taliban prisoners were determined by the administration to be 'unlawful combatants' and therefore not entitled to PoW status. According to an army reserve sergeant at Bagram, this classification led interrogators to believe that they 'could deviate slightly from the rules'.[70] Policy decisions were thus made that confused both the precise manner in which detainees were to be treated and the legal standing of detainees, both of which undermined important safeguards against mistreatment. In March 2005 the American Civil Liberties Union (ACLU) and Human Rights First brought a case on behalf of Iraqi and Afghan prisoners abused in US custody to a federal court in Illinois charging that the secretary of defense had violated constitutional and international laws prohibiting use of torture and cruel, inhuman and degrading treatment.[71] Submitting evidence on behalf of the plaintiffs, the 1997 to 2000 Navy Judge Advocate General stated 'in dealing with detainees, the attitude at the top was that they are all just terrorists, beneath contempt and outside the law so they could be treated inhumanely. . . . That attitude dropped like a rock down the chain of command'.[72]

The removal of proper safeguards against the mistreatment of prisoners held by the US military simultaneously provided opportunities for arbitrary arrests and detentions. Detainees were, for example, not afforded the opportunity to see an independent tribunal since, as Human Rights Watch representative John Sifton pointed out, 'the entire system operates outside the rule of law'.[73] Michael Posner of Human Rights First concurred that the detention system exists in a climate of secrecy outside of international norms.[74] As AHRC regional director Rafiullah Bidar explained '[n]o one is charged. No one is identified'.[75] Bidar also cites reports of foreign detainees being brought into this secretive prison network.[76] Given that the evidence reviewed above contradicts the role of human rights asserted in the hegemonic mythology, it is perhaps seductive to dismiss the human rights claims made by administration officials. The final section of this chapter urges against drawing such a conclusion by detailing the significance of the hegemonic mythology as a technique of governance.

Productive explanation

The productive explanation holds that there are politically significant internal consistencies in the application of the hegemonic discourse to the war in Afghanistan. In particular, the narrative provided by administration officials (i) highlighted human rights violations occurring in Afghanistan during the Taliban era, (ii) produced the identity of a free post-Taliban Afghanistan, (iii) identified Coalition Forces as responsible for this change in human rights observance in Afghanistan and (iv) asserted that liberating Afghanistan was a constitutive aim of the 2001 war. These four expressions of the hegemonic discourse can be identified as internally consistent in the sense that administration officials repeatedly asserted these messages. The four discursive expressions produce reality in terms of the hegemonic mythology by ascribing meanings to events and identities to actors as detailed below.

Human rights violations under the Taliban

The first internally consistent feature of the narrative provided by administration officials centers on the human rights violations conducted in Afghanistan during the Taliban era. These violations were consistently highlighted with the position of women drawn out for particular attention. President Bush stated that, '[w]omen were given no rights. Young girls did not go to school'.[77] The Taliban regime was identified as responsible for these violations since, '[i]t was a barbaric regime'.[78] On Women's Equality Day 2002 the president highlighted that '[i]n Afghanistan, the Taliban used violence and fear to deny Afghan women access to education, health care, mobility and the right to vote'.[79] The assistant secretary for democracy, human rights and labor likewise stated that

> [t]he human rights abuses that the Taliban have imposed on Afghanistan are in a class by themselves. In a number of categories they rate in the worst possible sector. There's no other country on earth that has this kind of treatment of women.[80]

Although a wealth of evidence exists to testify to the systematic violations of human rights in Afghanistan pre-October 2001, demonizing the Taliban overlooks those human rights abuses conducted by the warlords and their military commanders who subsequently became useful allies of Coalition Forces. It is in this sense of selectively highlighting those responsible for human rights abuses that the Lawyers Committee for Human Rights criticized the State Department for creating 'a misleading picture' of human rights abuses in Afghanistan in its *2002 Country Reports on Human Rights Practices*.[81] This misleading picture is consistent with the production of enemy identity as evil in line with the hegemonic mythology.

The discursive production of a free Afghanistan

The second internal consistency of the narrative provided by administration officials featured a post-Taliban era of human rights observance in Afghanistan. The underlying message was of an Afghanistan where the freedoms and human rights of citizens were protected from the vicissitudes of the Taliban regime. President Bush announced on separate occasions in 2004 that '[m]ore than 15 million Afghan citizens have been freed from the brutal zealotry of the Taliban',[82] that '[t]he people of Afghanistan are a world away from the nightmare of the Taliban'[83] and that '[p]eople are [now] free in that country [Afghanistan]'.[84] The underlying message contrasted a nightmare era of repression with a post-Taliban era of freedom. Repeating this message, Secretary

Powell assured that in Afghanistan 'human rights and democratic freedoms will be fully restored to people who have suffered years of oppression'.[85]

The production of reality in line with the underlying message was exemplified through the White House hosting a *Then and Now* website contrasting pre- and post-invasion circumstances in Afghanistan.[86] This website stressed how under the Taliban, listening to music, dancing and flying kites were all prohibited by edicts. The website stated that, a year after the liberation of Afghanistan, 'newspapers, radio and TV have been reborn. Individual and political freedoms are being re-established'.[87]

The official narrative provided by the administration produced a strategically simplified dichotomy. The *Then and Now* website made little mention of the endemic violence and ongoing violations of human rights in postwar Afghanistan or of the highly circumscribed capacity of the Karzai government to tackle these problems. The State Department produced the same strategic dichotomy in its *2002 Country Reports on Human Rights Practices* by 'generally overstat[ing] the progress of the new Karzai government in improving human rights performance'.[88] The 2006 *National Security Strategy* likewise reproduced this simplified dichotomy when it stated, '[a] few years ago, Afghanistan was condemned to a pre-modern nightmare. Now it has held two successful free elections'.[89] The document made no mention of the fact that international organizations refused to monitor the October 2004 presidential election, except in Kabul, on grounds that to do so would be too dangerous and for fear that they would have to publicize the failure of the election to be free and fair.[90]

The discursive production of the US military and its allies as liberators

The third internally consistent feature of the narrative provided by administration officials identified the US military and its allies as the agents responsible for transforming Afghanistan from serial human rights violator into aspiring land of the free. The president affirmed the US military as the force of freedom when declaring that

> [w]e have seen the character of the men and women who wear our country's uniform in places like Kabul and Kandahar, in Mosul and Baghdad. . . . Because of their fierce courage, America is safer. Two terror regimes are gone forever and more than 50 million souls now live in freedom.[91]

On another occasion, Bush identified Coalition Forces as liberators by stating that, '[t]hanks to the United States military and thanks to the coalition we have put together, we have freed the people of Afghanistan from one of the most repressive regimes in the history of mankind'.[92] The message was repeated when the president announced that, '[o]ur coalition has liberated Afghanistan and restored fundamental human rights and freedom to Afghan women and all the people of Afghanistan'.[93]

The identity of the US military as liberator was produced through two discursive features. First, history was sanitized of any reference to the US funds provided in the 1980s for the mujahedin groups that had gone on to form the basis of the Taliban regime. Second, the myth of the sanitized war held that high technology weapons targeted combatants with deadly accuracy leaving innocent civilians unharmed. In his October 7 address, President Bush, for example, stated that 'al Qaeda training camps and military installations of the Taliban regime' would be destroyed through the 'carefully targeted actions' of the US military.[94] The idea of a sanitized Afghanistan War can be identified as a myth, rather than unproblematic fact, for three reasons that have worked to make the civilian casualties inflicted during the campaign invisible.

First, civilian deaths have been made invisible through statements of intent that categorize any such deaths as unfortunate errors. Since the US military does not target civilians, there was no subsequent accountability for the 2000 pound bomb dropped by a US Navy jet on a residential neighborhood of Kabul on October 14, killing four and injuring eight, nor of the bombs dropped on October 16 and again on October 18 on a Red Cross complex in Kabul, nor of the 1000 pound bomb dropped on October 20 on a residential area in the western city of Heart, nor of the 500 pound bomb dropped on October 20 on a residential area of Kabul, nor of the gunning down of people in the village of Chowkar-Karez, nor of the December 29 bombing in the Tora Bora area which killed up to 100 people.[95] The stated intent to avoid civilian casualties also makes invisible the injuries and deaths resulting to men, women and children from the deployment by both US and UK forces of cluster bombs in residential areas during the Afghanistan War.[96] Second, civilian deaths were made invisible by the decisions not to compile authoritative statistics on the number of civilian deaths caused in the Afghanistan War and the refusal of US military spokespeople to respond to direct questions on this matter when raised by human rights groups.[97]

Third, the targeting of civilian infrastructure was made invisible by the capacity of the US military to unilaterally define identities. Donald Rumsfeld defended the decision to bomb the Kabul office of al Jazeera on October 10, 2001 on the grounds that media stations could be used as 'vehicles for the Taliban leadership and for al Qaeda to manage their affairs'.[98] A Department of Defense spokesperson similarly accounted for the targeting decision in terms of reported al Qaeda activity in the al Jazeera office, which was subsequently clarified to mean that interviews with Taliban officials had been broadcast from the station.[99] In this instance, the authorities were able to make invisible the targeting of a civilian office by redefining its identity in terms of a military objective.

Human rights and war aims

The fourth internally consistent feature of the narrative provided by administration officials was to state the liberation of an oppressed people as a component aim of the war. This feature expressed the hegemonic rule that human rights are integrated as genuine foreign policy goals.[100] Before the war began the president announced that military action would be an act of 'generosity of America and our allies' in aid of 'the oppressed people of Afghanistan'.[101] Donald Rumsfeld likewise explained that the US military was acting 'for the purpose of denying hostile regimes the opportunity to oppress their own people and other people'.[102] Following the invasion, Lorne Craner declared that '[t]he promotion of human rights, particularly the human rights of women and girls, is a high priority for us in Afghanistan today',[103] and correctly identified that '[a] number of people, from the Secretary of State and the President on down, have stated our commitment to human rights in Afghanistan'.[104] Thus, the ethical framework for the Afghanistan War was presented in terms of liberty, freedom and human rights.

This official narrative of the war was broadcast as widely and as loudly as possible in the name of the battle for hearts and minds. The Washington-, London- and Islamabad-based Coalition Information Center, was set up to get co-ordinated messages out to the news networks. Both radio and television stations were funded to further distribute the message.[105] Western-based news networks gave the air waves to an estimated 500 embedded reporters as well as to a plethora of on hand US military personnel.[106] In February 2002, the Office of Strategic Information, based in the Pentagon, became operational. This office was closed after one week following a number of allegations that the office had gone further than providing a favorable interpretation of events and was openly presenting misleading information to foreign media outlets.[107]

Conclusion: human rights as a technique of governance

This chapter has reviewed three differing explanations for the manner in which a human rights discourse has been integrated into the design and implementation of the Afghanistan War by the Bush Administrations. The reflective interpretation of the human rights discourse failed to explain the hostility demonstrated toward the universal and impartial integration of human rights. In contrast, the rejectionist explanation was found to overlook the political significance of the internally consistent messages of that discourse. In particular, four expressions of the hegemonic discourse highlighted in the final section of the chapter were argued to be politically significant by virtue of their capacity to produce, rather than reflect, reality.

This emphasis on human rights as a technique of governance is demonstrated in the events that forced the humanitarian NGO Médecins Sans Frontières (MSF) to close its medical programs in Afghanistan on July 28, 2004 after 24 years of working to help the Afghan people.[108] Its decision to pull out followed an attack by armed groups on a clearly marked MSF vehicle in the province of Badghis that killed five aid workers. The NGO observed in a press release that the provision of humanitarian aid had become impossible because of the extent to which Coalition Forces had politicized the delivery of aid in Afghanistan.[109] For example, in one instance in southern Afghanistan, Coalition Forces distributed leaflets requiring the local populace to provide 'information about the Taliban and al Qaeda' if the provision of aid was to continue.[110]

Rather than being a neutral and impartial response to human suffering, the provision of humanitarian aid had been co-opted by Coalition Forces into an instrument through which to elicit information and create discipline among the population. Such actions were identified by MSF as constituting 'attempts to co-opt humanitarian aid and use it to win hearts and minds'.[111] MSF attacked the broader trend that 'the US backed coalition has consistently sought to use humanitarian aid to build support for its military and political ambitions' in Afghanistan.[112] This politicization of aid jeopardized its delivery to those in most urgent need and compromised the lives of humanitarian volunteers. The dangers faced by aid volunteers was illustrated all too clearly when, in May 2005, three young Afghan women were found raped, hanged and dumped by the side of a road with a warning to others not to work for foreign relief organizations.[113] The politicization of aid is as antagonistic to an independent commitment to human rights as it is consistent with the use of human rights as a technique of discipline.

According to the productive account of discourse, language is itself an inherently political instrument.[114] By examining the internal consistencies and patterns within the hegemonic discourse, the productive account was found to offer an explanation of how discipline has been implemented through a language of freedom, human rights and democracy. The hypothesized deployment of language by administration officials to affect opinion and produce meaning rather than describe a corresponding reality is consistent with the divergence between public statements and what is known of behind the scenes discussions. According to information derived from interviews with the president, Donald Rumsfeld was for example opposed to relying solely on bombers and cruise missiles to fight the Afghanistan War. This opposition was predicated not upon military necessities, the aim of locating bin Laden or liberating an oppressed people. Instead, the secretary of defense 'was insistent on boots on the ground to change the psychology of how Americans viewed war'.[115] In particular, US soldiers fighting combat operations in foreign lands could be thereby made acceptable to a US public that still harbored suspicions following Vietnam.[116] Furthermore, the deployment of US troops could be understood in benevolent terms consistent with the hegemonic discourse, allowing policymakers the maximum remit in which to deploy military power in future scenarios.

Policymakers and close advisers saw the function and significance of the war extending beyond the borders of Afghanistan. Richard Perle stated that overthrowing the Taliban regime sent the important message to rogue states that 'you're next'.[117] The president is similarly reported to have viewed recourse to war in terms of signaling that 'this is a change from the past. We want to cause other countries like Syria and Iran to change their views'.[118] Consistent with this position, the president has demonstrated a keen interest in how policies were understood by the audience, lamenting at one point that 'the public relations war' was being lost since the administration was 'not getting credit' for its humanitarian operations in Afghanistan.[119] Therefore, through analyzing the consistencies in its application, this chapter has identified the principal importance of the hegemonic discourse as an instrument of governance that operates by producing understandings of the Afghanistan War as detailed above.

7 War on Iraq

Introduction

This chapter focuses on a case study of the US- and UK-led war against the Saddam Hussein regime of Iraq to address two aims. The chapter first aims to explain how the hegemonic discourse was integrated into the official narrative of the Iraq War asserted by the Bush Administrations. The second aim seeks to detail the patterns in how the official narrative produced a contingent and politicized understanding of the Iraq War.

Three sections will address these aims from the particular perspectives of the reflective, rejectionist and productive explanations of the hegemonic discourse. The first section explains how human rights concerns were integrated into the official narrative of the Iraq War in terms of the three rules of the hegemonic discourse. The first section proceeds to review the reflective explanation of the hegemonic discourse as a literal description of a corresponding reality. The second section details the inconsistencies in the reflective interpretation by focusing on the mistreatment of Iraqi prisoners. Under the rejectionist account, discursive appeals to human rights made by administration officials are interpreted as having little independent significance and are instead seen as a cover for the furtherance of political and economic interest.

The third section advances the productive explanation of the hegemonic discourse. This section analyzes how the narrative asserted by the Bush Administrations produced an understanding of the invasion and occupation of Iraq as a necessary and just war. This third section reviews evidence that a sanitized account of the Iraq War was disseminated to the audience as a component of the war effort. The hypothesis that the Iraq War was caused by faulty intelligence that left the Bush Administration with no option but to invade Iraq is disputed. This section also disputes the rejectionist conclusion that human rights were a political irrelevance in the invasion of Iraq. Instead, this section looks at how the threat from Iraq was discursively produced by the administration politicizing intelligence and emphasizing the human rights abuses committed by the Hussein regime. Thus, the third section of the chapter accounts for the role of the hegemonic discourse as a technique of governance that produced reality in line with predetermined conclusions.

Hegemonic discourse in the 2003 Iraq War

President Bush and British Prime Minister Blair advanced a range of reasons in defense of the decision to go to war against Saddam Hussein in March 2003. These included the liberation of the long oppressed Iraqi people, regional security concerns, regime change and pre-emptive self-defense.[1] The principal rationale was Iraq's perceived WMD capability which was argued to constitute an urgent threat to neighboring states and to Western states should such weapons be distributed to terrorist cells. On September 19, 2002, the president presented a resolution to Congress that would provide him with authorization to 'use all means that he determines to be appropriate, including force' to 'defend the national security interests of the United States against the threat posed by Iraq and restore international peace and security in the region'.[2] This war resolution was passed 296–133 in the House of Representatives on October 10, 2002 and by a margin of 77–23 in the Senate the following day.

Throughout the remainder of 2002 the Bush Administration exerted pressure on the United Nations to enforce existing Security Council resolutions relating to Iraq, most notably resolution 1284 that charged the United Nations Monitoring, Verification and Inspection Commission with overseeing the dismantling of Iraq's WMD program. Concerted diplomatic pressure resulted in the Security Council approving resolution 1441 in November 2002. Resolution 1441 found Iraq to be 'in material breach' of its commitments to disarm as required under previous Security Council resolutions. Resolution 1441 also required UN-coordinated weapons inspections to resume and ordered the Hussein regime to provide a complete declaration of its weapons program to the Security Council.[3] In line with the demands of 1441, Hans Blix led a team of weapons inspectors into Iraq on November 18, 2002.

The following month Iraq submitted a 12,000 page document declaring that it had no banned weapons, a conclusion that was immediately rejected as deliberately misleading by the US and UK governments. Preliminary inspections by the UN team did not uncover any WMD in Iraq but did identify 11 undeclared chemical weapons warheads.[4] These findings provided the background to the emergence of a split Security Council. The US, UK and Spain called for a second Security Council resolution explicitly authorizing the use of force to overthrow Saddam Hussein. France, Germany and Russia led a coalition of states who favored providing the Blix team with more time to complete their search for WMD.

In the absence of a Security Council consensus, President Bush announced on March 17, 2003 that 'all the decades of deceit and cruelty have now reached an end. Saddam Hussein and his sons must leave Iraq within 48 hours. Their refusal to do so will result in military conflict, commenced at a time of our choosing'.[5] War between Coalition Forces and the army of Iraq began two days later. After six weeks of fighting President Bush declared that the war had been won. This announcement simultaneously marked the start of a prolonged and bloody insurgency between competing sectarian, ethnic, religious, tribal and criminal factions in Iraq. As of 2006, no banned WMD had been located.

Human rights and freedoms as constitutive war aims

Bush Administration officials consistently appealed to the hegemonic mythology in calling for military action against the Hussein regime. The first hegemonic rule asserted that human rights were an independent policy goal. President Bush thus announced to the Iraqi people that '[w]e will help you build a peaceful and representative government that protects the rights of all citizens'.[6] The goal of military action was stated in terms of the liberation of a long oppressed people. The president proclaimed, for example, that 'we have no ambition in Iraq except the liberation of its people'.[7] Addressing the Iraqi people, the president announced that '[t]he goals of our coalition are the same as your goals – sovereignty for your country, dignity for your great culture, and for every Iraqi citizen, the opportunity for a better life'.[8] On another occasion the president stated that 'our agenda is freedom and independence, security and prosperity for the Iraqi people'.[9] Colin Powell repeated this stated aim by declaring that '[w]e will liberate Iraq'.[10]

As a component aspect of claiming the liberation of an oppressed people as a war aim, the human rights abuses committed during the Hussein era were highlighted. In 2001 the Hussein regime had, for example, been identified by the head of the US delegation to the UN Commission on Human Rights as 'one of the most repressive in the world'.[11] Acting Assistant Secretary of State for Democracy Michael Parmly, stated in March 2001 that 'there is a source of the human rights problems in Iraq and that is the regime of Saddam Hussein'.[12] Lorne Craner spoke of 'the horrors' of Saddam Hussein's regime 'with its capricious human rights violations'.[13] President Bush stated that under Hussein, Iraq was 'ruled by the cruelty and caprice of one man'.[14] Saddam Hussein was referred to by the president as a 'brutal man',[15] a 'brutal dictator',[16] and a 'cruel, cruel oppressor of the Iraq people',[17] who 'had used weapons of mass destruction on his own people'.[18] Websites further disseminated this stated identity by documenting vivid stories of the human rights abuses committed by the Hussein regime.[19]

The history of the war was subsequently written by the administrations to reify rule one of the hegemonic discourse. Following the war, the Department of State announced that 'a US led coalition has ended the brutal dictatorship of Saddam Hussein'.[20] The 2006 *National Security Strategy* justified the Iraq War on grounds that 'a tyrant has been toppled; over 8 million Iraqis voted in the nation's first free and fair election [and] a freely negotiated constitution was passed by a referendum in which almost 10 million Iraqis participated'.[21] The president explained that 'we're working to free the Iraqi people' from 'a regime that persecuted Iraqis'.[22] On another occasion the president reminded his audience that, had the US not acted against the Hussein regime

Iraq's torture chambers would still be filled with victims, terrified and innocent. The killing fields of Iraq where hundreds of thousands of men and women and children vanished into the sands would still be known only to the killers. For all who love freedom and peace, the world without Saddam Hussein's regime is a better and safer place.[23]

Human rights promotion is derived from a pre-existing US identity

Rule two of the hegemonic discourse defines US identity in terms of human rights and freedom. This rule featured prominently in the official narrative provided for the Iraq War. The president, for example, asserted that the US 'is at war with people who hate what we stand for. We love freedom',[24] and again, when he stated that 'America is pursuing a forward strategy of freedom in the Middle East'.[25] The president has asserted that 'America is a nation with a mission, and that mission comes from our most basic beliefs. We have no desire to dominate, no ambitions of empire'.[26] Military personnel serving in Iraq were said by the secretary of state to be 'serving humanity' by 'laying their lives on the line to liberate Iraq from the tyranny of Saddam Hussein'.[27]

According to this account of the Iraq War and its aftermath, Iraqi insurgents are not fighting a foreign army but rather the forces of freedom itself. The president, for example, accounted for the growing insurgency in Iraq following the overthrow of Hussein in terms that '[p]arts of Iraq are still dangerous because freedom has enemies inside of Iraq',[28] and that '[a]s democracy takes hold in Iraq, the enemies of freedom will do all in their power to spread violence and fear'.[29] Thus, Iraqis involved in the insurgency are opposing not US forces but rather freedom and democracy as represented by US forces. US identity was produced not only in repeated assertions that the US was acting to free the Iraqi people, but also in expunging from mention, previous US government support for Saddam Hussein during that period when the dictator was committing the worst of his atrocities, such as the Anfal campaign against the Kurds.[30]

US championing human rights complements broader foreign policy goals of promoting freedom, justice and democracy

The Bush Administrations consistently explained the Iraq War in terms of the third rule of the hegemonic discourse, which holds that freedom, justice and democracy are promoted alongside human rights as constitutive US policy objectives. The March 2003 attack itself was given the name Operation Iraqi Freedom. President Bush stated that the aim of invading Iraq was not only to liberate its people but also to create 'a democratic peace; a peace founded upon the dignity and rights of every man and woman'.[31] Administration officials have articulated US objectives in the war in terms of 'a free Iraq', to 'stop the Iraqi government's tyrannizing of its own population', to 'liberate the Iraqi people from tyranny' and to 'help Iraqis assume responsibility for their own defense and their own future'.[32] In line with asserting the future liberty of Iraqis as a key goal, billions of dollars were earmarked by the administrations for the reconstruction of Iraq. In the year following the overthrow of Hussein, 2600 schools, 240 hospitals and 1200 health clinics were, for example, built with US funding.

All three rules therefore feature prominently in the official narrative provided by the Bush Administration for the war in Iraq. The remainder of this chapter examines the political significance of this prominence from the perspectives of the three explanations described in Chapter 1.

A literal interpretation of the hegemonic discourse

The reflective explanation interprets the prominence ascribed to the hegemonic discourse in the Iraq War as indicating genuine, if not always overriding, foreign policy commitments to principles of human rights and liberty. Kagan and Kristol accounted for the war in part by recourse to Saddam Hussein's 'proven record of aggression and barbarity'.[33] Dombrowski and Payne argued that the Bush Administration respected international human rights norms in the lead up to the Iraq War.[34] Evidence for this assertion was identified in the form of 'the public statements of high-level officials'.[35] Under this assessment, the hegemonic discourse was therefore interpreted as a literal description of the aims of policy-makers. It was also in this sense that Drumbl concluded, 'Operation Iraqi Freedom was more than just a name. It also was a rationale'.[36]

Under the reflective explanation, the US is identified as the guarantor of the fundamental liberty and rights of all people and the last hope for the oppressed when internal politics prevents the UN from authorizing decisive action in defense of human rights. Kagan subsequently framed the deployment of US military power in Iraq in terms of protecting and promoting democracy.[37] Dueck similarly accounted for the Iraq War in terms of promoting democracy in the Middle East.[38] This goal was symbolized in the December 2005 national elections held in Iraq.

A further group of theorists argued the hegemonic discourse reflected a corresponding reality since humanitarian intervention was ethically warranted, indeed required, to put a stop to the well documented suffering inflicted by the Hussein regime on the Iraqi people. Thus, the argument went, for the human rights of long suffering Iraqis to be protected, toppling the Hussein regime was justified on humanitarian grounds. This justification provided retrospective validation of the claims made in the hegemonic discourse. Advancing this argument, Ignatieff for example contended that 'the disagreeable reality for those who believe in human rights is that there are some occasions – and Iraq may be one of them – when war is the only real remedy for regimes that live by terror'.[39] Lichtenberg similarly argued that, irrespective of motive, the Bush Administration was justified in invading Iraq on human rights grounds since it had valid reasons to believe that the humanitarian benefits of intervention outweighed the costs.[40] Hari likewise reasoned that '[t]he only moral factor in this war should be the Iraqi people, and their needs – and the Iraqi people's greatest need is for our help to get rid of one of the worst dictators on earth'.[41]

Advancing the reflective interpretation of the hegemonic discourse, many scholars from the realist camp of international relations concurred that the promotion of human rights constituted the basis of the war. Subsequent disagreement with the perceived promotion of human rights, democracy and freedom in foreign policy led 34 realist scholars to place an advertisement in the *New York Times* opposing the Iraq War on the grounds of the US national interest.[42] Whereas these realist scholars opposed the Iraq War on theoretical and ideological grounds, they joined their liberal and neo-conservative colleagues in interpreting the hegemonic discourse as describing the aims of the conflict.

Rejecting the hegemonic discourse

The rejectionist explanation points to the notable double standards employed by the Bush Administrations in the conduct of the Iraq War to demonstrate the contradictions in a literal interpretation of the hegemonic discourse. Falk, for example, pointed out that the Bush Administrations insisted on the prosecution of Hussein and his regime as war criminals while exempting Coalition Forces from accountability to crimes under international law.[43] Human Rights Watch noted that, following the war, Coalition Forces failed to secure (i) sites containing documented evidence of the human rights abuses committed under Hussein, (ii) sites containing the mass graves of the victims of his regime and (iii) the professional expertise necessary to ensure proper classification of evidence and exhumation of victims.[44] Had the egregious human rights abuses committed under Hussein been a genuine reason for the war, it is unclear why more effort had not been spent providing redress for the families of his victims following the overthrow of his regime.

The allocation of funds by the Bush Administrations likewise contradicted the asserted priority of securing human rights. In the month of February 2002 the UN High Commissioner for Refugees could not raise the $60 million required to provide for the basic needs of 600,000 refugees across the world. In that same month more than $2 billion was spent positioning US troops in the Gulf. When Congress approved $87.5 billion for operations in Iraq and Afghanistan on November 4, 2003, $51 billion was directed to military operations in Iraq and $18.6 billion was earmarked to restoring its oil industry, police, economic and political infrastructure.[45] This compares with the entire US foreign aid budget in 2002 of $10 billion. A focus on human rights cannot explain why resources were disproportionately channeled to military and oil-related activities, or for why Iraq was selected in the first instance for reconstruction in preference to other societies in equal or indeed more desperate need of assistance.

Given that (i) policymakers rarely provide public explanations devoid of political bias and (ii) motives can be neither proved nor disproved, rejectionist theorists hypothesize that the philanthropic ideals stated by administration officials to explain the basis of policies offers little insight into the policymaking process. Telhami reminds us, for example, of the contradiction between the rhetorical support asserted by the Bush Administrations for democracy in the Middle East and the fact that a clear majority of Arab peoples are hostile to US attempts to politically reshape the region.[46] A poll commissioned by the US-led Coalition Provisional Authority (CPA) in May 2004, and leaked the following month, revealed that while only 2 percent of Iraqis perceived coalition troops as liberators, 92 percent saw them as occupiers.[47] On this basis it is at best problematic to account for the Iraq War in terms of a democratic liberation. As the following section details, nowhere are the contradictions between the hegemonic discourse and actual practices clearer than in the mistreatment of Iraqi prisoners held in US-run correction facilities.

Prisoner abuse

Within three months of the 2003 invasion, allegations of prisoner abuse in US-run correction facilities were being reported by sources including Amnesty International and the UN Special Representative for Iraq, Sergio Vieira de Mello.[48] In April and May 2004 a major political crisis broke when hundreds of photos showing explicit acts of the physical and sexual abuse of persons under control (PUC) held in the US-run Abu Ghraib prison were printed in the global media. Senate and House members were shown a further 1800 images and video clips of abuse at the prison portraying forced sexual acts between male inmates, a soldier posing next to a dead prisoner and a video of one male prisoner being repeatedly banged into a cell door until he collapsed.[49] The internal Taguba report into the mistreatment of detainees, subsequently leaked to the public, described the abuse of prisoners held in Abu Ghraib as 'systematic and illegal', 'sadistic', 'blatant' and 'wanton'.[50] Examples of prisoner abuse identified in this leaked report included attaching wires to the fingers, toes and penises of prisoners to simulate electric torture, keeping prisoners naked for days at a time and forcing groups of detainees to perform sex acts while being photographed.[51]

The abuse of Iraqi prisoners was not limited to the Abu Ghraib facility. According to a leaked ICRC report dated February 2004, the mistreatment of Iraqi prisoners featured in the military intelligence sections of Camp Cropper correctional facility, Habbania Camp, the Tikrit holding area, a former mukhabarat office in Basra, as well as sections of Abu Ghraib.[52] Indeed, prisoner abuse had spread not only between US detention facilities but also to Iraqi security units who were torturing suspected insurgents through the use of strangulation, sexual abuse, hanging prisoners by the arms, breaking limbs and using an electric drill for kneecapping prisoners.[53] In November 2005 the bodies of 173 Iraqi detainees were, for example, found with signs of torture and malnourishment at an Interior Ministry basement lockup in Baghdad.[54] The Bush Administration responded to the political crisis surrounding the Abu Ghraib scandal by commissioning a number of official reports and by allocating fault not to the military and civilian leadership but rather to individual soldiers. The following section argues that these two mechanisms did more to obfuscate than to illuminate processes of prisoner abuse in Iraq.

Burying a problem in paperwork

The Abu Ghraib scandal resulted in a total of five hearings from the Senate Armed Services Committee, four hearings from the House Armed Services

Committee, three public hearings from the House Permanent Select Committee on Intelligence, numerous in-house investigations and a plethora of official reports. These reports pointed to a pattern of prisoner abuse that extended beyond isolated cases. When a report chaired by former Secretary of Defense James Schlesinger was published, panel member Tillie Fowler, for example, acknowledged that 'we found a string of failures that go well beyond an isolated cellblock in Iraq' and that 'these failures of leadership helped to set the conditions which allowed for the abusive practice to take place'.[55] The various investigations commissioned to examine the abuse of Iraqi prisoners can, nonetheless, be criticized on grounds of (i) assigned remit and (ii) independence.

First, none of the investigations that are publicly available were specifically tasked with investigating how official policies formulated by the civilian leadership contributed to prisoner abuses.[56] The Schlesinger report was, for example, commissioned to provide advice to the Department of Defense in the light of the mistreatment of prisoners.[57] The Fay-Jones report was charged only with examining the role of military intelligence forces at Abu Ghraib and did not examine the role of officers higher than Lieutenant General or of the civilian leadership.[58] Whilst the Church report was designed to look more holistically at the treatment of detainees, this report was not given the remit to assign responsibility for the abuse. Moreover, only a summary of the Church report has been made publicly available and the full report remains classified.[59]

Second, the Bush Administrations have not seen fit to establish any criminal inquiries into prisoner abuse that are truly independent of the US executive and the Pentagon. In particular, the administrations repeatedly refused to appoint a special prosecutor to investigate whether senior officials authorized torture and coercive interrogation.[60] The various publicly available reports therefore provide thousands of pages of descriptive material while neglecting the central question of how the policies made by the civilian leadership contributed to the abuse of prisoners.

The structure of prisoner abuse

Donald Rumsfeld assumed official responsibility for the abuses at Abu Ghraib.[61] Yet the Secretary of Defense simultaneously joined other administration officials in explaining the abuse in terms of isolated cases to be solved by prosecuting implicated individuals rather than investigating how military and civilian leadership failings contributed to the abuse.[62] There was, therefore, a notable disjuncture between the scale of prisoner abuse acknowledged by administration officials and more systematic accounts of abuse identified by organizations operating in the field. On the basis of visits to numerous detention facilities between March and November 2003, the director of operations for the ICRC, for example, characterized prisoner abuse as 'a broad pattern, not individual acts. There was a pattern and a system'.[63] As this following section demonstrates, five features point to the systematic, rather than individual, causes of prisoner abuse in Iraq, (i) multiple reports of the systematic nature of abuse, (ii) the lack of

effective external accountability facing Coalition Forces in Iraq, (iii) the inadequate provision of training to personnel relating to the proper treatment of prisoners, (iv) allegations that troops received orders to mistreat prisoners and (v) a
culture against reporting prisoner abuse.

Locating the causes of prisoner abuse in military structures rather than isolated incidents, a leaked 2004 ICRC report stated that the 'use of ill treatment
against persons deprived of their liberty went beyond exceptional cases and
might be considered as a practice tolerated' by Coalition Forces.[64] The report
cited 'brutality against protected persons upon capture and initial custody, sometimes causing death or serious injury' and the 'excessive and disproportionate
use of force against persons deprived of their liberty resulting in death or injury
during their period of internment' as the main violations of the rights of
prisoners.[65]

The ICRC reported that those prisoners deemed to have an intelligence value
were subject to 'both physical and psychological coercion, which in some cases
was tantamount to torture'.[66] Specific abuses reportedly employed by Coalition
Forces included tight handcuffing with flex-cuffs for extended periods so as to
cause skin lesions and nerve damage, beating, slapping, punching and kicking,
pressing the face into the ground with boots, using threats against family
members, stripping prisoners naked for days, holding prisoners in solitary confinement, providing insufficient sleep, food or water and forcing prisoners to
remain for long periods in stress positions.[67] The ICRC also reported estimates
from Coalition Force intelligence officers that between 70 and 90 percent of
Iraqi prisoners were not insurgents but had been arrested erroneously.[68]

Eyewitness reports from US troops serving in Iraq support the classification
of prisoner abuse as systematic rather than as isolated incidents. Officers sta-
tioned at Forward Operating Base Mercury,[69] stated that 'torture and other mistreatment of Iraqis in detention was systematic and was known at varying levels
of command'.[70] Officers described to Human Rights Watch how their battalion
'routinely used physical and mental torture as a means of intelligence gathering
and for stress relief'.[71] According to one account provided, soldiers would
'smoke' prisoners, which meant 'to put them in stress positions until they get
muscle fatigue and pass out'.[72] One soldier explained that extrajudicial punishments were an accepted norm of practice since '[i]f we were on patrol and catch
a guy that killed my captain or my buddy last week – man, it is human nature.
So we fucked them up bad ... you gotta understand, this was the norm. Every-
one would just sweep it under the rug'.[73]

The norm of prisoner abuse was facilitated by the lack of effective external
accountability facing Coalition Forces in Iraq. This lack of accountability was
revealed in the wake of the Abu Ghraib scandal when the US Army released a
summary of the circumstances of 27 Iraqis who had died in US custody.[74] This
summary revealed that in many cases no autopsies had been performed on the
deceased. In such cases no details of the cause of death were known, or the
extent to which abuse may have been a contributory factor. The holding of ghost
detainees in Iraq contributed further to this lack of accountability. An internal

Pentagon investigation into the Abu Ghraib scandal conducted by General Paul Kern revealed that up to 100 ghost detainees may have been kept in the prison, held secret even from the ICRC.[75] Supporting this assessment the Taguba investigation noted that the CIA 'routinely' requested military authorities at Abu Ghraib to hold suspects without listing them on the prison rolls.[76] As Chapter 5 detailed, there is no public knowledge or accountability of the conditions under which ghost detainees are held and interrogated.

In 2005, the ACLU used the Freedom of Information Act to obtain over 30,000 pages of official documentation relating to detainee abuse in Iraq. These documents revealed a lack of army accountability for numerous incidents. One document referred to the closing of an investigation into an elderly Iraqi women being sodomized with a stick on the basis of 'sanitized' internal investigations.[77] In another instance, documents revealed that army investigators had found 'probable cause' to believe that three members of Special Forces Group ODA 343 had committed murder and conspiracy and that a commander was an accessory after the fact. However, no action was taken against the commander in this instance and two of the soldiers involved were only given written reprimands.[78] Compounding the absence of external accountability revealed in these documents was the tendency of the US Army authorities to respond to clear cases of abuse through administrative hearings held behind closed doors in preference to criminal prosecutions before courts-martial.[79]

The systematic nature of prisoner abuse is furthermore evidenced in the inadequate training provided to US personnel on the proper treatment of prisoners.[80] Service personnel have reported receiving a lack of specific guidance in how to treat prisoners and were only informed that this should be 'lawful and humane'.[81] Concerned after witnessing what he considered to be the systematic abuse of prisoners, Captain Ian Fishback spent seventeen months contacting his superiors to clarify which specific procedures were humane and lawful and which were inhumane and unlawful. At the end of his considerable endeavors, Captain Fishback had gone through his entire chain of command from his direct commanding officer through to the Judge Advocate General's office and the most comprehensive response he had received was to 'use his judgment'.[82] This evident neglect to provide specific guidance to soldiers created a confusing situation for troops, whereby, the abuse of prisoners was an almost inevitable outcome. According to one soldier, abusive trends 'were accepted' by the authorities.[83] Military leadership, the soldier explained 'failed to provide clear guidance so we just developed it. They wanted intel. As long as no PUCs came up dead it happened'.[84]

Exemplifying the widespread confusion on the permissible treatment of prisoners, Donald Rumsfeld was, himself, unable to state in front of a Senate Armed Services Committee what specific instructions had been issued to the personnel involved in the abuses at Abu Ghraib.[85] After leaving the administration Colin Powell's chief of staff asserted that the abuse of prisoners was a 'concrete example' of 'the president and other top officials in effect giving the green light to soldiers to abuse detainees'.[86] Lawrence Wilkerson stated '[y]ou don't have this kind of pervasive attitude out there unless you've condoned it'.[87]

A number of troops have reported receiving actual instructions to mistreat prisoners. One soldier reported that 'interrogators pressed guards to beat up prisoners'.[88] Private Lynndie England became the face of the Abu Ghraib scandal after being photographed abusing Iraqi prisoners. England reported during her courts-martial on charges of assault and misconduct that she was ordered to perform the abuse. Referring to a photograph in which she was pictured holding an Iraqi prisoner like a dog on a leash, England stated, 'I was instructed by persons in higher ranks to stand there and hold this leash'.[89] Other soldiers charged in connection with the Abu Ghraib scandal have similarly alleged that they were 'told or encouraged to harshly treat prisoners by military intelligence officers, as part of a broader effort to soften the detainees up for interrogation'.[90] As commander of the 800th Military Police Brigade, Brigadier-General Janis Karpinski was in formal charge of the Abu Ghraib prison at the time that the abuse images were photographed. Karpinski claimed that a senior officer advised her that prisoners should be treated 'like dogs'.[91]

A number of orders issued by the military and civilian leadership suggest a tolerance for acts of prisoner mistreatment. On October 12, 2003 Lieutenant General Ricardo Sanchez issued an order authorizing military intelligence to manipulate the 'emotions and weaknesses' of detainees in Abu Ghraib.[92] Documents obtained by the ACLU under the Freedom of Information Act included an FBI e-mail that referred to an Executive Order, signed by the president, authorizing various abusive interrogation techniques including sleep deprivation and use of stress positions.[93] Seymour Hersh reported that Donald Rumsfeld had authorized a loosening of the rules under which information could be obtained from prisoners in Iraq. According to Hersh 'the Pentagon's operation, known inside the intelligence community by several code words, including Copper Green, encouraged physical coercion and sexual humiliation of Iraqi prisoners in an effort to generate more intelligence about the growing insurgency'.[94]

Tolerance of prisoner mistreatment is demonstrated nowhere more clearly than through the experiences faced by some soldiers who tried to report acts that they considered to constitute abuse. Human Rights Watch describe the experience faced by one such soldier who 'was consistently told to keep his mouth shut, turn a blind eye, or consider his career'.[95] Department of Defense documents released under the Freedom of Information Act included a memo from the head of the Defense Intelligence Agency (DIA), Vice Admiral Lowell Jacoby. This memo described how agents from the DIA who reported witnessing detainee abuse in Iraq were threatened, had their car keys confiscated, e-mails monitored and were told 'not to talk to anyone in the US'.[96]

Other documents made public under the Freedom of Information Act included a heavily redacted report written by an FBI agent who had witnessed 'numerous physical abuse incidents of Iraqi civilian detainees' including 'strangulation', 'beatings' and 'placement of lit cigarettes into the detainees ear openings'.[97] The document alluded to official cover-ups of the abuse by alleging that '[redacted] was providing this account to the FBI based on his knowledge that [redacted] were engaged in a cover-up of these abuses'.[98] In another incident, a soldier witnessing physical assaults by US troops on detainees held at Camp Red, Baghdad, filed a sworn statement that he had witnessed 'what I think were war crimes'.[99] The soldier reports that his chain of command 'did nothing to stop these war crimes, and allowed them to happen'.[100] In this case the internal army investigation was closed due to insufficient evidence.[101] Between September 2003 and September 2005 the US army had opened more than 400 inquiries into the abuse of prisoners at US detention facilities in Iraq and had punished 230 enlisted soldiers and officers.[102] The evidence reviewed above suggests that these cases are visible excesses of a more systematic pattern of tolerating prisoner abuse to obtain intelligence on a growing insurgency.

Blood for oil

The rejectionist explanation can point to the many changing reasons provided by administration officials to hypothesize a disjuncture between the expressed and actual causes of the Iraq War. A range of actual reasons for the Iraq War have subsequently been suggested, ranging from an enhanced US military presence in the Middle East to gaining political leverage over Saudi Arabia to protecting Israel through the removal of a hostile Ba'athist regime.[103] Perhaps the most common charge is that the language of freedom and human rights has acted as a cover for a war fought to implant a pro-Western regime in a state that contains 11 percent of known global oil reserves. Former South African President Nelson Mandela stated in January 2003 that '[a]ll that Mr Bush wants is Iraqi oil'.[104] Zunes claims that Washington views human rights in the Middle East in the context of maintaining leverage over Japanese and European markets heavily dependent upon imports of Middle Eastern oil.[105] Harvey meanwhile accounts for the war in terms of the US asserting control over the oil supplies of the greater Middle East as a means to control possible future economic and military competition from China.[106]

Supporting the hypothesis that human rights acted as a cover for the pursuit of an imperialist war, the president reportedly announced at a February 2003 National Security Council briefing that American corporations would help run the postwar oil sector under 'an Iraqi face'.[107] At the outset of the war on March 19, 2003, President Bush was meeting with his top advisers in the Roosevelt room. The main topic discussed at this meeting was not human rights, democracy nor freedom in Iraq, it was 'the international flow of oil' and in particular whether the president should use the strategic petroleum reserve.[108] Official statements that the Iraq War was unrelated to oil concerns also appear at odds with presidential announcements that 'America is addicted to oil' and the specific identification of US 'dependence' on Middle Eastern oil.[109]

There exist a plethora of ties between Bush Administration officials and the petrochemical corporations that have seen a rise in their profits in the wake of Iraq related contracts. These ties are exemplified in the Halliburton corporation that made political donations of $708,770 between 1999 and 2002, 95 percent of which went to the Republican party or Republican candidates.[110] Dick Cheney was CEO of Halliburton for five years before joining the Bush Administration.

When Cheney left in 2000 he reportedly received $33 million from the corporation.[111] On May 31, 2004 a leaked Pentagon memo revealed that the award of a multibillion-dollar contract to Halliburton had been 'coordinated' with the Vice Presidents office.[112]

There are numerous reports of Halliburton overcharging the government on Iraq-related contracts. The Pentagon launched one inquiry into claims that Halliburton had overcharged the US taxpayer by as much as $120 million.[113] Federal prosecutors opened a criminal probe following a Defense Contract Audit Agency finding that Halliburton had overcharged the government by $61 million for fuel deliveries from Kuwait to Iraq.[114] In May 2004, 12 Halliburton truck drivers reported that they were ordered to drive empty trucks around the desert and bill the Pentagon for the unnecessary work.[115] In June 2004, two former Halliburton employees, turned whistleblowers, alleged witnessing a range of instances of overcharging including the scrapping of an $80,000 truck because of a flat tyre, $45 for a case of soda and the use by corporate officials of five star hotels in Kuwait.[116] On January 23, 2004 Halliburton acknowledged that some employees were involved in a $6.3 million kickback deal with a Kuwaiti company.[117] The revelation did nothing to stop the government from awarding a $1.2 billion contract to Halliburton that same month.[118] The Democrat Senator for New Jersey summarized that '[t]he entire Halliburton affair represents the worst in government contracts with private companies: influence peddling, kickbacks, overcharging and no-bid deals'.[119]

On March 25, 2003 the US Army Corps of Engineers awarded Halliburton subsidiary Kellogg, Brown and Root (KBR) a contract to fight oil well fires and to reconstruct Iraqi oil fields.[120] The contract was open-ended, had no specified time or dollar limit and was awarded without any bidding process.[121] The 2003 third quarter revenues of KBR were up 80 percent to $2.3 billion, $900 million of which was income from Iraq-related contracts. KBR profits in the same quarter grew fourfold to $49 million, $34 million of which came from Iraqi contracts.[122] When seen in conjunction with the mistreatment of Iraqi prisoners detailed above, this evidence supports the argument that a discourse of human rights could have been utilized as a cover for a war fought to control oil supplies, support Israel, implant a pro-US regime in Iraq, promote US influence in the Middle East and as a welfare state for corporate allies. However, since these claims rely on inferring intent to policymakers, they cannot be proved or disproved beyond noting the consistencies detailed above. According to the third theoretical perspective, the rejectionist account joins that of the reflective explanation as employing an unduly restrictive view of the function of language and in particular neglecting how discourse can itself produce reality. The third section of the chapter therefore moves on to detail the productive explanation of the hegemonic discourse.

Producing reality

In November 2005 Senator McCain identified that '[w]e've got two wars going on: one a military one in Iraq, and then we've got a war for public opinion, for the hearts and minds of all the people in the world'.[123] The productive explanation accounts for the hegemonic discourse as a cue to how the audience should interpret events in Iraq. Thus conceptualized, the discourse of policymakers becomes itself a component aspect of the war by governing how the audience understands events. In this sense of governing understanding the discourse produces reality. The following section examines this productive application of discourse by analyzing how the Bush Administrations (i) sanitized the war effort, (ii) disseminated the desired messages from the war and (iii) politicized the threat posed by Saddam Hussein in the lead up to March 2003.

Sanitizing war

The following four features of the official narrative have worked to sanitize understandings of the Iraq War, (i) producing a simplified dichotomy, (ii) stating intent to avoid civilian casualties while opting not to record authoritative numbers of non-combatant casualties in occupied Iraq, (iii) unilaterally allocating identities and (iv) repackaging prisoner abuse in terms of the hegemonic mythology.

First, administration officials produced a simplistic dichotomy between an era of tyranny under Saddam Hussein and a liberated post-2003 Iraq. In line with the hegemonic mythology the US and its allies were identified as the agents responsible for bringing this freedom to Iraq. Addressing US military personnel in August 2003 the president declared that '[b]efore you went in, Iraqis were an oppressed people … Today, the Iraqis are liberated people'.[124] The president continued to explain that 'thanks to our military, Iraqi citizens do not have to fear a secret policy, arbitrary arrests or loved ones lost forever, and mass graves'.[125] On another occasion the president explained that the US military were 'bringing hope to the oppressed'.[126] The president has also defended the war by stating 'Iraqi men and women are no longer carried to torture chambers and rape rooms, and dumped in mass graves … Iraq is a free nation'.[127] This narrative of freedom replacing fear was asserted in the face of almost daily bombings and endemic violence in Iraq following the 2003 war. Indeed, in the three years following the invasion, much debate revolved around whether or not the scale of deaths, factional fighting, suicide attacks and revenge killings could be described as a civil war.

The narrative contrasting an oppressed Iraq under Saddam Hussein with a society liberated by the US military was also contradicted in assessments of post-war civil society made by the USAID. A conflict assessment attached to a 2006 invitation for contractors to bid on a project rehabilitating Iraqi cities described an Iraq in 'social breakdown' where criminals have 'almost free rein' and where competing religious, ethnic, criminal and tribal groups fight for power.[128] The conflict assessment explained that 'social liberties have been curtailed dramatically by roving bands of self-appointed religious-moral police'.[129] The top US commander in the Middle East mirrored this assessment of the security situation in Iraq when announcing to a Senate Committee in August 2006 that 'the sectarian violence is probably as bad as I have seen it'.[130] By highlighting the evils of the Hussein regime and playing down the endemic violence existing in post-2003 Iraq, the administration disseminated a sanitized understanding of events.

Second, the Iraq War was sanitized through prominent assertions of the intent to avoid civilian casualties. Creating the impression of a surgical military operation, precision bombings and laser guided missile strikes conducted by the US military were shown by Central Command to journalists on plasma televisions in an auditorium created by a Hollywood designer at a reported cost of $200,000.[131] Asserting the intent to avoid civilian casualties removed accountability for subsequent civilian deaths since these could be made politically invisible through being categorized as unfortunate errors. To legislate this lack of accountability, the Coalition Provisional Authority passed regulations exempting private security contractors that killed Iraqis from legal sanction. One human rights lawyer observed a year after the announced end to hostilities that the 30,000 employees of private security contractors operating in Iraq could effectively 'kill with impunity' because of the absence of legal regulations to hold them to account.[132]

Following the killing and mutilation of four American security personnel on March 31, 2004, a major US operation began in the city of Fallujah resulting in the deaths of an estimated 600 civilians.[133] The US attack on Fallujah included the use of white phosphorous which is fat soluble and capable of burning humans down to the bone. Until November 2005, the State Department maintained that shells containing white phosphorous had been used 'very sparingly in Fallujah, for illumination purposes'.[134] The department was forced to change this position following publication of a report in *Field Artillery*, which revealed that white phosphorous rounds had been used to flush out enemy fighters.[135] The stated intent to avoid civilian casualties appears inconsistent both with exempting contracted security personnel from independent legal sanction and with the use of a chemical weapon in Fallujah.

The intent to avoid civilian casualties faced little external scrutiny due, in part, to the decision of the occupying powers not to compile authoritative figures for the numbers of civilians killed and injured in occupied Iraq.[136] Vice Chairman of the Joint Chiefs, Marine General Pete Pace, reportedly stated in a meeting with Secretary Rumsfeld in March 2003 that, having learnt from the Vietnam experience, 'not once' would a number of predicted or actual civilian casualties in the Iraq War be reported.[137] A letter sent to Prime Minister Blair by 40 ambassadors, high commissioners and governors in April 2004 described as 'a disgrace' the fact that Coalition Forces were not keeping accurate figures of the numbers of Iraqis killed.[138]

The decision not to compile statistics on civilian casualties appeared to not only contradict the stated intent to avoid such casualties but also to violate the duty of occupying powers to record civilian losses stipulated in the Geneva Convention. The decision was however in accordance with the production of reality in terms of the hegemonic mythology since, in the absence of authoritative figures, Iraqi civilian losses were made politically invisible. Reports estimating numbers of civilians killed in Iraq that contradict the predetermined conclusions asserted in the hegemonic mythology can be subsequently disregarded. One such report, published in the medical journal the *Lancet*, found that the expressed intent to avoid civilian deaths had done little to actually prevent subsequent casualties since violence had replaced heart attacks, strokes and chronic illness as the main cause of death in postwar Iraq.[139] One of the contributors to the report commented in October 2004 that 'we think that about 100,000 excess deaths or more have happened since the 2003 invasion of Iraq. Violence accounted for most of the excess deaths and air strikes from Coalition Forces accounted for most violent deaths'.[140] This research was updated in July 2006 when it was estimated that in excess of 600,000 violent deaths had occurred in Iraq since the 2003 war.[141]

Third, the war effort was sanitized by the capacity of Coalition Forces to unilaterally designate identities. The Pentagon enjoyed broad discretion to authorize deaths by labeling those killed in bombing raids as 'militants', even applying the term to children who were killed in the village of Mukaradeeb in May 2004.[142]

The fourth mechanism adopted by the Bush Administration to sanitize the Iraq War was to repackage prisoner abuse in terms of the hegemonic mythology. In testimony before the Senate Armed Services Committee, Donald Rumsfeld announced

> to those Iraqis who were mistreated by members of the US armed forces, I offer my deepest apology. It was inconsistent with the values of our nation. It was inconsistent with the teachings of the military, to the men and women of the armed forces. And it was certainly fundamentally un-American.[143]

This apology restates the second hegemonic rule by categorizing the prisoner abuse as un-American. The abuse of prisoners is regretted not on the basis of violating humanitarian laws or the Geneva Conventions but rather through reference to American values and US military teachings. This response to the Abu Ghraib scandal thereby reasserted US identity in terms of the hegemonic mythology. The secretary of defense equated the 'teachings of the military' with American values in binary opposition to the mistreatment of prisoners.[144] Thus, conceptualized, the photos from Abu Ghraib are not principally images of US military personnel abusing prisoners but are instead redefined in terms of individuals abusing American values and the teachings of the US military. The secretary of defense continued to explain that by admitting that failures had occurred in Abu Ghraib the US would 'light the world as surely as the great ideas and beliefs that made this nation a beacon of hope and liberty for all who strive to be free'.[145] Thus, the systemic nature of prisoner abuse was denied and US identity was instead established as a beacon for freedom. In testimony before the Senate Armed Services Committee, Acting Secretary of the Army Les Brownlee articulated the underlying message that the abuse 'stand[s] in sharp contrast to the values of our Army and the nation it serves'.[146]

President Bush described the Abu Ghraib scandal on Al Arabiya television as a 'serious matter' on the basis that 'it's a matter that reflects badly on my country'.[147] The president went on to reassert the hegemonic identity of the US by assuring his audience that the mistreatment of prisoners 'does not represent the America that I know' and defended the 'goodness and character of the United States armed forces'.[148] A subsequent presidential announcement that Abu Ghraib would be completely rebuilt reinforced the impression that prisoner abuse was limited to this one facility and could be addressed by demolishing bricks. Administration officials therefore reinterpreted the abuse of prisoners to assert the predetermined conclusions defined as US commitment to human rights and freedom in Iraq. As detailed above, this contingent interpretation of events was employed in combination with other discursive techniques to produce a sanitized reality of the Iraq War in terms of the hegemonic discourse.

Disseminating the message

According to the productive explanation, knowledge of reality is a function of how events are assigned meaning through interpretation.[149] Six mechanisms can be subsequently identified as promoting the hegemonic discourse in public understandings of the Iraq War, (i) military power, (ii) legislation, (iii) establishing puppet media stations, (iv) allocating funds, (v) embedding reporters and (vi) producing images.

First, in the March 2003 attack on Iraq, the US military bombed radio and television transmitters, telephone exchanges and media stations critical of the US-led invasion.[150] A US missile destroyed the Baghdad office of al Jazeera. Revealing a political dimension to this campaign of bombing media targets, former UK cabinet official David Keogh was charged with violating the British Official Secrets Act for divulging the contents of a conversation held in April 2004 between President Bush and Tony Blair. In this conversation the president was reported to have expressed an interest in bombing the Qatar headquarters of al-Jazeera.[151] Targeting civilian media stations critical of US foreign policy raises serious questions over war crimes.

Second, legislation threatened to control the media message through the November 2004 decision of the Iraqi Media Commission to draft laws prohibiting journalists operating in Iraq from attaching patriotic descriptions to insurgents when reporting fighting. The proposed legislation would have required journalists to 'set aside space in your news coverage to make the position of the Iraqi government, which expresses the aspirations of most Iraqis, clear'.[152]

Third, US-established television stations repeatedly broadcast the hegemonic discourse to Iraqis. On April 10, 2003 the station, Towards Freedom, started broadcasting from a US C130 Hercules transport plane known as 'Commando Solo' flying over central Iraq.[153] The station began its broadcasts with messages from President Bush and Prime Minister Blair to the Iraqi people. President Bush used the opportunity to stress the message that Iraq was being liberated rather than conquered, announcing

[i]n the new era that is coming to Iraq, your country will no longer be held captive to the will of a cruel dictator.... You deserve better than tyranny and corruption and torture chambers. You deserve to live as a free people. And I assure every citizen of Iraq: your nation will soon be free.[154]

Towards Freedom celebrated this newfound freedom by broadcasting the evening bulletins of ABC, NBC and CBS dubbed into Arabic.[155] With a purpose described by the State Department of 'increasing access to unbiased news' and 'promoting understanding of the United States' the radio station Radio Sawa was established to broadcast in Arabic to the Middle East.[156] In February 2004 the president announced that al-Hurra, a new US-funded news, movie and entertainment television network would begin broadcasting in the Middle East. The president explained the purpose of the network as informing 'people in the Middle East the truth about the values and the policies of the United States'.[157]

Fourth, the hegemonic discourse was disseminated by allocating US funding to media outlets in Iraq that, according to the State Department, 'reported news in a fair and unbiased fashion'.[158] Clarifying the more precise meanings of fairness and unbiased in this context, one contracted public relations company paid Iraqi newspapers to print articles written by US soldiers 'to exercise influence in Iraqi communities on behalf of clients, including the military'.[159] Two former employees of the company reported that the Lincoln Group was awarded contracts worth tens of millions of dollars to fund the production of radio and television adverts, web sites and posters and to place opinion articles in Iraqi publications.[160] Illustrating the militarization of news reporting, the Pentagon awarded contracts for supplying Iraqi media outlets to a defense contractor, the Scientific Applications International Corporation.[161]

Fifth, media coverage of events in Iraq was influenced by the practice of embedding reporters. Embedded reporters live, talk and socialize with front line troops. The tendency of embedded journalists to empathize and report from the perspective of Coalition Force troops was illustrated in reports that some even took up arms and joined battles during the initial March 2003 war.[162]

Finally, the desired media message was disseminated by censoring imagery of the conflict in Iraq. Media relations were carefully coordinated to produce the image of a sanitized and humanitarian war. Based in the Pentagon with operations in Fort Meade, the Joint Combat Camera Program collated a daily total of 600–800 photos and 25–50 video clips showing the Iraqi frontline from the US military perspective.[163] Images emphasizing humanitarian actions and footage of the US military being welcomed by Iraqis were disseminated to the media and placed on internet sites which received 750,000 hits from the public per day.[164] Footage of hostile civilians, bombed out neighborhoods and civilian casualties were omitted. In an attempt to control the dissemination of images, the Pentagon initially attempted to ban photos taken by Tami Silico of returning flag-decked coffins from Iraq that vividly portrayed the negative costs of the conflict. The official explanation provided for this censorship was to protect the families of the dead. However, when one mother of a soldier killed in Iraq tried to meet the returning body of her 24-year-old son at the airport she was told 'absolutely not' by the military who 'don't want photographed scenes of distraught parents crying and yelling'.[165]

The events surrounding the capture, treatment and rescue of Private Jessica Lynch of 507th Maintenance Company exemplify how reality can be produced to validate predetermined messages. Private Lynch was captured on March 23, 2003 by Iraqi forces near Nassiriya. Journalists in Doha were summoned from their beds at 03:30 on April 2 for an urgent US Central Command presentation on the successful rescue of Lynch. At this presentation it was announced that Lynch had heroically resisted capture, having emptied her weapon at her attackers until the last minute.[166] Air Force Major-General Gene Renuart reported that elite units from the Army Rangers, Navy Seals and Marine Commandos facilitated the rescue by persuading an Iraqi doctor to lead them to Lynch.[167] It was revealed that the order to launch the rescue came personally from the overall commander of US troops in Iraq, General Tommy Franks, after he had briefed both the president and the secretary of defense about this urgent and daring mission.[168] The military operation to release Lynch involved a decoy attack launched by heavily armored troops near a bridge over the River Euphrates at Nassiriya. The rescue itself was captured on a night vision video that depicted heavily armed commandos in a Black Hawk helicopter firing guns in a combat operation.

Brigadier General Vincent Brooks explained the operation as a daring assault to rescue a captured US soldier from danger, when US forces had come under fire but had succeeded in their mission nonetheless.[169] Brooks stated that the hospital from which Lynch was rescued was being used as a military command post and that 'some brave souls put their lives on the line to make this happen'.[170] The stars and stripes was draped over the stretcher carrying Lynch out of the hospital reinforcing the image of a successful patriotic victory and 'America Loves Jessica Lynch' fridge magnets went on sale back home for $5.[171]

Eyewitness accounts provide a very different version of events from those presented in the military briefing. Lynch reported that her M16 rifle had clogged with sand, preventing her from firing a single shot in the initial March 23 firefight. In an interview conducted in November 2003, Lynch was asked whether the military's depiction of events had troubled her; to which the private replied '[y]eah, it's wrong ... I did not shoot, not a round, nothing. I went down praying to my knees. And that's the last I remember'.[172] According to another eyewitness, the information on the location of Private Lynch was not elicited at the initiative of US special forces as announced in the military briefing but was instead provided by a 32-year-old Iraqi lawyer who reported seeing Private Lynch while visiting his wife who worked at the hospital as a nurse.[173] In terms of her subsequent treatment in the Nassiriyan hospital Lynch has nothing but praise for the doctors that treated her, reporting that '[f]rom the time I woke up in that hospital, no one beat me, no one slapped me, no one, nothing. I'm so thankful for those people because that's why I'm alive today'.[174] In line with this account of events, doctors say they provided the best possible treatment to

Lynch, assigning to her the only specialist bed in the hospital and one of only two nurses on the floor.[175] Lynch was given three bottles of blood, two of which came from the medical staff in the hospital because there was no other source.

The operation to rescue Private Lynch appeared to be itself unnecessary for two reasons. First, two days before the rescue, a doctor at the hospital reported having arranged to deliver Lynch to the US military in an ambulance, but when this ambulance approached a checkpoint, US troops opened fire on the vehicle, forcing it to turn around.[176] Second, the rescue was not required since hostile armed forces had fled from the hospital the day before the rescue took place and this evacuation had been reported to the US military by both doctors and locals.[177] According to eyewitness reports, the only lives on the line during the rescue operation were those of the Iraqi doctors and other patients in the hospital who faced guns pointed at their heads. Dr Khudair al-Hazbar, deputy director of the hospital, reported that hospital patients were 'terrified' by the explosions and shots fired by the US military adding '[t]he Americans knew the Iraqi military had gone, so why they didn't come for her quietly, I don't know'.[178] Another doctor at the hospital, Dr Anman Uday reported that US forces created the spectacle of a daring rescue operation by restraining doctors and patients. Uday reports 'it was like a Hollywood film. They cried, "Go, go, go" with guns and blanks and the sound of explosions. They made a show – an action movie like Sylvester Stallone or Jackie Chan, with jumping and shouting, breaking down doors'.[179]

The US Army video of the contested events surrounding the rescue was heavily edited and the Pentagon has subsequently declined to make the full version public.[180] The capacity to produce a contingent and politicized account of events was subsequently evidenced in the plethora of headlines appearing around the world consisting of either 'Saving Private Ryan' or 'Saving Private Lynch' following the initial military briefing. *Time* noted that the operation 'buoyed a nation wondering what had happened to the short, neat liberation of Iraq'.[181] Writing in the *Washington Times*, Oliver North stressed the 'daring, drama and heroism' of the operation and that this proved that the Iraq War was 'a very successful military campaign, planned by talented senior officers and prosecuted by the finest fighting force the world has ever seen'.[182] Thus, history can be written to validate predetermined conclusions as detailed above.

The threat from Iraq

The main rationale for the 2003 war was arguably predicated not upon liberation but instead upon the threat posed by Iraqi WMD to international security. This following section details how this rationale discursively produced, rather than described, reality. A leaked memo from the British government dated eight months prior to the outbreak of the war revealed that in Washington '[m]ilitary action was now seen as inevitable. Bush wanted to remove Saddam, through military action, justified by the conjunction of terrorism and WMD'.[183] The memo continued by explaining 'the intelligence and facts were being fixed around the policy' of regime change in Iraq.[184] This following section supports the assessment of events by detailing how the threat that Iraq was said to pose was a function of predetermined beliefs in the Bush Administration rather than of erroneous intelligence. The section first reviews how administration officials highlighted the risks posed by Iraqi WMD. Second, the disjuncture of this narrative from the findings of weapons inspectors and publicly available intelligence assessments will be examined. Third, the section analyzes evidence of overt efforts made by administration officials to elicit and politicize the intelligence to justify the predetermined conclusion of the threat posed by Iraq.

Producing the risk from Saddam Hussein

Since they rely on assessments of future actions, perceptions of risks are matters of inference rather than of fact. Prior to March 2003, Bush Administration officials choose to emphasize the risks to international security posed by Iraq by making categorical statements on its WMD program and by ascribing future intents to the Hussein regime. In October 2002, President Bush stated that Iraq had a 'massive stockpile of biological weapons that has never been accounted for and is capable of killing millions'.[185] Prior to the war, Condoleezza Rice urged against waiting too long for conclusive proof of Hussein's WMD capabilities by raising the specter of Hussein launching a pre-emptive nuclear strike. The then national security advisor declared '[w]e don't want the smoking gun to be a mushroom cloud'.[186] On the eve of war in March 2003 Vice President Cheney likewise raised the prospect of a nuclear armed Iraq by stating that 'we believe that he [Saddam Hussein] has in fact reconstituted nuclear weapons'.[187] Officials emphasized the threat posed by these supposed WMD by ascribing aggressive intent to the Iraqi regime and alluding to links between Hussein and al Qaeda.[188] On August 26, 2002, Dick Cheney, for example, inferred threatening intent to Iraq by claiming there was 'no doubt' that Hussein was amassing WMD 'to use against our friends, against our allies and against us'.[189]

Contradictory intelligence

Unambiguous statements from administration officials identifying both WMD capability and aggressive intent in the Hussein regime were not consistently reflected in intelligence reports. While the CIA had concluded prior to the war that Iraq had WMD, the agency considered that these would only pose a threat to the US in the event of an invasion of Iraq. An October 2002 letter to Congress from CIA director George Tenet, for example, concluded that the likelihood of WMD use by Hussein would rise from 'low' to 'pretty high' in the event of a war.[190]

Other intelligence reports questioned the assumption that Hussein possessed any WMD in 2003. The Iraq Survey Group charged with detailing Hussein's WMD program reported to Congress on October 2, 2003 that there was no evidence that Iraq had reconstituted its chemical and nuclear weapons programs and that the only potential biological weapon had been the discovery of a single vial of botulinum toxin, which is also used in cosmetic surgery.[191] The following March, the head of the Iraq Survey Group, David Kay, called on the Bush Administration to 'come clean with the American people' and admit that it had been wrong about the existence of WMD in Iraq.[192] Likewise, an October 2004 report by Charles Duelfer found that 'Hussein posed a diminishing threat at the time the United States invaded and did not possess or have concrete plans to develop, nuclear, chemical or biological weapons'.[193]

Intelligence reports prior to the 2003 war were incomplete and subsequently did little to prove a definitive Iraqi WMD capability. Reporting to the United Nations Security Council on February 14, 2003, Hans Blix, for example, announced that his team had found no WMD in Iraq. On February 16, 2003, French President Jacques Chirac stated that Saddam Hussein posed no threat to the world and that war against Iraq would create a terrorist backlash.[194] David Kay claimed that President Bush and Prime Minister Blair 'should have been able to tell before the war that the evidence did not exist for drawing the conclusion that Iraq presented a clear, present and imminent threat on the basis of existing weapons of mass destruction'.[195] Accounting for the 2003 war, in terms of erroneous intelligence that left a skeptical administration with no choice but to launch a pre-emptive strike against Iraq, therefore, produces a highly dubious rendition of history.

Politicizing the intelligence

The perceived threat from Iraq was produced not solely by erroneous intelligence reports, but originated from within the Bush Administration itself. Former Treasury Secretary, Paul O'Neill described the Bush Administration as determined to oust Hussein from the beginning of the presidency.[196] According to O'Neill, as early as January 2001, NSC meetings were 'all about finding a way to do it' and the subject was 'Topic A' with the circulation of documents titled 'Post-Saddam Iraq'.[197] The Bush Administration subsequently applied three techniques to politicize the intelligence over Iraqi WMD, (i) ascribing threatening intent to Saddam Hussein, (ii) exerting pressure on analysts to find evidence of the threat posed by Hussein and (iii) exaggerating the intelligence against Hussein to support the argument for war. First, the administration ascribed intent to Hussein to provide retrospective justification of the decision to go to war. After the Duelfer report announced that Hussein possessed no WMD the president immediately insisted that Hussein had 'the intent of restarting his weapons program'.[198] Thus, the president inferred intent in line with the predetermined conclusion that Iraq posed a threat.

Second, intelligence analysts have reported coming under political pressure to provide evidence supporting the theory that Iraq posed a threat to the US and its allies. Cheney made a number of trips to the CIA prior to the war after which some analysts at the agency declared that they had 'felt pressed to find links between Iraq and al Qaeda to suit the administration'.[199] Counter terrorism coordinator Richard Clarke reported that the president had asked him three times to 'look into' whether Iraq had been involved in the 9/11 attacks or whether Hussein was 'linked in any way'.[200] Clark subsequently reported that the request was made 'in a very intimidating way, I mean, that we should come back with that answer'.[201] Hans Blix reported that administration officials had 'leaned on' UN weapons inspectors in order to extract more damning reports of Iraqi WMD prior to March 2003.[202] David Kay similarly reported that 'analysts were facing pressures to support the belief that Saddam had Weapons of Mass Destruction'.[203] Rather than the administration being misled into war by erroneous intelligence, these reports suggest the administration was itself exerting influence to establish intelligence that would justify the invasion of Iraq.

Third, as Hans Blix explained, administration officials 'exaggerat[ed] the risks they saw in order to get the political support for the war they would not otherwise have had'.[204] Blix summarized as 'spin and hype' the case presented by the Bush Administration for the war on Iraq.[205] The head of the UN weapons inspection team in Iraq compared the use of intelligence on Iraqi WMD by the Bush Administration to people in Europe in the Middle Ages who were convinced that witches existed and so found them when they looked for them.[206] Administration insiders have provided similar evidence testifying to the politicizing of prewar intelligence. Colonel Lawrence Wilkerson, for example, asserted that prewar intelligence had been 'spun', 'politicized' and 'cherry picked' by the White House and the Pentagon to justify the predetermined conclusions.[207]

Exemplifying exaggerated use of the intelligence, Cheney described as 'conclusive evidence' of Iraqi WMD programs the existence of two flatbed trailers that the vice president claimed had been used as biological weapons laboratories. David Kay in contrast reported that these trailers had most likely been used to produce hydrogen or rocket fuel rather than biological weapons.[208] In another instance, the Office of Special Plans (OSP), based in the Defense Department, disseminated reports with dubious credibility originating from Iraqi defectors. These reports included such allegations as Saddam Hussein hiding biological and chemical WMD under hospital beds.[209] Much of the evidence supplied by the OSP was later found to have been exaggerated or otherwise erroneous.[210]

Paul Wolfowitz reportedly acknowledged that the WMD justification for war was 'settled upon' by the administration 'for bureaucratic reasons'.[211] Likewise, a leaked 2002 memo authored by the British government suggested that WMD intelligence was offered more as pretext rather than a genuine reason for war. This memo categorized the case for military action against Hussein as 'thin'.[212] The memo acknowledged that 'Saddam was not threatening his neighbours and his WMD capability was less than that of Libya, North Korea or Iran'.[213] A brief comparison between Iraq and North Korea indeed demonstrates why Iraqi WMD did not pose a unique threat to the US. Under the dictatorship of Kim Jong Il, North Korea had a more advanced nuclear, biological and chemical weapons program than Iraq and was moreover exporting this technology as its main source of foreign currency earnings.[214] As Colin Powell addressed the UN

General Assembly on February 5, 2003 on the threat posed by Iraqi WMD, North Korea announced that it was restarting the facilities that lay at the center of its nuclear weapons program.[215] Ten days before the start of the Iraq War, North Korea declared a maritime exclusion zone in the Sea of Japan to undertake nuclear weapons tests. By the time that North Korea test fired short-, medium- and long-range missiles on July 4, 2006, the state was thought to have enriched sufficient weapons grade material for between four and ten nuclear warheads. Accounting for the Iraq War in terms of an administration misled by faulty intelligence is not only contradicted by the evidence reviewed above, it also overlooks how the intelligence was politicized in legitimizing that war.

Conclusion

This chapter has analyzed the political function of the hegemonic discourse in the narrative of the Iraq War asserted by the Bush Administrations. This case study analysis has resulted in three findings, each of which has been explained in a separate section of this chapter. The first section demonstrated how the constitutive rules of the hegemonic mythology comprised the ethical framework through which Bush Administration officials articulated the case for war.

The second section demonstrated the inconsistencies and contradictions of interpreting the hegemonic discourse as describing a corresponding reality in the Iraq War. This section found an evident disjuncture between human rights as an asserted rationale for the war and the systematic mistreatment of Iraqi prisoners. Interpreting the hegemonic discourse as a literal explanation of the Iraq War also failed to explain why Iraq was targeted for intervention in the first instance rather than, for example, the Darfur area of Sudan, whose population continued to suffer ongoing acts of genocide throughout the period 2001–06.[216] The rejectionist account subsequently dismissed the political significance of the official narrative as little more than rhetorical cover for the genuine reasons of the war. Rejectionist theorists have subsequently hypothesized these actual reasons in terms of the pursuit of perceived self-interest, geopolitics, securing the control of oil supplies or protecting the economic interests of corporate allies.

The third section of the chapter argued that both the reflective and rejectionist explanations of the hegemonic discourse employed an unduly restrictive view of language. Under the productive explanation, the significance of the official narrative of the Iraq War asserted by the Bush Administrations was not restricted to the extent to which it accurately described corresponding events. Instead, the hegemonic discourse was found to be significant for producing a rationale, meaning and purpose for foreign policy in the minds of the audience who conflate its mythology with an unproblematic account of reality. The section detailed how a contingent and sanitized version of the Iraq War was produced and disseminated in line with the hegemonic mythology.

The third section of the chapter also analyzed how the WMD rationale expressed by the administration produced a politicized understanding of the causes of the Iraq War. The efficacy of discourse as a means of reifying mythologies is directly proportionate to the extent to which the audience conflates the account provided with an unproblematic account of reality. In this context, a study by the Program on International Policy Attitudes found that, in summer 2003, 22 percent of Americans questioned thought that the US had found Iraqi WMD following the war, while 20 percent of those questioned thought that Iraq had actually deployed biological or chemical weapons in the 2003 war.[217] These beliefs that had attained the status of truth in the minds of the respondents were consistent with the identity of Hussein's Iraq promoted by Bush Administration officials as a ruthless state with a threatening WMD capacity.

According to the productive explanation, the principal battleground in the Iraq War was not military capabilities, economic strength or reliable intelligence. Instead, the principal battleground resided in how events were interpreted and understood, since it was this fundamentally ideological understanding that determined levels of popular support for different ideas and for the political organizations that represented those ideas. Depending upon the ideological perspective advanced, the Iraq War could be categorized either as an act of international aggression or as a necessary act of preventive self-defense; as a legal conflict, sanctioned by a number of Security Council resolutions working in combination, or as an illegal war; as an act of imperialism or as an act of humanitarian intervention; as an act of geopolitics or as an act of freedom and justice.

The hegemonic discourse is crucial to understanding the Iraq War not because of its capacity to describe reality but rather because of its capacity to produce an interpretation of inherently contestable events in the minds of the audience. This overtly political function of the official narrative is all the more significant since the stated intent of policymakers cannot be disproved. Underlying messages can be thus applied as a technique of governance to claim legitimacy in a range of circumstances while any criticism of the stated aims can be dismissed as undue cynicism. Indeed, the chapter detailed how the official response to the revelation of prisoner abuses in Abu Ghraib reinterpreted the scandal to illustrate the commitment of the US to freedom and human rights in Iraq. The hegemonic discourse was, therefore, more than a claim by the Bush Administrations to legitimacy in invading Iraq, the discourse was itself engaged in the production of that legitimacy.

Conclusion

Human rights have been employed in this research as an analytic instrument against which foreign policy decisions can be measured. The analytic utility of human rights has been derived from the necessary, rather than sufficient, conditions of the concept. The introduction explained how coherent claims to promote human rights, irrespective of which specific rights are advocated, are compelled to respect the principles of universal and impartial application. Asserting that only some people possess human rights, that some people possess more human rights than others, that different people possess different human rights or that the rights of some are more urgent than the same rights of others demonstrate that a criterion other than humanity is being used to advance rights claims. Such selective application therefore contradicts the necessary conditions of advancing human rights on the sole basis of a shared humanity.

Expecting any state to integrate the necessary requirements of human rights into its foreign policies could be argued to be an impractical expectation. There is much to commend this argument given that states have characteristically prioritized power concerns and self-interest over addressing the urgent needs of non-nationals. Yet the Bush Administrations have repeatedly presented foreign policies in terms of promoting freedom and human rights. This book has analyzed the political significance of this apparent paradox.

Three different approaches for conceptualizing the role of human rights in foreign policy have subsequently been considered. The reflective approach interpreted references to human rights as describing the aspirations underlying the decision-making process. This approach hypothesized that human rights can be integrated into foreign policies in certain circumstances but must at other times be overridden because of, for example, limited resources or security concerns. In contrast, the rejectionist approach highlighted those occasions where foreign policies condoned or violated human rights norms to dismiss official references to human rights as no more than rhetoric. The third explanation hypothesized that the human rights claims made by administration officials should be taken seriously, but not literally. This productive explanation examined the human rights discourse asserted by administration officials for evident patterns that departed from describing a corresponding reality in analytically discernable ways. This third explanation has been adopted in this book to detail how human rights have been politicized in the foreign policy of the Bush Administrations. The research findings are summarized in the following six conclusions.

The hegemonic discourse has internal consistencies

Chapter 1 categorized the human rights claims made by administration officials in terms of three internally consistent rules, (i) that human rights are impartially promoted as independent foreign policy goals; (ii) that rule one is derived from a pre-existing US identity and (iii) that championing human rights complements distinct foreign policy goals of freedom, justice and democracy promotion. These rules were identified as internally consistent in the sense that a number of administration officials repeated these messages in explaining a range of events. These three rules were also identified as internally consistent since administration officials did not contradict them. For example, in none of the post-9/11 public speeches analyzed for this research did an administration official assert that the human rights of non-nationals are inconsequential when compared to the self-interest of the US. These three internally consistent rules were referred to in this research as a discourse.

The discourse on human rights outlined above has been termed hegemonic since its political significance has been found to reside as a function of power that is implemented neither through overt coercion nor through appeals to self-interest. Instead, the hegemonic discourse operates as a technique of governance by disciplining the minds of the audience, both domestic and international. To the extent that the hegemonic discourse is internalized by the audience as reflecting a corresponding reality, it acts to coalesce domestic and international political support around foreign policies, to reduce criticisms of policies and to subsequently legitimize those policies as detailed in the foregoing pages of this research.

The hegemonic discourse is a mythology

References to democracy, freedom and liberty have featured at least as prominently in the foreign policy narrative expressed by the Bush Administrations as have values of human rights. However, the definition of freedom and democracy are inherently contestable and these emotive values can be subsequently applied to defend virtually any policy position. The absence of accepted criteria through which to define, measure and assess freedom and democracy renders meaningful examination of subsequent appeals to these concepts by administration officials analytically problematic. In contrast, claims to promote human rights can be evaluated against two necessary conditions as explained above. The claims made in the hegemonic discourse rest or fall upon the universal and impartial integration of human rights into foreign policy practice. This research has argued that the following two recurrent features of foreign policy under the Bush Administrations have eschewed the universal and impartial application of human rights, (i) selective integration and (ii) opposition to international human rights legislation.

First, this research adopted a country specific focus to document how human rights concerns have been selectively addressed by the Bush Administrations.[1] Systematic and genocidal violations of human rights occurring in areas of peripheral geopolitical concern were categorized as human tragedies undeserving of humanitarian intervention by US forces. Darfur stands out as one especially notable example where the entire Western world stood by and watched acts of genocide during the period 2000–06. Chapter 3 suggested that this selective neglect of human rights was not without pattern. In particular, human rights abuses were downplayed or emphasized to reaffirm the predetermined identities of states. Violations of human rights in designated enemy states were highlighted as proof of evil and despotic regimes. States including North Korea, Iran, Syria, Afghanistan under the Taliban and Iraq under Hussein were heavily criticized by the Bush Administrations for their human rights records. Whereas such criticisms were often entirely appropriate, their political function was revealed when juxtaposed with the sparse commentary leveled against designated friendly states. Human rights violations committed by friendly states were downplayed or else redefined as acts of counter terrorism, unproven allegations, unfortunate mistakes, unavoidable isolated incidents, uncharacteristic exceptions in an otherwise improving trend or as necessary responses to security threats.

Second, the research detailed antagonism to the universal and impartial enforcement of human rights through analyzing resistance from the Bush Administrations to international human rights law. Chapter 4 detailed hostility of the Bush Administrations toward the ICC as evidence of this opposition. An evident disparity therefore exists between the claims made in the hegemonic discourse and the selective integration of human rights in actual policy practice. The research explained this disparity in terms of the hegemonic discourse articulating predetermined conclusions that were asserted by administration officials irrespective of evidence to the contrary.

This research has not sought to infer intent to policymakers but has instead focused on analyzing the internal consistencies and external application of the asserted discourse. There is, however, no evidence to demonstrate any conscious conspiracy to mislead the public. Instead there is every reason to believe that administration officials have fully internalized the hegemonic discourse as common sense and fundamental truth. Indeed, this perceived self-evidence would remove the hegemonic discourse from any critical scrutiny and render its claims all the more convincing to the audience. The hegemonic discourse can therefore be categorized as a mythology in the sense of articulating a contingent and politicized account of reality and of articulating fundamental beliefs masquerading as truths.

The hegemonic discourse co-opts human rights

The evident disparity between the claims made in the hegemonic discourse and the selective integration of human rights in foreign policy practice is characteristically explained by the reflective account in terms of isolated exceptions, a gap between values and practice, competing security concerns or the basis of limited resources.² The reflective account effectively lowers the standards required for recognizing human rights in policy decisions by hypothesizing that human rights concerns can enter the policymaking process in a partial and selective fashion. This research has argued against such a contention on grounds of (i) internal coherence and (ii) the patterns evident in the selective integration of human rights into policy decisions. First, for the concept of human rights to maintain internal coherence, the necessary conditions of impartial and universal application must apply. The hypothesis that human rights can enter the policymaking process on a selective basis must, therefore, be rejected as internally contradictory. Second, this research has argued that accommodating the selective integration of human rights into foreign policy unduly removes from critical scrutiny evident patterns in how human rights have been co-opted. In particular, the reflective explanation depoliticizes two evident patterns of co-option, (i) that human rights have provided broad discretion for the unilateral deployment of US military force and (ii) that human rights have promoted favored aspects of domestic civil society.

First, the Bush Administrations have consistently co-opted human rights when explaining the deployment of US military force. Chapter 4 accounted for this co-option in terms of US exceptionalism. In line with the hegemonic mythology, US exceptionalism hypothesized human rights as the specific inheritance of the US. Chapter 4 examined how the only rights conferred under this conceptualization were to the US government who could thereby justify foreign policy. The myth of exceptionalism asserted a unilateral right for the US to wage war to free the oppressed while denying a similar right to others.³ Conceptualizing human rights in terms of US exceptionalism was found to co-opt the concept, since it works to empower the US government, while excluding vulnerable and marginalized individuals around the world from the capacity to enforce any actual rights in practice.⁴

Second, human rights have been co-opted by the Bush Administrations to export favored values of domestic civil society. The MCA has, for example, been analyzed as a policy initiative that diverted US aid away from addressing basic human requirements in favor of providing an incentive for states to liberalize their economies. A focus on the basic needs of the worlds dispossessed and vulnerable, therefore, provides little explanatory consistency for the application of human rights by the Bush Administrations. As Chapter 4 detailed, the hegemonic discourse has been more consistently applied in terms of co-opting human rights to justify the deployment of the US military and to promote favored elements of domestic civil society.

The hegemonic discourse produces a reality that legitimizes foreign policy

The political significance of the hegemonic discourse is not limited to the co-option of human rights in pursuit of geopolitical and economic goals. This research has hypothesized that a more fundamental significance involves the production of reality in the minds of the audience. This research has identified a capacity of the hegemonic discourse to produce reality through designating (i) identities, (ii) threats and (iii) intents. First, the hegemonic discourse produces the identities of political actors by differentiating the good from the evil, the threats from the normal, the friends from the enemies, the terrorists from the freedom fighters, the legitimate from the illegitimate, the dangerous from the safe and the oppressors from the oppressed. As detailed in the foregoing pages, the hegemonic discourse has produced an identity of the US as the source of human rights and freedom. In a speech at West Point in June 2002, President Bush expressed the underlying message that '[w]herever we carry it, the American flag will stand not only for power, but for freedom'.[5] To the extent that the audience accepts the identities stipulated in the hegemonic discourse, the reality of US foreign policy will be perceived in terms of promoting freedom against the forces of evil.

Second, the hegemonic discourse has produced reality by designating threats. In the case of nuclear proliferation in the Middle East, for example, threats have been stipulated to reaffirm predetermined conclusions.[6] Thus, the possible development of a nuclear weaponry capability by Iran can be categorized as an urgent threat to international security whereas the known possession of nuclear weapons by Israel demonstrates no such threat.[7] Rather than basing the threat assessment on the sole consideration of a state developing a nuclear weapons capability, the process of determining threats is politicized to reaffirm the predetermined identities of the actors involved. It is because the Bush Administrations can stipulate the reality of threats to international security that Israel can be understood by the audience as a peaceful friend and Iran as a destabilizing menace.

Third, the hegemonic discourse produced reality by stipulating foreign policy intents. The administrations enjoyed a broad remit to attach intents to policy decisions since motives can be neither proved nor disproved. As we have seen, US foreign policy intents have been defined in terms of democracy, freedom and human rights with any questioning of these intents being rejected as Un-American propaganda, undue cynicism or as outlandish conspiracy theory. As we have also seen, Bush Administration officials have simultaneously seen fit to rewrite the intents of designated enemies. Chapter 5 noted, for example, how the intent of bin Laden was inferred in terms of a hatred of freedom. Chapter 7 noted how, in the absence of any WMD being located in postwar Iraq, the Bush Administrations assigned Saddam Hussein with the intent to restart his WMD program at some future date had the US not intervened. Therefore, administration officials have consistently defined the intents of both the US and its enemies to produce the predetermined reality stipulated in the hegemonic discourse.

The commonality shared by these three discursive mechanisms has been to legitimize policy decisions. The first mechanism justified the deployment of US military power in terms of freedom. The second mechanism recognized or dismissed threats to international security on the basis of the perspective of the

Bush Administrations and its allies. The third mechanism defined the intent of the US, as well as the intents of its enemies, in terms of the hegemonic discourse.

A number of observers have hypothesized that legitimacy problems could confront a superpower operating in a unipolar world.[8] Charles Kupchan of Bill Clinton's National Security Council, for example, criticized the decision to invade Iraq in the absence of Security Council authorization on grounds that the US acted against the court of world opinion. Kupchan lamented that 'the United States has compromised perhaps its most precious asset – its international legitimacy'.[9] The above discussion highlights the consistent application of the hegemonic discourse as a technique to coalesce legitimacy around US foreign policy. The efficacy of discourse to produce legitimacy for policy decisions can be measured by the extent to which the audience has internalized the stated messages as truth. To the extent that the hegemonic discourse is treated with suspicion, the advantage that the US enjoys in military power is constrained by countervailing opinion that can readily transform into protest or opposition. Since the deployment of military force can change the actions but not the opinions of individuals, resistance against the US will most likely continue or intensify until the way that US power is understood first changes. Thus the fundamental function of the hegemonic discourse resides in its capacity to produce a reality that legitimizes foreign policy.

The hegemonic discourse resonates in previous administrations

Chapter 2 detailed how Presidents Woodrow Wilson and Jimmy Carter emphasized the same constitutive rules of the hegemonic discourse when explaining foreign policy. The dominance of the reflective explanation in interpreting these discourses is revealed in the established caricature image of President Wilson as an idealistic advocate of the rights of man and of President Carter as a utopian supporter of universal human rights. Chapter 2 detailed the problems with the literal interpretation of the hegemonic discourse under these democrat administrations by reviewing instances of policy decisions that contradicted the necessary conditions of human rights. The chapter went on to detail how the rejectionist account unduly dismissed the political relevance of the hegemonic discourse. Chapter 2 then examined how the Wilson and Carter Administrations demonstrated an awareness of the productive function of discourse as a precursor to explaining the consistent application of the hegemonic discourse by both Presidents as a technique of governance.

Analysis of the Wilson and Carter Administrations was found to inform our understanding of the role of the hegemonic discourse in the foreign policy of the Bush Presidencies since recurrent themes resonated in all administrations. In particular, the hegemonic discourse produced an identity of the US, coalesced support for political leadership and engendered geopolitical changes. Further research could test the historical record for how the hegemonic discourse resonates in the foreign policy narrative provided by other administrations. Further research could also examine the extent to which the hegemonic discourse resonates in the legislative and judicial branches of government and the extent to which the discourse is internalized or resisted among different sectors of the domestic and international audience.

Discourse analysis contributes to our understanding of human rights in foreign policy

The above conclusions point to a constitutive role for discourse analysis in understanding the significance of human rights in foreign policy. The narrative of policymakers is of political interest since this attaches intent, function and purpose to policy decisions. Yet assuming the literal interpretation of policy explanations has been found to be inadequate since this overlooks the productive, rather than simply descriptive, function of language. A method of discourse analysis has been adopted in this research to examine this political function of language. Rather than seeking to assume or infer the intent of policymakers, discourse analysis instead examines the narrative of administration officials for internal consistencies or rules. The ability of these rules to describe the role of human rights in actual foreign policy practice can then be evaluated on the basis of the necessary requirements for human rights defined in terms of impartial and universal application. By analyzing the resultant patterns, this method can detail how a human rights discourse has been employed as a technique to produce, rather than reflect, reality.

The second part of this book examined how discourse analysis could contribute to our understanding of the role and significance of human rights in the wars on terror, Afghanistan and Iraq. Chapters 5, 6 and 7 juxtaposed the application of the hegemonic discourse in each case study with the necessary conditions of human rights. Chapter 5 explained how the hegemonic discourse produced an identity of the US in line with human rights and freedom in binary opposition to the stated identity of a terrorist enemy. The chapter noted how the treatment of war on terror detainees excluded designated individuals from human rights norms and thus, contradicted the necessary requisites of universal implementation. The hegemonic discourse was, thereby, found to play an important role in the war on terror but as a technique of governance rather than as a literal account of policy decisions.

Chapter 6 detailed four ways in which the hegemonic discourse featured in the narrative provided by administration officials for the Afghanistan War, (i) by highlighting human rights violations occurring in Afghanistan during the Taliban era; (ii) by producing the identity of a free, post-Taliban Afghanistan; (iii) that Coalition Forces were identified as the bringers of this change in human rights observance in Afghanistan and (iv) that bringing freedom and human rights to Afghanistan was a constitutive aim of the 2001 war. The chapter examined how the account of the war asserted through these four features produced a mythological understanding of the military action in line with the predetermined conclusions defined by the hegemonic discourse. Thus, human rights were again applied consistently as a technique of governance by expressing a legitimizing rationale for the war. Through examining evidence relating to the treatment of prisoners and the choice of allies, the chapter noted how the actions of the US military were inconsistent with the necessary conditions of human rights.

Chapter 7 analyzed the significance of the hegemonic discourse for understanding the 2003 Iraq War. As with the previous two case studies, the chapter examined how reality was discursively produced to conform to the hegemonic mythology. The chapter demonstrated how the Iraq War was sanitized by the decision of Coalition Forces not to compile authoritative statistics on the number of civilian casualties. The chapter also challenged the contention that the war was caused by erroneous intelligence, by detailing how the Bush Administration had politicized prewar intelligence. Thus, the administration again employed discourse to produce reality in line with predetermined conclusions.

All three case studies concluded that the reflective and rejectionist accounts adopted an unduly restrictive view of the function and capacity of the hegemonic discourse. Both the reflective and rejectionist explanations restricted the possible significance of language to describing a corresponding reality. Refuting this claim, the case studies analyzed the capacity of the administration to produce an understanding of the intent, purpose and context of policy decisions in the minds of the audience. This research has subsequently accounted for the hegemonic discourse as a technique of governance through which the audience is led to understand power-based foreign policies in terms of human rights and freedom. The extent to which the promotion of human rights and freedom are understood by the audience as constituting the foreign policy of the Bush Administrations is itself the measure of the discursive capacity to produce reality in terms of the hegemonic discourse.

Notes

Introduction

1 For informative accounts of internal disagreements within the administration see Bob Woodward, *Plan of Attack*, London, Simon and Schuster, 2004 and Ron Suskind, *The Price of Loyalty*, New York, Simon and Schuster, 2004.

2 For the historical context of the rise in executive powers at the expense of the legislature see Michael Glennon, 'The Gulf War and the constitution', *Foreign Affairs*, 1991, vol. 70, no. 2, pp. 84–101.

3 See Jeffrey Lantis, 'Ethics and foreign policy', *International Studies Perspectives*, 2004, vol. 5, no. 2, pp. 117–33 at 118.

4 See George Kennan, 'On American principles', *Foreign Affairs*, 1995, vol. 74, no. 2, pp. 116–26 at 118.

5 W.B. Gallie, 'Essentially contested concepts', *Proceedings of the Aristotelian Society*, 1956, vol. 56, pp. 167–98.

6 For a defense of natural rights see John Locke, *Second Treatise of Government*, London, Macmillan, 1952. For informative debates over the historical and cultural contingency of these claims see Anthony Langlois, 'Human rights', *Review of International Studies*, 2002, vol. 28, no. 3, pp. 479–96; Michael Perry, 'Are human rights universal?' *Human Rights Quarterly*, 1997, vol. 19, no. 3, pp. 461–509 and Bilahari Kausikan, 'Asia's different standard', *Foreign Policy*, 1993, vol. 92, no. 3, pp. 24–41.

7 For details see David McLellan, *Karl Marx: Selected Writings*, Oxford, Oxford University Press, 1977, p. 59.

8 Attracta Ingram, *A Political Theory of Rights*, Oxford, Clarendon Press, 1994, p. 16.

9 See, for example, Thomas Pogge, *World Poverty and Human Rights*, Cambridge, MA, Polity Press, 2002.

10 Henry Shue, *Basic Rights: Subsistence, Affluence and United States Foreign Policy*, Princeton, NJ, Princeton University Press, 1980 and R.J. Vincent, *Human Rights and International Relations*, Cambridge, Cambridge University Press, 1986 and Johan Galtung, *Human Rights in Another Key*, Cambridge, MA, Polity Press, 1994.

11 See Douglas Long, *Bentham on Liberty*, Toronto, University of Toronto Press, 1977.

12 See, for example, John Gray, *Mill on Liberty: A Defense*, London, Routledge, 1983.

13 Joanne Bauer, 'International human rights and Asian commitment', *Human Rights Dialogue*, 1995, vol. 3. Online, available at: www.cceia.org/dialog3.html (accessed July 3, 1999).

14 Erik Kuhonta, 'The language of human rights in East Asia', *Human Rights Dialogue*, 1995, vol. 2. Online, available at: www.cceia.org/dialog2.html (accessed August 6, 2000).

15 Alan Gewirth, *Human Rights: Essays on Justification and Application*, Chicago, IL, University of Chicago Press, 1984.

16 Jack Donnelly, *International Human Rights*, 2nd edition, Boulder, CO, Westview Press, 1998, p. 22 and Jack Donnelly, 'Democracy and US foreign policy', in David Forsythe (ed.) *The United States and Human Rights: Looking Inward and Outward*, Lincoln, NE, University of Nebraska Press, 2000, pp. 199–226 at 206.

17 For a discussion see Tony Evans and Jan Hancock, 'International human rights law and the challenge of globalization', *The International Journal of Human Rights*, 1998, vol. 2, no. 3, pp. 1–21 and J. Watson, 'Legal theory, efficacy and validity in the development of human rights norms in international law', *University of Illinois Law Forum*, 1979, vol. 3, pp. 609–41.

18 David Howarth, *Discourse*, Buckingham, Open University Press, 2000, p. 9 and Richard Peet, Beate Born, Kendra Feher and Matthew Feinstein, *Unholy Trinity: The IMF, World Bank and WTO*, London, Zed Books, 2004, p. 16.

19 See Michel Foucault, *Ethics: Subjectivity and the Truth*, New York, The New Press, 1994, p. 16.

20 Narratives can be defined in terms of an internally consistent account of reality. See Jennifer Milliken, 'The study of discourse in international relations: a critique of research and methods', *European Journal of International Relations*, 1999, vol. 5, no. 2, pp. 225–54 at 229 and David Campbell, *Writing Security: US Foreign Policy and the Politics of Identity*, Manchester, Manchester University Press, 1998, pp. 4–5.

21 See Chapter 1.

22 Michel Foucault, quoted by David Owen in Simon Glendinning (ed.) *The Edinburgh Encyclopedia of Continental Philosophy*, Edinburgh, Edinburgh University Press, 1999, p. 599.

23 Michael Hechter, *Principles of Group Solidarity*, 4th edition, Berkley, CA, University of California Press, 1987, p. 87.

24 Ian Hurd, 'Legitimacy and authority in international politics', *International Organization*, 1999, vol. 53, no. 2, pp. 379–408 at 385.

25 For further discussion see Elina Penttinen, 'Capitalism as a system of global power', in Henri Goverde, Philip Cerny, Mark Haugaard and Howard Lentner (eds) *Power in Contemporary Politics*, London, Sage, 2000, pp. 205–20 at 206.

26 See Michel Foucault, *Power/Knowledge: Selected Interviews and Other Writings 1972–1977*, New York, Pantheon, 1980, p. 60 and Hurd, 'Legitimacy and authority in international politics', p. 388.

27 Andrew Kernohan, *Liberalism, Equality and Cultural Oppression*, Cambridge, Cambridge University Press, 1998, p. 22.

28 See Penttinen, 'Capitalism as a system of global power', in Goverde, Cerny, Haugaard and Lentner, *Power in Contemporary Politics*, p. 207.

29 Barry Allen, 'Foucault and modern political philosophy', in Jeremy Moss (ed.) *The Later Foucault*, London, Sage, 1998, pp. 164–98 at 179.

30 Andrew Hurrell, 'Legitimacy and the use of force: Can the circle be squared?' *Review of International Studies*, 2005, vol. 31, sp. iss., pp. 15–32 at 15. For further details on legitimacy in international politics see Ian Clark, *Legitimacy in International Society*, Oxford, Oxford University Press, 2005 and Hurd, 'Legitimacy and authority in international politics', pp. 379–408.

31 Hurrell, 'Legitimacy and the use of force', p. 16 and Martha Finnemore, 'Fights about rules: the role of efficacy and power in changing multilateralism', *Review of International Studies*, 2005, vol. 31, sp. iss., pp. 187–206 at 201.

32 Finnemore, 'Fights about rules', p. 201.

33 Finnemore, 'Fights about rules', p. 201.

34 For an excellent discussion on methodological reasoning in this area see Steve Smith, 'US democracy promotion: critical questions', in Michael Cox, John Ikenberry and Takashi Inoguchi (eds) *American Democracy Promotion: Impulses, Strategies and Impacts*, Oxford, Oxford University Press, 2000, pp. 63–82.

35 Tom Farer, 'The interplay of domestic politics, human rights and US foreign policy', in Thomas Weiss, Margaret Crahan and John Goering (eds) *Wars on Terrorism and Iraq: Human Rights, Unilateralism and US Foreign Policy*, London, Routledge, 2004, pp. 29–60 at 29.
36 Robert Keohane, 'International institutions: two approaches', *International Studies Quarterly*, 1988, vol. 44, no. 1, pp. 83–105 and John Mearsheimer, 'The false promise of international institutions', *International Security*, 1994, vol. 19, no. 3, pp. 5–49.
37 Stephen Walt, 'The renaissance of security studies', *International Studies Quarterly*, 1991, vol. 35, no. 2, pp. 211–40 and Milliken, 'The study of discourse in international relations', pp. 225–54.
38 For discussion see Jan Hancock, 'Understanding universal human rights discourse in times of exception', *International Studies Association Annual Conference*, San Diego, March 23, 2006.
39 Howarth, *Discourse*, p. 19.
40 Ferdinand de Saussure, *Course in General Linguistics*, London, Duckworth, 1983, p. 15.
41 See Véronique Pin Fat, 'The metaphysics of the national interest and the mysticism of the nation-state', *Review of International Studies*, 2005, vol. 31, no. 2, pp. 217–37 at 218.
42 See, for example, S. Silberstein, *War of Words: Language, Politics and 9/11*, London, Routledge, 2002 and M. Salter, *Barbarians and Civilization in International Relations*, London, Pluto Press, 2002.
43 Foucault, *Power/Knowledge*, p. 132.
44 See T. Brown, 'Ideological hegemony and global governance', *Journal of World-Systems Research*, 1997, vol. 3, no. 2, pp. 250–8 and Jonathan Clarke and Stefan Halper, *America Alone: The Neo Conservatives and the Global Order*, Cambridge, Cambridge University Press, 2004, pp. 206–7.

1 The hegemonic discourse

1 Shirin Tahir-Kheli (2001) *Item 4: Report of the High Commissioner for Human Rights*, 57th Session of the UN Commission on Human Rights, Geneva, March 21.
2 Colin Powell, quoted in Tahir-Kheli, *Item 4*.
3 Paula Dobriansky (2001) *Testimony Before the International Operations and Terrorism Subcommittee*, Senate Foreign Relations Committee, Washington, DC, May 24.
4 George W. Bush (2003) *President Bush Discusses Iraq Policy*, Whitehall Palace, London, November 19.
5 Colin Powell (2004) *Statement: Human Rights Week*, Brussels, December 8.
6 Colin Powell, 'A strategy of partnerships', *Foreign Affairs*, 2004, vol. 83, no. 1, pp. 22–30 at 29.
7 Robert Jackson (2004) *Human Rights and Democracy in Venezuela*, Statement before the Congressional Human Rights Caucus, Washington, DC, April 22.
8 Lorne Craner (2001) *Remarks to the Heritage Foundation*, Washington, DC, October 31.
9 National Security Council, *United States of America National Security Strategy*, Washington, DC, 2002, p. 14.
10 Minister Counselor for Public Affairs at the US Embassy in London Daniel Sreebny (2004) 'Research question'. E-mail. November 24.
11 Shirin Tahir-Kheli (2001) *Resolution L.13*, 57th Session of the UN Commission on Human Rights, Geneva, April 18.
12 Craner, *Remarks to the Heritage Foundation*.

13 Lorne Craner (2004) *Briefing on Supporting Human Rights and Democracy: The US Record 2003–2004 Report*, May 17.
14 Craner, *Remarks to the Heritage Foundation*.
15 Bureau of Democracy, Human Rights and Labor (2001) *Fact Sheet: Voluntary Principles on Security and Human Rights*, Washington, DC, February 20. Online, available at: www.state.gov (accessed January 2, 2002). On another occasion the State Department has asserted that 'a central goal of US foreign policy has been the promotion of respect for human rights, as embodied in the Universal Declaration of Human Rights'. See Jack Donnelly, 'International human rights: unintended consequences of the war on terrorism', in Thomas Weiss, Margaret Crahan and John Goering (eds) *Wars on Terrorism and Iraq: Human Rights, Unilateralism and US Foreign Policy*, London, Routledge, 2004, pp. 98–112 at 111 and Department of State, *Supporting Human Rights and Democracy: The US Record 2003–2004*, Washington, DC, 2004, p. 258.
16 Department of State, *Supporting Human Rights and Democracy*.
17 Department of State, *Supporting Human Rights and Democracy*.
18 Department of State, *Supporting Human Rights and Democracy*.
19 Paula Dobriansky, 'Democracy promotion', *Foreign Affairs*, 2003, vol. 82, no. 3, pp. 141–5 at 142.
20 Dobriansky, 'Democracy promotion', p. 142.
21 Dobriansky, 'Democracy promotion', pp. 142–3.
22 George W. Bush (2002) *State of the Union Address*, US Capitol, Washington, DC, January 29.
23 Lorne Craner (2004) *A Comprehensive Human Rights Strategy for China*, Carnegie Endowment for International Peace, Washington, DC, January 29.
24 George W. Bush (2003) *Remarks by the President at 2003 President's Dinner*, Washington Convention Center, Washington, DC, May 21.
25 George W. Bush (2006) *State of the Union Address*, US Capitol, Washington, DC, January 31.
26 George W. Bush (2001) *Proclamation on Human Rights Observances*, White House, Washington, DC, December 9.
27 George W. Bush (2005) *President Sworn-In to Second Term*, Inauguration Speech, Washington, DC, January 20.
28 Bush, 2002 *State of the Union Address*.
29 Shirin Tahir-Kheli (2001) *Item 9: Violation of Human Rights and Fundamental Freedoms in Any Part of the World*, 57th Session of the UN Commission on Human Rights, Geneva, March 30.
30 Craner, *Remarks to the Heritage Foundation*.
31 Powell, *Statement: Human Rights Week*.
32 Powell, *Statement: Human Rights Week*.
33 Powell, *Statement: Human Rights Week*.
34 Condoleezza Rice, quoted in Lorne Craner (2004) *Country Reports on Human Rights Practices for 2003*, Testimony Before the House International Relations Committee, Washington, DC, March 10.
35 Condoleezza Rice (2004) *Remarks at the McConnell Center for Political Leadership*, University of Louisville, Louisville, Kentucky, March, 8.
36 George W. Bush, quoted in Arkan Mohammed Ali, Thahe Mohammed Sabbar, Sherzad Kamal Khalid, Ali H., Mehboob Ahmad, Said Nabi Siddiqi, Mohammed Karim Shirullah and Haji Abdul Rahman v Donald H. Rumsfeld (2005) *District Court for the Northern District of Illinois*, p. 12. Online, available at: www.humanrightsfirst.org/us_law/etn/lawsuit/PDF/rums-complaint-022805.pdf (accessed March 14, 2005).

37 Dobriansky, *Testimony Before the International Operations and Terrorism Subcommittee*.
38 Bush, *President Sworn-In to Second Term*.
39 George W. Bush (2004) *A Proclamation: Human Rights Day, Bill of Rights Day and Human Rights Week*, Washington, DC, December 10.
40 George W. Bush (2003) *State of the Union Address*, US Capitol, Washington, DC, January 28.
41 Bush, *A Proclamation*.
42 George W. Bush and Tony Blair (2003) *Joint News Conference*, Camp David, Maryland, March 27.
43 Craner, *Remarks to the Heritage Foundation*.
44 Dobriansky, *Testimony Before the International Operations and Terrorism Subcommittee*.
45 Dick Cheney, quoted in Associated Press, 'Cheney thanks Italy for support in Iraq', *New York Times*, January 26, 2004. Online, available at: www.nytimes.com (accessed January 26, 2004).
46 George W. Bush (2002) *US Humanitarian Aid to Afghanistan*, Presidential Hall, Dwight David Eisenhower Executive Office Building, Washington, DC, October 11 and Bush, *Proclamation on Human Rights Observances*.
47 Bush, 2006 *State of the Union Address* and George W. Bush (2004) *First Kerry–Bush Presidential Debate*, Miami, Florida, September 30.
48 George W. Bush (2004) *Address to the United Nations General Assembly*, New York, September 21.
49 National Security Council, *National Security Strategy*, p. 29.
50 Powell, 'A strategy of partnerships', p. 29.
51 Powell, 'A strategy of partnerships', p. 29.
52 William Burke-White, 'Human rights and national security: the strategic correlation', *Harvard Human Rights Journal*, 2004, vol. 17, pp. 249–80 at 249.
53 Lawrence Freedman, 'The age of liberal wars', *Review of International Studies*, 2005, vol. 31, sp. iss., pp. 92–107 at 94.
54 Rosemary Foot, 'Bush, China and human rights', *Survival*, 2003, vol. 45, no. 2, pp. 167–86 at 173.
55 Adam Wolfson, 'Conservatives and neoconservatives', *Public Interest*, 2004, no. 154, pp. 32–40 at 36 and Adam Wolfson, 'How to think about humanitarian war', 2000, *Commentary*, July/August, pp. 44–8 at 48.
56 David Condron, 'Can there be an ethical foreign policy?' *Journal of Power and Ethics: An Interdisciplinary Review*, 2000, vol. 1, no. 3, pp. 234–43 at 241.
57 Randall Schweller, 'US democracy promotion: realist reflections', in Michael Cox, G. John Ikenberry and Takachi Inoguchi (eds) *American Democracy Promotion: Impulses, Strategies and Impacts*, Oxford, Oxford University Press, 2000, pp. 41–62 at 61.
58 Roger Rosenblatt, 'A patriot's progress: September 11 and freedom in America', *Global Issues*, 2002, vol. 7, no. 2, pp. 25–8 at 26.
59 Michael Warner, 'A new strategy for the new geopolitics', *Public Interest*, 2003, no. 153, pp. 94–9 at 98.
60 Michael Mazarr, 'George W. Bush, idealist', *International Affairs*, 2003, vol. 79, no. 3, pp. 503–22 at 506.
61 Mazarr, 'George W. Bush, idealist', p. 513.
62 Paul Wolfowitz, 'Remembering the future', *The National Interest*, Spring 2000, p. 5.
63 See Judith Goldstein and Robert Keohane, 'Ideas and foreign policy' in Judith Goldstein and Robert Keohane (eds) *Ideas and Foreign Policy: Beliefs, Institutions and Political Change*, Ithaca, NY, Cornell University Press, 1993, pp. 1–18 at 16.
64 Colin Dueck, 'Ideas and alternatives in American grand strategy, 2000–2004',

Review of International Studies, 2004, vol. 30, no. 3, pp. 511–35 at 534–5. For a defense of the independent role of principles in foreign policymaking see also G. John Ikenberry, 'Liberalism and empire: logics of order in the American unipolar age', *Review of International Studies,* 2004, vol. 30, no. 4, pp. 609–30 at 630.

65 See especially Hans Morgenthau, *Politics in the Twentieth Century*, Chicago, IL, University of Chicago Press, 1962 and Hans Morgenthau, *Politics Among Nations*, 5th edition, New York, Alfred Knopf, 1975.

66 Hans Morgenthau, *In Defense of the National Interest*, Washington, DC, University Press of America, 1982, p. 34.

67 See Paul Ransome, *Antonio Gramsci: A New Introduction*, New York, Harvester Wheatsheaf, 1992, pp. 123–4.

68 See Chapter 4 for details of administration opposition to specific international human rights legislation.

69 For details of these necessary conditions see Introduction.

70 For detailed analysis of these patterns see Chapters 3 and 4.

71 George W. Bush, *Bush–Gore Presidential Debate*, Wake Forest University, October 11, 2000.

72 George W. Bush, *Bush–Gore Presidential Debate*, Wake Forest University, October 3, 2000.

73 Bush, *Bush–Gore Presidential Debate*, October 11, 2000.

74 Condoleezza Rice, 'Promoting the national interest', *Foreign Affairs,* 2000, vol. 79, no.1, pp. 45–62.

75 Rice, 'Promoting the national interest', p. 63.

76 For a useful discussion see Julie Mertus, 'The new US human rights policy: a radical departure', *International Studies Perspectives*, 2003, vol. 4, no. 4, pp. 371–84 at 379.

77 Mertus, 'The new US human rights policy', p. 381.

78 See Kenneth Waltz, 'Evaluating theories', *The American Political Science Review*, 1997, vol. 91, no. 4, pp. 913–17.

79 John Pilger, *New Rulers of the World*, London, Verso, 2003; John Pilger, *Hidden Agendas*, London, Vintage, 1998 and William Blum, *Killing Hope: US and CIA Interventions Since World War II*, London, Zed, 2003.

80 George W. Bush revealed for example that it had left a deep impression when the college chaplain at Yale commented that his father had been beaten by a 'better man' in his 1964 run for Senate. See Fred Greenstein, 'The changing leadership of George W. Bush', in Eugene Wittkopf and James McCormick (eds) *The Domestic Sources of American Foreign Policy: Insights and Evidence*, Lanham, Rowman and Littlefield Publishers, 2004, pp. 353–62 at 354.

81 Michel Foucault, *The Archaeology of Knowledge*, London, Tavistock, 1972, p. 38.

82 Ivo Daalder and James Lindsay, *America Unbound: The Bush Revolution in Foreign Policy*, Washington, DC, Brookings Institution Press, 2003, p. 35.

83 See Bob Woodward, *Bush at War*, New York, Simon and Schuster, 2002, p. 137.

84 For a discussion see Alan Drengson, 'Shifting paradigms: From the technocratic to the person-planetary', *Environmental Ethics*, 1980, vol. 2, no. 3, pp. 221–40.

85 David Campbell, *Writing Security: US Foreign Policy and the Politics of Identity*, Manchester, Manchester University Press, 1998, p. 93.

86 Campbell, *Writing Security*, p. 92.

87 Gabriel Almond, *The American People and Foreign Policy*, New York, Harcourt, Brace, 1950, p. 53.

88 Otis Pike, quoted in William Blum, *Rogue State: A Guide to the World's Only Superpower*, London, Zed Books, 2002, p. 9.

89 For further discussion see Anthony Lang, 'Responsibility in the international

system: reading US foreign policy in the Middle East', *European Journal of International Relations*, 1999, vol. 5, no.1, pp. 67–107 at 99.

90 Michel Foucault, *Ethics: Subjectivity and the Truth*, New York, The New Press, 1994, p. 167.

91 Edward Bernays, *Propaganda*, New York, Horace Liveright, 1928, p. 71.

92 Bernays, *Propaganda*, p. 109.

93 Graham Wallas, *Human Nature in Politics*, London, Constable and Company, 1908, p. 86.

94 Wallas, *Human Nature in Politics*, p. 87.

95 Wallas, *Human Nature in Politics*, p. 107.

96 Almond, *The American People and Foreign Policy*, p. 232.

97 See also Stuart Ewen, *A Social History of Spin*, New York, Basic Books, 1996, p. 19.

98 Barry Allen, 'Foucault and modern political philosophy', in Jeremy Moss (ed.) *The Later Foucault*, London, Sage, 1998, pp. 164–98 at 174.

99 Robinson for example contended that ideological explanations of foreign policy decisions provided by successive postwar US administrations reflected those moral imperatives that defined the accepted criterion for justice in American society. See William Robinson, 'Globalization, the world system and "democracy promotion" in US foreign policy', *Theory and Society*, 1996, vol. 25, no. 5, pp. 615–65 at 621–2.

100 According to Bob Woodward, *Plan of Attack*, London, Simon and Schuster, 2004, p. 131.

101 For details see Ray Eldon Hiebert, 'Public relations and propaganda in framing the Iraq War: a preliminary review', *Public Relations Review*, 2003, vol. 29, no. 3, pp. 243–55 at 246.

102 Vince Vitto (2004) *Report of the Defense Science Board Task Force on Strategic Communication*, September, p. 1. Online, available at: www.publicdiplomacy.org/37.htm (accessed January 24, 2005).

103 Vitto, *Report of the Defense Science Board Task Force on Strategic Communication*, p. 4.

104 Vitto, *Report of the Defense Science Board Task Force on Strategic Communication*, p. 2.

105 Vitto, *Report of the Defense Science Board Task Force on Strategic Communication*, p. 2.

106 Hiebert, 'Public relations and propaganda in framing the Iraq War', p. 246.

107 Hiebert, 'Public relations and propaganda in framing the Iraq War', p. 246.

108 Lang, 'Responsibility in the international system', p. 76.

109 Lang, 'Responsibility in the international system', p. 76.

110 Campbell, *Writing Security*, p. 1.

111 See United States Senate Select Committee on Intelligence (2004) *Report on the US Intelligence Community's Prewar Intelligence Assessments on Iraq*, July 9. Online, available at: www.fas.org/irp/congress/2004_rpt/ssci_concl.pdf (accessed October 10, 2004) and Andrew Buncombe, 'Official verdict: White House misled world over Saddam', *Independent*, June 17, 2004. Online, available at: www.independent.co.uk (accessed June 18, 2004).

112 George W. Bush (2004) *Progress in the War on Terror*, January 22.

113 George W. Bush (2004) *President Outlines Steps to Help Iraq Achieve Democracy and Freedom*, United States Army War College, Carlisle, Pennsylvannia, May 24 and George W. Bush (2005) *President Outlines Strategy for Victory in Iraq*, US Naval Academy, Annapolis, Maryland, November 30.

114 George W. Bush, quoted in Buncombe, 'Official verdict'.

115 George W. Bush, quoted in Philip Shenon and Christopher Marquis, 'Panel finds no Qaeda–Iraq tie', *New York Times*, June 17, 2004. Online, available at:

www.nytimes.com (accessed June 20, 2004). The President also used 9/11 to produce an identity of Hussein's Iraq as a terrorist actor by asking the audience in his 2003 *State of the Union Address* to 'imagine those 19 hijackers with other weapons and other plans, this time armed by Saddam Hussein'.

116 Donald Rumsfeld, quoted in Suzanne Goldenberg, 'Bush allies admit war blunders', *The Guardian*, October 6, 2004. Online, available at: www.guardian.co.uk (accessed October 8, 2004) and Jim Lobe, 'The emperor within the empire', *Inter Press Service News Agency*, October 4, 2002. Online, available at: www.ipsnews.net (accessed December 16, 2003).

117 Donald Rumsfeld, quoted in Buncombe, 'Official verdict'.

118 Condoleezza Rice, quoted in Buncombe, 'Official verdict'.

119 Dick Cheney, quoted in Buncombe, 'Official verdict'.

120 Dick Cheney, quoted in Glenn Kessler and Jim Van de Hei, 'Misleading assertions cover Iraq War and voting records', *Washington Post*, October 6, 2004, p. A15.

121 Dick Cheney, quoted in Richard Stevenson, 'With 9/11 report, Bush's political thorn grows more stubborn', *New York Times*, June 17, 2004. Online, available at: www.nytimes.com (accessed June 18, 2004) and Mark Hosenball, Michael Isikoff and Evan Thomas, 'Cheney's long path to war', *Newsweek*, November 17, 2003, p. 38.

122 Wesley Clarke, quoted in Jim Lobe, 'Key officials used 9/11 as pretext for Iraq War', *Inter Press Service News Agency*, July 15, 2003. Online, available at: www.ipsnews.net/print.asp?idnews=19255 (accessed December 16, 2003).

123 Wesley Clarke, quoted in Lobe, 'Key officials used 9/11 as pretext for Iraq War'.

124 See Paul Pillar, *Terrorism and US Foreign Policy*, Washington, DC, Brookings Institution Press, 2003, p. xviii.

125 For details see Noam Chomsky, *Hegemony or Survival? America's Quest for Global Dominance*, London, Hamish Hamilton, 2003, p. 19.

126 See Buncombe, 'Official verdict'.

127 Pillar, *Terrorism and US Foreign Policy*, p. xviii. For authoritative accounts of how political information is manipulated in democracies as a mode of thought control see Noam Chomsky, *Knowledge of Language: Its Nature, Origins and Use*, New York, Praeger, 1986; Noam Chomsky, *On Power and Ideology: The Managua Lectures*, Boston, MA, South End Press, 1987; Noam Chomsky, *The Culture of Terrorism*, London, Pluto Press, 1988; Noam Chomsky, *Deterring Democracy*, Reading, Verso, 1992; Noam Chomsky, *Rethinking Camelot*, London, Verso, 1993 and Noam Chomsky, *Year 501: The Conquest Continues*, London, Verso, 1993.

128 Hiebert, 'Public relations and propaganda in framing the Iraq War', p. 244 and David Howarth, *Discourse*, Buckingham, Open University Press, 2000, p. 53.

129 CNN, 'US loses UN rights seat', May 4, 2001. Online, available at: www cnn.worldnews (accessed May 5, 2001).

130 George W. Bush, quoted in Dobriansky, *Testimony Before the International Operations and Terrorism Subcommittee*.

131 George W. Bush, quoted in Dobriansky, *Testimony Before the International Operations and Terrorism Subcommittee*.

132 Dobriansky, *Testimony Before the International Operations and Terrorism Subcommittee*.

133 Vitto, *Report of the Defense Science Board Task Force on Strategic Communication*, p. 2.

134 Bernays, *Propaganda*, p. 119.

135 For details on how liberty can be co-opted as an effective instrument of domination see Herbert Marcuse, *One Dimensional Man*, London, Sphere, 1964 and Ute Buhler, 'Who are we talking to? An addendum to recent RIS contributions on discourse ethics', *Review of International Studies*, 2002, vol. 28, no. 3, pp. 191–7 at 192.

136 See Lang, 'Responsibility in the international system', p. 76.
137 Condoleezza Rice, 'A balance of power that favors freedom', *United States Foreign Policy Agenda*, 2002, vol. 7, no. 4, pp. 5–9.

2 The hegemonic discourse of Wilson and Carter

1 For details of these necessary conditions see Introduction.
2 See, in particular, Tim Dunne, 'New thinking on international society', *British Journal of Politics and International Relations*, 2001, vol. 3, no. 2, pp. 223–44; Frances Harbour, *Thinking About International Ethics: Moral Cases from American Foreign Policy*, Boulder, CO, Westview Press, 1999; Michael MacKinnon, *The Evolution of US Peacekeeping Policy Under Clinton: A Fairweather Friend,* Portland, OR, Frank Cass, 2000; Joseph Nye, *The Paradox of American Power: Why the World's Only Superpower Can't Go It Alone*, New York, Oxford University Press, 2002 and Kathryn Sikkink, 'The power of principled ideas: human rights policies in the US and western Europe', in Judith Goldstein and Robert Keohane (eds) *Ideas and Foreign Policy: Beliefs, Institutions and Political Change*, Ithaca, NY, Cornell University Press, 1993, pp. 139–72. For details of the hegemonic rules see Chapter 1.
3 See, for example, Nicholas Wheeler, *Saving Strangers: Humanitarian Intervention in International Society*, Oxford, Oxford University Press, 2000 and Ward Thomas, *The Ethics of Destruction*, Ithaca, NY, Cornell University Press, 2001.
4 See Colin Dueck, 'Ideas and alternatives in American grand strategy, 2000–2004', *Review of International Studies*, 2004, vol. 30, no. 4, pp. 511–35 at 523 and Charles Kegley and Gregory Raymond, 'Preventive war and permissive normative order', *International Studies Perspectives*, 2003, vol. 4, no. 4, pp. 385–94 at 390.
5 Robert W. McElroy, *Morality and American Foreign Policy*, Princeton, NJ, Princeton University Press, 1992, p. 173.
6 Stephen Ambrose and Douglas Brinkley, *Rise to Globalism: American Foreign Policy Since 1938*, Harmondsworth, Penguin, 1997, p. 282.
7 Philip Bobbitt, *The Shield of Achilles*, New York, Knopf, 2001.
8 Mary Kaldor, 'American power: from "compellance" to cosmoplitanism?' *International Affairs*, 2003, vol. 79, no. 1, pp. 1–22 at 1.
9 For further examples see Graham Allison and Gregory Treverton, *Rethinking America's Security*, New York, W.W. Norton, 1992; Joseph Nye, *The Paradox of American Power*, New York, Oxford University Press, 2002; John Ruggie, *Winning the Peace*, New York, Columbia University Press, 1996; Larry Diamond, 'Promoting democracy', in Eugene Wittkopf (ed.) *The Future of American Foreign Policy*, New York, St. Martin's Press, 1994, pp. 101–7; Michael Ignatieff, 'Empire lite', *Prospect*, 2003, vol. 83, p. 36; Michael Cox, *US Foreign Policy After the Cold War: Superpower Without a Mission?* London, Pinter, 1995 and Thomas Carothers, 'Taking stock of democracy assistance', in Michael Cox, G. John Ikenberry and Takachi Inoguchi (eds) *American Democracy Promotion: Impulses, Strategies and Impacts*, Oxford, Oxford University Press, 2000, pp. 181–99.
10 McElroy, *Morality and American Foreign Policy*, pp. 10, 11 and 179.
11 McElroy, *Morality and American Foreign Policy*, p. 173.
12 McElroy, *Morality and American Foreign Policy*, p. 170.
13 McElroy, *Morality and American Foreign Policy*, p. 170.
14 Sikkink, 'The power of principled ideas', in Goldstein and Keohane (eds), *Ideas and Foreign Policy*, pp. 139–72.
15 See also Jason Ralph, 'High stakes and low intensity democracy: Understanding America's policy of promoting democracy', in Michael Cox, John Ikenberry and Takashi Inoguchi (eds) *American Democracy Promotion*, pp. 200–17 at 216.

16 David Callahan, *Between Two Worlds*, New York, HarperCollins, 1994, p. 283.

17 Sikkink, 'The power of principled ideas', in Goldstein and Keohane (eds) *Ideas and Foreign Policy*, p. 140.

18 For further details see Jan Hancock, *Environmental Human Rights: Power, Ethics and Law*, Aldershot; Ashgate, 2003, chs. 1 and 2. For an excellent discussion on how the literature on international ethics has tended to remain confined to an empiricist discourse that eschews normative questions and discussions of social power relations see Anthony Lang, 'Responsibility in the international system: reading US foreign policy in the Middle East', *European Journal of International Relations*, 1999, vol. 5, no. 1, pp. 67–107 at 98.

19 David Chandler, 'The limits of human rights and cosmopolitan citizenship', in David Chandler (ed.) *Rethinking Human Rights: Critical Approaches to International Politics*, Basingstoke, Palgrave, 2002, pp. 115–135 at 134.

20 Woodrow Wilson (1917) *Proclamation to the American People*, Washington, DC, April 15.

21 See, for example, Woodrow Wilson (1916) *Address to the Congress*, Washington, DC, April 19.

22 Wilson, *Address to the Congress*.

23 Wilson, *Address to the Congress*.

24 Woodrow Wilson, quoted in Noam Chomsky, *Hegemony or Survival? America's Quest for Global Dominance*, London, Hamish Hamilton, 2003, p. 42.

25 Woodrow Wilson, quoted in Ivo Daalder and James Lindsay, 'America unbound', *New York Times*, January 25, 2004. Online, available at: www.nytimes.com (accessed February 4, 2004).

26 Woodrow Wilson, quoted in US Department of State, 'The Tampico Affair', *Papers Relating to Foreign Affairs*, Washington, DC, 1914, pp. 474–6.

27 Woodrow Wilson (1917) *Address to Joint Session of Congress*, April 2.

28 Wilson, *Proclamation to the American People*.

29 Woodrow Wilson (1917) *Second Inaugural Address*, March 5.

30 See Woodrow Wilson (1918) *Speech Delivered to Congress in Joint Session*, January 8.

31 Kenneth Thompson, 'New reflections on ethics and foreign policy: the problem of human rights', *The Journal of Politics*, 1978, vol. 40, no. 4, pp. 984–1010 at 998.

32 Lawrence Freedman, 'The age of liberal wars', *Review of International Studies*, 2005, vol. 31, sp. iss., pp. 92–107 at 99.

33 McElroy, *Morality and American Foreign Policy*, p. 41.

34 See Henry Kissinger, *Diplomacy*, New York, Simon and Schuster, 1994, pp. 29–55.

35 Kissinger, *Diplomacy*, p. 46.

36 Walter Russell Mead, *Special Providence: American Foreign Policy and How it Changed the World*, New York, Routledge, 2002, p. 325.

37 Adam Wolfson, 'Conservatives and neoconservatives', *Public Interest*, 2004, no. 154, pp. 32–40 at 39.

38 Kevin Cole, 'The Wilsonian model of foreign policy and the post-cold war world', *Air and Space Power Chronicles*, 1999, vol. 13, no. 2. Online, available at: www.airpower.maxwell.af.mil/airchronicles/cc/Cole.html (accessed March 3, 2002).

39 Michael Warner, 'A new strategy for the new geopolitics', *Public Interest*, 2003, no. 153, pp. 94–8 at 96.

40 Letter from Nathan Boyd, Rio Grande Irrigation and Land Company Ltd, to Counselor Marshall Morgan, The American and British Claims Tribunal, Department of State, July 19, 1920, Presidential Papers Microfilm, Madison Building, Library of Congress, Washington, DC, Series 5, Paris Peace Conference 1914–21, sub series A, 'Policy Documents', reels 383–4.

41 Warner, 'A new strategy for the new geopolitics', pp. 94–8 and Wolfson, 'Conservatives and neoconservatives', pp. 32–40.

42 See Wilson, *Speech Delivered to Congress in Joint Session*.

43 Woodrow Wilson, quoted in William Robinson, 'Promoting capitalist polyarchy: the case of Latin America', in Michael Cox, John Ikenberry and Takashi Inoguchi (eds) *American Democracy Promotion*, pp. 308–25 at 313.

44 See Gabriel Kolko, *Main Currents in Modern American History*, New York, Pantheon, 1984, p. 47.

45 For details see Jack Donnelly, *International Human Rights*, 2nd edition, Boulder, CO, Westview Press, 1998, p. 96; see also Ivo Daalder and James Lindsay, *America Unbound: The Bush Revolution in Foreign Policy*, Washington, DC, Brookings Institution Press, 2003, p. 6.

46 See Edwin Lieuwin, *US Policy in Latin America*, London, Praeger, 1965 and Michael Cox, 'Wilsonianism resurgent? The Clinton Administration and the promotion of democracy', in Michael Cox, John Ikenberry and Takashi Inoguchi (eds) *American Democracy Promotion*, pp. 218–39 at 236.

47 See Cox, 'Wilsonianism resurgent?' in Cox, Ikenberry and Inoguchi (eds) *American Democracy Promotion*, p. 236.

48 Woodrow Wilson, quoted in Cox, 'Wilsonianism resurgent?' in Cox, Ikenberry and Inoguchi (eds) *American Democracy Promotion*, p. 236.

49 For details see M. Dennis, 'Looking backward: Woodrow Wilson, the new south and the question of race', *American Nineteenth Century History*, 2002, vol. 3, no. 1, pp. 77–104 at 77.

50 Hereafter referred to simply as the Mezes document.

51 S.E. Mezes, D.H. Miller and Walter Lippmann, *The Present Situation: The War Aims and Peace Terms it Suggests*, Woodrow Wilson Collection Microfilm, Madison Building, Library of Congress, Washington, DC, Series 5, Paris Peace Conference 1914–21, sub series A, 'Policy Documents', reels 383–4, p. 26.

52 The description on the original document reads, 'Brought by EM House to Woodrow Wilson Jan 4, 1918. WW had this before him when he wrote his 14-Points speech'. See Mezes, Miller and Lippmann, *The Present Situation*, p. 1.

53 For example, point seven related to the evacuation of Belgium. This is recommended in Mezes, Miller and Lippmann, *The Present Situation* p. 27. Point eight calls for the return to France of territories taken during the war by Germany. The Mezes document recommends the return of Northern France and Alsace Lorraine to France from Germany (pp. 27–8). Point nine calls for readjusted frontiers of Italy, 'along clearly recognizable lines of nationality', thereby resonating a recommendation in the Mezes document for 'a strong public move in the direction of Italy, emphasizing Italy's just claims to a rectification of her frontier, both for defensive and for nationalistic reasons' (pp. 17–18). Point 11 on self-determination for Serbia realizes a recommendation on pp. 22 and 30 of the Mezes document asserting Serbia's rights to independence and access to the sea. Point 13 calls for an independent Poland which the Mezes document calls for on pp. 32–3. Point 14 calling for a League of Nations resonates a discussion on pp. 37–8 of the Mezes document. See Wilson, *Speech Delivered to Congress in Joint Session*.

54 The PATRIOT Act was described as promoting security 'while also protecting our fundamental liberties' in National Security Council, *United States of America National Security Strategy*, Washington, DC, 2006, p. 8. For further details see David Cole, *Enemy Aliens: Double Standards and Constitutional Freedoms in the War on Terrorism*, New York, New York Press, 2004 and Christian Parenti, *The Soft Cage: Surveillance in America from Slavery to the War on Terror*, New York, Basic Books, 2004.

55 Mezes, Miller and Lippmann, *The Present Situation*, pp. 22–6.

56 Mezes, Miller and Lippmann, *The Present Situation*, p. 25.
57 Mezes, Miller and Lippmann, *The Present Situation*, p. 25.
58 Mezes, Miller and Lippmann, *The Present Situation*, p. 26.
59 Mezes, Miller and Lippmann, *The Present Situation*, pp. 34–5.
60 Mezes, Miller and Lippmann, *The Present Situation*, pp. 34–5.
61 Wilson, *Speech Delivered to Congress in Joint Session*.
62 Wilson, *Speech Delivered to Congress in Joint Session*.
63 Mezes, Miller and Lippmann, *The Present Situation*, pp. 17–18.
64 Mezes, Miller and Lippmann, *The Present Situation*, p. 24.
65 See Noam Chomsky, *Rethinking Camelot: JFK, the Vietnam War and US Political Culture*, London, Verso, 1993, p. 43.
66 Mezes, Miller and Lippmann, *The Present Situation*, pp. 9–10.
67 Mezes, Miller and Lippmann, *The Present Situation*, p. 20.
68 Mezes, Miller and Lippmann, *The Present Situation*, p. 15.
69 Mezes, Miller and Lippmann, *The Present Situation*, p. 10.
70 Mezes, Miller and Lippmann, *The Present Situation*, p. 14.
71 Walter LaFeber, *Inevitable Revolutions*, London, Norton, 1983, pp. 50 and 75.
72 Chomsky, *Hegemony or Survival*, p. 64.
73 Stephen Gill, *American Hegemony and the Trilateral Commission*, Cambridge, Cambridge University Press, 1990, pp. 220–1; Justin Rosenberg, *The Empire of Civil Society: A Critique of the Realist Theory of International Relations*, London, Verso, 1994, p. 37 and Tony Evans, *US Hegemony and the Project of Universal Human Rights*, London, St Martin's Press, 1996, p. 102.
74 Sikkink, 'The power of principled ideas', in Goldstein and Keohane (eds) *Ideas and Foreign Policy*, p. 139.
75 McElroy, *Morality and American Foreign Policy*, p. 173.
76 Warner, 'A new strategy for the new geopolitics', p. 94.
77 Diamond, 'Promoting democracy' in Wittkopf (ed.) *The Future of American Foreign Policy*, p. 105.
78 Alan Dobson, 'The dangers of US intervention', *Review of International Studies*, 2002, vol. 28, no. 3, pp. 577–97 at 580.
79 Jimmy Carter, quoted in Ambrose and Brinkley, *Rise to Globalism*, p. 282.
80 Jimmy Carter, quoted in Thompson, 'New reflections on ethics and foreign policy', p. 986.
81 Jimmy Carter (1981) *Farewell Address*, Washington, DC, January 14.
82 Jimmy Carter, quoted in Ambrose and Brinkley, *Rise to Globalism*, p. 281.
83 Jimmy Carter, quoted in Henry Kissinger, *Does America Need a Foreign Policy? Toward a Diplomacy for the 21st Century*, New York, Simon and Schuster, 2001, p. 250.
84 Jimmy Carter, quoted in Rosemary Foot, 'Credibility at stake: domestic supremacy in US human rights policy', in Eugene Wittkopf and James McCormick (eds) *The Domestic Sources of American Foreign Policy: Insights and Evidence*, Lanham, MD, Rowman and Littlefield Publishers, 2004, p. 105.
85 Carter, *Farewell Address*.
86 These were then sent to the Senate where, as of 2006, the International Covenant on Economic, Social and Cultural Rights (ICESCR) has still not been ratified. The International Covenant on Civil and Political Rights (ICCPR) was approved in 1992 but the Senate did not accept the First Optional Protocol, declared that the treaty was not self-executing and attached Reservations, Understandings and Declarations (RUDs) limiting US commitments under the covenant.
87 For details see Donnelly, *International Human Rights*, p. 99 and Sikkink, 'The power of principled ideas', in Goldstein and Keohane (eds) *Ideas and Foreign Policy*, p. 151.

88　Donnelly, *International Human Rights*, p. 98 and Ambrose and Brinkley, *Rise to Globalism*, p. 290.

89　For details see Ambrose and Brinkley, *Rise to Globalism*, p. 291.

90　Sikkink, 'The power of principled ideas', in Goldstein and Keohane (eds) *Ideas and Foreign Policy*, p. 151.

91　Ambrose and Brinkley, *Rise to Globalism*, p. 282.

92　Donnelly, *International Human Rights*, p. 102.

93　Donnelly, *International Human Rights*, p. 102.

94　The study compared the human rights situation of 59 states receiving US aid during the first two years of both the Reagan and Carter Administrations. It found that the situation improved in five states during the Carter years and deteriorated in four. The human rights situation improved in seven states and deteriorated in eight 1981–3. See D. Carleton and M. Stohl, 'The foreign policy of human rights: Rhetoric and reality from Jimmy Carter to Ronald Reagan', *Human Rights Quarterly*, 1985, vol. 7, no. 2, pp. 205–29 at 228.

95　Carleton and Stohl, 'The foreign policy of human rights', pp. 205–29.

96　Lars Schoultz, 'US foreign policy and human rights violations in Latin America: A comparative analysis of foreign aid distributions,' *Comparative Politics*, 1981, vol. 13, no. 2, pp. 149–70 at 167.

97　See Donnelly, *International Human Rights*, p. 102.

98　Zbigniew Brzezinski, *The Grand Chessboard: American Primacy and its Geostrategic Imperatives*, New York, Basic Books, 1997, p. 40.

99　See Chomsky, *Hegemony or Survival*, p. 22.

100　See William Blum, *Rogue State: A Guide to the World's Only Superpower*, London, Zed Books, 2002, p. 88.

101　United Nations, *General Assembly Resolution 34/46*, November 23, 1979. Blum, *Rogue State*, p. 186.

102　United Nations, *General Assembly Resolution 34/90A*, December 12, 1979. Blum, *Rogue State*, p. 186.

103　United Nations, *General Assembly Resolutions 34/93D*, December 12, 1979 and *34/199*, December 19, 1979 and Blum, *Rogue State*, p. 187.

104　Chomsky, *Hegemony or Survival*, p. 88.

105　Thompson, 'New reflections on ethics and foreign policy', p. 985.

106　See Thompson, 'New reflections on ethics and foreign policy', p. 985.

107　Jimmy Carter quoted in Phyllis Bennis, *Before and After: United States Foreign Policy and the War on Terrorism*, Moreton-in-Marsh, Arris Books, 2003, p. 48 and Ambrose and Brinkley, *Rise to Globalism*, pp. 288–9.

108　David Harvey, *The New Imperialism*, Oxford, Oxford University Press, 2003, p. 21.

109　Bennis, *Before and After*, p. 48.

110　See Ann Mayer, *Islam and Human Rights: Tradition and Politics*, 2nd edition, Boulder, CO, Westview Press, 1995, p. 5.

111　Jimmy Carter quoted in Ambrose and Brinkley, *Rise to Globalism*, p. 295.

3　Inconsistent application of human rights

1　The majority of whom were non-combatants and children. See Nicolas de Torrente, *Forgotten War: Democratic Republic of Congo*, New York, de.Mo, 2005.

2　The US Ambassador to Zimbabwe, Christopher Dell, has, for example, been so outspoken in his criticism of the repression carried out by Robert Mugabe's government that he has been threatened with expulsion.

3　Colin Powell, quoted in Shirin Tahir-Kheli (2001) *Item 9: Violation of Human Rights and Fundamental Freedoms in Any Part of the World*, 57th Session of the UN Commission on Human Rights, Geneva, March 30.

4 Colin Powell, quoted in Human Rights Watch (2005) *World Report*. Online, available at: www.hrw.org/wr2k5 (accessed March 3, 2005).
5 George W. Bush (2004) *President Speaks to the United Nations General Assembly*, New York, September 21.
6 Colin Powell, quoted in Toby Manhire, 'Darfur', *Guardian*, July 21, 2004. Online, available at: www.guardian.co.uk (accessed July 22, 2004).
7 See Human Rights Watch, *World Report*.
8 Jonathan Steele, 'Sudan urged to accept UN force as talks falter', *Guardian*, February 6, 2006. Online, available at: www.guardian.co.uk (accessed February 7, 2006).
9 George Moose (2001) *Briefing to the Press*, 57th Session of the UN Commission on Human Rights, Palais des Nations, Geneva, March 21.
10 Tahir-Kheli, *Item 9*.
11 See Michael Klare, 'Blood for oil: the Bush–Cheney energy strategy', in Leo Panitch and Colin Leys (eds) *Socialist Register 2004: The New Imperial Challenge*, London, Merlin Press, 2003, pp. 166–85 at 177.
12 Coletta Youngers, 'Latin America', in John Feffer (ed.) *Power Trip: US Unilateralism and Global Strategy After September 11*, New York, Seven Stories Press, 2003, pp. 150–61 at 154.
13 For further details see Ignacio Ramonet, 'Bolivia: When is a democracy not a democracy?' *La Monde Diplomatique*, November 2003. Online, available at: www.mondediplo.com (accessed December 13, 2003).
14 Youngers, 'Latin America', in Feffer (ed.) *Power Trip*, p. 155.
15 See David Harvey, *The New Imperialism*, Oxford, Oxford University Press, 2003, p. 9 and Department of State, *Supporting Human Rights and Democracy: The US Record 2003–2004*, Washington, DC, 2004, p. 258.
16 Ian James, 'Talk of US plot divides Venezuelans', *Associated Press*, November 19, 2005. Online, available at: www.washingtonpost.com (accessed November 20, 2005).
17 See Associated Press, 'Rumsfeld likens Chavez's rise to Hitler's', *Washington Post*, February 3, 2006. Online, available at: www.washingtonpost.com (accessed February 3, 2006).
18 Robert Jackson (2004) *Human Rights and Democracy in Venezuela*, Statement before the Congressional Human Rights Caucus, Washington, DC, April 22.
19 Center for Security Policy, *Precision-Guided Ideas*, Annual Report, Washington, DC, 2002, p. 21.
20 Associated Press, 'Rumsfeld likens Chavez's rise to Hitler's'.
21 Ramonet, 'Bolivia'.
22 Condoleezza Rice (2003) *Statement Made at the Interamerican Press Association*, Chicago, October 13.
23 Compared to Akbar Rafsanjani's 10 million votes. See Robert Tait, 'Shock as Iran elects hard-line president', *Observer*, June 26, 2005. Online, available at: www.guardian.co.uk (accessed June 27, 2005).
24 See Chapter 1 for details.
25 George W. Bush (2006) *State of the Union Address*, Washington, DC, January 31.
26 Bush, 2006 *State of the Union Address*.
27 Condoleezza Rice, quoted in Associated Press, 'Rice asks Congress for $75 million for Iran', *New York Times*, February 15, 2006. Online, available at: www.nytimes.com (accessed February 15, 2006).
28 Condoleezza Rice, quoted in Associated Press, 'Rice asks Congress for $75 Million for Iran'.
29 For further details see Human Rights Watch (2002) *Saudi Arabia: New Evidence of Torture*. Online, available at: www.hrw.org/ (accessed April 3, 2002); Amnesty International (2004) *Amnesty International Annual Report*. Online, available at:

web.amnesty.org/report2004/index-eng (accessed February 23, 2005); Michael Klare, 'Corporations, national security and war profiteering', *Multinational Monitor*, 2001, vol. 22, no. 11. Online, available at: www.multinational monitor.org/mm2001/01/nov01interviewklare.html (accessed March 22, 2002) and Christopher Joyner, 'US foreign policy, democracy and the Islamic world', in David Forsythe (ed.) *The United States and Human Rights: Looking Inward and Outward*, Lincoln, NE, University of Nebraska Press, 2000, pp. 246–70 at 264.

30 See Chalmers Johnson, *The Sorrows of Empire: How the Americans Lost Their Country*, New York, Metropolitan Book, 2003.

31 Fraser Cameron, *US Foreign Policy After the Cold War: Global Hegemon or Reluctant Sheriff?* London and New York, Routledge, 2002, p. 129.

32 National Energy Policy Development Group, *Report of the National Energy Policy Development Group*, 2001, Washington, DC, p. 8–4. Online, available at: www.whitehouse.gov/energy/ (accessed August 25, 2002).

33 Klare 'Corporations, national security and war profiteering'.

34 Klare, 'Blood for oil', in Panitch and Leys (eds) *Socialist Register 2004*, p. 171.

35 Kenneth Roth, 'The fight against terrorism: the Bush Administration's dangerous neglect of human rights', in Thomas G. Weiss, Margaret E. Crahan and John Goering (eds) *Wars on Terrorism and Iraq: Human Rights, Unilateralism and US Foreign Policy*, London, Routledge, 2004, pp. 113–31 at 115 and Stephen Zunes, 'Middle East', in Feffer (ed.) *Power Trip*, pp. 128–38 at 136.

36 Department of State (2004) *Supporting Human Rights and Democracy: The US Record 2003–2004*. Online, available at: www.state.gov/g/drl/rls/shrd/2003/31022.htm (accessed January 28, 2005).

37 See Stephen Zunes, 'US foreign policy, democracy and human rights', in David Forsythe (ed.) *The United States and Human Rights: Looking Inward and Outward*, Lincoln, NE, University of Nebraska Press, 2000, pp. 227–45 at 229.

38 National Security Council, *United States of America National Security Strategy*, Washington, DC, 2006, p. 2.

39 Thomas Carothers, 'Democracy promotion', *Foreign Affairs*, 2003, vol. 82, no. 3, pp.141–5 at 144.

40 For details see David Forsythe (2003) *US Foreign Policy and Human Rights in an Era of Insecurity: The Bush Administration and Human Rights After 9/11*, p. 20. Online, available at: www.unl.edu/polisci/faculty/forsythe/cuny-paper.pdf (accessed March 20, 2004).

41 For details see David Forsythe, 'US foreign policy and human rights in an era of insecurity', in Weiss, Crahan and Goering (eds) *Wars on Terrorism and Iraq*, pp. 80–97 at 87.

42 Forsythe, 'US foreign policy and human rights in an era of insecurity: the Bush Administration and human rights after 9/11', p. 21.

43 Lawyers Committee for Human Rights, *Imbalance of Powers*, Washington, DC, Human Rights First, 2003, p. 75.

44 Quoted in Lawyers Committee for Human Rights, *Imbalance of Powers*, p. 75.

45 George W. Bush (2000) *Presidential Debate at Wake Forest University*, October 11 and George W. Bush quoted in Ron Suskind, *The Price of Loyalty*, New York, Pocket Books, 2004, pp. 71–2.

46 For details see Jack Donnelly, 'International human rights: unintended consequences of the war on terrorism', in Weiss, Crahan and Goering (eds) *Wars on Terrorism and Iraq*, pp. 98–112 at 102.

47 Neumann quoted in Roger Burbach and Jim Tarbell, *Imperial Overstretch: George W. Bush and the Hubris of Empire*, London, Zed, 2004, p. 98.

48 See Dan Glaister, 'Bush foreign policy comes under renewed attack from within',

Guardian, June 14, 2004. Online, available at: www.guardian.co.uk (accessed June 15, 2004).

49 See especially George W. Bush (2006) *President's Radio Address*, Office of the Press Secretary, Englewood, Colorado, July 22.

50 General Dan Halutz quoted in David Clark, 'How can terrorism be condemned while war crimes go without rebuke?' *Guardian*, July 31, 2006. Online, available at: www.guardian.co.uk (accessed August 1, 2006) and leader, 'Death in Qana', *Guardian*, July 31, 2006. Online, available at: www.guardian.co.uk (accessed August 1, 2006).

51 Lebanese Health Minister Muhammed Jawad Khalifeh estimated that 600 Lebanese civilians had been killed with 382 confirmed dead and the remainder buried in rubble or missing. Nineteen Israeli citizens were reported killed in rocket attacks. See CBS (2006) *Rice to Return to Mideast*, July 28. Online, available at: www.cbsnews.com (accessed August 1, 2006).

52 Saree Makdisi, 'Lebanon's war with cluster bombs', *Los Angeles Times*, October 21, 2006. Online, available at: www.latimes.com (accessed October 22, 2006).

53 See Roth, 'The fight against terrorism', in Weiss, Crahan and Goering (eds) *Wars on Terrorism and Iraq*, p. 121.

54 See Lawyers Committee for Human Rights, *Holding the Line: A Critique of the Department of State's Annual Country Reports on Human Rights Practices*, Washington, DC, Human Rights First, 2003, p. 49.

55 See Donnelly, 'International human rights', in Weiss, Crahan and Goering (eds) *Wars on Terrorism and Iraq*, p. 102.

56 Frederick Gareau, *State Terrorism and the United States*, Atlanta, GA, Clarity Press, 2004, p. 199.

57 George W. Bush, quoted in Carothers, 'Democracy promotion', p. 144.

58 For details see Kate Gilmore (2002) *The War Against Terrorism: A Human Rights Perspective*. Online, available at: www.web.amnesty.org/web.nsf (accessed March 17, 2003).

59 Grace Livingstone, *Inside Colombia: Drugs, Democracy and War*, London, Latin American Bureau, 2003, pp. 29–32.

60 Amnesty International (2004) *Colombia*. Online, available at: www.amnesty.org (accessed September 6, 2004).

61 Livingstone, *Inside Colombia*, p. 29.

62 Youngers, 'Latin America', in Feffer (ed.) *Power Trip*, pp. 158–9 and Mario Murillo, *Colombia and the United States: War, Unrest and Destabilization*, New York, Seven Stories Press, 2004, p. 142.

63 Jim Lobe (2004) *US Militarizing Latin America*. Online, available at: www.LewRockwell.com (accessed October 7, 2004).

64 Lawyers Committee for Human Rights, *Holding the Line*, p. 124.

65 For details see Lawyers Committee for Human Rights, *Holding the Line*, pp. 25–6.

66 For details see Lawyers Committee for Human Rights, *Holding the Line*, pp. 25–6.

67 See Lawyers Committee for Human Rights, *Holding the Line*, p. 25.

68 See Lawyers Committee for Human Rights, *Holding the Line*, p. 26.

69 Department of State, *Supporting Human Rights and Democracy*, p. 234.

70 For example, reporting that regular military units went in advance of paramilitary forces and that locals have recognized members of the security forces among the ranks of the paramilitaries. See United Nations Commission on Human Rights, *Report of the United Nations High Commissioner for Human Rights on the Human Rights Situation in Colombia*, February 24, 2003, E/CN.4/2003/13, p. 14.

71 Human Rights Watch (2003) *Briefing to the 59th Session of the UN Commission on Human Rights: Colombia*, February 27. Online, available at: www.hrw.org/un/chr59/colombia.htm (accessed April 20, 2004).

72 Amnesty International concluded in 2003 that 'paramilitaries operating in collusion with the security forces were responsible for the vast majority of disappearances and killings of civilians'. See Amnesty International (2003) *Amnesty International Report 2003*. Online, available at: www.amnesty.org/report2003/col-summary-eng (accessed February 3, 2003).

73 Lawyers Committee for Human Rights, *Holding the Line,* p. 32.

74 For details see Youngers, 'Latin America', in Feffer (ed.) *Power Trip*, pp. 159–160; Steve Kretzmann, 'Oil, security, war: the geopolitics of US energy planning', *Multinational Monitor*, 2003, vol. 24, nos. 1–2. Online, available at: www.multinational-monitor.org (accessed April 21, 2005) and Klare, 'Blood for oil', in Panitch and Leys (eds) *Socialist Register 2004*, p. 178.

75 C. Chivers and Ethan Wilensky-Lanford, 'Uzbeks say troops shot recklessly at civilians', *New York Times*, May 17, 2005. Online, available at: www.nytimes.com (accessed May 18, 2005).

76 Richard Boucher, quoted in Reuters, 'US "disturbed" by Uzbek crackdown, urges reform', *New York Times*, May 16, 2005. Online, available at: www.nytimes.com (accessed May 17, 2005).

77 Nicholas Burns, quoted in Reuters, 'Top US diplomat postponing Uzbekistan trip', *New York Times*, July 31, 2005. Online, available at: www.nytimes.com (accessed August 1, 2005).

78 Nick Walsh, 'Brutality and poverty fuel wave of unrest', *Guardian*, May 16, 2005, p. 15.

79 According to estimates provided by *Human Rights Watch* see Gareau, *State Terrorism and the United States*, p. 199.

80 Theo van Boven, quoted in Craig Murray, 'What drives support for the torturer?' *Guardian*, May 16, 2005, p. 20.

81 See Murray, 'What drives support for the torturer?' p. 20.

82 Murray, 'What drives support for the torturer?' p. 20.

83 See Lawyers Committee for Human Rights, *Imbalance of Powers*, p. 74. This figure includes military and security aid. In addition an undisclosed sum has been provided to Uzbekistan from the Pentagon budget. See Murray, 'What drives support for the torturer?' p. 20.

84 Talib Yakubov, quoted in Lawyers Committee for Human Rights, *Imbalance of Powers*, p. 75.

85 Craig Murray, quoted in Jane Meyer, 'Outsourcing torture', *The New Yorker*, February 14, 2005. Online, available at: www.newyorker.com (accessed February 16, 2005).

86 Craig Murray, quoted in Meyer, 'Outsourcing torture'. For further details see also Noam Chomsky, *Hegemony or Survival? America's Quest for Global Dominance*, London, Hamish Hamilton, 2003, p. 114.

87 See Forsythe, 'US foreign policy and human rights in an era of insecurity', in Weiss, Crahan and Goering (eds) *Wars on Terrorism and Iraq*, p. 87.

88 See Murray, 'What drives support for the torturer?' p. 20.

89 Lawyers Committee for Human Rights, *Holding the Line*, pp. 62–5.

90 See Lawyers Committee for Human Rights, *Holding the Line*, p. 64.

91 See Bagila Bukharbayeva, 'Hundreds dead in Uzbek uprising', *Associated Press*, May 15, 2005. Online, available at: www.nytimes.com (accessed May 16, 2005).

92 Scott McClellan, quoted in Murray, 'What drives support for the torturer?' p. 20.

93 Lawyers Committee for Human Rights, *Holding the Line*, p. 77.

94 Lawyers Committee for Human Rights, *Holding the Line*, p. 2.

95 Lawyers Committee for Human Rights, *Holding the Line*, p. iii.

96 Quoted in Lawyers Committee for Human Rights, *Holding the Line*, p. iii.

97 Lawyers Committee for Human Rights, *Holding the Line*, p. 9.

98 Amnesty International, *2004 Amnesty International Annual Report*; see also Amnesty International (2004) *Building an International Human Rights Agenda*. Online, available at: web.amnesty.org/web/web.nsf (accessed February 17, 2005).

99 Emphasis added. Paul Wolfowitz, 'Remembering the Future', *The National Interest*, Spring 2000, p. 4.

100 Lorne Craner (2001) *Remarks to the Heritage Foundation*, Washington, DC, October 31.

4 Consistent application of human rights

1 Henry Kissinger, 'America at the apex', *The National Interest*, 2001, Summer, p. 15.

2 See David Harvey, *The New Imperialism*, Oxford, Oxford University Press, 2003, pp. 190–1.

3 See Andrew Kohut, *Bush's Gains Broad-Based*, Washington, DC, Pew Research Center, 2004, p. 1.

4 See Kohut, *Bush's Gains Broad-Based*, p. 2.

5 Kohut, *Bush's Gains Broad-Based*, p. 4.

6 For details see Roger Burbach and Jim Tarbell, *Imperial Overstretch: George W. Bush and the Hubris of Empire*, London, Zed, 2004, p. 95.

7 Christian Coalition of America (2005) *Our Mission*. Online, available at: www.cc.org/mission.cfm (accessed January 3, 2005) and Christian Coalition of America (2005) *About Us*. Online, available at: www.cc.org/about.cfm (accessed January 3, 2005).

8 See George W. Bush (2001) *News Conference*, October 11 and George W. Bush (2001) *President Says US Attorneys are Front Line in War*, US Attorneys Conference, November 29.

9 George W. Bush, quoted in Julian Borger, 'How born-again George became a man on a mission', *Guardian*, October 7, 2005. Online, available at: www.guardian.co.uk (accessed October 8, 2005).

10 George W. Bush, quoted in Rupert Cornwall, 'Bush: God told me to invade Iraq', *Independent*, October 7, 2005. Online, available at: www.news.independent.co.uk (accessed October 8, 2005).

11 George W. Bush, quoted in Tim Reid, 'Bush begs for support to fight "evil radicals" waging war on humanity', *Times*, October 7, 2005, p. 46.

12 George W. Bush, quoted in Cornwall, 'Bush: God told me to invade Iraq'.

13 George W. Bush, quoted in Bob Woodward, *Plan of Attack*, London, Simon and Schuster, 2004, p. 379.

14 George W. Bush (2005) *President Sworn-In to Second Term*, Inauguration Speech, Washington, DC, January 20.

15 George W. Bush (2006) *State of the Union Address*, Washington, DC, January 31.

16 See Tom Barry and Jim Lobe, 'The people', in John Feffer (ed.) *Power Trip: US Unilateralism and Global Strategy After September 11*, New York, Seven Stories Press, 2003, pp. 39–49 at 44.

17 See the Project for the New American Century, *Rebuilding America's Defenses: Strategy, Forces and Resources for a New Century*, Washington, DC, 2000, p. iv.

18 American Enterprise Institute, *Annual Report*, Washington, DC, 2004, p. 1.

19 See Burbach and Tarbell, *Imperial Overstretch*, p. 93.

20 Quoted in Burbach and Tarbell, *Imperial Overstretch*, p. 93.

21 Donald Rumsfeld, quoted in Center for Security Policy, *Precision-Guided Ideas*, Annual Report, Washington, DC, 2002, p. 2.

22 George W. Bush, February 2003, quoted in American Enterprise Institute (2005), *Becoming a Donor*. Online, available at: www.aei.org/ (accessed January 5, 2005).

23 For further details see American Enterprise Institute, *Annual Report*, p. 36.

24 See editors, 'Bush's corporate cabinet', *Multinational Monitor*, 2001, vol. 22, no. 5. Online, available at: www.multinationalmonitor.org/mm2001/01may/may01toc.html (accessed August 18, 2002).

25 Editors, 'Bush's corporate cabinet'.

26 See Jim Lobe, 'North Korean attack on US diplomat spotlights ultra-hawk', *Inter Press Service News Agency*, August 4, 2003. Online, available at: www.ipsnews.net/print.asp?idnews=19517 (accessed December 16, 2003).

27 Project for the New American Century, *Rebuilding America's Defenses*, preface and Jim Lobe, 'Key officials used 9/11 as pretext for Iraq War', *Inter Press Service News Agency*, July 15, 2003. Online, available at: www.ipsnews.net/print.asp?idnews=19255 (accessed December 16, 2003).

28 Henry Luce Booth, 'The American century', in Michael Hogan (ed.) *The Ambiguous Legacy*, Cambridge, Cambridge University Press, 1999, pp. 11–29 at 20 (originally published in *Life Magazine*, 1942).

29 Project for the New American Century, *Rebuilding America's Defenses*, p. 4.

30 For details see Burbach and Tarbell, *Imperial Overstretch*, p. 89; see also Chalmers Johnson, *The Sorrows of Empire: How the Americans Lost Their Country*, New York, Metropolitan Books, 2003; Barry and Lobe, 'The people', in Feffer (ed.) *Power Trip*, p. 45 and Project for a New American Century (1998) *Letter to President Clinton on Iraq*, January 26. Online, available at: www.dartmouth.edu/~govdocs/iraq/letter.htm (accessed June 23, 2004).

31 Appointed by President Bush to the position of director for the Near East on the National Security Council in 2002.

32 Deputy secretary of state.

33 Undersecretary of state for arms control and international security.

34 Undersecretary of state for global affairs.

35 Secretary of defense.

36 Deputy secretary of defense.

37 Adviser to and former chairman of the Defense Policy Board.

38 Education secretary.

39 Representative to Afghanistan and Iraq.

40 Steve Smith, 'US democracy promotion: critical questions', in Michael Cox, G. John Ikenberry and Takachi Inoguchi (eds) *American Democracy Promotion: Impulses, Strategies and Impacts*, Oxford, Oxford University Press, 2000, pp. 63–82 at 73.

41 National Security Council, *United States of America National Security Strategy*, Washington, DC, 2006, p. 4.

42 In the cases of Bolivia, Chile, Guatemala, Haiti, Iran, Liberia, Pakistan, Paraguay, Somalia, South Africa, Sudan, South Vietnam, South Korea and Zaire. See Jack Donnelly, *International Human Rights*, 2nd edition, Boulder, CO, Westview Press, 1998, p. 87.

43 See Natalie Hevener Kaufman and David Whiteman, 'Opposition to human rights treaties in the United States Senate: the legacy of the Bricker Amendment', *Human Rights Quarterly*, 1988, vol. 10, no. 3, p. 309.

44 Senator Bricker, quoted in Kaufman and Whiteman, 'Opposition to human rights treaties in the United States Senate', p. 309.

45 Louis Henkin, 'Foreign affairs and the constitution', *Foreign Affairs*, 1987, vol. 66, no. 2, p. 305.

46 Lorne Craner (2004) *Briefing on Supporting Human Rights and Democracy*, Washington, DC, May 17.

47 George W. Bush (2003) *UK/US Joint Statement on Multilateralism*, 10 Downing St, London, November 20.

48 National Security Council, *United States of America National Security Strategy*, Washington, DC, 2002, p. v.
49 For an analysis of the market causing human rights violations see Jan Hancock, *Environmental Human Rights*, Aldershot, Ashgate, 2003.
50 Jeffrey Sachs, quoted in Warren Hoge, 'Bolton makes his case at UN for a new focus for aid projects', *New York Times*, September 1, 2005. Online, available at: www.nytimes.com (accessed September 3, 2005).
51 For details see Colum Lynch, 'US wants changes in UN agreement', *Washington Post*, August 25, 2005, p. A01 and op. ed., 'That's no way to treat visitors', *New York Times*, August 30, 2005. Online, available at: www.nytimes.com (accessed September 1, 2005).
52 See Colum Lynch, 'US wants changes in UN agreement'.
53 George Moose (2001) *Item 7: The Right to Development*, 57th Session of the UN Commission on Human Rights, Geneva, March 27.
54 Moose, *Item 7*.
55 United States Government (2003) *Comment on the Working Group on the Right to Development*, Statement at the UN Commission on Human Rights, 59th Session, February 10, quoted in Stephen Marks, 'The human right to development: between rhetoric and reality', *Harvard Human Rights Journal,* 2004, vol. 17, pp. 137–67 at 146–7.
56 Quoted in Marks, 'The human right to development', p. 147.
57 Moose, *Item 7*.
58 For details see Rosemary Foot, 'Credibility at stake: domestic supremacy in US human rights policy', in Eugene Wittkopf and James McCormick (eds) *The Domestic Sources of American Foreign Policy: Insights and Evidence*, Lanham, MD, Rowman and Littlefield Publishers, 2004, pp. 95–115 at 109.
59 National Security Council, *National Security Strategy*, 2002, p. 17.
60 See, for example, George W. Bush (2002) *President Bush Announces a New Initiative for Cuba*, May 18.
61 See Department of State, *Supporting Human Rights and Democracy: The US Record 2003–2004*, Washington, DC, 2004, p. vii.
62 For further details see George W. Bush (2002) *Remarks at the International Conference on Financing for Development in Monterrey*, Monterrey, March 22; Liz Sidoti, 'House cuts foreign aid request', *Washington Times*, June 30, 2002, p. A15; USAID Press Release (2002) *Millennium Challenge Account Update Fact Sheet*, June 3. Online, available at: www.usaid.gov/press/releases/2002/fs_mca.html (accessed August 5, 2002) and Marks, 'The human right to development', p. 161.
63 See Mark Weisbrot, 'Foreign economic policy', in Feffer (ed.) *Power Trip*, pp. 85–96 at 85.
64 George W. Bush (2000) *Bush-Gore Presidential Debate*, Wake Forest University, October 11.
65 Heritage Foundation, *Our Business is Solutions*, Annual Report, Washington, DC, 2002, p. 3.
66 Heritage Foundation, *Our Business is Solutions*, p. 3.
67 Heritage Foundation, *Our Business is Solutions*, p. 16.
68 Heritage Foundation, *Our Business is Solutions*, p. 16.
69 Larry Nowels, quoted in Marks, 'The human right to development', p. 163.
70 Colin Powell, quoted in Noy Thrupkaew, 'Culture', in Feffer (ed.) *Power Trip*, pp. 106–116 at 109.
71 For details see Center for Responsive Politics (2002) *Donald Rumsfeld*. Online, available at: www.opensecrets.org/bush/cabinet/cabinet.rumsfeld.asp (accessed December 16, 2003) and editors, 'Bush's corporate cabinet'.
72 Center for Responsive Politics, *Donald Rumsfeld*.

73 For details see Center for Responsive Politics (2002) *John Ashcroft: Attorney General*. Online, available at: www.opensecrets.org/bush/cabinet/cabinet. ashcroft.asp (accessed December 16, 2003).

74 For details see Center for Responsive Politics (2002) *Andrew H. Card Jr.* Online, available at: www.opensecrets.org/bush/cabinet/cabinet.card.asp (accessed December 16, 2003).

75 For details see editors, 'Bush's corporate cabinet'.

76 For details see Center for Responsive Politics (2002) *Ann M. Veneman: Agriculture Secretary*. Online, available at: www.opensecrets.org/bush/cabinet/cabinet. norton.asp (accessed December 16, 2003) and editors, 'Bush's corporate cabinet'.

77 For details see editors, 'Bush's corporate cabinet'.

78 For details see Center for Responsive Politics (2002) *Tommy G. Thompson: Health and Human Services Secretary*. Online, available at: www.opensecrets.org/bush/ cabinet/cabinet.thompson.asp (accessed December 16, 2003).

79 See editors, 'Bush's corporate cabinet'.

80 For further details see editors, 'Bush's corporate cabinet'.

81 For details see Center for Responsive Politics (2002) *Gale Norton: Interior Secretary*. Online, available at: www.opensecrets.org/bush/cabinet/cabinet.norton.asp (accessed December 16, 2003) and editors, 'Bush's corporate cabinet'.

82 See Center for Responsive Politics (2002) *Donald Evans: Commerce Secretary*. Online, available at: www.opensecrets.org/bush/cabinet/cabinet.evans.asp (accessed December 16, 2003).

83 See editorial, 'The corporate conservative administration takes shape', *Multinational Monitor*, 2001, vol. 22, nos. 1 and 2. Online, available at: www.multinationalmonitor.org/mm2001/01jan-feb/editorial.html (accessed January 31, 2005).

84 For further details see William Hartung and Michelle Ciarocca, 'Corporate think tanks and the doctrine of aggressive militarism', *Multinational Monitor*, 2003, vol. 24, nos. 1 and 2. Online, available at: www.multinational monitor.org (accessed December 2, 2004).

85 For further details see Hartung and Ciarocca, 'Corporate think tanks and the doctrine of aggressive militarism'.

86 For further details see Hartung and Ciarocca, 'Corporate think tanks and the doctrine of aggressive militarism'.

87 For further details see Hartung and Ciarocca, 'Corporate think tanks and the doctrine of aggressive militarism'.

88 For further details see Hartung and Ciarocca, 'Corporate think tanks and the doctrine of aggressive militarism'.

89 For details see Center for Responsive Politics (2002) *President George W. Bush: Introduction*. Online, available at: www.opensecrets.org/bush/index.asp (accessed December 16, 2003).

90 Figures provided by Center for Responsive Politics (2001) *President Bush's First 100 Days: A Look at How the Special Interests Have Fared*. Online, available at: www.opensecrets.org/bush/100days/energy.asp (accessed December 16, 2003).

91 Figures based on contributions of $200 or more, released by the Federal Election Commission, see Center for Responsive Politics (2002) *Oil and Gas: Top 20 Recipients*. Online, available at: www.opensecrets.org/industries/recips.asp?Ind= E01&cycle=2000&recipdetail= (accessed December 16, 2003).

92 According to figures from Center for Responsive Politics (2001) *A Money in Politics Backgrounder on the Energy Industry*. Online, available at: www.opensecrets.org/ pressreleases/energybriefing.htm (accessed on December 16, 2003).

93 Figures based on contributions of $200 or more, released by the Federal Election Commission. See Center for Responsive Politics (2003) *Coal Mining: Long Term*

Contribution Trends. Online, available at: www.opensecrets.org/industries/ indus.asp?Ind=E1210 (accessed December 16, 2003).

94 Figures obtained from Sheryl Fred, Center for Responsive Politics (2003) *The Best Defense.* Online, available at: www.opensecrets.org/news/defensebudget/index1.asp (accessed on December 16, 2003).

95 For further details see Fred, *The Best Defense.*

96 For details see Fred, *The Best Defense* and David Teather, 'Oil firm linked to Cheney gets Iraq boost', *Guardian*, October 30, 2003. Online, available at: www.guardian.co.uk/print/03858,4785553–110373,00.html (accessed November 1, 2003).

97 For details see Fraser Cameron, *US Foreign Policy After the Cold War: Global Hegemon or Reluctant Sheriff?* London and New York, Routledge, 2002, p. 96.

98 See Teather, 'Oil firm linked to Cheney gets Iraq boost'.

99 See Teather, 'Oil firm linked to Cheney gets Iraq boost'.

100 A point forcibly made at the time by Syrian Ambassador to the UN Mikhail Wehber. See Ian Traynor, 'Censored version of declaration provokes anger', *Guardian*, December 19, 2002. Online, available at: www.guardian.co.uk (accessed December 20, 2002).

101 For details see John Kampfner, *Blair's Wars*, London, Simon and Schuster, 2003, p. 229.

102 See Kampfner, *Blair's Wars*, p. 229.

103 See staff and agencies, 'UN row over Iraqi report', *Guardian*, December 10, 2002. Online, available at: www.guardian.co.uk (accessed December 11, 2002).

104 Quoted in Traynor, 'Censored version of declaration provokes anger'.

105 For details see Kampfner, *Blair's Wars*, p. 229; see also Traynor, 'Censored version of declaration provokes anger'.

106 See Jules Lobel and Michael Ratner, 'International Law', in Feffer (ed.) *Power Trip*, pp. 74–84 at 84.

107 See Lobel and Ratner, 'International Law', in Feffer (ed.) *Power Trip*, p. 83.

108 For details see Cameron, *US Foreign Policy After the Cold War*, p. 177.

109 Memo quoted in Paul Brown, 'Oil giant bids to replace climate expert', *Guardian*, April 5, 2002. Online, available at: www.guardian.co.uk (accessed April 6, 2002).

110 For details see Brown, 'Oil giant bids to replace climate expert'.

111 See Michael Klare, 'Blood for oil: the Bush–Cheney energy strategy', in Leo Panitch and Colin Leys (eds) *Socialist Register 2004: The New Imperial Challenge*, London, Merlin Press, 2003, pp. 166–85 at 167.

112 See Dana Milbank and Justin Blum, 'Document says oil chiefs met with Cheney Task Force', *Washington Post*, November 16, 2005, p. A01.

113 For details see Milbank and Blum, 'Document says oil chiefs met with Cheney Task Force'.

114 Frank Lautenberg, quoted in Milbank and Blum, 'Document says oil chiefs met with Cheney Task Force'.

115 See Lee Drutman, 'Repetitively straining workers', *Multinational Monitor*, 2004, vol. 25, no. 1. Online, available at: multinationalmonitor.org/mm2004/05012004/ may-june04corp2.html (accessed January 31, 2005).

116 For details see Drutman, 'Repetitively straining workers'.

117 For details see Drutman, 'Repetitively straining workers'.

118 For details see Garry Leech, 'Bush places corporate interests over human rights', *Dissident Voice*, June 10, 2003. Online, available at: www.dissidentvoice.org/Art-icles5/Leech_Victims-Rights.htm (accessed November 20, 2003).

119 For details see Leech, 'Bush places corporate interests over human rights'.

120 See David Forsythe (2003) *US Foreign Policy and Human Rights in an Era of Insecurity: The Bush Administration and Human Rights After 9/11*. Online, available at:

www.unl.edu/polisci/faculty/forsythe/cuny-paper.pdf (accessed March 20, 2004); Deborah Madsen, *American Exceptionalism*, Edinburgh, Edinburgh University Press, 1998, pp. 1–2 and Benjamin Barber, 'Imperialism or interdependence?', *Security Dialogue*, 2004, vol. 35, no. 2, pp. 237–242 at 239.

121 Adam Wolfson, 'Humanitarian Hawks?' *Policy Review*, December 1999, pp. 29–42.
122 Paula Dobriansky, 'United States human rights policy: an overview', *Department of State Bulletin*, Washington, DC, Department of State, 1988, p. 54.
123 George W. Bush (2002) *President Bush Delivers Graduation Speech at West Point*, June 1.
124 Lorne Craner (2001) *Speech to the Heritage Foundation*, October 31, quoted in Julie Mertus, 'The new US human rights policy: a radical departure', *International Studies Perspectives*, 2003, vol. 4, no. 4, pp. 371–84 at 373.
125 George W. Bush (2001) *President Discusses Stronger Economy and Homeland Defense*, Glen Burnie, Maryland, October 24.
126 George W. Bush (2003) *President Bush Announces Combat Operations in Iraq Have Ended*, USS Abraham Lincoln, May 1.
127 George W. Bush (2003) *President Bush Discusses Iraq Policy*, Whitehall Palace, London, November 19.
128 George W. Bush (2001) *President Speaks to the United Nations General Assembly*, New York, September 21.
129 See Mary Kaldor 'American Power', *International Affairs*, 2003, vol. 79, no. 1, pp. 1–22 and Jean Bethke Elshtain, *Just War Against Terror: Ethics and the Burden of American Power in a Violent World*, New York, Basic Books, 2003.
130 For well informed critiques of international human rights law see J. Watson, 'Legal theory, efficacy and validity in the development of human rights norms in international law', *University of Illinois Law Forum*, 1979, vol. 3, pp. 609–41 and Tony Evans, *US Hegemony and the Project of Universal Human Rights*, Basingstoke, Macmillan, 1996.
131 David Forsythe, 'The United States and international criminal justice', *Human Rights Quarterly*, 2002, vol. 24, no. 4, pp. 974–91 at 980.
132 The other being Somalia, see Amnesty International (2004) *More Than Words Needed This Human Rights Day*, AI Index: AMR 51/171/2004. Online, available at: www.amnestyusa.org (accessed January 4, 2005).
133 See Kenneth Roth, 'The fight against terrorism: the Bush Administration's dangerous neglect of human rights', in Thomas G. Weiss, Margaret E. Crahan and John Goering (eds) *Wars on Terrorism and Iraq: Human Rights, Unilateralism and US Foreign Policy*, London, Routledge, 2004, pp. 113–31 at 122.
134 Jim Lobe, 'New human rights network denounces selectivity in Bush Administration's human rights agenda', *Foreign Policy in Focus*, December 11, 2003, p. 2.
135 Lobel and Ratner, 'International Law', in Feffer (ed.) *Power Trip*, p. 78.
136 See, for example, National Security Council, *National Security Strategy*, 2002, p. 31.
137 John Bolton, quoted in Lobe, 'North Korean attack on US diplomat spotlights ultrahawk'.
138 See David Forsythe, 'The United States and international criminal justice', p. 984.
139 See Georg Nolte, 'The United States and the International Criminal Court', in David Malone and Yuen Khong (eds) *Unilateralism and United States Foreign Policy*, Boulder, CO, Lynne Rienner, 2003, pp. 71–93 at 81.
140 For details see Mertus, 'The new US human rights policy', p. 377 and Lobel and Ratner, 'International Law', in John Feffer (ed.) *Power Trip*, p. 80.
141 For details see Amnesty International, *More Than Words Needed This Human Rights Day* and Amnesty International (2003) *United States of America*. Online, available at: web.amnesty.org (accessed February 3, 2004).

142 The 'Hague Invasion Act'. See Roth, 'The fight against terrorism', in Weiss, Crahan and Goering (eds) *Wars on Terrorism and Iraq*, p. 123.

143 See Ajiz Ahmad, 'Imperialism of our time', in Panitch and Leys (eds) *Socialist Register 2004*, pp. 43–62 at 50.

144 Emphasis added. John Bolton, quoted in Colum Lynch, 'Bolton voices opposition to UN proposals', *Washington Post*, September 1, 2003, p. A23.

145 John Bolton, quoted in Colum Lynch, 'Bolton voices opposition to UN proposals', p. A23.

146 John Bolton, quoted in Colum Lynch, 'Bolton voices opposition to UN proposals', p. A23.

147 Emphasis added. National Security Council, 2006 *National Security Strategy*, p. 6.

148 David Chandler, 'Rhetoric without responsibility: the attraction of ethical foreign policy', *British Journal of Politics and International Relations*, 2003, vol. 5, no. 3, pp. 295–316 at 307.

149 See Leo Panitch and Sam Gindin, 'Global capitalism and American Empire', in Panitch and Leys (eds) *Socialist Register 2004*, pp. 1–42 at 31.

5 War on Terror

1 George W. Bush (2005) *President Bush Meets with President Torrijos of Panama*, Casa Amarilla, Panama City, November 7.

2 George W. Bush, quoted in Lawyers Committee for Human Rights, *Assessing the New Normal: Liberty and Security for the Post-September 11 United States*, Washington, DC, Human Rights First, 2003, p. 81.

3 Colin Powell (2004) *Statement: Human Rights Week*, Brussels, Belgium, December 8.

4 Richard Armitage, 'Allies, friends and partners on every page: international cooperation in the national security strategy', *US Foreign Policy Agenda*, 2002, vol. 7, no. 4, pp. 10–13 at 10.

5 Lorne Craner (2001) *Remarks to the Heritage Foundation*, Washington DC, October 31.

6 George W. Bush (2001) *Proclamation on Human Rights Observances*, White House, Washington, DC, December 9; see also George W. Bush (2004) *President Bush Discusses Importance of Democracy in Middle East*, Library of Congress, Washington, DC, February 4, in which the president spoke of advancing 'moral clarity' in fighting the war on terror since 'we are the heirs of the tradition of liberty, defenders of the freedom, the conscience and the dignity of every person'.

7 Bush, *Proclamation on Human Rights Observances*.

8 Bush, *Proclamation on Human Rights Observances*.

9 Signatories of the group include David Blankenthorn, Gerard Bradley, Paul Ekman, Jean Bethke Elshtain, Amitai Etzioni, Hillel Fradkin, Samuel Freedman, Neil Gilbert, David Gutmann, James Davison Hunter, James Turner Johnson, Daniel Patrick Moynihan, Michael Novak, Robert Putnam, Paul Vitz and Michael Walzer. Institute for American Values (2002) *What We're Fighting For: A Letter From America*. Online, available at: www.americanvalues.org/html/wwff.html (accessed July 12, 2003).

10 Institute for American Values, *What We're Fighting For: A Letter From America*.

11 Institute for American Values, *What We're Fighting For: A Letter From America*.

12 Henry Kissinger (2001) *Foreign Policy in the Age of Terrorism*, Ruttenberg lecture. Online, available at: ics.leeds.ac.uk/papers/pmt/exhibits/817/kissinger.pdf#search=%22Kissinger%20Foreign%20Policy%20in%20the%20Age%20of%20terrorism%20Ruttenberg%22 (accessed March 27, 2002).

13 Shattuck goes on to argue that fighting such human rights wars may be counterproductive on grounds that they engender rather than eliminate terrorists. John

Shattuck, *Freedom on Fire: Human Rights Wars and America's Response*, Boston, MA, Harvard University Press, 2003, p. 6.

14 Human Rights Watch, quoted in Frederick Gareau, *State Terrorism and the United States*, Atlanta, GA, Clarity Press, 2004, p. 191.

15 Human Rights Watch, quoted in Gareau, *State Terrorism and the United States*, p. 191.

16 George Will, 'Why didn't he ask Congress?' *Washington Post*, December 20, 2005, p. A31 and Peter Baker and Charles Babington, 'Bush addresses uproar over spying', *Washington Post*, December 20, 2005, p. A01.

17 For details see Baker and Babington, 'Bush addresses uproar over spying', p. A01.

18 For details see Cynthia Brown (ed.) *Lost Liberties: Ashcroft and the Assault on Personal Freedom*, New York, The New Press, 2004 and Nat Hentoff, *The War on the Bill of Rights and the Gathering Resistance*, New York, Seven Stories Press, 2004.

19 See editorial, 'Feds say Patriot Act not for homeless', *Washington Times*, June 30, 2005, p. A8.

20 Editorial, 'Feds say Patriot Act not for homeless', p. A8.

21 Department of Defense (1987) *US Army Field Manual on Intelligence Interrogation*. Online, available at: www.globalsecurity.org/intell/library/policy/army/fm/fm34–52/ (accessed November 4, 2005) and Arkan Mohammed Ali, Thahe Mohammed Sabbar, Sherzad Kamal Khalid, Ali H., Mehboob Ahmad, Said Nabi Siddiqi, Mohammed Karim Shirullah and Haji Abdul Rahman v Donald H. Rumsfeld, District Court for the Northern District of Illinois, February 2005, p. 2.

22 For details see Human Rights First (2005) *The Case Against Rumsfeld: Hard Facts Timeline*. Online, available at: www.humanrightsfirst.org/us_law/etn/lawsuit/PDF/rums-timeline-022805.pdf (accessed March 30, 2005).

23 See Lawyers Committee for Human Rights, *Holding the Line: A Critique of the Department of State's Annual Country Reports on Human Rights Practices*, Washington, DC, Human Rights First, 2003, p. 19.

24 State Department, *2002 State Department Country Report*, quoted in Lawyers Committee for Human Rights, *Holding the Line*, p. 19.

25 State Department, *2002 State Department Country Report*, quoted in Amnesty International (2004) *More than Words Needed this Human Rights Day*, AI Index: AMR 51/171/2004. Online, available at: www.amnestyusa.org (accessed February 23, 2005).

26 For details see Human Rights Watch (2003) *US State Department Criticism of Stress and Duress Interrogation Around the World*, April 16. Online, available at: www.hrw.org (accessed June 23, 2003).

27 See Human Rights First, *The Case Against Rumsfeld*.

28 For details see Human Rights First, *The Case Against Rumsfeld*.

29 See Amnesty International (2005) *An Appeal to President George W. Bush on the Occasion of His Re-Inauguration*, AI Index: AMR 51/012/2005. Online, available at: www.amnestyusa.org (accessed January 25, 2005).

30 Erik Saar and Viveca Novak, *Inside the Wire: A Military Intelligence Soldier's Eyewitness Account of Life at Guantanamo*, New York, Penguin Press, 2005, p. 222.

31 Quoted in Human Rights Watch, *World Report 2005*. Online, available at: www.hrw.org/english/docs/2005 (accessed February 2, 2006).

32 See Sheldon Alberts, 'Cheney defends Guantanamo methods', *National Post*, June 14, 2005, p. A9.

33 Alberts, 'Cheney defends Guantanamo methods', p. A9.

34 For details see American Civil Liberties Union (2004) *FBI E-Mail Refers to Presidential Order Authorizing Inhumane Interrogation Techniques*, December 20. Online, available at: www.aclu.org (accessed January 17, 2005).

35 Quoted in American Civil Liberties Union, *FBI E-Mail*.

36 See American Civil Liberties Union, *FBI E-Mail*.
37 For details see Dana Priest and Dan Eggen, 'Terror suspect alleges torture', *Washington Post*, January 6, 2005, p. A01.
38 See Human Rights Watch, *World Report 2005*.
39 Allegations reported in Tania Branigan and Vikram Dodd, 'Afghanistan to Guantanamo Bay: the story of three British detainees', *Guardian*, August 4, 2004. Online, available at: www.guardian.co.uk (accessed August 6, 2004).
40 Vikram Dodd and Tania Branigan, 'Questioned at gunpoint, shackled and forced to pose naked', *Guardian*, August 4, 2004. Online, available at: www.guardian.co.uk (accessed August 6, 2004).
41 According to Camp Echo prisoner 00558 Moazzam Begg, letter published in *Guardian*, July 12, 2004. Online, available at: www.imageguardian.co.uk (accessed July 13, 2004).
42 Leila Zerrougui, Leandro Despouy, Manfred Nowak, Asma Jahangir and Paul Hunt, *Report of the Chairperson of the Working Group on Arbitrary Detention*, United Nations Commission on Human Rights, E/CN.4/2006/120, February 15, 2006, p. 25.
43 Zerrougui *et al.*, *Report of the Chairperson of the Working Group on Arbitrary Detention*, p. 25.
44 Zerrougui *et al.*, *Report of the Chairperson of the Working Group on Arbitrary Detention*, p. 26.
45 Zerrougui *et al.*, *Report of the Chairperson of the Working Group on Arbitrary Detention*, p. 37.
46 Zerrougui *et al.*, *Report of the Chairperson of the Working Group on Arbitrary Detention*, p. 37.
47 See Colum Lynch, 'UN draft decries US on detainee treatment', *Washington Post*, February 14, 2006, p. A09.
48 Scott McClellan, quoted in staff and agencies, 'UN calls for Guantanamo Bay to close', *Guardian*, February 16, 2006. Online, available at: www.guardian.co.uk (accessed February 17, 2006).
49 Bryan Whitman, quoted in Robert Burns, 'Bad publicity puts Pentagon on defensive', *Associated Press*, February 17, 2006. Online, available at: www.wasingtonpost.com (accessed February 17, 2006).
50 Manfred Nowak, quoted in Nick Wadhams, 'UN report criticizes US for Gitmo', *Washington Post*, February 13, 2006. Online, available at: www.washingtonpost.com (accessed February 13, 2006).
51 J. Gordon quoted in Lynch, 'UN draft decries US on detainee treatment', p. A09.
52 See David Forsythe (2003) *US Foreign Policy and Human Rights in an Era of Insecurity: The Bush Administration and Human Rights After 9/11*, p. 15. Online, available at: www.unl.edu/polisci/faculty/forsythe/cuny-paper.pdf (accessed March 20, 2004).
53 Zerrougui *et al.*, *Report of the Chairperson of the Working Group on Arbitrary Detention*, p. 11.
54 See Mark Drumbl, 'Judging the 11 September terrorist attacks', *Human Rights Quarterly*, 2002, vol. 24, no. 2, pp. 323–60 at 340–1 and Human Rights Watch, *World Report 2005*.
55 Alberto Gonzales, quoted in Neil Lewis, 'US charges two with war crimes, setting stage for tribunals', *New York Times*, February 24, 2004. Online, available at: www.nytimes.com (accessed February 24, 2004).
56 For details see James Schlesinger (2004) *Final Report of the Independent Panel to Review DoD Detention Operations*, August 24, p. 7. Online, available at: news.findlaw.com/wp/docs/dod/abughraibrpt.pdf (accessed September 1, 2004).
57 Quoted in Human Rights Watch, *World Report 2005*.
58 For details see Kenneth Roth, 'The fight against terrorism: the Bush Administra-

tion's dangerous neglect of human rights', in Thomas G. Weiss, Margaret E. Crahan and John Goering (eds) *Wars on Terrorism and Iraq: Human Rights, Unilateralism and US Foreign Policy*, London, Routledge, 2004, pp. 113–31 at 117.

59 See Jules Lobel and Michael Ratner, 'International law', in John Feffer (ed.) *Power Trip: US Unilateralism and Global Strategy After September 11*, New York, Seven Stories Press, 2003, pp. 74–84 at 81 and Forsythe, *US Foreign Policy and Human Rights in an Era of Insecurity*, p. 14.

60 President George W. Bush, quoted in Amnesty International, *An Appeal to President George W. Bush on the Occasion of His Re-Inauguration*.

61 See Michael Ignatieff, 'International justice, war crimes and terrorism', *Social Research*, 2002, vol. 69, no. 4, pp. 1135–59 at 1144.

62 Revised February 2003, April 2003 and July 2003.

63 See Human Rights First, *Trials Under Military Order: A Guide to the Final Rules for Military Commissions*, Washington, DC, 2004, p. 1 and Avidan Cover (2004) *Military Commission Proceedings Violate International Law*. Online, available at: www.humanrightsfirst.org/media/2004_alerts/0817.htm (accessed September 13, 2004).

64 Roth, 'The fight against terrorism', in Weiss, Crahan and Goering (eds) *Wars on Terrorism and Iraq*, p. 119.

65 Protocol addition to protocol 1, article 75, Geneva Convention, August 12, 1949.

66 See Andrew Buncombe, 'Military tribunals at Guantanamo ruled illegal by US judge', *Independent*, November 10, 2004. Online, available at: www.independent.co.uk (accessed November 11, 2004).

67 For details see Human Rights First, *Trials Under Military Order*, pp. 2–3.

68 Military commission order no. 1, quoted in Human Rights First, *Trials Under Military Order*, p. 3.

69 See Human Rights First, *Trials Under Military Order*, p. 3.

70 Article 105, quoted in Human Rights First, *Trials Under Military Order*, p. 3. For further details see Michael Byers, 'Not yet havoc: geopolitical change and the international rules on military force', *Review of International Studies*, 2005, vol. 31, sp. iss., pp. 51–70.

71 Quoted in Saar and Novak, *Inside the Wire*, p. 55.

72 George W. Bush (2003) *President Bush, Prime Minister Hold Joint Press Conference*, White House, Washington, DC, November 20.

73 Dick Cheney, quoted in Alberts, 'Cheney defends Guantanamo methods', p. A9.

74 Quoted in staff and agencies, 'UN calls for Guantanamo Bay to close'.

75 Quoted in Tim Golden, 'After ruling, uncertainty hovers at Cuba prison', *New York Times*, June 30, 2006. Online, available at: www.nytimes.com (accessed June 30, 2006).

76 George W. Bush, quoted in Reuters, 'Bush speaks of closing Guantanamo prison', *New York Times*, May 8, 2006. Online, available at: www.nytimes.com (accessed May 8, 2006).

77 David Rose, 'Revealed: the full story of the Guantanamo Bay Britons', *Observer*, March 14, 2004. Online, available at: www.observer.guardian.co.uk (accessed March 15, 2004).

78 *Hamdan* v *Rumsfeld*, November 8, 2004. See Buncombe, 'Military tribunals at Guantanamo ruled illegal by US judge'.

79 John Ashcroft, quoted in Amnesty International, *More than Words*.

80 Associated Press, 'Bush must regroup after combatant ruling', June 29, 2004. Online, available at: www.nytimes.com (accessed June 29, 2004).

81 For discussion regarding the administration's response to these rulings see Human Rights Watch, *World Report 2005*.

82 See Buncombe, 'Military tribunals at Guantanamo ruled illegal by US judge'.

83 For details see Zerrougui *et al.*, *Report of the Chairperson of the Working Group on Arbitrary Detention*, p. 15.

84 See Linda Greenhouse, 'Justices, 5–3, broadly reject Bush plan to try detainees', *New York Times*, June 30, 2006. Online, available at: www.nytimes.com (accessed June 30, 2006).

85 Greenhouse, 'Justices, 5–3, broadly reject Bush plan to try detainees'.

86 For further details see Helen Kinsella, 'Discourses of differences: civilians, combatants and compliance with the rules of war', *Review of International Studies*, 2005, vol. 31, sp. iss., pp. 163–85.

87 Former intelligence official, quoted in James Risen, David Johnston and Neil Lewis, 'Harsh CIA methods cited in top Qaeda interrogations', *New York Times*, May 13, 2004. Online, available at: www.nytimes.com (accessed May 13, 2004).

88 See Dana Priest, 'CIA holds terror suspects in secret prisons', *Washington Post*, November 2, 2005, p. A01 and Isabel Hilton, 'The 800lb gorilla in American foreign policy', *Guardian*, July 28, 2004. Online, available at: www.guardian.co.uk (accessed July 28, 2004). The origins of the rendition program lie in a Presidential Directive signed by President Clinton which reads

> [i]f we do not receive adequate cooperation from a state that harbors a terrorist whose extradition we are seeking, we shall take appropriate measures to induce cooperation. Return of suspects by force may be effected without the cooperation of the host government, consistent with the procedures outlined in NSD-77, which shall remain in effect.
> See Bill Clinton (1995) *Presidential Decision Directive 39*, June 21. Online, available at: www.fas.org/irp/offdocs/pdd39.htm (accessed June 29, 2002).

89 For details see Risen, Johnston and Lewis, 'Harsh CIA methods cited in top Qaeda interrogations'.

90 See Human Rights Watch, *World Report 2005* and Priest, 'CIA holds terror suspects in secret prisons', p. A01.

91 Lawyers Committee for Human Rights, *Assessing the New Normal*, p. 80.

92 Quoted in Lawyers Committee for Human Rights, *Assessing the New Normal*, p. 81.

93 See Priest and Eggen, 'Terror suspect alleges torture', p. A01.

94 See Amnesty International, *An Appeal to President George W. Bush on the Occasion of His Re-Inauguration*.

95 Nigel Rodley, quoted in Adrian Levy and Cathy Scott-Clark, 'One huge US jail', *Guardian*, March 19, 2005. Online, available at: www.guardian.co.uk (accessed March 19, 2005).

96 John Radsan, quoted in Jane Meyer, 'Outsourcing torture', *The New Yorker*, February 14, 2005. Online, available at: www.newyorker.com (accessed February 18, 2005).

97 See Human Rights Watch, *World Report 2005*. A Council of Europe investigation estimated that over 100 individuals had been subjected to extraordinary rendition. See staff and agencies, 'European governments knew of CIA flights', *Guardian*, January 24, 2006. Online, available at: www.guardian.co.uk (accessed January 25, 2006).

98 Quoted in staff and agencies, 'European governments knew of CIA flights'.

99 Ian Cobain and Richard Norton-Taylor, 'Destination Cairo: Human rights fears over CIA flights', *Guardian*, September 12, 2005. Online, available at: www.guardian.co.uk (accessed September 13, 2005).

100 Tailfin no. N379P, see Levy and Scott-Clark, 'One huge US jail'.

101 See Meyer, 'Outsourcing torture'.

102 For details see Priest, 'CIA holds terror suspects in secret prisons', p. A01 and Dana

Priest and Robin Wright, 'Cheney fights for detainee policy', *Washington Post*, November 7, 2005, p. A01.

103 See Luke Harding, 'Rice admits US mistakes in war on terror after wave of criticism across Europe', *Guardian*, December 7, 2005. Online, available at: www.guardian.co.uk (accessed December 7, 2005).

104 Detainee known as Al Qadasi, see Zerrougui *et al.*, *Report of the Chairperson of the Working Group on Arbitrary Detention*, p. 27.

105 See Meyer, 'Outsourcing torture'.

106 Quoted in Meyer, 'Outsourcing torture'.

107 See Christopher Pyle, 'Torture by proxy', *San Francisco Chronicle*, January 4, 2004. Online, available at: www.sfgate.com (accessed January 24, 2004).

108 According to a motion filed in a US federal court in November 2004, see Priest and Eggen, 'Terror suspect alleges torture', p. A01 and Amnesty International, *An Appeal to President George W. Bush on the Occasion of His Re-Inauguration*.

109 See Amnesty International, *An Appeal to President George W. Bush on the Occasion of His Re-Inauguration*.

110 George W. Bush, quoted in Ian Cobain and Richard Norton-Taylor, 'Destination Cairo'.

111 *The President's Power as Commander in Chief to Transfer Captive Terrorists to the Control and Custody of Foreign Nations*, memo, March 13, 2002.

112 See Risen, Johnston and Lewis, 'Harsh CIA methods cited in top Qaeda interrogations'.

113 Article 3, Convention against Torture and other Cruel, Inhuman or Degrading Treatment or Punishment, adopted and opened for signature, ratification and accession by General Assembly Resolution 39/46, ratified by the US in 1994 and Human Rights First (2002) *A Year of Loss: Re-examining Civil Liberties Since September 11*. Online, available at: www.humanrightsfirst.org/us_law/loss/loss_ch5a.htm (accessed April 20, 2004).

114 Quoted in Meyer, 'Outsourcing torture'.

115 For details see Roth, 'The fight against terrorism', in Weiss, Crahan and Goering (eds) *Wars on Terrorism and Iraq*, p. 117.

116 Roth, 'The fight against terrorism', in Weiss, Crahan and Goering (eds) *Wars on Terrorism and Iraq*, p. 122.

117 Quoted in Jim Lobe (2004) *US Media Ignore Rumsfeld's 'Dirty Wars' Talk*, November 24. Online, available at: www.lewrockwell.com (accessed November 24, 2004).

118 See Ivo Daalder and James Lindsay, *America Unbound: The Bush Revolution in Foreign Policy*, Washington, DC, Brookings Institution Press, 2003, p. 102.

119 National Security Council, *United States of America National Security Strategy*, Washington, DC, 2002, p. 6.

120 George W. Bush (2001) *No Nation can be Neutral in this Conflict*, White House, Washington, DC, November 6.

121 George W. Bush (2004) *President Bush Discusses Importance of Democracy in Middle East*, Library of Congress, Washington, DC, February 4.

122 George W. Bush (2004) *Remarks by the President to the National Governors Association*, State Dining Room, February 23.

123 George W. Bush (2006) *State of the Union Address*, Washington, DC, January 31.

124 Article 1, Convention against Torture and other Cruel, Inhuman or Degrading Treatment or Punishment, adopted and opened for signature, ratification and accession by General Assembly Resolution 39/46, December 10, 1984.

125 Article 4.2, International Covenant on Civil and Political Rights, 1966.

126 Zerrougui *et al.*, *Report of the Chairperson of the Working Group on Arbitrary Detention*, p. 22.

127 Department of Justice Working Group Report, *Detainee Interrogations in the*

Global War on Terrorism: Assessment of Legal, Historical, Policy and Operational Considerations, March 6, 2003, leaked to the *Wall Street Journal*, June 2004, p. 4. Online, available at: www.online.wsj.com/public/resources/documents/military_0604.pdf (accessed August 5, 2004).

128 Department of Justice Working Group Report, *Detainee Interrogations in the Global War on Terrorism*, p. 4.

129 Department of Justice Working Group Report, *Detainee Interrogations in the Global War on Terrorism*, p. 4.

130 Department of Justice Working Group Report, *Detainee Interrogations in the Global War on Terrorism*, p. 21.

131 Department of Justice Working Group Report, *Detainee Interrogations in the Global War on Terrorism*, p. 24.

132 Department of Justice Working Group Report, *Detainee Interrogations in the Global War on Terrorism*, p. 27.

133 Announced December 30, 2004. For details see Amnesty International, *An Appeal to President George W. Bush on the Occasion of His Re-Inauguration*.

134 See Human Rights Watch (2005) *US: Justifying Abuse of Detainees*. Online, available at: www.hrw.org/English/docs/2005/01/12/usint10072_txt.htm (accessed February 9, 2005).

135 See Human Rights Watch, *US: Justifying Abuse of Detainees*.

136 McCain cited in Zerrougui *et al.*, *Report of the Chairperson of the Working Group on Arbitrary Detention*, p. 23.

137 See, for example, Priest and Wright, 'Cheney fights for detainee policy', p. A01; Foster Klug, 'McCain: torture ban needed for US image', *Associated Press*, November 13, 2005. Online, available at: www.washingtonpost.com (accessed November 14, 2005) and Jonathan Weisman, 'Senators agree on detainee rights', *Washington Post*, November 15, 2005, p. A01.

138 For further details see Priest and Wright, 'Cheney fights for detainee policy', p. A01.

139 According to Klug, 'McCain: torture ban needed for US image'.

140 Senate: 90–9, House: 308–122.

141 George W. Bush, quoted in Eric Schmitt, 'President backs McCain measure on inmate abuse', *New York Times*, December 16, 2005. Online, available at: www.nytimes.com (accessed December 16, 2005).

142 George W. Bush, quoted in Dan Froomkin, 'Bush's tortured logic', *Washington Post*, November 8, 2005. Online, available at: www.washingtonpost.com (accessed November 8, 2005).

143 George W. Bush (2003) *United Nations International Day in Support of Victims of Torture*, June 26, quoted in Lawyers Committee for Human Rights, *Assessing the New Normal*, p. 81.

144 George W. Bush, Presidential Memorandum, February 7, 2002, quoted in Amnesty International, *An Appeal to President George W. Bush on the Occasion of His Re-Inauguration*.

145 For details see Priest, 'CIA holds terror suspects in secret prisons', p. A01.

146 See staff and agencies, 'European governments knew of CIA flights'.

147 Priest, 'CIA holds terror suspects in secret prisons', p. A01.

148 See Risen, Johnston and Lewis, 'Harsh CIA methods cited in top Qaeda interrogations'.

149 Senator John Rockefeller, Democrat Senator for West Virginia and Vice Chairman of the Senate Select Committee on Intelligence. See Priest and Wright, 'Cheney fights for detainee policy', p. A01.

150 Cofer Black, quoted in Duncan Campbell, 'US interrogators turn to torture lite', *Guardian*, January 25, 2003, p. 17.

151 For details see Roth, 'The fight against terrorism', in Weiss, Crahan and Goering (eds) *Wars on Terrorism and Iraq*, p. 123.
152 Marty quoted in staff and agencies, 'European governments knew of CIA flights'.
153 The document states that, if questioned over rendition, 'we should try to avoid getting drawn on detail and try to move the debate on'. The leaked briefing paper was written by Irfan Siddiq of the UK Foreign Secretary's private office, dated December 7, 2005, to Grace Cassy of the Prime Minister's Office and passed to the *New Statesman*. See Richard Norton-Taylor, 'Torture flights: What no. 10 knew and tried to cover up', *Guardian*, January 19, 2006. Online, available at: www.guardian.co.uk (accessed January 19, 2006).
154 George W. Bush (2001) *Statement by the President in His Address to the Nation*, September 11.
155 George W. Bush (2001) *'President Discusses War on Terrorism in Address to the Nation'*, World Congress Center, Atlanta, Georgia, November 8. Bush stated in his 2006 *State of the Union Address*, '[t]errorists like bin Laden ... seek to impose a heartless system of totalitarian control throughout the Middle East'. Bush has also stated terrorists 'hate us and they hate freedom and they hate people who embrace freedom'. See George W. Bush, 'Transcript of President Bush's interview on Al Arabiya television', *New York Times*, May 5, 2004. Online, available at: www.nytimes.com (accessed May 6, 2004). President Bush has also stated that terrorists 'hate what we see right here in this chamber – a democratically elected government. Their leaders are self-appointed. They hate our freedoms – our freedom of religion, our freedom of speech, our freedom to vote and assemble and disagree with each other'. See George W. Bush (2001) *Address to a Joint Session of Congress and the American People*, Washington, DC, September 20.
156 George W. Bush (2005) *President Addresses Nation*, Fort Bragg, North Carolina, June 28.
157 Condoleezza Rice (2004) *Remarks at the McConnell Center for Political Leadership*, University of Louisville, Louisville, Kentucky, March 8.
158 See, for example, Mary Kaldor, 'American Power: from "compellance" to cosmopolitanism?' *International Affairs*, 2003, vol. 79, no. 1, pp. 1–22 at 17.
159 See Michael Klare, 'Corporations, national security and war profiteering', *Multinational Monitor*, 2001, vol. 22, no. 11. Online, available at: www.multinationalmonitor.org/mm2001/01/nov01interviewklare.html (accessed February 23, 2002).
160 Osama bin Laden, 'Text: Osama bin Laden's 1998 interview', *Guardian*, October 8, 2001. Online, available at: www.guardian.co.uk (accessed October 9, 2001) and Hamid Mir, 'Muslims have the right to attack America', *Independent*, November 11, 2001, pp. 2–3.
161 Bin Laden quoted in Bruce Lincoln, *Holy Terror: Thinking About Religion After September 11*, Chicago, IL, University of Chicago Press, 2003, p. 102.
162 Government officials also pressured print media to adopt similar policies. See Lincoln, *Holy Terror*, p. 19.
163 See Lincoln, *Holy Terror*, p. 20.
164 George W. Bush (2005) *President Outlines Strategy for Victory in Iraq*, US Naval Academy, Annapolis, Maryland, November 30.
165 George W. Bush (2004) *President Bush Reaffirms Resolve to War on Terror, Iraq and Afghanistan*, East Room, White House, Washington, DC, March 19.
166 Bush, *President Bush Reaffirms Resolve to War on Terror, Iraq and Afghanistan*.
167 A proposal that was withdrawn in the face of strong opposition. See William Hartung, 'Military', in Feffer (ed.) *Power Trip*, pp. 60–74 at 70.
168 For further details see William Blum, *Rogue State: A Guide to the World's Only Superpower*, London, Zed Books, 2002, p. 32.
169 See Lawyers Committee for Human Rights, *Holding the Line*, p. 11.

170 See Human Rights First, *A Year of Loss*.

171 See Roth, 'The fight against terrorism', in Weiss, Crahan and Goering (eds) *Wars on Terrorism and Iraq*, p. 124.

172 See Jack Donnelly, 'International human rights: unintended consequences of the war on terrorism', in Weiss, Crahan and Goering (eds) *Wars on Terrorism and Iraq*, pp. 98–112 at 102.

173 See Human Rights Watch, *Human Rights Situation in Chechnya*, Briefing paper, 59th session of the UN Commission on Human Rights, April 7, 2003, p. 1.

174 See Lawyers Committee for Human Rights, *Imbalance of Powers*, Washington, DC, Human Rights First, 2003, p. 77.

175 See Roth, 'The fight against terrorism', in Weiss, Crahan and Goering (eds) *Wars on Terrorism and Iraq*, p. 124.

176 See Human Rights First, *A Year of Loss*.

177 See Lawyers Committee for Human Rights, *Imbalance of Powers*, p. 72.

178 United Nations Press Release (2003) *Menace of Terrorism Requires Global Response Says Secretary General*, January 20. Online, available at: www.un.org/News/Press/docs/2003/sgsm8583.doc.htm (accessed January 21, 2003).

179 The president, for example, stated that the aim of the terrorists was 'to frighten to the point where our nation would not act'. See George W. Bush (2001) *News Conference*, East Room, White House, Washington, DC, October 11.

180 John Ashcroft in testimony to Senate Judiciary Committee, December 2001, quoted in Dan Eggen and Mike Allen, 'Ashcroft to leave cabinet', *Washington Post*, November 10, 2004, p. A01.

6 War on Afghanistan

1 Including stinger missiles. See Frederick Gareau, *State Terrorism and the United States*, Atlanta, GA, Clarity Press, 2004, p. 193.

2 Gareau, *State Terrorism and the United States*, p. 193.

3 Norah Niland, 'Justice postponed', in Antonio Donini, Norah Niland and Karin Wermester (eds) *Nation-Building Unraveled? Aid, Peace and Justice in Afghanistan*, London, Kumarian Press, 2004, pp. 61–82 at 73.

4 Niland, 'Justice postponed', in Donini, Niland and Wermester (eds) *Nation-Building Unraveled?* pp. 61–82.

5 See Rick Fawn, 'From ground zero to the war in Afghanistan', in Mary Buckley and Rick Fawn (eds) *Global Responses to Terrorism: 9/11, Afghanistan and Beyond*, London and New York, Routledge, 2003, pp. 11–24 at 15.

6 See Mark Drumbl, 'Self-defense and the use of force: breaking the rules, making the rules or both?' *International Studies Perspectives*, 2003, vol. 4, no. 4, pp. 409–31 at 419 and Sean Murphy (ed.) 'Terrorist attacks on World Trade Center and Pentagon', *American Journal of International Law*, 2002, vol. 96, no. 1, pp. 237–55.

7 United Nations, *Security Council Resolution 1378*, November 14, 2001. Online, available at: usinfo.state.gov/topical/pol/terror/01111512.htm (accessed July 5, 2004).

8 George W. Bush, quoted in Murphy (ed.) 'Terrorist attacks on World Trade Center and Pentagon', pp. 237–55.

9 George W. Bush (2002) *US Humanitarian Aid to Afghanistan*, Presidential Hall, Dwight David Eisenhower Executive Office Building, Washington, DC, October 11.

10 Donald Rumsfeld, quoted in Helen Kinsella, 'Discourses of differences: civilians, combatants and compliance with the rules of war', *Review of International Studies*, 2005, vol. 31, sp. iss., pp.163–85 at 168.

11 General Myers, quoted in Kinsella, 'Discourses of differences', p. 168.

12 For details see Barnett Rubin, 'Transitional justice and human rights in Afghanistan', *International Affairs*, 2003, vol. 79, no. 3, pp. 567–581 at 574.

13 For details see David Chandler, 'Introduction: Rethinking human rights', in David Chandler (ed.) *Rethinking Human Rights: Critical Approaches to International Politics*, Basingstoke, Palgrave, 2002, pp. 1–15 at 9.

14 See Department of State (2001) *Summary of US Assistance to the Afghan People Since October 1, 2001*, Washington, DC, November 23. Online, available at: www.state.gov/r/pa/prs/ps/2001/6303.htm (accessed February 5, 2002).

15 White House Office of the Press Secretary (2002) *American Assistance to the People of Afghanistan*, Washington, DC, October 11. Online, available at: www.state.gov/p/sca/rls/fs/14786.htm (accessed October 13, 2002).

16 See, for example, USAID Administrator Andrew Natsios (2002) *Reconstruction and Rebuilding Efforts in Afghanistan*, State Department Briefing Room, Washington, DC, December 23.

17 See, for example, Amnesty International (2002) *Amnesty International Report 2002*, AI Index POL 10/001/2002. Online, available at: web.amnesty.org/web/ar2002.nsf (accessed March 13, 2003).

18 See, for example, Robert Lieber, 'A new era in US strategic thinking', *Global Issues*, 2002, vol. 7, no. 2, pp. 5–8 at 7.

19 Quoted in Peter Singer, *The President of Good and Evil: Taking George W. Bush Seriously*, London, Granta Books, 2004, p. 146.

20 Quoted in Singer, *The President of Good and Evil*, p. 146.

21 Jean Bethke Elshtain, *Just War Against Terror: Ethics and the Burden of American Power in a Violent World*, New York, Basic Books, 2003.

22 Jean Bethke Elshtain, 'Intellectual dissent and the war on terror', *Public Interest*, 2003, no. 151, pp 86–97 at 91.

23 For details see Amnesty International (2003) *Amnesty International 2003 Annual Report*. Online, available at: web.amnesty.org/report2003/Afg-summary-eng (accessed May 11, 2005).

24 Amnesty International, *Amnesty International 2003 Annual Report*.

25 Niland, 'Justice postponed', in Donini, Niland and Wermester (eds) *Nation-Building Unraveled?* p. 75.

26 Amnesty International, *Amnesty International 2003 Annual Report*.

27 Amnesty International, *Amnesty International 2003 Annual Report*.

28 See John Kampfner, *Blair's Wars*, London, Simon and Schuster, 2003, p. 151.

29 For details see Amnesty International, *Amnesty International 2003 Annual Report*.

30 See Amnesty International, *Amnesty International 2003 Annual Report* and Peter Oborne, 'On the roads of ruin', *Observer*, May 25, 2003. Online, available at: observer.guardian.co.uk (accessed May 28, 2003).

31 Oborne, 'On the roads of ruin'.

32 See Niland, 'Justice postponed', in Donini, Niland and Wermester (eds) *Nation-Building Unraveled?* p. 73.

33 See Kampfner, *Blair's Wars*, p. 143.

34 See Jenny Warren (2002) *Military Intervention in Afghanistan: Implications for British Foreign and Defence Policy*, BASIC Occasional Papers on International Security Policy, no. 40. Online, available at: www.basicint.org/pubs/Papers/BP40.htm (accessed July 23, 2003).

35 Niland, 'Justice postponed', in Donini, Niland and Wermester (eds) *Nation-Building Unraveled?* p. 76 and Rubin, 'Transitional justice and human rights in Afghanistan', p. 574.

36 See Rubin, 'Transitional justice and human rights in Afghanistan', p. 574 and Amnesty International, *Amnesty International Report 2002*.

37 Amnesty International, *Amnesty International 2003 Annual Report*.

38 Request made in May 2003. See Isabel Hilton, 'Now we pay the warlords to tyrannize the Afghan people', *Guardian*, July 31, 2003. Online, available at: www.guardian.co.uk (accessed August 2, 2003).

39 Quoted in Kenneth Roth, 'The fight against terrorism: the Bush Administration's dangerous neglect of human rights', in Thomas G. Weiss, Margaret E. Crahan and John Goering (eds) *Wars on Terrorism and Iraq: Human Rights, Unilateralism and US Foreign Policy*, London, Routledge, 2004, pp. 113–131 at 121.

40 Gareau, *State Terrorism and the United States*, p. 196.

41 Niland, 'Justice postponed', in Donini, Niland and Wermester (eds) *Nation-Building Unraveled?* p. 75.

42 Niland, 'Justice postponed', in Donini, Niland and Wermester (eds) *Nation-Building Unraveled?* p. 79.

43 Human Rights Watch (2005) *2005 World Report*. Online, available at: www.hrw.org/wr2k5 (accessed February 20, 2006).

44 Human Rights Watch (2004) *Enduring Freedom: Abuses by US Forces in Afghanistan*, vol. 16, no. 3 (C). Online, available at: hrw.org/reports/2004/afghanistan0304/ (accessed April 12, 2005).

45 Duncan Campbell and Suzanne Goldenberg, 'They said this is America', *Guardian*, June 23, 2004. Online, available at: www.guardian.co.uk (accessed June 23, 2004).

46 For details see Tim Golden, 'In US report, brutal details of 2 Afghan inmates' deaths', *New York Times,* May 20, 2005. Online, available at: www.nytimes.com (accessed May 21, 2005).

47 See Dana Priest, 'CIA holds terror suspects in secret prisons', *Washington Post*, November 2, 2005, p. A01.

48 Adrian Levy and Cathy Scott-Clark, 'One huge US jail', *Guardian*, March 19, 2005. Online, available at: www.guardian.co.uk (accessed March 20, 2005).

49 Levy and Scott-Clark, 'One huge US jail'.

50 Moazzam Begg, 'Letter', *Guardian*, July 12, 2004. Online, available at: image.guardian.co.uk (accessed July 13, 2004).

51 For details see editorial, 'Patterns of abuse', *New York Times*, May 23, 2005. Online, available at: www.nytimes.com (accessed May 23, 2005) and Roth, 'The fight against terrorism', in Weiss, Crahan and Goering (eds) *Wars on Terrorism and Iraq*, p. 119.

52 See Human Rights Watch, *Enduring Freedom*.

53 Quoted in Tim Golden, 'Army faltered in investigating detainee abuse', *New York Times*, May 22, 2005. Online, available at: www.nytimes.com (accessed May 23, 2005).

54 See Golden, 'Army faltered in investigating detainee abuse' and Brad Adams (2004) *An Open Letter to US Secretary of Defense Donald Rumsfeld*, December 13. Online, available at: www.hrw.org (accessed December 16, 2004).

55 Quoted in Golden, 'In US report, brutal details of 2 Afghan inmates' deaths'.

56 Lieutenant Colonel Elizabeth Rouse, quoted in Golden, 'In US report, brutal details of 2 Afghan inmates' deaths'.

57 Golden, 'In US report, brutal details of 2 Afghan inmates' deaths'.

58 Quoted in Golden, 'In US report, brutal details of 2 Afghan inmates' deaths'.

59 See Adams, *An Open Letter to US Secretary of Defense Donald Rumsfeld*.

60 Human Rights Watch, *Enduring Freedom*.

61 Human Rights Watch, *Enduring Freedom*.

62 Human Rights Watch, *Enduring Freedom*.

63 Dr Rafiullah Bidar quoted in Levy and Scott-Clark, 'One huge US jail'.

64 Dr Rafiullah Bidar quoted in Levy and Scott-Clark, 'One huge US jail'.

65 Quoted in Rupert Cornwell, 'Cheney "created climate for US war crimes"',

Independent, November 30, 2005. Online, available at: www.news.independent. co.uk (accessed November 30, 2005).

66 Quoted in Cornwell, 'Cheney "created climate for US war crimes"'.

67 For details see Human Rights First (2005) *The Case Against Rumsfeld: Hard Facts Timeline*. Online, available at: www.humanrightsfirst.org/us_law/etn/lawsuit/PDF/ rums-timeline-022805.pdf (accessed March 16, 2005).

68 See editorial, 'Patterns of abuse'.

69 Colonel Berg. See Tim Golden, 'Years after 2 Afghans died, abuse case falters', *New York Times*, February 13, 2006. Online, available at: www.nytimes.com (accessed February 15, 2006).

70 See James Schlesinger (2004) *Final Report of the Independent Panel to Review DoD Detention Operations*, August 24, p. 7. Online, available at: news.findlaw.com/ wp/docs/dod/abughraibrpt.pdf (accessed September 1, 2004).

71 American Civil Liberties Union (2005) *Legal Claims in Ali et al. v Rumsfeld*, Fact Sheet, March 1. Online, available at: www.aclu.org/SafeandFree/SafeandFree. cfm?ID=17590&c=207 (accessed April 1, 2005).

72 Rear Admiral John Hutson, (2005) *The Case Against Rumsfeld*, March 1. Online, available at: www.humanrightsfirst.org/us_law/etn/lawsuit/statements/lit-hutson-030105.htm (accessed April 1, 2005).

73 Quoted in Campbell and Goldenberg, 'They said this is America'.

74 See Levy and Scott-Clark, 'One huge US jail'.

75 Dr Rafiullah Bidar, quoted in Levy and Scott-Clark, 'One huge US jail'.

76 Dr Rafiullah Bidar, quoted in Levy and Scott-Clark, 'One huge US jail'.

77 George W. Bush (2004) *Remarks on Freedom for the People of Afghanistan*, Hershey, Pennsylvannia, April 19.

78 Bush, *Remarks on Freedom for the People of Afghanistan*.

79 George W. Bush (2002) *Proclamation 7584 Women's Equality Day 2002*, Code of Federal Regulations, title 3, vol. 1, ref. 3CFR7584, August 23. Online, available at: www.presidency.ucsb.edu/ws/print.php?pid=61878 (accessed July 29, 2003).

80 Lorne Craner (2001) *Human Rights and the Taliban*, Remarks at the Foreign Press Center, Washington, DC, November 6.

81 Lawyers Committee for Human Rights, *Holding the Line: A Critique of the Department of State's Annual Country Reports on Human Rights Practices*, Washington, DC, Human Rights First, 2003, pp. 21–2.

82 George W. Bush (2004) *Progress in the War on Terror*, White House, Office of the Press Secretary, January 22.

83 George W. Bush (2004) *President Bush Reaffirms Resolve to War on Terror, Iraq and Afghanistan*, East Room, White House, Washington, DC, March 19.

84 Bush, *Remarks on Freedom for the People of Afghanistan*.

85 Colin Powell (2004) *Statement: Human Rights Week*, Brussels, Belgium, December 8.

86 White House (2002) *Afghanistan: Then and Now*. Online, available at: www.white-house.gov/afac/thenandnow.html (accessed March 20, 2003).

87 White House *Afghanistan: Then and Now*.

88 Lawyers Committee for Human Rights *Holding the Line*, p. 22. The Lawyers Committee also note that the *2002 Country Reports* overstates the degree to which the regional warlords acknowledge the Karzai Administration as a legitimate central authority.

89 National Security Council, *United States of America National Security Strategy*, Washington, DC, 2006, p. 12.

90 Monitors from the OSCE and the EU, see Justin Huggler, 'Afghanistan hits fever pitch as warlords turn "democrat"', *Independent*, October 6, 2004. Online, available at: news.independent.co.uk (accessed October 6, 2004).

91 George W. Bush, quoted in Rupert Cornwell, 'Bush praises "fierce courage" of US soldiers in memorial day speech', *Independent*, June 1, 2004. Online, available at: www.news.independent.co.uk (accessed June 1, 2004).
92 George W. Bush (2002) *Remarks at the Knoxville, Tennessee, Civic Center*, April 8.
93 Bush, *Proclamation 7584*.
94 George W. Bush, quoted in Bruce Lincoln, *Holy Terror: Thinking About Religion After September 11*, Chicago, IL, University of Chicago Press, 2003, p. 99.
95 For details see Murphy (ed.) 'Terrorist attacks on World Trade Center and Pentagon', pp. 237–55 and Kampfner, *Blair's Wars*, p. 147.
96 The October 22, 2001 dropping of a cluster bomb in the village of Herat effectively turned the village into a minefield. See Murphy (ed.) 'Terrorist attacks on World Trade Center and Pentagon', pp. 237–55. UN officials reported that cluster bombs landing on the village of Shaker Qala killed nine civilians and injured 14 more. *Human Rights Watch* estimate that B-1 bombers dropped 50 CBU-87 cluster bombs in five missions during the first week of the war. See Human Rights Watch (2001) *Cluster Bombs in Afghanistan: A Human Rights Watch Backgrounder*. Online, available at: www.hrw.org/backgrounder/arms/cluster-bck1031.htm (accessed January 10, 2002).
97 See Amnesty International, *Amnesty International Report 2002*.
98 Donald Rumsfeld, quoted in Amnesty International, *Amnesty International Report 2002*.
99 For details see David Miller, 'The domination effect', *Guardian*, January 8, 2004. Online, available at: www.guardian.co.uk (accessed January 8, 2004).
100 Hegemonic rule one, Chapter 1.
101 George W. Bush, quoted in David Chandler, 'Rhetoric without responsibility: the attraction of ethical foreign policy', *British Journal of Politics and International Relations*, 2003, vol. 5, no. 3, pp. 295–316 at 297.
102 Donald Rumsfeld, quoted in Chandler, 'Introduction', in Chandler (ed.) *Rethinking Human Rights*, p. 9.
103 Craner, *Human Rights and the Taliban*.
104 Craner, *Human Rights and the Taliban*.
105 Such as the Voice of America. See George W. Bush (2004) *State of the Union Address*, Washington, DC, January 20.
106 See Gareau, *State Terrorism and the United States*, p. 206.
107 For details see Noy Thrupkaew, 'Culture', in John Feffer (ed.) *Power Trip: US Unilateralism and Global Strategy After September 11*, New York, Seven Stories Press, 2003, pp. 106–116 at 112–13.
108 Médecins Sans Frontières (2004) *MSF Pulls Out of Afghanistan*, Press Release, July 28. Online, available at: www.msf.org (accessed July 28, 2004).
109 Médecins Sans Frontières, *MSF Pulls Out of Afghanistan*.
110 May 2004. See Médecins Sans Frontières, *MSF Pulls Out of Afghanistan*.
111 Médecins Sans Frontières, *MSF Pulls Out of Afghanistan*.
112 Médecins Sans Frontières, *MSF Pulls Out of Afghanistan*.
113 Stephen Graham, 'Slaying of Afghan women concerns UN', *Washington Post*, May 5, 2005. Online, available at: www.washingtonpost.com (accessed May 6, 2005).
114 See Chapters 1–4.
115 According to Bob Woodward, *Plan of Attack*, London, Simon and Schuster, 2004, p. 26.
116 Woodward, *Plan of Attack*, p. 26.
117 Richard Perle (2001) *Next Stop Iraq*, Remarks at the Foreign Policy Research Institute's Annual Dinner, Philadelphia, November 14.
118 George W. Bush, quoted in Singer, *The President of Good and Evil*, p. 150.

119 NSC meeting, October 31, 2001. See Bob Woodward, *Bush at War*, London, Simon and Schuster, 2002, p. 279.

7 War on Iraq

1 For a discussion on how the official explanation for the Iraq War shifted between security and liberation see Judith Lichtenberg, 'Pre-emption and exceptionalism in US foreign policy', in Thomas Weiss, Margaret Crahan and John Goering (eds) *Wars on Terrorism and Iraq: Human Rights, Unilateralism and US Foreign Policy*, London, Routledge, 2004, pp. 61–73 at 70.

2 Quoted in Al Gore, 'Transcript of the former US vice-president's speech on Iraq and the war on terrorism', *Guardian*, September 23, 2002. Online, available at: www.guardian.co.uk (accessed September 25, 2002).

3 United Nations (2003) *Press Release: Resolution 1441*, November 8. Online, available at: www.un.org/News (accessed November 9, 2003).

4 Hans Blix (2003) *Hans Blix Address to the UN*, January 27. Online, available at: www.un.org (accessed February 1, 2003).

5 George W. Bush (2003) *President Says Saddam Hussein Must Leave Iraq Within 48 Hours*, Cross Hall, Washington, DC, March 17.

6 George W. Bush (2003) *President Bush's Message to the Iraqi People*, Washington, DC, April 10.

7 George W. Bush (2003) *Address at MacDill Air Base*, Florida, March 26. See also George W. Bush (2004) *State of the Union Address*, Washington, DC, January 20.

8 George W. Bush (2003) *President Bush Addresses Nation on the Capture of Saddam Hussein*, Cabinet Room, White House, Washington, DC, December 14.

9 George W. Bush (2004) *President Outlines Steps to Help Iraq Achieve Democracy and Freedom*, United States Army War College, Carlisle, Pennsylvania, May 24.

10 Colin Powell (2003) Speech to the American Israel Public Affairs Committee's Annual Policy Conference, Washington, DC, March 30.

11 Shirin Tahir-Kheli (2001) *Item 9: Violation of Human Rights and Fundamental Freedoms in Any Part of the World*, 57ty Session on the UN Commission on Human Rights, Geneva, March 30.

12 Michael Parmly (2001) Briefing to the Press: 57th Session of the UN Commission on Human Rights, Geneva, March 21.

13 Lorne Craner (2004) *Country Reports on Human Rights Practices for 2003*, Testimony Before House International Relations Committee, Washington, DC, March 10.

14 George W. Bush (2004) *Importance of Democracy in Middle East*, Library of Congress, Washington, DC, February 4.

15 Bush, 2004 *State of the Union Address*.

16 George W. Bush (2003) *President Bush Thanks Military*, MCAS Miramar, California, August 14.

17 George W. Bush (2003) *Moment of Truth for World on Iraq*, Azores, March 16 .

18 George W. Bush (2004) *Remarks by the President to the National Governors Association*, State Dining Room, White House, Washington, DC, February 23.

19 See, for example, White House (2003) *Tales of Saddam's Brutality*, September 29. Online, available at: www.whitehouse.gov/news/releases/2003/09/20030929–14. html (accessed April 14, 2005) and Department of State Office of International Information Programs (2003) *Focus on Human Rights in Saddam's Iraq: The Violent Coercion and Repression of the Iraqi People*. Online, available at: www.usembassy.it/pdf/other/iraqfocus1.pdf#search=%22The%20Violent%20Coercion%20and%20Repression%20of%20the%20Iraqi%20People%22   (accessed March 4, 2005).

20 Department of State, *Supporting Human Rights and Democracy: The US Record 2003–2004*, Washington, DC, 2004.

21 National Security Council, *United States of America National Security Strategy*, Washington, DC, 2006, p. 2.

22 Bush, *President Bush Thanks Military*. See also George W. Bush and Tony Blair (2003) *Joint News Conference*, Camp David, Maryland, March 27.

23 Bush, 2004 *State of the Union Address*.

24 Bush, *President Bush Thanks Military*.

25 Bush, *Importance of Democracy in Middle East*.

26 Bush, 2004 *State of the Union Address*.

27 Powell, Speech to the American Israel Public Affairs Committee's Annual Policy Conference.

28 Bush, *President Bush Thanks Military*.

29 Bush, 2004 *State of the Union Address*.

30 For details see William Blum, *Rogue State: A Guide to the World's Only Superpower*, London, Zed Books, 2002, pp. 121–2.

31 Bush, 2004 *State of the Union Address*.

32 Paula Dobriansky, 'Democracy promotion', *Foreign Affairs*, 2003, vol. 82, no. 3, pp. 141–5 at 143; Richard Armitage, 'Allies, friends and partners on every page', *US Foreign Policy Agenda*, 2002, vol. 7, no. 4, p. 10 and Bob Woodward, *Plan of Attack*, London, Simon and Schuster, 2004, pp. 154–5.

33 Robert Kagan and William Kristol, 'Why we went to war', *Weekly Standard*, October 20, 2003, p. 5.

34 Peter Dombrowski and Rodger Payne, 'Global debate and the limits of the Bush doctrine', *International Studies Perspectives*, 2003, vol. 4, no. 4, pp. 395–408 at 395.

35 Dombrowski and Payne, 'Global debate and the limits of the Bush doctrine', p. 395.

36 Mark Drumbl, 'Self-defense and the use of force: breaking the rules, making the rules or both?' *International Studies Perspectives*, 2003, vol. 4, no. 4, pp. 409–31 at 424.

37 Robert Kagan, 'A tougher war for the US is one of legitimacy', *New York Times*, January 24, 2004. Online, available at: www.nytimes.com (accessed January 25, 2004).

38 Colin Dueck, 'Ideas and alternatives in American grand strategy, 2000–2004', *Review of International Studies*, 2004, vol. 30, no. 4, pp. 511–35 at 531.

39 Michael Ignatieff, 'The Burden', *New York Times Magazine*, January 5, 2003. Online, available at: www.mtholyoke.edu/acad/intrel/bush/burden.htm (accessed January 8, 2003).

40 Lichtenberg, 'Pre-emption and exceptionalism in US foreign policy', in Weiss, Crahan and Goering (eds) *Wars on Terrorism and Iraq*, p. 71.

41 Johann Hari, 'The case for war', *Guardian*, February 15, 2003, p. 6.

42 September 26, 2002, noted in Mary Kaldor 'American Power', *International Affairs*, 2003, vol. 79, no. 1, pp. 1–22 at 15.

43 For details see Richard Falk, 'Legality and legitimacy: the quest for principled flexibility and restraint', *Review of International Studies*, 2005, vol. 31, sp. iss., pp. 31–50 at 37.

44 See Human Rights Watch, 'Iraq: state of the evidence', *Human Rights Watch Report*, 2004, vol. 16, no. 9(E), p. 2. Online, available at: www.hrw.org/reports/2004/iraq1104/ (accessed February 3, 2005).

45 Associated Press, 'Bush wins $87 billion for Iraq and Afghanistan', *Guardian*, November 4, 2003. Online, available at: www.guardian.co.uk (accessed November 6, 2003).

46 Shibley Telhami, 'After a war with Iraq: democracy, militancy and peacemaking', *International Studies Perspectives*, 2003, vol. 4, no. 2, pp. 182–5 at 183.

47 Anne Penketh, 'Poll reveals hostility to US and support for rebel cleric', *Independent*, June 17, 2004. Online, available at: www.independent.co.uk (accessed June 18, 2004).

48 See Michael Byers, 'Not yet havoc: geopolitical change and the international rules on military force', *Review of International Studies*, 2005, vol. 31, sp. iss., pp. 51–70 at 65.

49 Carl Hulse and Sheryl Stolberg, 'Lawmakers view images from Iraq', *New York Times*, May 13, 2004. Online, available at: www.nytimes.com (accessed May 13, 2004).

50 Antonio Taguba (2004) *Hearing Article 15–6 Investigation of the 800th Military Police Brigade*, March. Online, available at: www.agonist.org/annex/taguba.htm (accessed July 12, 2005).

51 Taguba, *Hearing Article 15–6*, p. 12.

52 International Committee of the Red Cross (2004) Report of the International Committee of the Red Cross on the Treatment by the Coalition Forces of Prisoners of War and Other Protected Persons by the Geneva Conventions in Iraq During Arrest, Internment and Interrogation, February, p. 7. Leaked to the *Wall Street Journal*, May 2004.

53 Editorial, 'New charges of abuse surface', *Washington Times*, July 3, 2005, p. A7.

54 Bradley Klapper, 'UN urges Iraq torture probe', *Associated Press*, November 16, 2005. Online, available at: www.washingtonpost.com (accessed November 16, 2005).

55 Fowler quoted in Douglas Jehl, 'A trail of "major failures" leads to defense secretary's office', *New York Times*, August 25, 2004. Online, available at: www.nytimes.com (accessed August 26, 2004).

56 Notable questions include the decision to involve private contractors in the prisoner interrogation process.

57 See James Schlesinger (2004) *Final Report of the Independent Panel to Review DoD Detention Operations*, August 24, p. 7. Online, available at: news.findlaw.com/wp/docs/dod/abughraibrpt.pdf (accessed September 1, 2004).

58 Anthony Jones and George Fay (2004) *Investigation of Intelligence Activities at the Abu Ghraib Prison and 205th Military Intelligence Brigade*, August 23. Online, available at: www.slate.com/features/whatistorture/pdfs/FayJonesReport.pdf (accessed November 5, 2004).

59 See Amnesty International (2005) *Abu Ghraib: One Year Later, Who's Accountable?* Online, available at: www.amnestyusa.org/stoptorture/agfactsheet.html (accessed August 17, 2005).

60 For further details see Human Rights Watch (2005) *World Report 2005*. Online, available at: www.hrw.org/english/docs/2005 (accessed February 2, 2006).

61 See transcript, 'Rumsfeld testifies before Senate Armed Services Committee', *Washington Post*, May 7, 2004. Online, available at: www.washingtonpost.com (accessed August 28, 2004).

62 See David Stout, 'Rumsfeld offers apology for abuse of Iraq prisoners', *New York Times*, May 7, 2004. Online, available at: www.nytimes.com (accessed May 8, 2004); Lorne Craner (2004) *Briefing on Supporting Human Rights and Democracy*, Washington, DC, May 17 and George W. Bush (2004) *Statement at the Pentagon*, May 10.

63 Pierre Kraehenbuehl quoted in Simon Jeffrey, 'Rumsfeld apologises for Iraq jail abuse', *Guardian*, May 7, 2004. Online, available at: www.guardian.co.uk (accessed May 8, 2004).

64 International Committee of the Red Cross, Report, p. 4.

65 International Committee of the Red Cross, Report, p. 3.

66 International Committee of the Red Cross, Report, pp. 3–4.

67 International Committee of the Red Cross, Report, p.12.

68 International Committee of the Red Cross, Report, p. 8.

69 US Army's 82nd Airborne Division, 1st Battalion, 504th Parachute Infantry Regiment.

70 Quoted in Human Rights Watch, 'Leadership failure: firsthand accounts of torture of Iraqi detainees by the US Army's 82nd Airborne Division', *Human Rights Watch Report*, 2005, vol. 17, no. 3(G). Online, available at: www.hrw.org/reports/2005/us0905/index.htm (accessed November 12, 2005).

71 Quoted in Human Rights Watch, 'Leadership Failure'.

72 Quoted in Human Rights Watch, 'Account of Sergeant A, 82nd Airborne Division', *Human Rights Watch Report*, 2005, vol. 17, no. 3(G). Online, available at: www.hrw.org/reports/2005/us0905/2.htm (accessed November 12, 2005).

73 Quoted in Human Rights Watch, 'Account of Sergeant A'.

74 See Douglas Jehl, Steven Myers and Eric Schmitt, 'Abuse of captives more widespread, says Army survey', *New York Times*, May 26 2004. Online, available at: www.nytimes.com (accessed May 28, 2004).

75 See editorial, 'A failed investigation', *Washington Post*, September 10, 2004, p. A28 and Bradley Graham and Josh White, 'General cites hidden detainees', *Washington Post*, September 10, 2004, p. A24.

76 Taguba, *Hearing Article 15–6*.

77 American Civil Liberties Union (2005) *Newly Released Investigative Files Provide Further Evidence Soldiers Not Held Accountable for Abuse*, January 24. Online, available at: www.aclu.org (accessed January 29, 2005).

78 American Civil Liberties Union, *Newly Released Investigative Files Provide Further Evidence Soldiers Not Held Accountable for Abuse*.

79 For details see Human Rights Watch, 'Leadership Failure'.

80 As noted in Taguba, *Hearing Article 15–6*, p. 10.

81 See Human Rights Watch (2005) *Did President Bush Order Torture?* Online, available at: www.hrw.org/English/docs/2004/12/21/usint9925_txt.htm (accessed February 9, 2005).

82 See Human Rights Watch, 'Leadership Failure'.

83 See Human Rights Watch, 'Account of Sergeant A'.

84 Quoted in Human Rights Watch, 'Account of Sergeant A'.

85 See Sheryl Stolberg, 'Prisoner abuse scandal puts McCain in spotlight once again', *New York Times*, May 10, 2004. Online, available at: www.nytimes.com (accessed May 10, 2004).

86 Colonel Lawrence Wilkerson quoted in Dan Froomkin, 'Former insider lashes out', October 20, 2005. Online, available at: www.washingtonpost.com (accessed October 20, 2005).

87 Quoted in Froomkin, 'Former insider lashes out'.

88 Eric Schmitt, '3 in 82nd Airborne say beating Iraqi prisoners was routine', *New York Times*, September 24, 2005. Online, available at: www.nytimes.com (accessed September 24, 2005).

89 Speaking on KCNC-TV in Denver in May 2004. See Kirk Johnson, 'Guard featured in abuse photos says she was following orders', *New York Times*, May 12, 2004. Online, available at: www.nytimes.com (accessed May 12, 2004) and Kate Zernike, 'Woman with leash appears in court on Abu Ghraib abuse charges', *New York Times*, August 4, 2004. Online, available at: www.nytimes.com (accessed August 4, 2004).

90 Douglas Jehl and Eric Schmitt, 'Afghan policies on questioning prisoners taken to

Iraq', *New York Times*, May 21, 2004. Online, available at: www.nytimes.com (accessed August 4, 2004).

91 See Eric Schmitt, 'Four top officers cleared by Army in prison abuse', *New York Times*, April 23, 2005. Online, available at: www.nytimes.com (accessed April 24, 2004) and George Wright, 'Commander a scapegoat for Abu Ghraib,' *Guardian*, June 15, 2004. Online, available at: www.guardian.co.uk (accessed June 15, 2004).

92 For details see Julian Borger, 'US general linked to Abu Ghraib abuse', *Guardian*, May 22, 2004, p. 12.

93 American Civil Liberties Union (2004) *FBI E-Mail Refers to Presidential Order Authorizing Inhumane Interrogation Techniques*, December 20. Online, available at: www.aclu.org (accessed February 17, 2005).

94 Hersh quoted in David Usborne, 'Rumsfeld loosened interrogation rules claims New Yorker', *Independent*, May 17, 2004. Online, available at: www.independent.co.uk (accessed May 17, 2004).

95 Human Rights Watch, 'Leadership Failure'.

96 Quoted in American Civil Liberties Union (2004) *Special Ops Task Force Threatened Government Agents Who Saw Detainee Abuse in Iraq*, December 7. Online, available at: www.aclu.org (accessed December 18, 2004).

97 Report dated June 2004, quoted in American Civil Liberties Union, *FBI E-Mail Refers to Presidential Order Authorizing Inhumane Interrogation Techniques*.

98 Quoted in American Civil Liberties Union, *FBI E-Mail Refers to Presidential Order Authorizing Inhumane Interrogation Techniques*.

99 Quoted in American Civil Liberties Union, *Newly Released Investigative Files Provide Further Evidence Soldiers Not Held Accountable for Abuse*.

100 Quoted in American Civil Liberties Union, *Newly Released Investigative Files Provide Further Evidence Soldiers Not Held Accountable for Abuse*.

101 See American Civil Liberties Union, *Newly Released Investigative Files Provide Further Evidence Soldiers Not Held Accountable for Abuse*.

102 See Schmitt, '3 in 82nd Airborne say beating Iraqi prisoners was routine'.

103 See Charles Kupchan, *The End of the American Era*, New York, Vintage Books, 2003, p. xiii. For information on administration concerns of Iraq targeting Israel see Woodward, *Plan of Attack*, pp. 42, 258, 320 and 387.

104 Quoted by Tom Fenton (2003) *Mandela Slams Bush on Iraq*, January 30. Online, available at: www.cbsnews.com (accessed January 30, 2003).

105 Stephen Zunes, 'US foreign policy, democracy and human rights', in David Forsythe (ed.) *The United States and Human Rights: Looking Inward and Outward*, Lincoln, NE, University of Nebraska Press, 2000, pp. 227–45 at 230.

106 David Harvey, *The New Imperialism*, Oxford, Oxford University Press, 2003, p. 19.

107 NSC meeting February 24, 2003. For details see Woodward, *Plan of Attack*, pp. 322–3.

108 Woodward, *Plan of Attack*, p. 381.

109 George W. Bush (2006) *State of the Union Address*, Washington, DC, January 31.

110 Including PAC, soft money and individual contributions to federal candidates, party committees and leadership PACs. See Center for Responsive Politics (2003) *Rebuilding Iraq: The Contractors*. Online, available at: www.opensecrets.org/bush/100days/environment.asp (accessed December 16, 2003).

111 Charlie Cray, 'The Halliburton fix', *Multinational Monitor*, 2004, vol. 25, no. 5. Online, available at: multinationalmonitor.org/mm2004/05012004/may-june04 corp1.html (accessed January 31, 2005) and David Teather, 'Oil firm linked to Cheney gets Iraq boost', *Guardian*, October 30, 2003. Online, available at: www.guardian.co.uk/print/03858,4785553–110373,00.html (accessed October 30, 2003).

112 Memo dated March 2003. See Rupert Cornwell, 'E-Mail links Cheney to Hallibur-

ton Deal', *Independent*, June 1, 2004. Online, available at: www.independent.co.uk (accessed June 1, 2004).

113 For details see Mark Tran, 'Pentagon launches Halliburton inquiry', *Guardian*, December 12, 2004. Online, available at: www.guardian.co.uk (accessed December 12, 2004).

114 For details see Cray, 'The Halliburton fix'.

115 For details see Cray, 'The Halliburton fix'.

116 For details see Cray, 'The Halliburton fix'.

117 Michael Janofsky, 'Halliburton turns over $6.3 million to government', *New York Times*, January 24, 2004. Online, available at: www.nytimes.com (accessed January 24, 2004) and David Teather, 'Halliburton staff sacked for taking bribes', *Guardian*, January 24, 2004. Online, available at: www.guardian.co.uk (accessed January 24, 2004).

118 See Teather, 'Halliburton staff sacked for taking bribes'.

119 Senator Frank Lautenberg quoted in Cray, 'The Halliburton fix'.

120 Center for Responsive Politics, *Rebuilding Iraq: The Contractors*.

121 See Teather, 'Oil firm linked to Cheney gets Iraq boost' and Center for Responsive Politics, *Rebuilding Iraq: The Contractors*.

122 Teather, 'Oil firm linked to Cheney gets Iraq boost'.

123 Quoted in Foster Klug, 'McCain: torture ban needed for US image', *Associated Press*, November 13, 2005. Online, available at: www.washingtonpost.com (accessed November 14, 2005).

124 Bush, *President Bush Thanks Military*.

125 Bush, *President Bush Thanks Military*.

126 Bush, 2004 *State of the Union Address*.

127 Bush, *Importance of Democracy in Middle East*. See also George W. Bush, 'In Bush's Words', *New York Times*, December 15, 2003. Online, available at: www.nytimes.com (accessed December 15, 2003).

128 Assessment attached to the $1.3 billion *Focused Stabilization in Strategic Cities Initiative*, quoted in Julian Borger, 'Official US agency paints dire picture of "out of control" Iraq', *Guardian*, January 20, 2006. Online, available at: www.guardian. co.uk (accessed January 20, 2006).

129 Quoted in Borger, 'Official US Agency paints dire picture of "out of control" Iraq'.

130 General John Abizaid quoted in BBC News (2006) *US Echoes Iraq Civil War Warning*. Online, available at: news.bbc.co.uk/go/pr/fr/-/1/hi/world/middle_east/5243042.stm (accessed August 3, 2006).

131 See Ray Hiebert, 'Public relations and propaganda in framing the Iraq War: a preliminary review', *Public Relations Review*, 2003, vol. 29, no. 3, pp. 243–55 at 250.

132 Phil Shiner, 'End this lawlessness', *Guardian*, June 10, 2004. Online, available at: www.guardian.co.uk (accessed June 10, 2004).

133 See Amnesty International (2004) *Killings of Civilians in Basra and Al-Amara*, May 11. Online, available at: web.amnesty.org/library/print/ENGMDE140072004 (accessed May 12, 2004).

134 Quoted in George Monbiot, 'The US used chemical weapons in Iraq and then lied about it', *Guardian*, November 15, 2005. Online, available at: www.guardian.co.uk (accessed November 15, 2005).

135 Monbiot, 'US used chemical weapons'.

136 The US Army only released numbers of 'Saddamists' and 'al Qaeda' elements killed. See Kim Sengupta and Marie Woolf, 'Allies accused of breaking Geneva Convention on civilian losses', *Independent*, May 17, 2004. Online, available at: www.independent.co.uk (accessed May 17, 2004).

137 Quoted in Woodward, *Plan of Attack*, p. 327.

138 Brian Barder *et al.*, 'A letter to Blair: Your Middle East policy is doomed say diplo-

mats', *Independent*, April 27, 2004. Online, available at: www.independent.co.uk (accessed April 27, 2004).

139 Les Roberts, Riyadh Lafta, Richard Garfield, Jamal Khudhairi and Gilbert Burnham, 'Mortality before and after the 2003 invasion of Iraq: cluster sample survey', *Lancet,* 2004, vol. 364, no. 9448, pp. 1857–64.

140 Les Roberts quoted in Jeremy Laurance and Colin Brown, 'Revealed: War has cost 100,000 Iraqi lives', *Independent*, October 29, 2004. Online, available at: www.independent.co.uk (accessed October 29, 2004).

141 Gilbert Burnham, Riyadh Lafta, Shannon Doocy and Les Roberts, 'Mortality after the 2003 invasion of Iraq: A cross-sectional cluster sample survey', *Lancet*, 2006, vol. 368, no. 9545, pp. 1421–8.

142 Leader, 'Lies about crimes', *Guardian*, May 21, 2004. Online, available at: www.guardian.co.uk (accessed May 21, 2004).

143 Rumsfeld in transcript, 'Rumsfeld testifies before Senate Armed Services Committee'.

144 Rumsfeld in transcript, 'Rumsfeld testifies before Senate Armed Services Committee'.

145 Rumsfeld in transcript, 'Rumsfeld testifies before Senate Armed Services Committee'.

146 Les Brownlee in transcript, 'Rumsfeld testifies before Senate Armed Services Committee'.

147 Quoted in Richard Stevenson, 'Bush on Arab TV denounces abuse of Iraqi captives', *New York Times*, May 6, 2004. Online, available at: www.nytimes.com (accessed May 6, 2004).

148 George W. Bush quoted in Stevenson, 'Bush on Arab TV denounces abuse of Iraqi captives' and George W. Bush (2004) *Statement at the Pentagon*, May 10.

149 For details see Chapter 1.

150 See Hiebert, 'Public relations and propaganda in framing the Iraq War' p. 248 and David Forsythe (2003) *US Foreign Policy and Human Rights in an Era of Insecurity: The Bush Administration and Human Rights After 9/11*, p. 13. Online, available at: www.unl.edu/polisci/faculty/forsythe/cuny-paper.pdf (accessed July 28, 2003).

151 Kevin Sullivan and Walter Pincus, 'Paper says Bush talked of bombing Arab TV network', *Washington Post*, November 23, 2005, p. A14 and Raymond Whitaker and Marie Woolf, 'PM on the defensive over Official Secrets Act trial', *Independent*, November 27, 2005. Online, available at: www.independent.co.uk (accessed November 27, 2005).

152 See Jim Lobe (2004) 'Press watchdog "deeply disturbed" by Iraqi regime's media threat', November 16. Online, available at: www.LewRockwell.com (accessed March 4, 2005).

153 George Jones, 'Bush and Blair message beamed in', *Daily Telegraph*, April 11, 2003. Online, available at: www.telegraph.co.uk/news (accessed April 12, 2003).

154 George W. Bush, 'Bush's address on Towards Freedom', *Guardian*, April 10, 2003. Online, available at: www.guardian.co.uk (accessed April 10, 2003).

155 Charles Stewart-Smith, 'Why should the Iraqis believe US TV?' *Guardian*, April 14, 2003. Online, available at: www.guardian.co.uk (accessed April 14, 2003).

156 See Department of State (2004) *Supporting Human Rights and Democracy: The US Record 2003–2004*. Online, available at: www.state.gov/g/drl/rls/shrd/2003/ 31022.htm (accessed January 28, 2005).

157 Bush, *Importance of Democracy in Middle East*.

158 Department of State, *Supporting Human Rights and Democracy*.

159 The Lincoln Group. See David Cloud and Jeff Gerth, 'Muslim scholars were paid to aid US propaganda', *New York Times*, January 2, 2006. Online, available at: www.nytimes.com (accessed January 2, 2006).

160 Cloud and Gerth, 'Muslim scholars were paid to aid US propaganda'.

161 David Miller, 'The domination effect', *Guardian*, January 8, 2004. Online, available at: www.guardian.co.uk (accessed January 8, 2004).

162 Hiebert, 'Public relations and propaganda in framing the Iraq War', p. 250.

163 See Hiebert, 'Public relations and propaganda in framing the Iraq War', p. 251.

164 See Hiebert, 'Public relations and propaganda in framing the Iraq War', p. 251.

165 Jane Bright quoted in Mark Borkowski, 'Body blow', *Guardian*, April 26, 2004. Online, available at: media.guardian.co.uk (accessed April 26, 2004).

166 See Gary Younge, 'Private Lynch's media war continues as Iraqi doctors deny rape claim', *Guardian*, November 12, 2003. Online, available at: www.guardian.co.uk (accessed November 12, 2003).

167 See Nicole Winfeld, 'US tells how its troops rescued Army heroine', *Observer*, April 6, 2003. Online, available at: www.observer.guardian.co.uk (accessed April 6, 2003).

168 See John Kampfner, 'The truth about Jessica', *Guardian*, May 15, 2003. Online, available at: media.guardian.co.uk (accessed May 15, 2003).

169 See Kampfner, 'The truth about Jessica'.

170 Quoted in Rory McCarthy, 'Saving Private Lynch', *Guardian*, April 3, 2003. Online, available at: www.guardian.co.uk (accessed April 3, 2003).

171 Kampfner, 'The truth about Jessica'.

172 Quoted in Younge, 'Private Lynch's media war continues as Iraqi doctors deny rape claim'.

173 For details see Tania Branigan, 'Iraqi lawyer risked life to help rescue of PoW Jessica Lynch', *Guardian*, April 5, 2003. Online, available at: www.guardian.co.uk (accessed May 15, 2003).

174 Younge, 'Private Lynch's media war continues as Iraqi doctors deny rape claim'.

175 Kampfner, 'The truth about Jessica'.

176 Dr Harith Al-Houssona. See Kampfner, 'The truth about Jessica'.

177 For details see Kampfner, 'The truth about Jessica'.

178 Quoted in Younge, 'Private Lynch's media war continues as Iraqi doctors deny rape claim'.

179 Quoted in Kampfner, 'The truth about Jessica'.

180 See Kampfner, 'The truth about Jessica'.

181 Quoted in Toby Manhire, 'Private's life becomes public property', *Guardian*, April 8, 2003. Online, available at: www.guardian.co.uk (accessed April 8, 2003).

182 Quoted in Manhire, 'Private's life becomes public property'.

183 Matthew Rycroft (2002) *Downing Street Memo*, July 23, leaked to the *Sunday Times*, May 1, 2005. Online, available at: www.downingstreetmemo.com/memos.html (accessed August 2, 2005).

184 Rycroft, *Downing Street Memo*.

185 Quoted in Katherine Pfleger and Dafna Linzer, 'Kay doubts presence of illicit Iraq arms', *New York Times*, January 26, 2004. Online, available at: www.nytimes.com (accessed January 26, 2004).

186 Quoted in Bob Herbert, 'The wrong war', *New York Times*, March 26, 2004. Online, available at: www.nytimes.com (accessed March 26, 2004).

187 Quoted in Mark Hosenball, Michael Isikoff and Evan Thomas, 'Cheney's long path to war', *Newsweek*, November 17, 2003, p. 38.

188 See Chapter 1 for details of how the administration discursively linked the wars on Iraq and al Qaeda.

189 Cheney speech to the VFW National Convention quoted by Andrew Rosenthal, 'Decoding the Senate intelligence committee investigation on Iraq', *New York Times*, July 18, 2004. Online, available at: www.nytimes.com (accessed July 18, 2004).

190 Tenet quoted in Julian Borger, 'CIA in blow to Bush attack plans', *Guardian*, October 10, 2002. Online, available at: www.guardian.co.uk (accessed October 10, 2002).

191 For details see Julian Borger, 'In wake of WMD report, Bush struggles to convince public he was right to go to war', *Guardian*, October 4, 2003. Online, available at: www.guardian.co.uk (accessed October 4, 2003).

192 Quoted in Julian Borger, 'Admit WMD mistake, survey chief tells Bush', *Guardian*, March 3, 2004. Online, available at: www.guardian.co.uk (accessed October 4, 2003).

193 Charles Duelfer (2004) *Comprehensive Report of the Special Advisor to the DCI on Iraq's WMD*, September 30. Online, available at: news.findlaw.com/nytimes/docs/iraq/cia93004wmdrpt.html (accessed October 24, 2004).

194 Toby Harnden, 'America rejects Chirac's claim that Saddam is no threat', *Daily Telegraph*, February 17, 2003. Online, available at: www.telegraph.co.uk/news (accessed February 17, 2003).

195 Quoted in Associated Press, 'Kay criticizes Bush, Blair on Iraq intel', *New York Times*, July 18, 2004. Online, available at: www.nytimes.com (accessed July 18, 2004).

196 Ron Suskind, *The Price of Loyalty*, New York, Pocket Books, 2004.

197 Quoted in Martin Kettle, 'Topic A and how the Iraq game was given away', *Guardian*, January 13, 2004. Online, available at: www.guardian.co.uk (accessed January 13, 2004).

198 George W. Bush (2004) *President Bush Discusses Iraq Report*, South Grounds, White House, Washington, DC, October 7.

199 Reuters, 'Democrats call for probe of Iraq weapons claims', *New York Times*, January 25, 2004. Online, available at: www.nytimes.com (accessed January 25, 2004) and James Risen, 'Ex-inspector says CIA missed disarray in Iraqi arms program', *New York Times*, January 26, 2004. Online, available at: www.nytimes.com (accessed January 26, 2004).

200 Richard Clarke, *Against All Enemies*, New York, Simon and Schuster, 2004, p. 54.

201 Richard Clarke, *60 Minutes*, CBS, quoted in Todd Purdum, 'An accuser's insider status puts the White House on the defensive', *New York Times*, March 23, 2004. Online, available at: www.nytimes.com (accessed January 26, 2004).

202 See John O'Farrell, 'Hands off the UN', *Guardian*, June 13, 2003. Online, available at: www.guardian.co.uk (accessed June 13, 2003); Helena Smith, 'Blix: I was smeared by the Pentagon', *Guardian*, June 11, 2003. Online, available at: www.guardian.co.uk (accessed June 11, 2003) and Amy Bartholomew and Jennifer Breakspear, 'Human rights as swords of Empire', in Leo Panitch and Colin Leys (eds) *Socialist Register 2004: The New Imperial Challenge*, London, Merlin Press, 2003, pp. 125–145 at 130.

203 Quoted in Associated Press, 'Kay criticizes Bush, Blair on Iraq intel'.

204 Hans Blix quoted in Reuters, 'Iraq charges against Bush begin to mount', *New York Times*, March 23, 2004. Online, available at: www.nytimes.com (accessed March 23, 2004).

205 Quoted in Barnaby Mason (2003) *Blix Adds to US and UK Worries*, September 18. Online, available at: newsvote.bbc.co.uk (accessed September 18, 2003).

206 See Mason, *Blix Adds to US and UK Worries*.

207 Quoted in Rupert Cornwell, 'Cheney "created climate for US war crimes"', *Independent*, November 30, 2005. Online, available at: www.news.independent.co.uk (accessed November 30, 2005).

208 For details see editorial, 'Mr Cheney, meet Mr Kay', *New York Times*, January 27, 2004. Online, available at: www.nytimes.com (accessed January 28, 2004).

209 See John Kampfner, *Blair's Wars*, London, Simon and Schuster, 2003, pp. 162–3 and Hosenball, Isikoff and Thomas, 'Cheney's long path to war', p. 41.
210 Maureen Dowd, 'I spy a screw-up', *New York Times*, March 31, 2005. Online, available at: www.nytimes.com (accessed March 31, 2004).
211 Quoted in Bartholomew and Breakspear, 'Human rights as swords of Empire', pp. 125–45.
212 Rycroft, *Downing Street Memo*.
213 Rycroft, *Downing Street Memo*.
214 For details see Ivo Daalder and James Lindsay, *America Unbound: The Bush Revolution in Foreign Policy*, Washington, DC, Brookings Institution Press, 2003, p. 175.
215 Marcus Warren and Toby Harnden, 'The case against Saddam', *The Daily Telegraph*, February 6, 2003. Online, available at: www.telegraph.co.uk/news (accessed February 8, 2003).
216 See Chapter 3.
217 Steven Kull, *Misperceptions, the Media and the Iraq War*, Baltimore, MD, University of Maryland, Program on International Policy Attitudes, 2003, p. 5.

Conclusion

1 See Chapter 3.
2 See, for example, Colin Dueck, 'Ideas and alternatives in American grand strategy, 2000–2004', *Review of International Studies*, 2004, vol. 30, no. 3, pp. 511–35.
3 See John Laughland, 'Human rights and the rule of law', in David Chandler (ed.) *Rethinking Human Rights: Critical Approaches to International Politics*, Basingstoke, Palgrave, 2002, pp. 38–56 at 46.
4 For details see Chapter 4.
5 George W. Bush (2002) *Remarks by the President at 2002 Graduation Exercise of the United States Military Academy*, West Point, New York, June 1.
6 See James Der Derian, 'Decoding the National Security Strategy of the United States of America', *Boundary*, 2003, vol. 30, no. 3, pp. 19–27 at 24.
7 Indeed, US government officials have never spoken openly about Israeli nuclear weapons since foreign aid legislation enacted in 1977 bans aid to states that secretly develop nuclear weapons.
8 See, for example, G. John Ikenberry, 'Liberalism and empire: logics of order in the American unipolar age', *Review of International Studies*, 2004, vol. 30, no. 4, pp. 609–30 at 624; Larry Diamond, 'Promoting democracy', in Eugene Wittkopf (ed.) *The Future of American Foreign Policy*, New York, St Martin's Press, 1994, pp. 101–7 at 103 and Robert McElroy, *Morality and American Foreign Policy*, Princeton, NJ, Princeton University Press, 1992, pp. 44–5.
9 Charles Kupchan, *The End of the American Era*, New York, Vintage Books, 2003, p. ix.

Bibliography

Books

Allison, Graham and Gregory Treverton, *Rethinking America's Security*, New York, W.W. Norton, 1992.

Almond, Gabriel, *The American People and Foreign Policy*, New York, Harcourt, Brace, 1950.

Ambrose, Stephen and Douglas Brinkley, *Rise to Globalism: American Foreign Policy Since 1938*, Harmondsworth, Penguin, 1997.

Bennis, Phyllis, *Before and After: United States Foreign Policy and the War on Terrorism*, Moreton-in-Marsh, Arris Books, 2003.

Bernays, Edward, *Propaganda*, New York, Horace Liveright, 1928.

Blum, William, *Rogue State: A Guide to the World's Only Superpower*, London, Zed Books, 2002.

Blum, William, *Killing Hope: US and CIA Interventions Since World War II*, London, Zed Books, 2003.

Bobbitt, Philip, *The Shield of Achilles*, New York, Knopf, 2001.

Brown, Cynthia (ed.) *Lost Liberties: Ashcroft and the Assault on Personal Freedom*, New York, The New Press, 2004.

Brzezinski, Zbigniew, *The Grand Chessboard: American Primacy and its Geostrategic Imperatives*, New York, Basic Books, 1997.

Buckley, Mary and Rick Fawn (eds) *Global Responses to Terrorism: 9/11, Afghanistan and Beyond*, London and New York, Routledge, 2003.

Burbach, Roger and Jim Tarbell, *Imperial Overstretch: George W Bush and the Hubris of Empire*, London, Zed Books, 2004.

Callahan, David, *Between Two Worlds*, New York, HarperCollins, 1994.

Cameron, Fraser, *US Foreign Policy After the Cold War: Global Hegemon or Reluctant Sheriff?* London and New York, Routledge, 2002.

Campbell, David, *Writing Security: US Foreign Policy and the Politics of Identity*, Manchester, Manchester University Press, 1998.

Chandler, David (ed.) *Rethinking Human Rights: Critical Approaches to International Politics*, Basingstoke, Palgrave, 2002.

Chomsky, Noam, *Knowledge of Language: Its Nature, Origins and Use*, New York, Praeger, 1986.

Chomsky, Noam, *On Power and Ideology: The Managua Lectures*, Boston, MA, South End Press, 1987.

Chomsky, Noam, *The Culture of Terrorism*, London, Pluto Press, 1988.

Chomsky, Noam, *Deterring Democracy*, Reading, Verso, 1992.

Chomsky, Noam, *Rethinking Camelot: JFK, the Vietnam War and US Political Culture*, London, Verso, 1993.

Chomsky, Noam, *Year 501: The Conquest Continues*, London, Verso, 1993.

Chomsky, Noam, *Hegemony or Survival? America's Quest for Global Dominance*, London, Hamish Hamilton, 2003.

Clark, Ian, *Legitimacy in International Society*, Oxford, Oxford University Press, 2005.

Clarke, Jonathan and Stefan Halper, *America Alone: The Neo Conservatives and the Global Order*, Cambridge, Cambridge University Press, 2004.

Clarke, Richard, *Against All Enemies*, New York, Simon and Schuster, 2004.

Cole, David, *Enemy Aliens: Double Standards and Constitutional Freedoms in the War on Terrorism*, New York, New York Press, 2004.

Cox, Michael, *US Foreign Policy After the Cold War: Superpower Without a Mission?* London, Pinter, 1995.

Cox, Michael, G. John Ikenberry and Takachi Inoguchi (eds) *American Democracy Promotion: Impulses, Strategies and Impacts*, Oxford, Oxford University Press, 2000.

Daalder, Ivo and James Lindsay, *America Unbound: The Bush Revolution in Foreign Policy*, Washington, DC, Brookings Institution Press, 2003.

de Saussure, Ferdinand, *Course in General Linguistics*, London, Duckworth, 1983.

de Torrente, Nicolas, *Forgotten War: Democratic Republic of Congo*, New York, de.Mo, 2005.

Donini, Antonio, Norah Niland and Karin Wermester (eds) *Nation-Building Unraveled? Aid, Peace and Justice in Afghanistan*, London, Kumarian Press, 2004.

Donnelly, Jack, *International Human Rights*, 2nd edition, Boulder, CO, Westview Press, 1998.

Elshtain, Jean Bethke, *Just War Against Terror: Ethics and the Burden of American Power in a Violent World*, New York, Basic Books, 2003.

Evans, Tony, *US Hegemony and the Project of Universal Human Rights*, Basingstoke, Macmillan, 1996.

Ewen, Stuart, *A Social History of Spin*, New York, Basic Books, 1996.

Feffer, John (ed.) *Power Trip: US Unilateralism and Global Strategy After September 11*, New York, Seven Stories Press, 2003.

Forsythe, David (ed.) *The United States and Human Rights: Looking Inward and Outward*, Lincoln, NE, University of Nebraska Press, 2000.

Foucault, Michel, *The Archaeology of Knowledge*, London, Tavistock, 1972.

Foucault, Michel, *Power/Knowledge: Selected Interviews and Other Writings 1972-1977*, New York, Pantheon, 1980.

Foucault, Michel, *Ethics: Subjectivity and the Truth*, New York, The New Press, 1994.

Galtung, Johan, *Human Rights in Another Key*, Cambridge, MA, Polity Press, 1994.

Gareau, Frederick, *State Terrorism and the United States*, Atlanta, GA, Clarity Press, 2004.

Gewirth, Alan, *Human Rights: Essays on Justification and Application*, Chicago, IL, University of Chicago Press, 1984.

Gill, Stephen, *American Hegemony and the Trilateral Commission*, Cambridge, Cambridge University Press, 1990.

Glendinning, Simon (ed.) *The Edinburgh Encyclopedia of Continental Philosophy*, Edinburgh, Edinburgh University Press, 1999.

Goldstein, Judith and Robert Keohane (eds) *Ideas and Foreign Policy: Beliefs, Institutions and Political Change*, Ithaca, NY, Cornell University Press, 1993.

Goverde, Henri, Philip Cerny, Mark Haugaard and Howard Lentner (eds) *Power in Contemporary Politics*, London, Sage, 2000.

Gray, John, *Mill on Liberty: A Defense*, London, Routledge, 1983.

Hancock, Jan, *Environmental Human Rights: Power, Ethics and Law*, Aldershot, Ashgate, 2003.

Harbour, Frances, *Thinking About International Ethics: Moral Cases from American Foreign Policy*, Boulder, CO, Westview Press, 1999.

Harvey, David, *The New Imperialism*, Oxford, Oxford University Press, 2003.

Hechter, Michael, *Principles of Group Solidarity*, 4th edition, Berkley, CA, University of California Press, 1987.

Hentoff, Nat, *The War on the Bill of Rights and the Gathering Resistance*, New York, Seven Stories Press, 2004.

Hogan, Michael (ed.) *The Ambiguous Legacy*, Cambridge, Cambridge University Press, 1999.

Howarth, David, *Discourse*, Buckingham, Open University Press, 2000.

Ingram, Attracta, *A Political Theory of Rights*, Oxford, Clarendon Press, 1994.

Johnson, Chalmers, *The Sorrows of Empire: How the Americans Lost Their Country*, New York, Metropolitan Book, 2003.

Kampfner, John, *Blair's Wars*, London, Simon and Schuster, 2003.

Kernohan, Andrew, *Liberalism, Equality and Cultural Oppression*, Cambridge, Cambridge University Press, 1998.

Kissinger, Henry, *Diplomacy*, New York, Simon and Schuster, 1994.

Kissinger, Henry, *Does America Need a Foreign Policy? Toward a Diplomacy for the 21st Century*, New York, Simon and Schuster, 2001.

Kohut, Andrew, *Bush's Gains Broad-Based*, Washington, DC, Pew Research Center, 2004.

Kolko, Gabriel, *Main Currents in Modern American History*, New York, Pantheon, 1984.

Kull, Steven, *Misperceptions, the Media and the Iraq War*, Baltimore, MD, University of Maryland, Program on International Policy Attitudes, 2003.

Kupchan, Charles, *The End of the American Era*, New York, Vintage Books, 2003.

LaFeber, Walter, *Inevitable Revolutions*, London, Norton, 1983.

Lawyers Committee for Human Rights, *Assessing the New Normal: Liberty and Security for the Post-September 11 United States*, Washington, DC, Human Rights First, 2003.

Lawyers Committee for Human Rights, *Holding the Line: A Critique of the Department of State's Annual Country Reports on Human Rights Practices*, Washington, DC, Human Rights First, 2003.

Lawyers Committee for Human Rights, *Imbalance of Powers*, Washington, DC, Human Rights First, 2003.

Lieuwin, Edwin, *US Policy in Latin America*, London, Praeger, 1965.

Lincoln, Bruce, *Holy Terror: Thinking About Religion After September 11*, Chicago, IL, University of Chicago Press, 2003.

Livingstone, Grace, *Inside Colombia: Drugs, Democracy and War*, London, Latin American Bureau, 2003.

Locke, John, *Second Treatise of Government*, London, Macmillan, 1952.

Long, Douglas, *Bentham on Liberty*, Toronto, University of Toronto Press, 1977.

MacKinnon, Michael, *The Evolution of US Peacekeeping Policy Under Clinton: A Fairweather Friend,* Portland, OR, Frank Cass, 2000.

Madsen, Deborah, *American Exceptionalism*, Edinburgh, Edinburgh University Press, 1998.

Malone, David and Yuen Khong (eds) *Unilateralism and United States Foreign Policy*, Boulder, CO, Lynne Rienner, 2003.

Marcuse, Herbert, *One Dimensional Man*, London, Sphere, 1964.

Mayer, Ann, *Islam and Human Rights: Tradition and Politics*, 2nd edition, Boulder, CO, Westview Press, 1995.

McElroy, Robert, *Morality and American Foreign Policy*, Princeton, NJ, Princeton University Press, 1992.

McLellan, David, *Karl Marx: Selected Writings*, Oxford, Oxford University Press, 1977.

Mead, Walter, *Special Providence: American Foreign Policy and How it Changed the World*, New York, Routledge, 2002.

Moss, Jeremy (ed.) *The Later Foucault*, London, Sage, 1998.

Morgenthau, Hans, *Politics in the Twentieth Century*, Chicago, IL, University of Chicago Press, 1962.

Morgenthau, Hans, *Politics Among Nations*, 5th edition, New York, Alfred Knopf, 1975.

Morgenthau, Hans, *In Defense of the National Interest*, Washington, DC, University Press of America, 1982.

Murillo, Mario, *Colombia and the United States: War, Unrest and Destabilization*, New York, Seven Stories Press, 2004.

Nye, Joseph, *The Paradox of American Power: Why the World's Only Superpower Can't Go It Alone*, New York, Oxford University Press, 2002.

Panitch, Leo and Colin Leys (eds) *Socialist Register 2004: The New Imperial Challenge*, London, Merlin Press, 2003.

Parenti, Christian, *The Soft Cage: Surveillance in America from Slavery to the War on Terror*, New York, Basic Books, 2004.

Peet, Richard, Beate Born, Kendra Feher and Matthew Feinstein, *Unholy Trinity: The IMF, World Bank and WTO*, London, Zed Books, 2004.

Pilger, John, *Hidden Agendas*, London, Vintage, 1998.

Pilger, John, *New Rulers of the World*, London, Verso, 2003.

Pillar, Paul, *Terrorism and US Foreign Policy*, Washington, DC, Brookings Institution Press, 2003.

Pogge, Thomas, *World Poverty and Human Rights*, Cambridge, MA, Polity Press, 2002.

Ransome, Paul, *Antonio Gramsci: A New Introduction*, New York, Harvester Wheatsheaf, 1992.

Rosenberg, Justin, *The Empire of Civil Society: A Critique of the Realist Theory of International Relations*, London, Verso, 1994.

Ruggie, John, *Winning the Peace*, New York, Columbia University Press, 1996.

Saar, Erik and Viveca Novak, *Inside the Wire: A Military Intelligence Soldier's Eyewitness Account of Life at Guantanamo*, New York, Penguin Press, 2005.

Salter, M., *Barbarians and Civilization in International Relations*, London, Pluto Press, 2002.

Shattuck, John, *Freedom on Fire: Human Rights Wars and America's Response*, Boston, MA, Harvard University Press, 2003.

Shue, Henry, *Basic Rights: Subsistence, Affluence and United States Foreign Policy*, Princeton, NJ, Princeton University Press, 1980.

Silberstein, S., *War of Words: Language, Politics and 9/11*, London, Routledge, 2002.

Singer, Peter, *The President of Good and Evil: Taking George W. Bush Seriously*, London, Granta Books.

Suskind, Ron, *The Price of Loyalty*, New York, Simon and Schuster, 2004.

Thomas, Ward, *The Ethics of Destruction*, Ithaca, NY, Cornell University Press, 2001.

Vincent, R.J., *Human Rights and International Relations*, Cambridge, Cambridge University Press, 1986.

Wallas, Graham, *Human Nature in Politics*, London, Constable and Company, 1908.

Weiss, Thomas, Margaret Crahan and John Goering (eds) *Wars on Terrorism and Iraq: Human Rights, Unilateralism and US Foreign Policy*, London, Routledge, 2004.

Wheeler, Nicholas, *Saving Strangers: Humanitarian Intervention in International Society*, Oxford, Oxford University Press, 2000.

Wittkopf, Eugene (ed.) *The Future of American Foreign Policy*, New York, St. Martin's Press, 1994.

Wittkopf, Eugene and James McCormick (eds) *The Domestic Sources of American Foreign Policy: Insights and Evidence*, Lanham, MD, Rowman and Littlefield Publishers, 2004.

Woodward, Bob, *Bush at War*, New York, Simon and Schuster, 2002.

Woodward, Bob, *Plan of Attack*, London, Simon and Schuster, 2004.

Journal articles

Armitage, Richard, 'Allies, friends and partners on every page: international cooperation in the national security strategy', *US Foreign Policy Agenda*, 2002, vol. 7, no. 4.

Barber, Benjamin, 'Imperialism or interdependence?' *Security Dialogue*, 2004, vol. 35, no. 2.

Bauer, Joanne, 'International human rights and Asian commitment', *Human Rights Dialogue*, 1995, vol. 3.

Brown, T., 'Ideological hegemony and global governance', *Journal of World-Systems Research*, 1997, vol. 3, no. 2.

Buhler, Ute, 'Who are we talking to? An addendum to recent RIS contributions on discourse ethics', *Review of International Studies*, 2002, vol. 28, no. 3.

Burke-White, William, 'Human rights and national security: the strategic correlation', *Harvard Human Rights Journal*, 2004, vol. 17.

Burnham, Gilbert, Riyadh Lafta, Shannon Doocy and Les Roberts, 'Mortality after the 2003 invasion of Iraq: A cross-sectional cluster sample survey', *Lancet*, 2006, vol. 368, no. 9545.

Byers, Michael, 'Not yet havoc: geopolitical change and the international rules on military force', *Review of International Studies*, 2005, vol. 31, sp. iss.

Carleton D. and M. Stohl, 'The foreign policy of human rights: Rhetoric and reality from Jimmy Carter to Ronald Reagan', *Human Rights Quarterly*, 1985, vol. 7, no. 2.

Carothers, Thomas, 'Democracy promotion', *Foreign Affairs*, 2003, vol. 82, no. 3.

Chandler, David, 'Rhetoric without responsibility: the attraction of ethical foreign policy', *British Journal of Politics and International Relations,* 2003, vol. 5, no. 3.

Cole, Kevin, 'The Wilsonian model of foreign policy and the post-cold war world', *Air and Space Power Chronicles*, 1999, vol. 13, no. 2.

Condron, David, 'Can there be an ethical foreign policy?' *Journal of Power and Ethics: An Interdisciplinary Review*, 2000, vol. 1, no. 3.

Cray, Charlie, 'The Halliburton fix', *Multinational Monitor*, 2004, vol. 25, no. 5.

Dennis, M., 'Looking backward: Woodrow Wilson, the new south and the question of race', *American Nineteenth Century History*, 2002, vol. 3, no. 1.

Der Derian, James, 'Decoding the National Security Strategy of the United States of America', *Boundary*, 2003, vol. 30, no. 3.

Dobriansky, Paula, 'Democracy promotion', *Foreign Affairs*, 2003, vol. 82, no. 3.

Dobson, Alan, 'The dangers of US intervention', *Review of International Studies*, 2002, vol. 28, no. 3.

Dombrowski, Peter and Rodger Payne, 'Global debate and the limits of the Bush doctrine', *International Studies Perspectives*, 2003, vol. 4, no. 4.

Drengson, Alan, 'Shifting paradigms: From the technocratic to the person-planetary', *Environmental Ethics*, 1980, vol. 2, no. 3.

Drumbl, Mark, 'Judging the 11 September terrorist attacks', *Human Rights Quarterly*, 2002, vol. 24, no. 2.

Drumbl, Mark, 'Self-defense and the use of force: breaking the rules, making the rules or both?' *International Studies Perspectives*, 2003, vol. 4, no. 4.

Drutman, Lee, 'Repetitively straining workers', *Multinational Monitor*, 2004, vol. 25, no. 1.

Dueck, Colin, 'Ideas and alternatives in American grand strategy, 2000-2004', *Review of International Studies*, 2004, vol. 30, no. 3.

Dunne, Tim, 'New thinking on international society', *British Journal of Politics and International Relations*, 2001, vol. 3, no. 2.

Editorial, 'Bush's corporate cabinet', *Multinational Monitor*, 2001, vol. 22, no. 5.

Editorial, 'The corporate conservative administration takes shape', *Multinational Monitor*, 2001, vol. 22, nos. 1 and 2.

Elshtain, Jean Bethke, 'Intellectual dissent and the war on terror', *Public Interest*, 2003, no. 151.

Evans, Tony and Jan Hancock, 'International human rights law and the challenge of globalization', *The International Journal of Human Rights*, 1998, vol. 2, no. 3.

Falk, Richard, 'Legality and legitimacy: the quest for principled flexibility and restraint', *Review of International Studies*, 2005, vol. 31, sp. iss.

Finnemore, Martha, 'Fights about rules: the role of efficacy and power in changing multilateralism', *Review of International Studies*, 2005, vol. 31, sp. iss.

Foot, Rosemary, 'Bush, China and human rights', *Survival*, 2003, vol. 45, no. 2.

Forsythe, David, 'The United States and international criminal justice', *Human Rights Quarterly*, 2002, vol. 24, no. 4.

Freedman, Lawrence, 'The age of liberal wars', *Review of International Studies*, 2005, vol. 31, sp. iss.

Gallie, W., 'Essentially contested concepts', *Proceedings of the Aristotelian Society*, 1956, vol. 56.

Glennon, Michael, 'The Gulf War and the constitution', *Foreign Affairs*, 1991, vol. 70, no. 2.

Hartung, William and Michelle Ciarocca, 'Corporate think tanks and the doctrine of aggressive militarism', *Multinational Monitor*, 2003, vol. 24, nos. 1 and 2.

Henkin, Louis, 'Foreign affairs and the constitution', *Foreign Affairs*, 1987, vol. 66, no. 2.

Hiebert, Ray Eldon, 'Public relations and propaganda in framing the Iraq War: a preliminary review', *Public Relations Review*, 2003, vol. 29, no. 3.

Hurd, Ian, 'Legitimacy and authority in international politics', *International Organization*, 1999, vol. 53, no. 2.

Hurrell, Andrew, 'Legitimacy and the use of force: Can the circle be squared?' *Review of International Studies*, 2005, vol. 31, sp. iss.

Ignatieff, Michael, 'International justice, war crimes and terrorism', *Social Research*, 2002, vol. 69, no. 4.

Ignatieff, Michael, 'Empire lite', *Prospect*, 2003, vol. 83.

Ikenberry, G. John, 'Liberalism and empire: logics of order in the American unipolar age', *Review of International Studies*, 2004, vol. 30, no. 4.

Kaldor, Mary, 'American Power: from "compellance" to cosmopolitanism?' *International Affairs*, 2003, vol. 79, no. 1.

Kaufman, Natalie and David Whiteman, 'Opposition to human rights treaties in the United States Senate: the legacy of the Bricker Amendment', *Human Rights Quarterly*, 1988, vol. 10, no. 3.

Kausikan, Bilahari, 'Asia's different standard', *Foreign Policy*, 1993, vol. 92, no. 3.

Kegley, Charles and Gregory Raymond, 'Preventive war and permissive normative order', *International Studies Perspectives*, 2003, vol. 4, no. 4.

Kennan, George, 'On American principles', *Foreign Affairs*, 1995, vol. 74, no. 2.

Keohane, Robert, 'International institutions: two approaches', *International Studies Quarterly*, 1988, vol. 44, no. 1.

Kinsella, Helen, 'Discourses of differences: civilians, combatants and compliance with the rules of war', *Review of International Studies*, 2005, vol. 31, sp. iss.

Kissinger, Henry, 'America at the apex', *The National Interest*, 2001, Summer.

Klare, Michael, 'Corporations, national security and war profiteering', *Multinational Monitor*, 2001, vol. 22, no. 11.

Kretzmann, Steve, 'Oil, security, war: the geopolitics of US energy planning', *Multinational Monitor*, 2003, vol. 24, nos. 1 and 2.

Kuhonta, Erik, 'The language of human rights in East Asia', *Human Rights Dialogue*, 1995, vol. 2.

Lang, Anthony, 'Responsibility in the international system: reading US foreign policy in the Middle East', *European Journal of International Relations*, 1999, vol. 5, no.1.

Langlois, Anthony, 'Human rights', *Review of International Studies*, 2002, vol. 28, no. 3.

Lantis, Jeffrey, 'Ethics and foreign policy', *International Studies Perspectives*, 2004, vol. 5, no. 2.

Lieber, Robert, 'A new era in US strategic thinking', *Global Issues*, 2002, vol. 7, no. 2.

Lobe, Jim, 'New human rights network denounces selectivity in Bush Administration's human rights agenda', *Foreign Policy in Focus*, 2003, December 11.

Marks, Stephen, 'The human right to development: between rhetoric and reality', *Harvard Human Rights Journal,* 2004, vol. 17.

Mazarr, Michael, 'George W. Bush, idealist', *International Affairs*, 2003, vol. 79, no. 3.

Mearsheimer, John, 'The false promise of international institutions', *International Security*, 1994, vol. 19, no. 3.

Mertus, Julie, 'The new US human rights policy: a radical departure', *International Studies Perspectives*, 2003, vol. 4, no. 4.

Milliken, Jennifer, 'The study of discourse in international relations: a critique of research and methods', *European Journal of International Relations*, 1999, vol. 5, no. 2.

Murphy, Sean (ed.) 'Terrorist attacks on World Trade Center and Pentagon', *American Journal of International Law*, 2002, vol. 96, no. 1.

Perry, Michael, 'Are human rights universal?' *Human Rights Quarterly*, 1997, vol. 19, no. 3.

Pin Fat, Véronique, 'The metaphysics of the national interest and the mysticism of the nation-state', *Review of International Studies*, 2005, vol. 31, no. 2.

Powell, Colin, 'A strategy of partnerships', *Foreign Affairs*, 2004, vol. 83, no. 1.

Rice, Condoleezza, 'Promoting the national interest', *Foreign Affairs,* 2000, vol. 79, no.1.

Rice, Condoleezza, 'A balance of power that favors freedom', *United States Foreign Policy Agenda*, 2002, vol. 7, no. 4.

Roberts, Les, Riyadh Lafta, Richard Garfield, Jamal Khudhairi and Gilbert Burnham,

'Mortality before and after the 2003 invasion of Iraq: cluster sample survey', *Lancet*, 2004, vol. 364, no. 9448.

Robinson, William, 'Globalization, the world system and "democracy promotion" in US foreign policy', *Theory and Society*, 1996, vol. 25, no. 5.

Rosenblatt, Roger, 'A patriot's progress: September 11 and freedom in America', *Global Issues*, 2002, vol. 7, no. 2.

Rubin, Barnett, 'Transitional justice and human rights in Afghanistan', *International Affairs*, 2003, vol. 79, no. 3.

Schoultz, Lars, 'US foreign policy and human rights violations in Latin America: A comparative analysis of foreign aid distributions,' *Comparative Politics*, 1981, vol. 13, no. 2.

Telhami, Shibley, 'After a war with Iraq: democracy, militancy and peacemaking', *International Studies Perspectives*, 2003, vol. 4, no. 2.

Thompson, Kenneth, 'New reflections on ethics and foreign policy: the problem of human rights', *The Journal of Politics*, 1978, vol. 40, no. 4.

Walt, Stephen, 'The renaissance of security studies', *International Studies Quarterly*, 1991, vol. 35, no. 2.

Waltz, Kenneth, 'Evaluating theories', *The American Political Science Review*, 1997, vol. 91, no. 4.

Warner, Michael, 'A new strategy for the new geopolitics', *Public Interest*, 2003, no. 153.

Watson, J., 'Legal theory, efficacy and validity in the development of human rights norms in international law', *University of Illinois Law Forum*, 1979, vol. 3.

Wolfowitz, Paul, 'Remembering the Future', *The National Interest*, Spring 2000.

Wolfson, Adam, 'Humanitarian Hawks?' *Policy Review*, December 1999.

Wolfson, Adam, 'How to think about humanitarian war', 2000, *Commentary*, July/August.

Wolfson, Adam, 'Conservatives and neoconservatives', *Public Interest*, 2004, no. 154.

Newspaper articles

Alberts, Sheldon, 'Cheney defends Guantanamo methods', *National Post*, June 14, 2005.

Baker, Peter and Charles Babington, 'Bush addresses uproar over spying', *Washington Post*, December 20, 2005.

Barder, Brian *et al.*, 'A letter to Blair: Your Middle East policy is doomed say diplomats', *Independent*, April 27, 2004.

Begg, Moazzam, 'Letter', *Guardian*, July 12, 2004.

bin Laden, Osama, 'Text: Osama bin Laden's 1998 interview', *Guardian*, October 8, 2001.

Borger, Julian, 'CIA in blow to Bush attack plans', *Guardian*, October 10, 2002.

Borger, Julian, 'In wake of WMD report, Bush struggles to convince public he was right to go to war', *Guardian*, October 4, 2003.

Borger, Julian, 'Admit WMD mistake, survey chief tells Bush', *Guardian*, March 3, 2004.

Borger, Julian, 'US general linked to Abu Ghraib abuse', *Guardian*, May 22, 2004.

Borger, Julian, 'How born-again George became a man on a mission', *Guardian*, October 7, 2005.

Borger, Julian, 'Official US agency paints dire picture of "out of control" Iraq', *Guardian*, January 20, 2006.

Borkowski, Mark, 'Body blow', *Guardian*, April 26, 2004.

Branigan, Tania, 'Iraqi lawyer risked life to help rescue of PoW Jessica Lynch', *Guardian*, April 5, 2003.

Branigan, Tania and Vikram Dodd, 'Afghanistan to Guantanamo Bay: the story of three British detainees', *Guardian*, August 4, 2004.

Brown, Paul, 'Oil giant bids to replace climate expert', *Guardian*, April 5, 2002.

Bukharbayeva, Bagila, 'Hundreds dead in Uzbek uprising', *New York Times*, May 15, 2005.

Buncombe, Andrew, 'Official verdict: White House misled world over Saddam', *Independent*, June 17, 2004.

Buncombe, Andrew, 'Military tribunals at Guantanamo ruled illegal by US judge', *Independent*, November 10, 2004.

Burns, Robert, 'Bad publicity puts Pentagon on defensive', *Washington Post*, February 17, 2006.

Bush, George W., 'Bush's address on Towards Freedom', *Guardian*, April 10, 2003.

Bush, George W., 'In Bush's Words', *New York Times*, December 15, 2003.

Bush, George W., 'Transcript of President Bush's interview on Al Arabiya television', *New York Times*, May 5, 2004.

Campbell, Duncan, 'US interrogators turn to torture lite', *Guardian*, January 25, 2003.

Campbell, Duncan and Suzanne Goldenberg, 'They said this is America', *Guardian*, June 23, 2004.

Chivers, C. and Ethan Wilensky-Lanford, 'Uzbeks say troops shot recklessly at civilians', *New York Times*, May 17, 2005.

Clark, David, 'How can terrorism be condemned while war crimes go without rebuke?' *Guardian*, July 31, 2006.

Cloud, David and Jeff Gerth, 'Muslim scholars were paid to aid US propaganda', *New York Times*, January 2, 2006.

Cobain, Ian and Richard Norton-Taylor, 'Destination Cairo: Human rights fears over CIA flights', *Guardian*, September 12, 2005.

Cornwell, Rupert, 'Bush praises "fierce courage" of US soldiers in memorial day speech', *Independent*, June 1, 2004.

Cornwell, Rupert, 'E-Mail links Cheney to Halliburton Deal', *Independent*, June 1, 2004.

Cornwall, Rupert, 'Bush: God told me to invade Iraq', *Independent*, October 7, 2005.

Cornwell, Rupert, 'Cheney created climate for US war crimes', *Independent*, November 30, 2005.

Daalder, Ivo and James Lindsay, 'America unbound', *New York Times*, January 25, 2004.

Dodd, Vikram and Tania Branigan, 'Questioned at gunpoint, shackled and forced to pose naked', *Guardian*, August 4, 2004.

Dowd, Maureen, 'I spy a screw-up', *New York Times*, March 31, 2005.

Editorial, 'Mr Cheney, meet Mr Kay', *New York Times*, January 27, 2004.

Editorial, 'A failed investigation', *Washington Post*, September 10, 2004.

Editorial, 'Patterns of abuse', *New York Times*, May 23, 2005.

Editorial, 'Feds say Patriot Act not for homeless', *Washington Times*, June 30, 2005.

Editorial, 'New charges of abuse surface', *Washington Times*, July 3, 2005.

Editorial, 'That's no way to treat visitors', *New York Times*, August 30, 2005.

Eggen, Dan and Mike Allen, 'Ashcroft to leave cabinet', *Washington Post*, November 10, 2004.

Froomkin, Dan, 'Former insider lashes out', *Washington Post*, October 20, 2005.

Froomkin, Dan, 'Bush's tortured logic', *Washington Post*, November 8, 2005.

Glaister, Dan, 'Bush foreign policy comes under renewed attack from within', *Guardian*, June 14, 2004.

Golden, Tim, 'In US report, brutal details of 2 Afghan inmates' deaths', *New York Times,* May 20, 2005.

Golden, Tim, 'Army faltered in investigating detainee abuse', *New York Times*, May 22, 2005.

Golden, Tim, 'Years after 2 Afghans died, abuse case falters', *New York Times*, February 13, 2006.

Golden, Tim, 'After ruling, uncertainty hovers at Cuba prison', *New York Times*, June 30, 2006.

Goldenberg, Suzanne, 'Bush allies admit war blunders', *Guardian*, October 6, 2004.

Gore, Al, 'Transcript of the former US vice-president's speech on Iraq and the war on terrorism', *Guardian*, September 23, 2002.

Graham, Bradley and Josh White, 'General cites hidden detainees', *Washington Post*, September 10, 2004.

Graham, Stephen, 'Slaying of Afghan women concerns UN', *Washington Post*, May 5, 2005.

Greenhouse, Linda, 'Justices, 5-3, broadly reject Bush plan to try detainees', *New York Times*, June 30, 2006.

Harding, Luke, 'Rice admits US mistakes in war on terror after wave of criticism across Europe', *Guardian*, December 7, 2005.

Hari, Johann, 'The case for war', *Guardian*, February 15, 2003.

Harnden, Toby, 'America rejects Chirac's claim that Saddam is no threat', *Daily Telegraph*, February 17, 2003.

Herbert, Bob, 'The wrong war', *New York Times*, March 26, 2004.

Hilton, Isabel, 'Now we pay the warlords to tyrannize the Afghan people', *Guardian*, July 31, 2003.

Hilton, Isabel, 'The 800lb gorilla in American foreign policy', *Guardian*, July 28, 2004.

Hoge, Warren, 'Bolton makes his case at UN for a new focus for aid projects', *New York Times*, September 1, 2005.

Hosenball, Mark, Michael Isikoff and Evan Thomas, 'Cheney's long path to war', *Newsweek*, November 17, 2003.

Huggler, Justin, 'Afghanistan hits fever pitch as warlords turn democrat', *Independent*, October 6, 2004.

Hulse Carl and Sheryl Stolberg, 'Lawmakers view images from Iraq', *New York Times*, May 13, 2004.

Ignatieff, Michael, 'The Burden', *New York Times Magazine*, January 5, 2003.

James, Ian, 'Talk of US plot divides Venezuelans', *Washington Post*, November 19, 2005.

Janofsky, Michael, 'Halliburton turns over $6.3 million to government', *New York Times*, January 24, 2004.

Jeffrey, Simon, 'Rumsfeld apologises for Iraq jail abuse', *Guardian*, May 7, 2004.

Jehl, Douglas and Eric Schmitt, 'Afghan policies on questioning prisoners taken to Iraq', *New York Times*, May 21, 2004.

Jehl, Douglas, Steven Myers and Eric Schmitt, 'Abuse of captives more widespread, says Army survey', *New York Times*, May 26, 2004.

Jehl, Douglas, 'A trail of "major failures" leads to defense secretary's office', *New York Times*, August 25, 2004.

Johnson, Kirk, 'Guard featured in abuse photos says she was following orders', *New York Times*, May 12, 2004.

Jones, George, 'Bush and Blair message beamed in', *Daily Telegraph*, April 11, 2003.

Kagan, Robert, 'A tougher war for the US is one of legitimacy', *New York Times*, January 24, 2004.

Kagan, Robert and William Kristol, 'Why we went to war', *Weekly Standard*, October 20, 2003.

Kampfner, John, 'The truth about Jessica', *Guardian*, May 15, 2003.

Kessler, Glenn and Jim Van de Hei, 'Misleading assertions cover Iraq War and voting records', *Washington Post*, October 6, 2004.

Kettle, Martin, 'Topic A and how the Iraq game was given away', *Guardian*, January 13, 2004.

Klapper, Bradley, 'UN urges Iraq torture probe', *Washington Post*, November 16, 2005.

Klug, Foster, 'McCain: Torture ban needed for US image', *Washington Post*, November 13, 2005.

Laurance, Jeremy and Colin Brown, 'Revealed: War has cost 100,000 Iraqi lives', *Independent*, October 29, 2004.

Leader, 'Lies about crimes', *Guardian*, May 21, 2004.

Leader, 'Death in Qana', *Guardian*, July 31, 2006.

Levy, Adrian and Cathy Scott-Clark, 'One huge US jail', *Guardian*, March 19, 2005.

Lewis, Neil, 'US charges two with war crimes, setting stage for tribunals', *New York Times*, February 24, 2004.

Lynch, Colum, 'Bolton voices opposition to UN proposals', *Washington Post*, September 1, 2003.

Lynch, Colum, 'US wants changes in UN agreement', *Washington Post,* August 25, 2005.

Lynch, Colum, 'UN draft decries US on detainee treatment', *Washington Post*, February 14, 2006.

Makdisi, Saree, 'Lebanon's war with cluster bombs', *Los Angeles Times*, October 21, 2006.

Manhire, Toby, 'Private's life becomes public property', *Guardian*, April 8, 2003.

Manhire, Toby, 'Darfur', *Guardian*, July 21, 2004.

McCarthy, Rory, 'Saving Private Lynch', *Guardian*, April 3, 2003.

Meyer, Jane, 'Outsourcing torture', *The New Yorker*, February 14, 2005.

Milbank, Dana and Justin Blum, 'Document says oil chiefs met with Cheney Task Force', *Washington Post*, November 16, 2005.

Miller, David, 'The domination effect', *Guardian*, January 8, 2004.

Mir, Hamid, 'Muslims have the right to attack America', *Independent*, November 11, 2001.

Monbiot, George, 'The US used chemical weapons in Iraq and then lied about it', *Guardian*, November 15, 2005.

Murray, Craig, 'What drives support for the torturer?' *Guardian*, May 16, 2005.

Norton-Taylor, Richard, 'Torture flights: What no. 10 knew and tried to cover up', *Guardian*, January 19, 2006.

O'Farrell, John, 'Hands off the UN', *Guardian*, June 13, 2003.

Oborne, Peter, 'On the roads of ruin', *Observer*, May 25, 2003.

Penketh, Anne, 'Poll reveals hostility to US and support for rebel cleric', *Independent*, June 17, 2004.

Pfleger, Katherine and Dafna Linzer, 'Kay doubts presence of illicit Iraq arms', *New York Times*, January 26, 2004.

Priest, Dana, 'CIA holds terror suspects in secret prisons', *Washington Post*, November 2, 2005.

Priest, Dana and Dan Eggen, 'Terror suspect alleges torture', *Washington Post*, January 6, 2005.

Priest, Dana and Robin Wright, 'Cheney fights for detainee policy', *Washington Post*, November 7, 2005.

Purdum, Todd, 'An accuser's insider status puts the White House on the defensive', *New York Times*, March 23, 2004.

Pyle, Christopher, 'Torture by proxy', *San Francisco Chronicle*, January 4, 2004.

Ramonet, Ignacio, 'Bolivia: When is a democracy not a democracy?' *La Monde Diplomatique*, November 2003.

Reid, Tim, 'Bush begs for support to fight "evil radicals" waging war on humanity', *Times*, October 7, 2005.

Risen, James, 'Ex-inspector says CIA missed disarray in Iraqi arms program', *New York Times*, January 26, 2004.

Risen, James, David Johnston and Neil Lewis, 'Harsh CIA methods cited in top Qaeda interrogations', *New York Times*, May 13, 2004.

Rose, David, 'Revealed: the full story of the Guantanamo Bay Britons', *Observer*, March 14, 2004.

Rosenthal, Andrew, 'Decoding the Senate intelligence committee investigation on Iraq', *New York Times*, July 18, 2004.

Schmitt, Eric, 'Four top officers cleared by Army in prison abuse', *New York Times*, April 23, 2005.

Schmitt, Eric, '3 in 82nd Airborne say beating Iraqi prisoners was routine', *New York Times*, September 24, 2005.

Schmitt, Eric, 'President backs McCain measure on inmate abuse', *New York Times*, December 16, 2005.

Sengupta, Kim and Marie Woolf, 'Allies accused of breaking Geneva Convention on civilian losses', *Independent*, May 17, 2004.

Shenon, Philip and Christopher Marquis, 'Panel finds no Qaeda-Iraq tie', *New York Times*, June 17, 2004.

Shiner, Phil, 'End this lawlessness', *Guardian*, June 10, 2004.

Sidoti, Liz, 'House cuts foreign aid request', *Washington Times*, June 30, 2002.

Smith, Helena, 'Blix: I was smeared by the Pentagon', *Guardian*, June 11, 2003.

Staff and agencies, 'UN row over Iraqi report', *Guardian*, December 10, 2002.

Staff and agencies, 'European governments knew of CIA flights', *Guardian*, January 24, 2006.

Staff and agencies, 'UN calls for Guantanamo Bay to close', *Guardian*, February 16, 2006.

Steele, Jonathan, 'Sudan urged to accept UN force as talks falter', *Guardian*, February 6, 2006.

Stevenson, Richard, 'Bush on Arab TV denounces abuse of Iraqi captives', *New York Times*, May 6, 2004.

Stevenson, Richard, 'With 9/11 report, Bush's political thorn grows more stubborn', *New York Times*, June 17, 2004.

Stewart-Smith, Charles, 'Why should the Iraqis believe US TV?' *Guardian*, April 14, 2003.

Stolberg, Sheryl, 'Prisoner abuse scandal puts McCain in spotlight once again', *New York Times*, May 10, 2004.

Stout, David, 'Rumsfeld offers apology for abuse of Iraq prisoners', *New York Times*, May 7, 2004.

Sullivan, Kevin and Walter Pincus, 'Paper says Bush talked of bombing Arab TV network', *Washington Post*, November 23, 2005.

Tait, Robert, 'Shock as Iran elects hard-line president', *Observer*, June 26, 2005.

Teather, David, 'Oil firm linked to Cheney gets Iraq boost', *Guardian*, October 30, 2003.

Teather, David, 'Halliburton staff sacked for taking bribes', *Guardian*, January 24, 2004.

Tran, Mark, 'Pentagon launches Halliburton inquiry', *Guardian*, December 12, 2004.

Transcript, 'Rumsfeld testifies before Senate Armed Services Committee', *Washington Post*, May 7, 2004.

Traynor, Ian, 'Censored version of declaration provokes anger', *Guardian*, December 19, 2002.

Usborne, David, 'Rumsfeld loosened interrogation rules claims New Yorker', *Independent*, May 17, 2004.

Wadhams, Nick, 'UN report criticizes US for Gitmo', *Washington Post*, February 13, 2006.

Walsh, Nick, 'Brutality and poverty fuel wave of unrest', *Guardian*, May 16, 2005.

Warren, Marcus and Toby Harnden, 'The case against Saddam', *The Daily Telegraph*, February 6, 2003.

Whitaker, Raymond and Marie Woolf, 'PM on the defensive over Official Secrets Act trial', *Independent*, November 27, 2005.

Will, George, 'Why didn't he ask Congress?' *Washington Post*, December 20, 2005.

Winfeld, Nicole, 'US tells how its troops rescued Army heroine', *Observer*, April 6, 2003.

Wright, George 'Commander a scapegoat for Abu Ghraib,' *Guardian*, June 15, 2004.

Younge, Gary, 'Private Lynch's media war continues as Iraqi doctors deny rape claim', *Guardian*, November 12, 2003.

Zernike, Kate, 'Woman with leash appears in court on Abu Ghraib abuse charges', *New York Times*, August 4, 2004.

Web addresses

Adams, Brad (2004) *An Open Letter to US Secretary of Defense Donald Rumsfeld*, December 13. Online, available at: www.hrw.org.

American Civil Liberties Union (2004) *FBI E-Mail Refers to Presidential Order Authorizing Inhumane Interrogation Techniques*, December 20. Online, available at: www.aclu.org.

American Civil Liberties Union (2004) *Special Ops Task Force Threatened Government Agents Who Saw Detainee Abuse in Iraq*, December 7. Online, available at: www.aclu.org.

American Civil Liberties Union (2005) *Legal Claims in Ali et al.* v. *Rumsfeld*, Fact Sheet, March 1. Online, available at: www.aclu.org/SafeandFree/SafeandFree.cfm?ID=17590&c=207.

American Civil Liberties Union (2005) *Newly Released Investigative Files Provide Further Evidence Soldiers Not Held Accountable for Abuse*, January 24. Online, available at: www.aclu.org.

American Enterprise Institute (2005) *Becoming a Donor*. Online, available at: www.aei.org/.

Amnesty International (2002) *Amnesty International Report 2002*, AI Index POL 10/001/2002. Online, available at: web.amnesty.org/web/ar2002.nsf.

Amnesty International (2003) *Amnesty International Report 2003*. Online, available at: www.amnesty.org/report2003/col-summary-eng.

Amnesty International (2003) *United States of America.* Online, available at: web.amnesty.org.

Amnesty International (2004) *Amnesty International Annual Report.* Online, available at: web.amnesty.org/report2004/index-eng.

Amnesty International (2004) *Building an International Human Rights Agenda.* Online, available at: web.amnesty.org/web/web.nsf.

Amnesty International (2004) *Colombia.* Online, available at: www.amnesty.org.

Amnesty International (2004) *Killings of Civilians in Basra and Al-Amara,* May 11. Online, available at: web.amnesty.org/library/print/ENGMDE140072004.

Amnesty International (2004) *More Than Words Needed This Human Rights Day,* AI Index: AMR 51/171/2004. Online, available at: www.amnestyusa.org.

Amnesty International (2005) *Abu Ghraib: One Year Later, Who's Accountable?* Online, available at: www.amnestyusa.org/stoptorture/agfactsheet.html.

Amnesty International (2005) *An Appeal to President George W. Bush on the Occasion of His Re-Inauguration,* AI Index: AMR 51/012/2005. Online, available at: www.amnestyusa.org.

Arkan Mohammed Ali, Thahe Mohammed Sabbar, Sherzad Kamal Khalid, Ali H., Mehboob Ahmad, Said Nabi Siddiqi, Mohammed Karim Shirullah and Haji Abdul Rahman v. *Donald H. Rumsfeld* (2005) District Court for the Northern District of Illinois. Online, available at: www.humanrightsfirst.org/us_law/etn/lawsuit/PDF/rums-complaint-022805.pdf.

Associated Press (2004) 'Bush must regroup after combatant ruling', *New York Times,* June 29. Online, available at: www.nytimes.com.

Associated Press (2003) 'Bush wins $87 billion for Iraq and Afghanistan', *Guardian,* November 4. Online, available at: www.guardian.co.uk.

Associated Press (2004) 'Cheney thanks Italy for support in Iraq', *New York Times,* January 26. Online, available at: www.nytimes.com.

Associated Press (2004) 'Kay criticizes Bush, Blair on Iraq intel', *New York Times,* July 18. Online, available at: www.nytimes.com.

Associated Press (2006) 'Rice asks Congress for $75 million for Iran', *New York Times,* February 15. Online, available at: www.nytimes.com.

Associated Press (2006) 'Rumsfeld likens Chavez's rise to Hitler's', *Washington Post,* February 3. Online, available at: www.washingtonpost.com.

BBC News (2006) *US Echoes Iraq Civil War Warning.* Online, available at: news.bbc.co.uk/go/pr/fr/-/1/hi/world/middle_east/5243042.stm.

Blix, Hans (2003) *Hans Blix Address to the UN,* January 27. Online, available at: www.un.org.

Bureau of Democracy, Human Rights and Labor (2001) *Fact Sheet: Voluntary Principles on Security and Human Rights,* Washington, DC, February 20. Online, available at: www.state.gov.

Bush, George W. (2002) *Proclamation 7584 Women's Equality Day 2002,* Code of Federal Regulations, title 3, vol. 1, ref. 3CFR7584, August 23. Online, available at: www.presidency.ucsb.edu/ws/print.php?pid=61878.

CBS (2006) *Rice to Return to Mideast,* July 28. Online, available at: www.cbsnews.com.

Center for Responsive Politics (2001) *A Money in Politics Backgrounder on the Energy Industry.* Online, available at: www.opensecrets.org/pressreleases/energybriefing.htm.

Center for Responsive Politics (2001) *President Bush's First 100 Days: A Look at How the Special Interests Have Fared.* Online, available at: www.opensecrets.org/bush/100days/energy.asp.

Center for Responsive Politics (2002) *Andrew H. Card Jr.* Online, available at: www.opensecrets.org/bush/cabinet/cabinet.card.asp.

Center for Responsive Politics (2002) *Ann M. Veneman: Agriculture Secretary.* Online, available at: www.opensecrets.org/bush/cabinet/cabinet.norton.asp.

Center for Responsive Politics (2002) *Donald Evans: Commerce Secretary.* Online, available at: www.opensecrets.org/bush/cabinet/cabinet.evans.asp.

Center for Responsive Politics (2002) *Donald Rumsfeld.* Online, available at: www.opensecrets.org/bush/cabinet/cabinet.rumsfeld.asp.

Center for Responsive Politics (2002) *Gale Norton: Interior Secretary.* Online, available at: www.opensecrets.org/bush/cabinet/cabinet.norton.asp.

Center for Responsive Politics (2002) *John Ashcroft: Attorney General.* Online, available at: www.opensecrets.org/bush/cabinet/cabinet.ashcroft.asp.

Center for Responsive Politics (2002) *Oil and Gas: Top 20 Recipients.* Online, available at: www.opensecrets.org/industries/recips.asp?Ind=E01&cycle=2000&recipdetail=.

Center for Responsive Politics (2002) *President George W. Bush: Introduction.* Online, available at: www.opensecrets.org/bush/index.asp.

Center for Responsive Politics (2002) *Tommy G. Thompson: Health and Human Services Secretary.* Online, available at: www.opensecrets.org/bush/cabinet/cabinet. thompson.asp.

Center for Responsive Politics (2003) *Coal Mining: Long Term Contribution Trends.* Online, available at: www.opensecrets.org/industries/indus.asp?Ind=E1210.

Center for Responsive Politics (2003) *Rebuilding Iraq: The Contractors.* Online, available at: www.opensecrets.org/bush/100days/environment.asp.

Christian Coalition of America (2005) *About Us.* Online, available at: www.cc. org/about.cfm.

Christian Coalition of America (2005) *Our Mission.* Online, available at: www.cc. org/mission.cfm.

Clinton, Bill (1995) *Presidential Decision Directive 39*, June 21. Online, available at: www.fas.org/irp/offdocs/pdd39.htm.

CNN (2001) 'US loses UN rights seat', May 4. Online, available at: www cnn.world-news.

Cover, Avidan (2004) *Military Commission Proceedings Violate International Law.* Online, available at: www.humanrightsfirst.org/media/2004_alerts/0817.htm.

Department of Defense (1987) *US Army Field Manual on Intelligence Interrogation.* Online, available at: www.globalsecurity.org/intell/library/policy/army/fm/fm34-52/.

Department of Justice Working Group Report (2003) *Detainee Interrogations in the Global War on Terrorism: Assessment of Legal, Historical, Policy and Operational Considerations*, March 6, leaked to the *Wall Street Journal*, June 2004. Online, available at: www.online.wsj.com/public/resources/documents/military_0604.pdf.

Department of State (2001) *Summary of US Assistance to the Afghan People Since October 1, 2001*, November 23. Online, available at: www.state.gov/r/pa/prs/ ps/2001/6303.htm.

Department of State (2004) *Supporting Human Rights and Democracy: The US Record 2003-2004.* Online, available at: www.state.gov/g/drl/rls/shrd/2003/31022.htm.

Department of State Office of International Information Programs (2003) *Focus on Human Rights in Saddam's Iraq: The Violent Coercion and Repression of the Iraqi People.* Online, available at: www.usembassy.it/pdf/other/iraqfocus1.pdf#search= %22The%20Violent%20Coercion%20and%20Repression%20of%20the%20Iraqi%20 People%22.

Duelfer, Charles (2004) *Comprehensive Report of the Special Advisor to the DCI on Iraq's WMD*, September 30. Online, available at: news.findlaw.com/nytimes/docs/iraq/cia93004wmdrpt.html.

Fenton, Tom (2003) *Mandela Slams Bush on Iraq*, January 30. Online, available at: www.cbsnews.com.

Forsythe, David (2003) *US Foreign Policy and Human Rights in an Era of Insecurity: The Bush Administration and Human Rights After 9/11*. Online, available at: www.unl.edu/polisci/faculty/forsythe/cuny-paper.pdf.

Fred, Sheryl (2003) *The Best Defense*. Online, available at: www.opensecrets.org/news/defensebudget/index1.asp.

Gilmore, Kate (2002) *The War Against Terrorism: A Human Rights Perspective*. Online, available at: www.web.amnesty.org/web.nsf.

Human Rights Watch (2001) *Cluster Bombs in Afghanistan: A Human Rights Watch Backgrounder*. Online, available at: www.hrw.org/backgrounder/arms/cluster-bck1031.htm.

Human Rights First (2002) *A Year of Loss: Re-examining Civil Liberties Since September 11*. Online, available at: www.humanrightsfirst.org/us_law/loss/loss_ch5a.htm.

Human Rights Watch (2002) *Saudi Arabia: New Evidence of Torture*. Online, available at: www.hrw.org/.

Human Rights Watch (2003) *Briefing to the 59th Session of the UN Commission on Human Rights: Colombia*, February 27. Online, available at: www.hrw.org/un/chr59/colombia.htm.

Human Rights Watch (2003) *US State Department Criticism of Stress and Duress Interrogation Around the World*, April 16. Online, available at: www.hrw.org.

Human Rights Watch (2004) *Enduring Freedom: Abuses by US Forces in Afghanistan*, vol. 16, no. 3 (C). Online, available at: hrw.org/reports/2004/afghanistan0304/.

Human Rights Watch (2004) 'Iraq: state of the evidence', *Human Rights Watch Report*, vol. 16, no. 9(E). Online, available at: www.hrw.org/reports/2004/iraq1104/.

Human Rights Watch (2005) *Did President Bush Order Torture?* Online, available at: www.hrw.org/English/docs/2004/12/21/usint9925_txt.htm.

Human Rights Watch (2005) 'Account of Sergeant A, 82nd Airborne Division', *Human Rights Watch Report*, vol. 17, no. 3(G). Online, available at: www.hrw.org/reports/2005/us0905/2.htm.

Human Rights Watch (2005) 'Leadership failure: firsthand accounts of torture of Iraqi detainees by the US Army's 82nd Airborne Division', *Human Rights Watch Report*, vol. 17, no. 3(G). Online, available at: www.hrw.org/reports/2005/us0905/index.htm.

Human Rights Watch (2005) *US: Justifying Abuse of Detainees*. Online, available at: www.hrw.org/English/docs/2005/01/12/usint10072_txt.htm.

Human Rights First (2005) *The Case Against Rumsfeld: Hard Facts Timeline*. Online, available at: www.humanrightsfirst.org/us_law/etn/lawsuit/PDF/rums-timeline-022805.pdf.

Human Rights Watch (2005) *World Report*. Online, available at: www.hrw.org/wr2k5.

Hutson, Rear Admiral John (2005) *The Case Against Rumsfeld*, March 1. Online, available at: www.humanrightsfirst.org/us_law/etn/lawsuit/statements/lit-hutson-030105.htm.

Institute for American Values (2002) *What We're Fighting For: A Letter From America*. Online, available at: www.americanvalues.org/html/wwff.html.

Jones, Anthony and George Fay (2004) *Investigation of Intelligence Activities at the Abu Ghraib Prison and 205th Military Intelligence Brigade*, August 23. Online, available at: www.slate.com/features/whatistorture/pdfs/FayJonesReport.pdf.

Kissinger, Henry (2001) *Foreign Policy in the Age of Terrorism*, Ruttenberg lecture. Online, available at: ics.leeds.ac.uk/papers/pmt/exhibits/817/kissinger.pdf#search=%22 Kissinger%20Foreign%20Policy%20in%20the%20Age%20of%20terrorism%20 Ruttenberg%22.

Leech, Garry (2003) 'Bush places corporate interests over human rights', *Dissident Voice*, June 10. Online, available at: www.dissidentvoice.org/Articles5/Leech_Victims-Rights.htm.

Lobe, Jim (2002) 'The emperor within the empire', *Inter Press Service News Agency*, October 4. Online, available at: www.ipsnews.net.

Lobe, Jim (2003) 'Key officials used 9/11 as pretext for Iraq War', *Inter Press Service News Agency*, July 15. Online, available at: www.ipsnews.net/print.asp?idnews=19255.

Lobe, Jim (2003) 'North Korean attack on US diplomat spotlights ultra-hawk', *Inter Press Service News Agency*, August 4. Online, available at: www.ipsnews.net/print.asp?idnews=19517.

Lobe, Jim (2004) 'Press watchdog "deeply disturbed" by Iraqi regime's media threat', November 16. Online, available at: www.LewRockwell.com.

Lobe, Jim (2004) *US Media Ignore Rumsfeld's 'Dirty Wars' Talk*, November 24. Online, available at: www.lewrockwell.com.

Lobe, Jim (2004) *US Militarizing Latin America*. Online, available at: www.LewRock-well.com.

Mason, Barnaby (2003) *Blix Adds to US and UK Worries*, September 18. Online, available at: newsvote.bbc.co.uk.

Médecins Sans Frontières (2004) *MSF Pulls Out of Afghanistan*, July 28. Online, available at: www.msf.org.

National Energy Policy Development Group (2001) *Report of the National Energy Policy Development Group*, Washington, DC. Online, available at: www.whitehouse.gov/energy/.

Project for a New American Century (1998) *Letter to President Clinton on Iraq*, January 26. Online, available at: www.dartmouth.edu/~govdocs/iraq/letter.htm.

Reuters (2004) 'Democrats call for probe of Iraq weapons claims', *New York Times*, January 25. Online, available at: www.nytimes.com.

Reuters (2004) 'Iraq charges against Bush begin to mount', *New York Times*, March 23. Online, available at: www.nytimes.com.

Reuters (2005) 'US "disturbed" by Uzbek crackdown, urges reform', *New York Times*, May 16. Online, available at: www.nytimes.com.

Reuters (2005) 'Top US diplomat postponing Uzbekistan trip', *New York Times*, July 31. Online, available at: www.nytimes.com.

Reuters (2006) 'Bush speaks of closing Guantanamo prison', *New York Times*, May 8. Online, available at: www.nytimes.com.

Rycroft, Matthew (2002) *Downing Street Memo*, July 23, leaked to the *Sunday Times*, May 1, 2005. Online, available at: www.downingstreetmemo.com/memos.html.

Schlesinger, James (2004) *Final Report of the Independent Panel to Review DoD Detention Operations*, August 24. Online, available at: news.findlaw.com/wp/docs/dod/abughraibrpt.pdf.

Taguba, Antonio (2004) *Hearing Article 15-6 Investigation of the 800th Military Police Brigade*, March. Online, available at: www.agonist.org/annex/taguba.htm.

United Nations (2001) *Security Council Resolution 1378*, November 14. Online, available at: usinfo.state.gov/topical/pol/terror/01111512.htm.

United Nations (2003) *Press Release: Menace of Terrorism Requires Global Response Says Secretary General*, January 20. Online, available at: www.un.org/News/Press/docs/2003/sgsm8583.doc.htm.

United Nations (2003) *Press Release: Resolution 1441*, November 8. Online, available at: www.un.org/News.

United States Senate Select Committee on Intelligence (2004) *Report on the US Intelligence Community's Prewar Intelligence Assessments on Iraq*, July 9. Online, available at: www.fas.org/irp/congress/2004_rpt/ssci_concl.pdf.

USAID Press Release (2002) *Millennium Challenge Account Update Fact Sheet*, June 3. Online, available at: www.usaid.gov/press/releases/2002/fs_mca.html.

Vitto, Vince (2004) *Report of the Defense Science Board Task Force on Strategic Communication*, September. Online, available at: www.publicdiplomacy.org/37.htm.

Warren, Jenny (2002) *Military Intervention in Afghanistan: Implications for British Foreign and Defence Policy*, BASIC Occasional Papers on International Security Policy, no. 40. Online, available at: www.basicint.org/pubs/Papers/BP40.htm.

White House (2002) *Afghanistan: Then and Now*. Online, available at: www.whitehouse.gov/afac/thenandnow.html.

White House Office of the Press Secretary (2002) *American Assistance to the People of Afghanistan*, October 11. Online, available at: www.state.gov/p/sca/rls/fs/14786.htm.

White House (2003) *Tales of Saddam's Brutality*, September 29. Online, available at: www.whitehouse.gov/news/releases/2003/09/20030929-14.html.

Others

American Enterprise Institute, *Annual Report*, Washington, DC, 2004.

Boyd, Nathan, Rio Grande Irrigation and Land Company Ltd (1920) *Letter to Counselor Marshall Morgan*, The American and British Claims Tribunal, Department of State, July 19, Presidential Papers Microfilm, Madison Building, Library of Congress, Washington, DC, Series 5, Paris Peace Conference 1914-21, sub series A, 'Policy Documents'.

Bush, George W. (2000) *Bush-Gore Presidential Debate*, Wake Forest University, October 11.

Bush, George W. (2001) *Statement by the President in His Address to the Nation*, September 11.

Bush, George W. (2001) *Address to a Joint Session of Congress and the American People*, Washington, DC, September 20.

Bush, George W. (2001) *President Speaks to the United Nations General Assembly*, New York, September 21.

Bush, George W. (2001) *News Conference*, East Room, White House, Washington, DC, October 11.

Bush, George W. (2001) *President Discusses Stronger Economy and Homeland Defense*, Glen Burnie, Maryland, October 24.

Bush, George W. (2001) *No Nation can be Neutral in this Conflict*, White House, Washington, DC, November 6.

Bush, George W. (2001) *'President Discusses War on Terrorism in Address to the Nation'*, World Congress Center, Atlanta, Georgia, November 8.

Bush, George W. (2001) *President Says US Attorneys are Front Line in War*, US Attorneys Conference, November 29.

Bush, George W. (2001) *Proclamation on Human Rights Observances*, White House, Washington, DC, December 9.

Bush, George W. (2002) *State of the Union Address*, US Capitol, Washington, DC, January 29.

Bush, George W. (2002) *Remarks at the International Conference on Financing for Development in Monterrey*, Monterrey, March 22.

Bush, George W. (2002) *Remarks at the Knoxville, Tennessee, Civic Center*, April 8.

Bush, George W. (2002) *President Bush Announces a New Initiative for Cuba*, May 18.

Bush, George W. (2002) *Remarks by the President at 2002 Graduation Exercise of the United States Military Academy*, West Point, New York, June 1.

Bush, George W. (2002) *US Humanitarian Aid to Afghanistan*, Presidential Hall, Dwight David Eisenhower Executive Office Building, Washington, DC, October 11.

Bush, George W. (2003) *State of the Union Address*, US Capitol, Washington, DC, January 28.

Bush, George W. (2003) *Moment of Truth for World on Iraq*, Azores, March 16.

Bush, George W. (2003) *President Says Saddam Hussein Must Leave Iraq Within 48 Hours*, Cross Hall, Washington, DC, March 17.

Bush, George W. (2003) *Address at MacDill Air Base*, Florida, March 26.

Bush, George W. (2003) *President Bush's Message to the Iraqi People*, Washington, DC, April 10.

Bush, George W. (2003) *President Bush Announces Combat Operations in Iraq Have Ended*, USS Abraham Lincoln, May 1.

Bush, George W. (2003) *Remarks by the President at 2003 President's Dinner*, Washington Convention Center, Washington, DC, May 21.

Bush, George W. (2003) *President Bush Thanks Military*, MCAS Miramar, California, August 14.

Bush, George W. (2003) *President Bush Discusses Iraq Policy*, Whitehall Palace, London, November 19.

Bush, George W. (2003) *President Bush, Prime Minister Hold Joint Press Conference*, 10 Downing St, London, November 20.

Bush, George W. (2003) *President Bush Addresses Nation on the Capture of Saddam Hussein*, Cabinet Room, White House, Washington, DC, December 14.

Bush, George W. (2004) *State of the Union Address*, Washington, DC, January 20.

Bush, George W. (2004) *Progress in the War on Terror*, White House, Washington, DC, January 22.

Bush, George W. (2004) *Importance of Democracy in Middle East*, Library of Congress, Washington, DC, February 4.

Bush, George W. (2004) *Remarks by the President to the National Governors Association*, State Dining Room, February 23.

Bush, George W. (2004) *President Bush Reaffirms Resolve to War on Terror, Iraq and Afghanistan*, East Room, White House, Washington, DC, March 19.

Bush, George W. (2004) *Remarks on Freedom for the People of Afghanistan*, Hershey, Pennsylvania, April 19.

Bush, George W. (2004) *Statement at the Pentagon*, May 10.

Bush, George W. (2004) *President Outlines Steps to Help Iraq Achieve Democracy and Freedom*, United States Army War College, Carlisle, Pennsylvania, May 24.

Bush, George W. (2004) *Address to the United Nations General Assembly*, New York, September 21.

Bush, George W. (2004) *First Kerry–Bush Presidential Debate*, Miami, Florida, September 30.

Bush, George W. (2004) *President Bush Discusses Iraq Report*, South Grounds, White House, Washington, DC, October 7.

Bush, George W. (2004) *A Proclamation: Human Rights Day, Bill of Rights Day and Human Rights Week*, Washington, DC, December 10.

Bush, George W. (2005) *President Sworn-In to Second Term*, Inauguration Speech, Washington, DC, January 20.

Bush, George W. (2005) *President Addresses Nation*, Fort Bragg, North Carolina, June 28.

Bush, George W. (2005) *President Bush Meets with President Torrijos of Panama*, Casa Amarilla, Panama City, November 7.

Bush, George W. (2005) *President Outlines Strategy for Victory in Iraq*, US Naval Academy, Annapolis, Maryland, November 30.

Bush, George W. (2006) *State of the Union Address*, US Capitol, Washington, DC, January 31.

Bush, George W. (2006) *President's Radio Address*, Office of the Press Secretary, Englewood, Colorado, July 22.

Bush, George W. and Tony Blair (2003) *Joint News Conference*, Camp David, Maryland, March 27.

Carter, Jimmy (1981) *Farewell Address*, Washington, DC, January 14.

Center for Security Policy (2002) *Precision-Guided Ideas*, Annual Report, Washington, DC.

Convention against Torture and other Cruel, Inhuman or Degrading Treatment or Punishment, adopted and opened for signature, ratification and accession by General Assembly Resolution 39/46, December 10, 1984.

Craner, Lorne (2001) *Remarks to the Heritage Foundation*, Washington, DC, October 31.

Craner, Lorne (2001) *Human Rights and the Taliban*, Remarks at the Foreign Press Center, Washington, DC, November 6.

Craner, Lorne (2004) *A Comprehensive Human Rights Strategy for China*, Carnegie Endowment for International Peace, Washington, DC, January 29.

Craner, Lorne (2004) *Country Reports on Human Rights Practices for 2003*, Testimony Before the House International Relations Committee, Washington, DC, March 10.

Craner, Lorne (2004) *Briefing on Supporting Human Rights and Democracy: The US Record 2003-2004 Report*, Washington, DC, May 17.

Department of State (2004) *Supporting Human Rights and Democracy: The US Record 2003-2004*, Washington, DC.

Dobriansky, Paula (1988) 'United States human rights policy: an overview', *Department of State Bulletin*, Washington, DC.

Dobriansky, Paula (2001) *Testimony Before the International Operations and Terrorism Subcommittee*, Senate Foreign Relations Committee, Washington, DC, May 24.

Geneva Convention (1949) August 12.

Heritage Foundation (2002) *Our Business is Solutions*, Annual Report, Washington, DC.

Human Rights First (2004) *Trials Under Military Order: A Guide to the Final Rules for Military Commissions*, Washington, DC.

Human Rights Watch (2003) *Human Rights Situation in Chechnya*, Briefing paper, 59th session of the UN Commission on Human Rights, April 7.

International Committee of the Red Cross (2004) Report of the International Committee of the Red Cross on the Treatment by the Coalition Forces of Prisoners of War and Other Protected Persons by the Geneva Conventions in Iraq During Arrest, Internment and Interrogation, February.

International Covenant on Civil and Political Rights (1966).

Jackson, Robert (2004) *Human Rights and Democracy in Venezuela*, Statement before the Congressional Human Rights Caucus, Washington, DC, April 22.

Mezes, S, D. Miller and Walter Lippmann (1918) *The Present Situation: The War Aims and Peace Terms it Suggests*, Woodrow Wilson Collection Microfilm, Madison Building. Library of Congress, Washington, DC, Series 5, Paris Peace Conference 1914-21, sub series A, 'Policy Documents'.

Mohammed Ali, Arkan, Thahe Mohammed Sabbar, Sherzad Kamal Khalid, Ali H., Mehboob Ahmad, Said Nabi Siddiqi, Mohammed Karim Shirullah and Haji Abdul Rahman v. Donald H. Rumsfeld (2005) District Court for the Northern District of Illinois, February.

Moose, George (2001) *Briefing to the Press*, 57th Session of the UN Commission on Human Rights, Palais des Nations, Geneva, March 21.

Moose, George (2001) *Item 7: The Right to Development*, 57th Session of the UN Commission on Human Rights, Geneva, March 27.

National Security Council (2002) *United States of America National Security Strategy*, Washington, DC.

National Security Council (2006) *United States of America National Security Strategy*, Washington, DC.

Natsios, Andrew, USAID Administrator (2002) *Reconstruction and Rebuilding Efforts in Afghanistan*, State Department Briefing Room, Washington, DC, December 23.

Parmly, Michael (2001) *Briefing to the Press*, 57th Session of the UN Commission on Human Rights, Geneva, March 21.

Perle, Richard (2001) *Next Stop Iraq*, Remarks at the Foreign Policy Research Institute's Annual Dinner, Philadelphia, November 14.

Powell, Colin (2003) *Speech to the American Israel Public Affairs Committee's Annual Policy Conference*, Washington, DC, March 30.

Powell, Colin (2004) *Statement: Human Rights Week*, Brussels, Belgium, December 8.

Project for the New American Century (2000), *Rebuilding America's Defenses: Strategy, Forces and Resources for a New Century*, Washington, DC.

Rice, Condoleezza (2003) *Statement Made at the Interamerican Press Association*, Chicago, October 13.

Rice, Condoleezza (2004) *Remarks at the McConnell Center for Political Leadership*, University of Louisville, Louisville, Kentucky, March 8.

Sreebny, Daniel, Minister Counselor for Public Affairs at the US Embassy in London (2004) 'Research question'. E-mail. November 24.

Tahir-Kheli, Shirin (2001) *Item 4: Report of the High Commissioner for Human Rights*, 57th Session of the UN Commission on Human Rights, Geneva, March 21.

Tahir-Kheli, Shirin (2001) *Item 9: Violation of Human Rights and Fundamental Freedoms in Any Part of the World*, 57th Session of the UN Commission on Human Rights, Geneva, March 30.

Tahir-Kheli, Shirin (2001) *Resolution L.13*, 57th Session of the UN Commission on Human Rights, Geneva, April 18.

The President's Power as Commander in Chief to Transfer Captive Terrorists to the Control and Custody of Foreign Nations (2002) memo, March 13.

United Nations Commission on Human Rights (2003) *Report of the United Nations High Commissioner for Human Rights on the Human Rights Situation in Colombia*, February 24, E/CN.4/2003/13.

US Department of State (1914) 'The Tampico Affair', *Papers Relating to Foreign Affairs*, Washington, DC.

Wilson, Woodrow (1916) *Address to the Congress*, Washington, DC, April 19.

Wilson, Woodrow (1917) *Second Inaugural Address*, Washington, DC, March 5.

Wilson, Woodrow (1917) *Address to Joint Session of Congress*, Washington, DC, April 2.

Wilson, Woodrow (1917) *Proclamation to the American People*, Washington, DC, April 15.

Wilson, Woodrow (1918) *Speech Delivered to Congress in Joint Session*, Washington, DC, January 8.

Zerrougui, Leila, Leandro Despouy, Manfred Nowak, Asma Jahangir and Paul Hunt (2006) *Report of the Chairperson of the Working Group on Arbitrary Detention*, United Nations Commission on Human Rights, E/CN.4/2006/120, February 15.

Index

Abu Ghraib 129–33, 138–9, 147
Afghanistan 96, 109–11, 150; Afghanistan
    Human Rights Commission 111–12,
    116–17; hegemonic discourse 109–11,
    120–1, 154–5; human rights violations
    112–13, 120; humanitarian aid 111;
    prisoner abuse 98, 114–16
African Union 54–5
Ahmadinejad, Mahmoud 57
aid 74–5, 128
AIDS 54
al Jazeera 120, 139
al Qaeda 28, 94, 98, 105, 110, 120
Algeria 59
Almond, Gabriel 26–7
American Civil Liberties Union 92, 117,
    132–3
American Enterprise Institute 70–1
Amnesty International 61–2, 67, 91, 112
Andizhan massacre 63–4
Annan, Kofi 77, 107
Anti-Ballistic Missile Treaty 78
Argentina 46–7
Austria–Hungary 43

Bagram 114–16
basic rights 3, 74, 151
Bernays, Edward 26, 31
bin Laden, Osama 95, 105, 110, 122, 152
Biological Weapons Convention 78
Blair, Tony 100, 104, 124, 137, 139, 144
Blix, Hans 124, 144–5
Blum, William 23–4
Bolivia 56
Bolsheviks 34, 44–5
Bolton, John 71, 82–3
Bricker amendment 72
Brzezinski, Zbigniew 48
Bureau of Democracy, Human Rights and
    Labor 15, 18

Burma 79
Burns, William 59
Bush, George W. 21–2, 24–5, 71, 80, 95,
    118, 134, 136, 138–9, 143, 152; and
    human rights promotion 14, 16, 18, 30,
    53, 104, 118, 125, 140

Campbell, David 25–6, 28
Carter, Jimmy 45–50, 153
Center for Security Policy 70–1
Central Intelligence Agency 56, 64, 97–8,
    102–3, 109, 114, 132, 143–4
Chávez, Hugo 55–6
Chechnya 67, 107
Cheney, Dick 18, 29, 79, 95, 102–3, 116,
    134, 143, 145
Chile 46–7
Christian Coalition 69
civil rights 89–90
Clark, Wesley 29
climate change 78
cluster munitions 61, 120
Colombia 61–2, 67
combatant status review tribunals 96
Commission on Human Rights 29–30, 92,
    125
Committee on Public Information 41
Comprehensive Test Ban Treaty 78
Congressional Human Rights Caucus 56, 64
Convention against Torture 93, 99, 101, 104
Craner, Lorne 125; and human rights
    promotion 14–18, 72, 121
creationism 69
Creel, George 41
Cuba 55, 74

Darfur 54–5, 146, 150
Defense Science Board 27, 30–1
democracy promotion 18–19, 22–3, 33,
    43–4, 126–8, 149

Democratic Republic of Congo 54
discourse 149, 153; analysis method 7–8,
  154–5; defined 4; productive function of
  24–31
Dobriansky, Paula 71, 80; and human
  rights promotion 14–15, 17–18, 30
Downing Street memo 142–3, 145
Duelfer, Charles 144

Egypt 59, 97, 105, 110
England, Lynndie 133
Espionage and Sedition Acts 42
ethics: defined 2
evangelical Protestantism 69
exceptionalism 68, 80–1, 83–4, 151

First World War *see* World War I
France 48
free trade 45, 72–3
Freedom House 75
Foreign Relations Committee 57, 75
Foucault, Michel 5–6, 8, 26
Fourteen Point Plan 38–9, 41, 43

Geneva Convention 81, 94–5, 117, 137–8
genocide 54–5
Germany 44–5
Gerson, Michael 27
ghost detainees 103, 131–2
Gomez, Juan 45
Gramsci, Antonio 21
Grenada 49
Guantanamo Bay 90–8, 107
Guatemala 47
Gulf War 28

Hadley, Stephen 76
Haiti 22
Halliburton 134–5
hegemonic discourse 13–19, 27, 35, 106,
  117–23, 136–9, 146–7, 149–55; defined
  4–5; and Woodrow Wilson 37–8, 153
Helsinki agreements 49
Heritage Foundation 67, 75, 80
Hezbollah 59–61
HIV 54
human rights: defined 2–4, 148; negative
  human rights 3; positive human rights 3,
  72–4; production of 36, 82–3, 134,
  139–42, 152; and the state system 7,
  148; as technique of governance 31, 36,
  42, 82–3, 121–2, 147, 151, 154–5
Human Rights First 117
Human Rights Watch 62, 89, 114, 116–17,
  128, 131, 133

Hussein, Saddam 123–7, 136, 143–5, 152

Institute for American Values 88
International Atomic Energy Agency 78
International Committee of the Red Cross
  91–3, 97, 129–32
International Criminal Court 68, 81–2,
  150
international human rights law 21, 81–2,
  101, 150
International Monetary Fund 75
Iran 28, 50, 57, 145, 150, 152
Iraq 77, 124, 136, 142–3, 153, 155;
  hegemonic discourse 124–7, 140,
  146–7; human rights violations 128,
  137–9; humanitarian aid 126, 128; Iraq
  Survey Group 143–4; links to al Qaeda
  28–9, 124, 143–4; private security
  contractors 137; Weapons of Mass
  Destruction 78, 124–5, 137, 142–8, 152
Israel 48, 59–61, 105, 107, 152

Jackson, Robert 14
Jewish Institute for National Security
  Affairs 59

Kay, David 144–5
Karimov, Islam 63–4
Karzai, Hamid 111, 113–14, 119
Khmer Rouge 48

Lansing, Robert 40
Lawyers Committee for Human Rights 62,
  66, 118
League of Nations 40
Lebanon 59–61
legitimacy 6–7, 28, 54, 146–7, 151–2;
  defined 6
Lockheed Martin 76
long war *see* war on terror
Lynch, Jessica 141–2

McCain, John 135
Marx, Karl 2–3
Médecins Sans Frontières 121–2
Millennium Challenge Account 68, 74–5,
  151
millennium development goals 73
Minh, Ho Chi 44
Monroe doctrine 40, 45
Morgenthau, Hans 20
Monterrey 73
mujahedin 109, 120
Murray, Craig 64

mythology 25, 31, 54, 57, 83, 149–50;
    defined 5

National Endowment for Democracy 56
National Energy Policy Development
    Group 58, 79
National Security Strategy: 2002 14,
    18–19, 72, 74, 100; *2006* 58, 71, 83,
    100, 119, 125
natural rights 2, 32
neo-conservatism 70
Nicaragua 47
North Atlantic Treaty Organization 82
North Korea 145–6, 150
Northrop 76–7

Office of Special Plans 145
Office of Strategic Influence 27
oil 50, 55–6, 58, 63, 78–9, 128, 134–5
O'Neill, John 144

Pakistan 61, 99, 110
Panama Canal 34, 47
PATRIOT Act *see* Uniting and
    Strengthening America by Providing
    Appropriate Tools Required to Intercept
    and Obstruct Terrorism Act
Powell, Colin 75, 110, 132, 145; and
    human rights promotion 14, 17, 19, 88,
    119
prisoner abuse 88, 90–1, 101–4, 114–17,
    129–34, 138
Project for the New American Century
    70–1

Qana 61

rendition 97–9, 104
Republican Party 69
Rice, Condoleezza 31, 56–7, 103–4, 110,
    143; and human rights promotion 17,
    22, 104
rights of man *see* natural rights
Robertson, Pat 69
Roosevelt, Franklin 58
Rumsfeld, Donald 29, 70–1, 76, 90, 102,
    114, 116, 122, 130, 132–3; and human
    rights promotion 121, 138
Russia 34, 44–5

Sanchez, Gonzalo 56
Saudi Arabia 57–8, 99, 105, 110
Schlesinger report 130
Second World War *see* World War II

Security Council *see* United Nations
    Security Council
self-determination 34, 39–40, 43–4
Sharon, Ariel 59
slavery 22
social and economic rights *see* human
    rights
social power 26, 31; defined 5–6
Somalia 22
South Africa 48
Soviet Union 49
State Department 58, 75, 93, 125, 137,
    140; *Country Report on Human Rights
    Practices* 62, 65–6, 90, 118–19; and
    human rights promotion 15, 47, 62, 74
Supreme Court 96
Syria 97–8

Taguba report 129, 132
Taliban 110, 113, 117–18, 120
Tampico 37–8
terrorism *see* War on Terror
torture *see* prisoner abuse

United Kingdom 48
United Nations 46, 48, 60–2, 74, 77, 82–3,
    93, 101, 124, 127
United Nations Security Council 77, 83,
    110, 124, 147
Uniting and Strengthening America by
    Providing Appropriate Tools Required
    to Intercept and Obstruct Terrorism Act
    42, 89–90
Universal Declaration of Human Rights
    15, 18, 80
universal human rights *see* human rights
Uruguay 46
utilitarianism 3
Uzbekistan 63–6, 97

values 31, 33, 149; American 15–20, 22,
    88, 138, 140; defined 2
Venezuela 45, 55–7

Wallas, Graham 26–7
Waltz, Kenneth 23
war on terror 59, 66, 79; and hegemonic
    discourse 87–9, 100, 104, 106, 154; and
    human rights 99
Wilkerson, Lawrence 132, 145
Wilson, Woodrow 37–45
Wolfowitz, Paul 67, 71, 76, 145
World Bank 75
World War I 37–8, 41, 44
World War II 58

For Product Safety Concerns and Information please contact our EU
representative GPSR@taylorandfrancis.com
Taylor & Francis Verlag GmbH, Kaufingerstraße 24, 80331 München, Germany